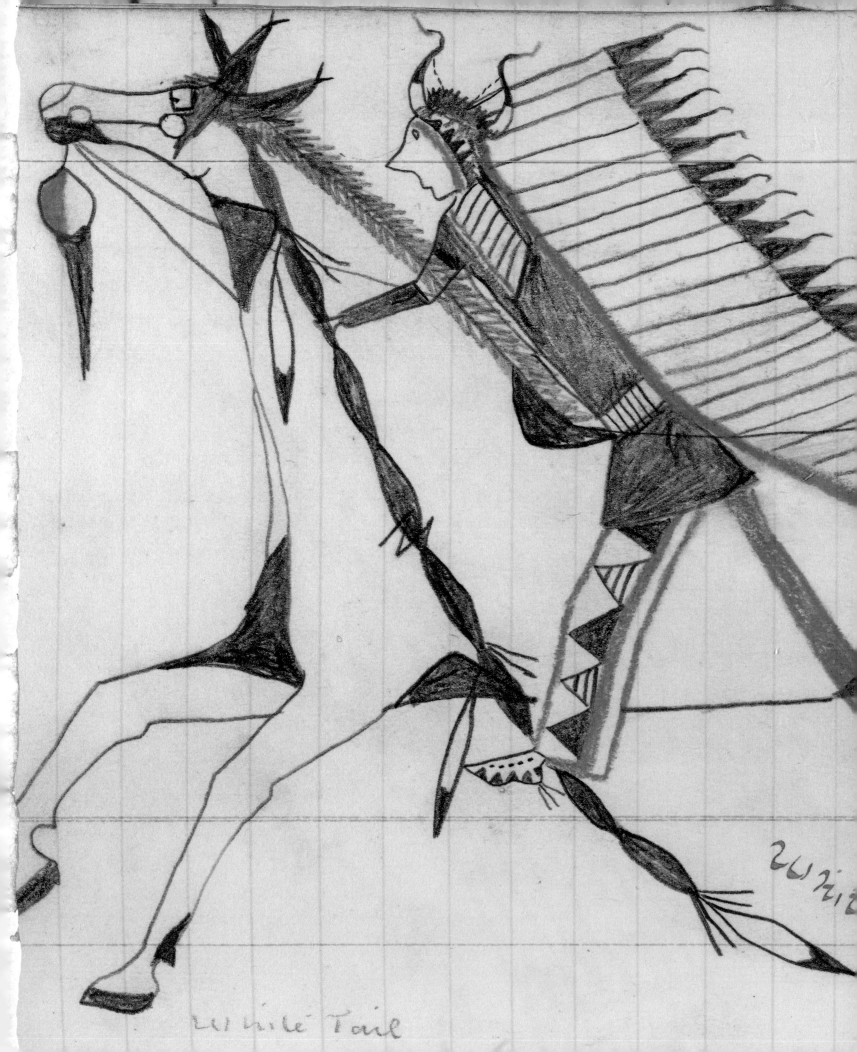

White Tail

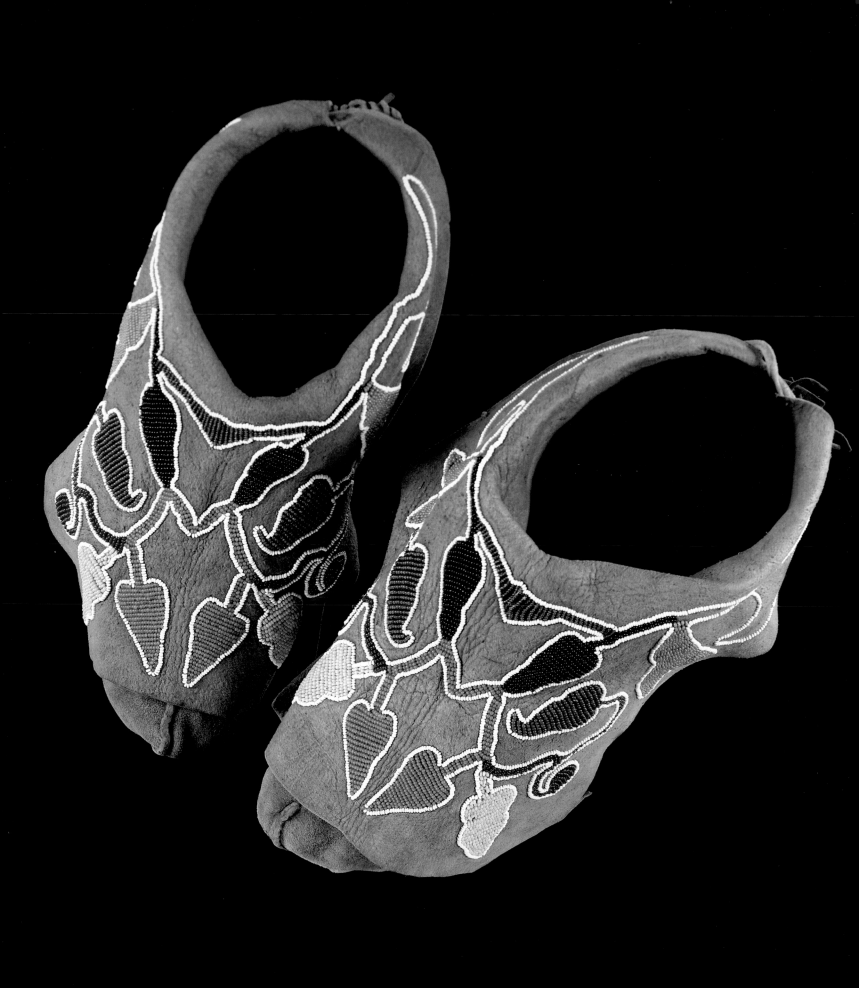

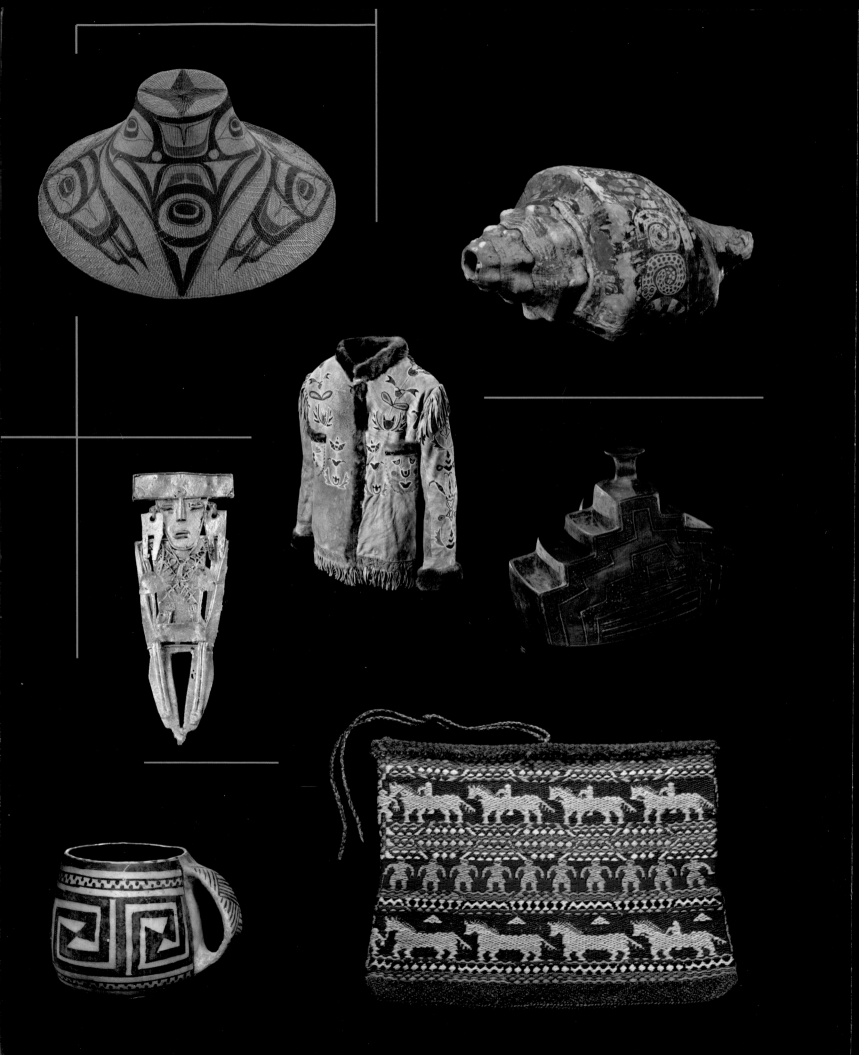

INFINITY
of
NATIONS

ART AND HISTORY IN THE COLLECTIONS OF THE NATIONAL MUSEUM OF THE AMERICAN INDIAN

Edited by Cécile R. Ganteaume

HARPER

An Imprint of HarperCollins*Publishers*
www.harpercollins.com

in association with the
National Museum of the American Indian · Smithsonian Institution

The publication *Infinity of Nations: Art and History in the Collections of the National Museum of the American Indian* has been sponsored by the Leon Levy Foundation.

INFINITY OF NATIONS, © 2010 by the National Museum of the American Indian. All rights reserved. No part of this book may be used or reproduced in any manner whatsoever without written permission except in the case of brief quotations embodied in critical articles and reviews. For information, address HarperCollins Publishers, 10 East 53rd Street, New York, NY 10022.

HarperCollins books may be purchased for educational, business, or sales promotional use. For information, please write: Special Markets Department, HarperCollins Publishers, 10 East 53rd Street, New York, NY 10022.

FIRST EDITION
Printed in China by RR Donnelley

Published in conjunction with the exhibition *Infinity of Nations: Art and History in the Collections of the National Museum of the American Indian*, opening at the Smithsonian's National Museum of the American Indian George Gustav Heye Center in New York City in October 2010.

Director: Kevin Gover
Associate Director for Museum Programs: Tim Johnson
Publications Manager: Tanya Thrasher
Editor: Holly Stewart
Designer: Steve Bell
Color separations by Robert J. Hennessey Photography

The National Museum of the American Indian, Smithsonian Institution, is dedicated to working in collaboration with the indigenous peoples of the Americas to foster and protect Native cultures throughout the Western Hemisphere. The museum's publishing program seeks to augment awareness of Native American beliefs and lifeways and to educate the public about the history and significance of Native cultures.

For information about the National Museum of the American Indian, please visit the NMAI website at www.AmericanIndian.si.edu. To become a member, please visit www.AmericanIndian.si.edu/give or call 1-800-242-NMAI (6624).

The name of the "Smithsonian," "Smithsonian Institution," and the sunburst logo are registered trademarks of the Smithsonian Institution.

10   11   12   13   14   SCPC 10   9   8   7   6   5   4   3   2   1

ISBN: 978-0-06-154731-7

The paper used in this publication meets the minimum requirements of the American National Standard for Permanence of Paper for Printed Library Materials 239.48-1984.

The Smithsonian National Museum of the American Indian wishes to thank the following for their support of *Infinity of Nations*:

The United States Congress; the Lower Manhattan Development Corporation, which is funded through Community Development Block Grants from the U.S. Department of Housing and Urban Development; and the City of New York, with support from the Office of the Mayor and the New York City Council through the Department of Cultural Affairs. Public support has also been provided by the New York State Council on the Arts. *Infinity of Nations* has received additional federal support from the Latino Initiatives Pool, administered by the Smithsonian Latino Center, and the Smithsonian School Programming Fund.

Leadership foundation support has been provided by the Leon Levy Foundation and the Henry Luce Foundation. Generous support has also been provided by Booth Ferris Foundation and through a grant from Carnegie Corporation of New York that was made possible by an anonymous donor.

Leadership program support has been provided by the Leona M. and Harry B. Helmsley Charitable Trust. Generous program support has also been provided by Education Sponsors Valerie and Jack Rowe and the Rowe Family Foundation, Barbara and James Block, and Corporate Program Sponsor American Express. Exhibition support has been provided by John and Margot Ernst.

The University of Michigan historian Michael Witgen (Ojibwe) introduced editor and curator Cécile Ganteaume to the expression "infinity of nations," from his original research into 17th-century French colonial documents. The museum is most grateful to Professor Witgen for generously sharing his scholarship on Anishinaabe and French relations, and for his consultations on Native contributors to this book.

 Smithsonian
National Museum of the American Indian

Contents

Wealth of nations

Objects created in the past are the only historical occurrences that continue to exist in the present.

—Jules David Prown

THESE PAGES PRESENT a brief overview of the extraordinary collections of the National Museum of the American Indian—two hundred iconic examples selected for their aesthetic quality and power as emblems of Native beliefs, the perspectives they offer on the place in history of prominent Indian men and women, and the stories they illustrate of cultural encounter among Native peoples and between Indians and non-Indians.

This book marks a departure for the museum in a few important ways. It is our first geographical survey of the collections. The regions described here—neither static nor defined by boundaries—reflect the importance of place to Native cultures and help clarify the connections among peoples. *Infinity of Nations* also represents the first time the museum has used the word "art" without qualification to describe objects in the archaeological and historic collections. This is not in any way intended to distance these objects from their original cultural context, but rather to acknowledge, as the images on these pages make clear, the value Native American cultures have always given to aesthetics and to artistic achievement.

In the essays that follow, regional specialists and Native authorities, from traditional knowledge keepers to university professors, reveal a rich and dynamic history shaped from its earliest days by long-distance trade, intellectual exchange, political expansionism, and the movement of peoples. Far from a vast and empty wilderness, the New World the authors explore is home to complex societies ranging from loose federations of villages to empires administered from great cities—an infinity of nations. An essay on modern and contemporary art by Native artists from throughout the Americas brings that story into the present day.

The significance of the objects illustrated here, however, goes beyond our appreciation of their beauty or our wish to understand the past. These objects preserve the vision and ideas of their makers. As the museum works in partnership with Native people to study and conserve this legacy, the collections provide an irreplaceable resource for Native communities committed to sustaining cultural traditions, and for Native artists engaged in culture's continual renewal. For all of us, Indian and non-Indian, these objects remain relevant as long as their messages remain true.

Thanks are due to many individuals for their contributions to this book and to the exhibition of the same title, on view at the museum's George Gustav Heye Center in New York, but especially to Cécile R. Ganteaume, who conceived of the content and assembled an outstanding group of collaborating scholars. University of Michigan historian Michael Witgen (Ojibwe) introduced the museum to the phrase "infinity of nations," from his original research into 17th-century French colonial documents. The expression still resonates with meaning—for the image it captures of the Americas at contact and for the respect it accords Native sovereignty. Finally, the museum is grateful to the many supporters whose generosity made the exhibition possible—including city, state, and federal agencies; foundations; individuals; and members of the Heye Center Board of Directors—and to the Leon Levy Foundation, which sponsored the publication of this book.

—Kevin Gover (Pawnee), director, and
Tim Johnson (Mohawk), associate director for museum
programs, National Museum of the American Indian

Tłı̨chǫ elders Melanie Weyallon, Bernadette Williah, and Mary Madeline Champlain use red ochre to add a spirit line to a newly made caribou skin lodge, 2000. Russell Lake Camp near Behchokǫ̀, Northwest Territories, Canada. In 2007 and 2008, members of the Tłı̨chǫ community studied the caribou skin lodge in the museum's collections.

Face to face with the past

At their best, museums invite us to extraordinary encounters

FOR ME, IT ALL BEGAN WITH AN ARROW—twenty-three inches long and of surprisingly small diameter, with a somewhat dubious curve to the shaft. Hardened sinew bound three neatly trimmed feathers to the nock end; a similar wrapping, with an "x" pattern, held a small arrowhead to the tip. I could tell that the shaft had been carefully worked, for it was darkened in several places and shaped by the long strokes of a knife. A "practice arrow," I've been told, probably from the northern Great Plains, probably mid- to late-19th century. With its too-thin, too-curved shaft, the arrow seems willing to confirm this interpretation. For me, at age thirteen, the object called forth an act of imagination. When I looked at the arrow, I saw a boy my own age, working under the tutelage of a master arrow-maker. A century earlier, he had sat practicing under a cottonwood, along the Powder River perhaps, binding the wet sinew with wood and stone. Now I held his work in my hands and I conjured his story.

In the years that followed, I confronted a number of objects that called me to imagine. And those imaginings led me to make emotional connections to objects, to experience them in empathic terms. Objects, I found, could move me to feelings of joy, bewilderment, sadness, even fear. It was a bison robe one year, an antique wooden flute the next. There was that ancient headdress, which seemed so frighteningly animal that it might spring to life. In graduate school, I found myself reviewing a collection of Overland Trail diaries from the mid-19th century. Written in the same mass-produced, leather-bound notebooks, each diary threatened to lose its individuality, to be absorbed into the collection. Then a friend pointed me to a singular journal whose back pages were crusted

with blood. I imagined the story of the owner's fate: a member of the Mormon Battalion, perhaps he had been shot in the war with Mexico. At the same time, I felt the powerful emotional pull of a thing from the past—here were life and death, painted on the page in the most literal way. Even as I savored those experiences, however, I found myself resisting them, perhaps for the first time. Why should I assume that the blood was human, that it belonged to the journal's owner, that it was contemporaneous with the writing? I couldn't know these things without more research, and even then, much of my knowledge would take the form of imaginative, if logical, speculations, grounded by minimal actual data. Still, it seemed to me that, at the very least, I should try to figure things out. Perhaps I owed the object a debt of scholarship.

One more memory. As the National Museum of the American Indian was preparing this book, I had the opportunity to walk through the museum's collections and conservation rooms and see a few of the objects up close. Laid out on trays and shelves, with no glass separating us, the objects spoke to me in yet another way. Lingering on the skilled workmanship, the shapes and forms, the colors and textures, I saw the objects in deeply aesthetic terms as things of beauty. I wanted to draw them near, look at them from all angles, hold them so as to close the gaps of time and space, culture and history. I wanted, in some inarticulate way, to possess something of them. The desire was not new. The watchful curators silently let me know that "drawing close" and "possessing" would be a really bad idea.

Why have I dragged you into this little history of my encounters with arrows and journals and headdresses? I have a deep suspicion that others have

Selk´nam arrows, ca. 1900. Tierra del Fuego Province, Argentina.
Beech wood, sinew, wood, glass, feathers; each 79 x 3.5 cm. 14/2402

experienced objects in similar ways. If so, it is worth thinking a bit more about the nature of these encounters. And since we turn to museums to experience objects, it may be worth wondering how such encounters do or do not take place in museum settings. This book rests, at least in part, upon the premise that individual writers have certain kinds of experiences with the objects in the collections. Each of the essays and descriptions in this book participates, in some measure, in the curious encounter between individual subject and material object.

I have not chosen my very few objects at random, though these encounters were undoubtedly powerful. Rather, each of my little stories suggests a distinct way that we might conceptualize such encounters: the imagination that leads to storytelling; affect, or the experience of emotion; the scholarly will to historical and cultural contextualization; and the sensual desires encoded in aesthetic appreciation.

Caveat time. We build these kinds of categories as tools to "think with." They never describe the entirety of experience and can just as easily be put aside. Likewise it is worth reminding ourselves that there are other encounters as well; it's not difficult to identify a class of spiritual objects that exceeds these categories. And of course, these forms of experience blur together constantly. Imaginative storytelling, for example, can rely primarily on critical history and traditional knowledge, even as it takes its power from affect and channels its narrative toward aesthetics. But for all the caveats—and I'm certain there are more—these categories can serve as a useful map for thinking about the mysterious *qualities* of objects, the ways we interact with them, and the role of museums in making those qualities available as experiences.

Objects take us to a peculiar order of experience, for they possess their own fields of force. In addition to the five perceptual senses—and the serious observer moves beyond the visual, into realms of touch, smell, sound, and perhaps even taste—objects activate in us another sort of sense, one that incites our imagination and affect. Objects do not simply wait to be perceived. They have curious autonomies

of their own. We might think usefully, then, not of "perceiving," but of "meeting with objects," or "engaging objects," or even "confronting objects." And being confronted by them. Objects are not docile. They are surprisingly active.

The German modernist critic Walter Benjamin framed such possibilities around the concept of *aura*. "To perceive the aura of an object we look at," Benjamin suggested, "means to invest it with the ability to look at us in return."[1] At one point, Benjamin speculated that the aura was constituted around the apparatus of high art: exhibition, criticism, genealogy, provenance. At other moments, however, he pointed to the aura as a quality of objects themselves, and to an archaic moment in time when humans had fully experienced the immediacy of the world of things. "'To read what was never written,'" Benjamin mused. "Such reading is the most ancient: reading before all languages, from the entrails, the stars, or dances."[2] Benjamin imagined an original moment in which humans understood direct correspondences between the world and the character of things, when we were able to perceive what he cryptically, but evocatively, called "nonsensuous similarities."[3] Undeniably mystical, Benjamin's dreamscape asks us to consider the ways objects engage our imagination and emotion. If objects carry with them a kind of presence, how could our encounters with them be anything other than extraordinary?

It would be a mistake to follow Benjamin's musing back to a primordial time in human history, just as it would be a mistake to claim that American Indian producers of objects have enjoyed special access to an "auratic" sense of correspondence. Benjamin was no crude social evolutionist, imagining a "primitive" origin from which "modernity" developed. His thought aimed at something much deeper than those troubled categories. What mattered were those great and mysterious moments when stars and entrails lined up with earthly time and space—just as time and space have lined up with the deep forms found in objects such as shamans' tools, warriors' shields, pipes, masks, clothing.

Indigenous artisans have, in fact, sought to capture the world through objects. Sometimes that effort has taken shape in symbols or representations. Sometimes the impulse has been aesthetic. At many other times, however, it has been concerned with the possibilities for *mimesis*—that curious capturing of essences and correspondences that we might associate with an experience of "nonsensuous similarity." Consider Sherry Farrell Racette's description in these pages of an 18th-century Cree coat. Made from a single moose hide, the coat aligns the wearer's spine with that of the animal, with the hide draping over the wearer in the same way it once covered the moose. Decorative patterns follow the vertebrae of the spinal column, further closing the gap between human and moose. Beautiful in its conception and execution, the coat offers an experience that is far beyond symbolism or representation. Its alignment between moose and human is something other than mimicry or imitation; it's not quite a simulation either. Rather, the coat's mimetic power stems from its ability to establish correspondences that exist beyond the realm of sensuous perception. And despite the fact that we, museum viewers, cannot wear the coat, it is nonetheless capable of summoning deep emotional and imaginative responses—that eerie feeling that the object has come close, that it returns our gaze.

Perhaps nowhere is this odd sense of closeness more apparent than in objects that originate in the past. The happenings of the past disappear forever into time. If an event is fortunate, it is recorded or remembered, put into an archive of memory, paper, stone, or other media. But unlike historical accounts or collective memory, objects carry the material past palpably forward.[4] In the object, the past is literally present. What was *there*, in the past, is now *here*, in our own time. The touch of the arrow-maker is imprinted on the arrow I hold in my hand. This pipe—or basket, or gorget, or pot—was as close to people a century or millennium ago as it is to me *right now*. The object's collapsing of time creates a particular form of closeness—my hand to the maker's hand, her hand to mine. It spurs us to imagine those other hands, to feel their presence.

For the most part, these acts of imagination and emotion conjure no knowledge. Rather, they create a longing for lost stories. Who were the arrow-maker, the Overland Trail diarist, and the maker of the Cree coat? What were the particular stories of their lives? It is very, very difficult to say. The paradox can drive you crazy: you hold in your hand a fragment of the past that works powerfully upon your mind, and yet remains a stranger to you.

From that paradox emerges a desire for knowledge and contextualization. If we cannot know the individual tale of this basket or that pot, perhaps we may be able to understand the broader story of which it is a part. And in that quest, objects stand as our best evidence of the past. So we make close examinations, produce deductions, conjure reasonable speculations. We surround the object with others from the same time and place. Consult tribal elders, artists, and craft experts, and place objects in cultural contexts. Search for historical documents. Make comparisons to other times and places. Build analytical categories and populate them with similar objects. All these things bring an object close to us in new ways—through cognitive strategies that are as powerful as our affective or imaginative encounters.

And so consider a Tlingit basketry hat crafted in the shape of an oversized sailor's cap. Even as Teri Rofkar encourages the hat itself to speak, she makes a series of informed deductions: a Western fashion in a Tlingit medium places the hat in a long, complex story of trade and encounter on the northern Pacific coast. Because wool and woolen sailor's hats quickly became common to that trade, this particular hat—woven of grass and spruce root—must mark an early moment in that story. Negative spaces in the design and the abundance of roots needed for a large hat suggest the weaver lived near Yakutat. Similar sailor's hats continue to be worn today in dances that reflect upon the history of contact with Russians and Aleutics. Rofkar applies her knowledge through an exercise in deductive logic. In doing so, she does the hat a form of justice, creating a rich context that allows us to understand something about that past that this object carries forward into the present.

Other objects offer even greater opportunities for this contextual knowing. If the makers of objects frequently remain anonymous, their owners are often not so obscure. How do we think about E. Pauline Johnson's burden strap, Susette La Flesche's wedding dress, or objects belonging to Joseph Brant, Osceola, and Tecumseh? We can insert these things into the well-documented life stories of their owners, transferring some part of our knowledge from owner to object. When we do so, however—and who can resist the temptation to fetishize these objects around such famous figures?—it seems to me that we create another curious paradox: the more we actually know about an object's maker or owner, the more the object itself seems to recede into the past, to slip from our hands. The anonymity of arrow-makers and weavers of sailor's hats incites us to imagine them. Our relatively deep knowledge of Tecumseh or Brant or La Flesche gives us a sense of closeness to them and to history, but limits, in an odd way, our ability to imagine.

Our encounters with objects navigate a knife's edge among forms of experience at once complementary and incommensurable. Imagination and emotion create in us a sense of obligation to an object, a desire to understand its nature, context, and history. And yet this debt of scholarship is also a will to knowledge. In that sense, it is a will to a kind of power over the object. As we come to know an object, we draw it close to us in an intellectual way. This is a good thing. We understand it, and we understand the story in which it might be embedded: survival and subsistence, spirituality and ritual, social and cultural practice, commemoration and memory, cross-cultural trade and diplomacy. How does this cognitive closeness sit in relation to an emotional, affective closeness? Unevenly, it would seem to me. There are objects and contexts in which your gut, your head, and your mind work as one, allowing objects to draw you close in multiple ways. These can be among the most powerful sorts of moments in human existence. But there are also moments when history or context seems to overwrite those other experiences, when the words on the exhibition label outpace the object itself.

The collectors who gathered the objects featured in *Infinity of Nations* had numerous motives: salvage and salary, competitive instinct, the institutionalization of the museum, connoisseurship and aesthetic pleasure, and for artists, generosity with their own work. These things are well and widely known. Nor do we need to offer more than a quick gesture to the fact that many older objects were not created in relation to a Western notion of "art" or aesthetics. When a functional or ceremonial object or a trade or tourist good appears in a museum or collection, it has necessarily been recontextualized to suit the conceptual needs of institutions and their audiences. It is *always* worth remembering that the histories of collection and display are necessarily histories of uneven power and contest. The very presence of objects in a collection inevitably refracts the traumas of that past. Reminding ourselves of this may qualify any notion of aesthetic pleasure, but it does not necessarily eliminate it.

The delight and desire I experienced while looking at some of these objects on shelves and in drawers had everything to do with aesthetic pleasure, and it followed two distinct forms. I took pleasure, for myself alone, in the objects themselves. The geometric patterns found in a Karajá or Mebêngôkre war club from Brazil. The graceful forms of 2,000-year-old duck decoys from present-day Nevada. The carefully chosen color palette that springs a Kootenai baby carrier to life. The proliferation of decorative fringe, which makes an Assiniboine rifle case something more. The intricate skill on display in a knife, fork, and spoon set carved from ivory. These things—and hundreds more—all correspond with my own sense of beauty, making me acutely aware that aesthetic pleasure is not bound by culture or history.

But I also find myself wishing to grasp another experience: I want to know the possibilities for aesthetic pleasure that must have rested in the objects' relation to their original makers, owners, wearers, users, and viewers. In contemplating the (im)possibilities of this aesthetic, I am drawn not simply to form, symmetry, style, and color, but to *material*, and most particularly to the organic nature of these objects. I am pulled back to my encounter with an eagle feather headdress. So *avian*, so animal—that object spun me out of any simple contemplation of surface beauty. The people who made the things shown here attached aesthetic pleasures to the life found in stone, bone, wood, clay, ivory, horn, tusk, shell, tooth, gourd, grass, roots, bark, hair, wool, cotton, fur, copper, bronze, and, yes, gold and silver.

These two possibilities play out differently—for me, at least. With "beautiful" objects, I experience a desire to possess and to linger, to close the gaps and enjoy a kind of universal closeness, the human commonality of maker and viewer. In the presence of those other aesthetics—of the relationship of the objects' makers to their world—I experience a similar desire to possess, though it is not about bringing the object close. Rather, I want to savor the ways it estranges me—through a particular medium of beauty—from everything I think I know.

Across all these ranges—imagination, emotion, knowledge, and aesthetics—objects call us simultaneously to human commonality and to a particular sense of disorientation and defamiliarization. They encapsulate the otherness of time, culture, and the power inherent in an object itself. How can we be touching both the past and the present? How can we be touching another culture? Is this object focusing its auratic gaze upon me even now?

The museum is the place we go to play with these experiences. Sometimes it works out well, but not always—and perhaps not even very often. The Frankfurt School critic Theodor Adorno once famously, purposefully, misread the etymologies surrounding "museum," linking the word to "mausoleum" and pronouncing museums the homes of dead objects to which we no longer have a vital relationship.[5] And we can see his rather grim point: All that glass, separating us from the things themselves. All those gift shops, which necessarily help fund the museum, but also make it a commodity spectacle. All those object-corpses from the past, taxidermical trophies for visitors who are

expected—and who came to the museum—to pay homage to cultural treasures. There is too much to see, and we move too quickly. Our feet hurt. And before we know it, we've said the appropriate things—How beautiful! How interesting!—and moved on to whatever comes next.

Museums do not seek these results, of course, and work hard to counteract our tendency to be distracted or overwhelmed. For museum curators, a far better etymology leads to the Greek muses—the spirits of creative knowledge—and to "musing" itself. The museum, in this sense, is a living place, and museum people seek to set up situations in which visitors can take active musing seriously. They hope we consider the museum as a place of amusement, where our experience leaves us bemused, lost in thought.

Musing has typically been encouraged in its intellectual form and has followed two paths toward narrowing the gaps of history and culture, or bringing viewers and objects into closer proximity. The first has emphasized possibilities for contextualization; the second, the dynamics of universalism and difference that characterize aesthetic responses to objects. In other words, our culture has tended to create museums structured around History and Art, two cognitive ways of experiencing objects. Labels and captions feed us knowledge that enables us to perceive objects in light of what we know, and to deepen that knowledge. Sometimes—and often in relation to codes of display and lighting—museums help clarify for us the formal properties that signify aesthetic beauty. Both are critical strategies for musing, and I'm not dismissing them. They make up an important half of my own framework for thinking about our experiences with objects. It may well be that these are exactly the kinds of memory and culture apparatus that Walter Benjamin believed created an aura that inhered in objects.

But it matters that "musing" really isn't quite the same thing as "thinking" or "interpreting" or "analyzing." The word suggests that we are moving slowly and almost randomly around a topic, letting thoughts come as they will, letting the topic—dare I say, the object—set the pace and direction of our contemplation. This

Diaguita bowl, AD 950–1450. Elqui Province, Chile. Clay, paint; 8 x 23 cm. Collected during the Thea Heye Chile Expedition led by Samuel K. Lothrop. 17/5128

kind of musing, it seems to me, is exactly what might lead us to invest an object with the ability to return our gaze. It meanders slowly around the possibility that an object might possess its own logic, meaning, and mysterious power. In that meandering, musing moment, we open ourselves up to the possibilities.

It seems to me that *Infinity of Nations* asks us to contemplate experiences beyond the familiar possibilities captured by historical contextualization and aesthetic appreciation. We are asked to muse. Even as historical and cultural context and an appreciation for artistic and craft skills allow us to bring objects cognitively and aesthetically close, these same strategies open us to the importance of their radical difference. When history seeks to close the gap between now and then, or us and them, we should remind ourselves to muse on the otherness of objects. And when we are tempted to think *only* in terms of universal artistry, we should

acknowledge those many distinct aesthetics to which we have only the slightest access.

Feeling that otherness ought to remind us that these objects have auratic power that can create a radically different way of closing the gap in our understanding. These objects bring the material past into the present. They call us to acts of imaginative empathy. And if we recognize their ability to return our gaze, we might—if we are extraordinarily fortunate—find that they have churned our stomachs and altered our minds. For these kinds of musings, rich with knowledge and appreciation, imagination and emotion, the museum remains the place: imperfect, but perfectly full of possibility.

—Philip J. Deloria (Standing Rock Sioux)

Pipe tomahawk presented to Chief Tecumseh (Shawnee, 1768–1813), ca. 1812. Canada. Wood, iron, lead; 66 x 22.5 cm. Gift of Sarah Russell Imhof and Joseph A. Imhof. 17/6249

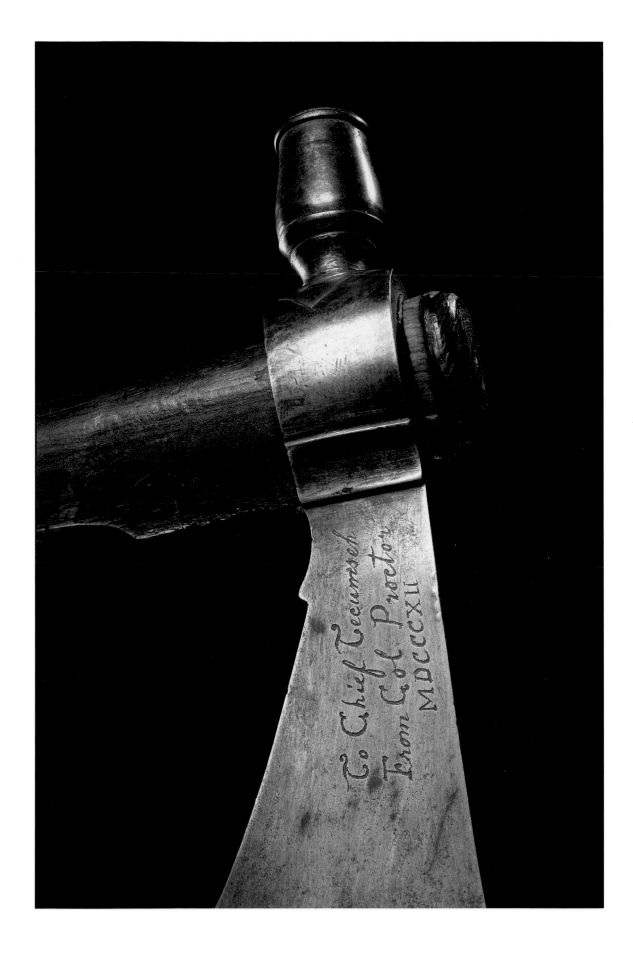

Mapuche Machi beating *kultrung* during a Rewe renewal ceremony, 2001. Chile. N56591

Choyümpelu che

"The place where people grow"—the Mapuche language, Mapudungun

THE COLLECTIONS OF THE NATIONAL MUSEUM of the American Indian show the rich history and creative genius of several past and present Native groups in the Southern Cone of South America from roughly AD 1000 to the early 1900s. All of the peoples represented are related historically and are part of the same general stream of technological and artistic development. They worked with bone, hide, hair, fibers, wood, bark, precious metals, stone, clay, feathers, pigments, teeth, hooves, and horns, and made objects of symbolic significance. These are objects of the deities and ancestors, of fertility, and of belief and faith. Weapons and hunting implements, costumes, tools, images of gods, jewelry, containers, and musical instruments—all have facilitated the survival and interrelationships of these peoples through time.

People settled throughout the Paraguayan Chaco, the Pampas of Argentina and Uruguay, and the Patagonian area of southern Argentina. The largest group is the Mapuche, Araucanians of the forest lands of the south-central Andes, primarily in Chile but also in neighboring Argentina.[1] Their population probably numbered between 400,000 and 700,000 at the time of Spanish contact. The northern Araucanians, known as the Picunche, were absorbed by the Spanish during the first century of the Colonial era (AD 1550–1650). The southern Araucanians—the Mapuche and Huilliche—remained outside the influences of Spanish institutions until the late 19th century. Numbering between 600,000 and 800,000 today, they remain the largest surviving Native nationality in southern South America.

Little is known of the Mapuche between roughly AD 1450 and 1600. Until recently the archaeological and historical evidence suggested that most Mapuche lived in scattered, loosely confederated agricultural communities, under rulers with a kinship-based structure of authority.[2] They had a mixed economy with regional variations that largely depended upon the type of environment (coast, central valley, mountains). Farming and herding were the primary food-producing activities in the central valley, though hunting, fishing, and gathering plant foods also contributed to the diet. Scholars now believe some Mapuche also moved around, migrating from one valley to another, probably looking for new economic opportunities, and defending themselves from outsiders or against each other. Communities often fought with their neighbors over land, women, and resources, as suggested by the first Spanish chroniclers and by the presence of hilltop fortresses that may have been built in late pre-Hispanic times. Most areas never had a centralized political network, but were headed by formal rulers or toqui (war chiefs) during periods of military conflict. In times of peace, ülmen and lonko held respected, but informal, leadership roles. Other chroniclers indicate that some Mapuche agriculturalists were more centralized, as numerous toqui came together to form larger butanmapu—political organizations created to resist the Spanish.[3]

As the Inka and Spanish empires encountered the Mapuche and moved through Chile and Argentina, a domino effect of shifting formal and informal frontiers impacted populations in distant neighboring

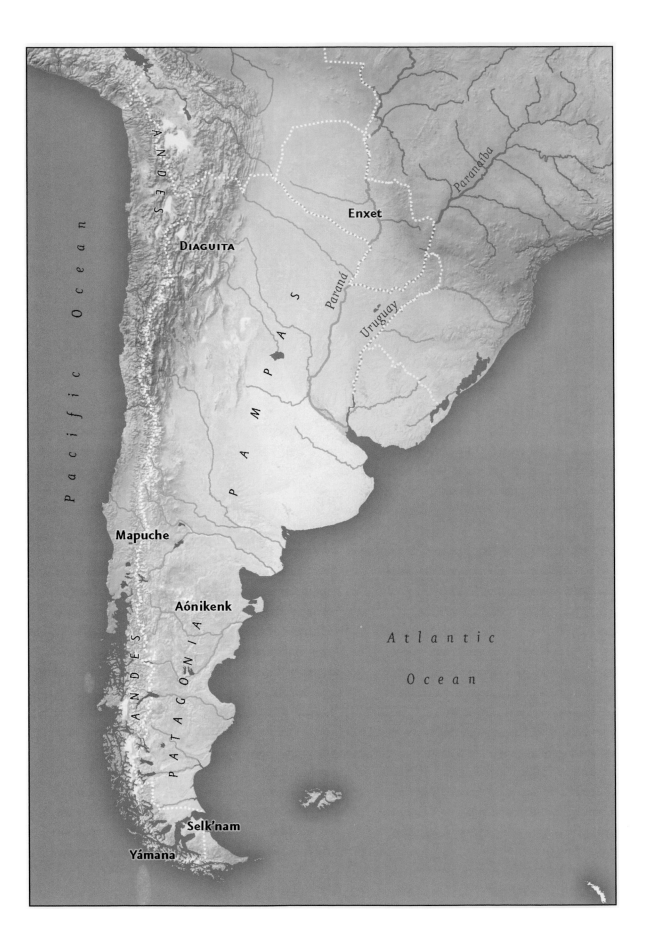

lands, including the Huilliche, who lived to the south. Contact between Mapuche populations and Inka and Spanish personnel often led to greater cultural, ethnic, and racial mixing than in more politically controlled areas of the two empires. Engagement along the frontiers not only provided occasions for military conflict, but also opportunities for the exchange of ideas, goods, and peoples, and influenced the technological development of some Mapuche communities. Encounter with the Spanish brought knowledge of new cereals and other plants; new domestic animals, such as the horse and cow; new uses of metals; and continued impetus toward union in tribal government to repel the Spanish.

In contrast to the Native nations in core areas of the Spanish Empire, the southern Mapuche were less impacted by contact with the European world. During the Colonial era, all the peoples of the Southern Cone quickly developed into equestrian societies that used horses for hunting, stealing Spanish cattle, and raiding Spanish villages. Throughout this era, southern South America was peripheral to Spanish development. Lacking the large amounts of gold, silver, and Native labor of the central Andes, from the perspective of the Spanish, the Southern Cone was primarily suited to European mixed farming. Immigrants gradually pushed out small Native populations, with the exception of the Mapuche. Unable to defeat the Mapuche and preoccupied with the control and administration of many other regions throughout the continent, the Spanish decided to employ a sporadic defensive stance and established formal frontiers between the Mapuche and themselves. In fact, the Spanish signed a royal treaty in 1643 that recognized the sovereignty of the Araucanian nation between the Bio Bio and Bueno rivers. For the next two centuries, Spanish and Mapuche relationships consisted mainly of guerilla raids by both sides. The price for the Mapuche of their relative

independence was social upheaval and population dispersion in many areas. Eventually, the Mapuche were strongly influenced by Spanish culture, as shown in two beautifully carved wooden stirrups that exhibit both Mapuche and Spanish design motifs (see page 31).

In 1884 the Chilean government began to move the Mapuche onto reservations, or *reducciones*. Since the early 20th century, the Mapuche have been semi-integrated into non-Native Chilean society through this mandatory concentration. As a result, the Mapuche people have experienced social and cultural change, but they have held onto their own social structure, ideology, religion, and land-use patterns. They are still a patrilineal and patrilocal society—Mapuche couples make their homes near the husbands' family—living in dispersed communities, although more than half the population today lives in large urban areas.[4]

Other indigenous societies in Latin America also were successful in resisting Spanish control, but none survived or flourished the way the southern Mapuche did over a period of nearly 350 years.

The Mapuche religion pervades the people's lives. The religion consists of a pantheon of deities, ancestral figures, good and evil forces, and other, less important, beings hierarchically nested in an ideologically conceived framework of time and space.[5] The core of Mapuche religion and cosmology focuses on practices—including ritual performances enacted by the entire community—that link the living with their ancestors and deities, and that use past knowledge to guide future behavior.[6] Continuity in form and meaning of rituals and of many other cultural patterns extends back at least to the 15th and 17th centuries AD. The Mapuche believe in a unity between the living and the dead, between the natural and visible world and the supernatural world. Sickness and death have no natural causes but come from *wekufes*, or evil forces. The evil spirits will do no harm if religious rituals are performed correctly, according to traditional ways. *Nguillatufes*, or ritual priests concerned with restraining evil, represent the people before the deities at ceremonial events. On a daily basis and at some public rituals, the shaman, or Machi, is preoccupied with the external struggle between good and evil.

The protecting center of the Mapuche world is Wenu Mapu, a celestial land where the deities and powerful ancestors live. The Mapuche pray to Ngünechen, the supreme being who lives in this land, for food, prosperity, peace, victory in battle, and a wholesome life. Another deity, Pillan, resides in the high Andean mountains and controls such catastrophic events as tidal waves, droughts, earthquakes, and volcanic eruptions. He is the omnipotent protector and embodiment of the good spirits of the ancestors, especially those of famous leaders and warriors.

Although there are pan-Mapuche religious forms, there is considerable local and regional variation in the different sets of figures that are deified and propitiated, particularly beliefs and sanctions specific to individual male lineages. Different emphasis is often placed, for example, on local sets of deities and on animal forms that certain zoomorphic figures may take. Human figures, animalistic symbols, and motifs woven into textiles all metaphorically represent the continued relationship among ancestors, the living, and the natural world.

Much of this variation relates to social nature, meaning that each network of lineages taking part in a ceremony brings in ancestors and spirits of local importance, but within a framework of great cultural homogeneity. Such figures may also reflect differences in the economy and the ecological order, or food chain, of plant and animal communities from which the organizational model of both the living and the ancestors is metaphorically drawn. Anthropomorphic and zoomorphic forms—such as the crescent-shaped axe, or *cura*, made of basalt stone shown on page 23—and textile designs express these relationships and metaphors in the material world of real life. The stepped-diamond motif of the woven poncho shown at the far right, symbolizes the cosmological world of the Mapuche; the poncho's red-and-black color scheme is associated with authority and power. During public events usually only the lonko, a lineage leader, wears it. The axe was an important instrument, probably used by toqui and lonko as a symbol of authority. Toqui cura are mentioned by early Spanish chroniclers and are occasionally used today by lonkos in ceremony. Typically, they have a handle, as seen here, and are in the form of a bird's head, probably a hawk. Hawks represent important ancestors among the Mapuche.

The Mapuche are highly skilled weavers who created an extraordinary quality and design in their textiles. Textiles had many functions in daily life and were used for ponchos, belts, women's dresses and shawls, rugs, storage bags, head bands, and sleeping blankets, as well as trade items. Textiles continue to play an important part in the expression of individual differences in wealth and status, as well as to identify the social group to which women belong. Weaving techniques are passed from generation to generation through the female line.

The pottery of the Mapuche is of high quality, but not very well known among the many outstanding regional traditions of pottery-making in the Andes.

Mapuche woman wearing a silver breast ornament, ca. 1920, Temuco, Chile. P10455

Mapuche leader's poncho, ca. 1920. Chol Chol, Chile. Wool, dye; 156 x 147 cm. Collected during the Thea Heye Chile Expedition led by Samuel K. Lothrop. 17/5656

Although utilitarian ceramics were made for cooking and storing food, and for preparing *chicha* (corn beer), the highest forms of pottery-making are the chicha drinking vessel and the burial urn. The making of these vessels may have been a specialized occupation, and some of them were traded long distances.

Late pre-Hispanic Mapuche archeological culture is a hybridization of local cultures, central Chilean cultures, and various cultures from the eastern flanks of the Andes in west-central Argentina, all of which invariably expressed Andean and probably Amazonian influences. There also are Inka and Spanish features in Mapuche material culture; Mapuche pottery exhibits pre-Hispanic Andean and probable Inka influences in vessel forms and in the color and design of decorations. Andean and some Amazonian influences also are suggested in the organization of Mapuche political and religious space; in the art and iconography of some motifs on wooden statues and textiles; and in myths, tales, and legends. Genetic and linguistic evidence, including linguistic ties with the Tupi–Guarani and other language groups in the tropical lowlands of Bolivia or Brazil, also suggests that the Mapuche are related to peoples across a wider geographic area.[7] How these affinities were established in pre-Hispanic times is not yet known.

—Tom Dillehay

Aónikenk bolas, ca. 1900. Patagonia, Argentina. Animal hide, stone; 99 x 22 x 6.5 cm. Collected during the Thea Heye Chile Expedition led by Samuel K. Lothrop. 18/4932

The peoples of Fuego–Patagonia and Gran Chaco

The southernmost end of the hemisphere, Fuego–Patagonia was surely the last part of the Americas to be settled by people. Nevertheless, a number of archaeological sites in Patagonia date to ca. 10,000 BC, and in Tierra del Fuego to ca. 8500 BC.[1] In historic times only a few groups of people have lived here. On the southern mainland of Patagonia lived the Aónikenk (also called Tehuelche). Related to the Aónikenk both ethnically and linguistically— and like them, hunters—were the Selk´nam (Ona), who lived on the island of Tierra del Fuego. The Manek´enk (Haush), farther south on Tierra del Fuego, are thought to have been different from their immediate neighbors both ethnically and

linguistically, although by historic times they were relatively integrated with the Selk´nam. The two groups even carried out their main ceremonies together.

On the southern and western coasts of Tierra del Fuego, the Yámana (Yahgan) were maritime hunters and foragers. They also inhabited smaller islands as far as Cape Horn to the south and the region of the Straits of Magellan to the north. North of the Yámana in the Fuegian archipelago lived the Kawesqar (Alakaluf), another group of hunters and foragers on the sea, whose material goods were very like those of the Yámana.

Selk'nam arrows, ca. 1900.
Tierra del Fuego Province, Argentina. Beech wood, sinew, wood, glass, feathers; each 79 x 3.5 cm. 14/2402

Puppup (center), watched by his nephew and close friend Chalshoat and other Selk'nam while making an arrow in front of a guanaco-skin windbreak, January 1908. Najmishk, near Cape Viamonte and the tributaries of the Rio Fuego, Tierra del Fuego.

Yámana (Yahgan) model canoe, ca. 1900. Navarino Island, Chile. Beech bark, wood, whale gut, plant fiber, turf; 75 x 21 x 14 cm. Collected by Charles W. Furlong. 5/8572

The Yámana and Kawesqar were "canoe people," in contrast to the land-centered Aónikenk, Selk´nam, and Manek´enk. All of these groups except the Manek´enk overlapped and met in the western area of the Straits of Magellan. They were not in contact at all times, but in areas where groups met, intermarriage was not uncommon. People of these overlapping zones could be bilingual, or even trilingual.

With limited plant life and few large animals, Fuego–Patagonia is not a hospitable land. It can be divided into three major environmental zones: the western archipelago, islands that are really the peaks of the Andean foothills; the Andes themselves; and lower lands east of the Andes to the Atlantic. The islands of the archipelago have a cool and very wet maritime climate. Glaciers come down to the sea in

many spots, and coastlines are rugged and steep, with little flat land near the shore. The Andean range is lower here than in most of the rest of the continent. Nevertheless, many of the mountains are covered with snow all year. On the eastern side of the Andes, on Tierra del Fuego and mainland Patagonia, rainfall is much less than in the western zone, and average annual temperatures are a few degrees higher. This eastern zone progresses from rugged foothills in the west to undulating, mostly treeless terrain extending as far as the Atlantic. The zone east of the Andes is a steppe of tussock grasses, while forest predominates in the archipelago and in the foothills of the Andes.

The Aónikenk were highly nomadic, moving constantly in search of food. Their main prey were guanacos (an American camelid) and rheas (the American ostrich). By the time the Aónikenk got horses, they had probably begun to use bolas and lances as their primary hunting weapons, and bows and arrows had become less important.[2]

The Selk´nam, too, were nomadic. They gathered berries, mushrooms, and other seasonal plant foods, as well as shellfish, and fished and hunted various animals. But guanaco, hunted by the men, were their main source of food and clothing. Selk´nam bows and arrows, the main weapon of the hunt, were very skillfully made. The arrowheads were finely chipped stone until late in historic times, when discarded glass became widely used. Neither men nor women wore tailored clothing. Men slung guanaco skins around their shoulders, dropping these capes to shoot their bows or to perform other tasks. Women wore similar skins but wrapped around their bodies. The men also wore the fine fur from the chest of the guanaco as frontlets or headbands. In winter, when there was snow on the ground, all wore sandals of skins insulated with grasses. The name "Patagonia" almost certainly comes from *patagones*, meaning "big feet," a name given by Ferdinand Magellan to the Aónikenk, who also wore such sandals. Selk´nam women did most of the work in camp, scraping skins used for clothing and for windbreaks and huts. They also carried most of the camp goods, as well as the small children.

The Yámana have been called water nomads, and their canoes were the most essential implements of their wandering lives. All adult men owned a canoe and were of necessity married—it was the wives who paddled and steered the canoe and maintained the fire that was kept going, insulated by sod, at the bottom of the hull. The Yámana used their canoes mostly in the fringe of calm sea that lies between land and the underwater forest of kelp close to shore, within the more protected channels of the archipelago. They often crossed more difficult waters, however, in their nomadic rounds, and even reached the Wollaston Islands, where Cape Horn is found.

Yámana canoes were made of three large pieces of bark sewn together and supported by a framework of poles. Because the canoes lasted only some

six months, making them was an almost continual task for the men. Canoes varied in size but generally were made to carry a whole family. The men traveled in front with the harpoons and spears close at hand. They used harpoons to catch sea lions, seals, and the smaller dolphins and whales. Yámana women fished and used special spears to collect crabs, lobsters, and sea urchins from the sea bottom. The women also dived and swam to collect enormous amounts of shellfish. Other objects of daily living carried and used in the canoe included baskets, dip-net baskets, bark or leather buckets that doubled as bailers—though well caulked with grass, mud, and fat, the canoes leaked continually—and paddles. Poignantly, the Yámana model canoe shown here dates to the period when the Yámana people were severely threatened by the dramatic increase of settlers in Tierra del Fuego. The model is accurately rendered to the last detail. Its gear includes a piece of turf used to keep a fire going in the canoe at all times, paddles, a harpoon, a dip-net lashed to the end of a pole, a bark canoe bailer, a storage basket for carrying shellfish, and mooring rope.

The Yámana made all their equipment of local materials: the wood and bark of southern beeches; the bone and skins of whales, sea lions, and other animals; and various plant products. Their knives and scrapers were made of stone or shell. The Yámana were not reluctant, though, to use metal and other materials—and ideas—adopted from other groups, including Europeans. Their canoes, for example, changed from bark boats to hollowed logs and, eventually, to planked boats.[3]

The Yámana practiced two important ceremonies for the initiation of young men and women, the Chiexaus and the Kina. Their purpose was to educate the initiates in the oral traditions of society, moral behavior, and adult roles. The Chiexaus took place when abundant food was available so that a large group could come together for a considerable period; a beached whale was the most common source of food for these ceremonies. The ceremony lasted as long as the food did—sometimes months. The Kina was a more specialized initiation for men. Dances were

Yámana (Yahgan) bark mask, ca. 1910. Tierra del Fuego Province, Argentina. Bark, paint, baleen; 24 x 18 x 72 cm. Collected by Samuel K. Lothrop. 14/2258

Nellie Lawrence and two Yámana men wearing bark masks, standing at the entrance to the Great Hut of the Kina initiation ceremony, 1922. Punta Remolino, north coast of the Beagle Channel, Tierra del Fuego.

performed at both ceremonies, at which participants held painted wands while spirits were impersonated by already-initiated men and wearing body paint and bark or leather masks.

The Enxet (Lengua) are one of a number of different ethnic and linguistic groups living in the Gran Chaco, a lowland area covering about a quarter of a million square miles in the northwestern two-thirds of Paraguay and the surrounding areas of Argentina and Bolivia. The northeast of the Gran Chaco is a dry, open thorn forest; the southeast is a mix of grasslands and savanna. The eastern half can become impassable in the wet season and is dry to semiarid in the dry season. It has been one of the last areas in South America to be developed, and its indigenous

inhabitants resisted colonization until well into the 1800s. Originally, the Enxet were nomadic. In historic times, they also practiced agriculture, maintaining garden plots that they visited during their wanderings. Still numbering some 17,000 people, the Enxet are no longer nomadic, though they still retain the egalitarian ethics of their hunting and gathering past.[4]

—Paul Ossa

Mapuche stirrups with tapaderos

Mapuche stirrups with tapaderos (hoods), ca. 1910. Chile. Wood, iron; 23 x 24 x 25 cm. Collected during the Thea Heye Chile Expedition led by Samuel K. Lothrop. 17/7324

Between 1560 and 1580, toward the beginning of the war against the Spanish conquerors, the Mapuche appropriated the horse, becoming skillful riders and breeders who adapted the horse to new grasslands and mountains.

For important rituals and celebrations, each chief ornamented his horse with the finest possible equipment and decorations. These stirrups are wooden replicas of silver stirrup designs made at the end of the 19th century. This particular design may well have belonged to a wealthy chief or Mapuche cacique. The geometrical lines and figures, which are also found in Mapuche silver jewelry and weaving, contain the Mapuche worldview and ideas about sociocultural organization. These include the almighty guide Ngünechen, the earth, nature, and human beings within the circles that replicate the form of the earth.

This cacique may have been in charge of a large community divided into nine areas called Ayllarewe where, in times of war, the ancestors lived in accordance with Native ways. This social structure is represented here by nine sculpted caskets in the downward part of the central figure. The sun over a geometrically designed human figure means that life is possible with the integration of the star clusters, that nature and human beings are governed by the divinities. The four bulges or mounds in each corner of the stirrups, together with straight upward lines, represent sacred spaces and communication with the deities.

—María Catrileo (Mapuche)

Mapuche *kultrung* (ceremonial drum)

Many Mapuche people still observe their Native rituals, although many also profess Catholic or Protestant faith. Especially in rural areas, many families practice Ngillatun (prayer, thanksgiving, or supplication) and Machitun (healing), and they turn to the Machi as their fundamental religious leader.

The Mapu, or land, has always been the central core of Mapuche life and beliefs. This view is represented by the *kultrung*, or ritual drum, which each Machi designs according to the particular knowledge and spiritual strength given to her or him by Ngünechen, a deity encompassing the spiritual family that governs and controls nature and life.

The circular shape of the kultrung symbolizes the world infinitum. The cross on its surface indicates the spaces into which the world is divided—the four natural and spiritual positive and negative strengths that correspond to the land of the east, land of the north, land of the sea (to the west), and land of the south. The central part contains the core and strength that sustains equilibrium among the vertical spaces formed by Wenu Mapu (the land above), where the beneficial deities and the old ancestors live; Nag Mapu (the land downward), where all the living, both good and bad, are; and Minche Mapu (the land underneath), where some good and evil spirits dwell. Nature, life, and the astral zone are coordinated in a circular space that represents eternity and makes life possible in a world where good and evil live in communion.

The sculptor who makes a kultrung must be trustworthy, because he has to keep the carving process and the symbols secret. He first chooses a piece of dried laurel trunk for the concave base. The hide of a female goat is used to make the drumhead, in part because it represents fertility, but also because it produces a pleasant tune. The second step is purification and the installation of the Machi's spirit within the drum. The secret language of the Machi calls the kultrung *kawiñ kura*. "Kawiñ" refers to the aureole that surrounds the moon; "kura" means stone. The inside of the kultrung contains small bright *likan kura* (living stones) that represent stars given by Ngünechen to illuminate and empower the Machi in rituals. Coins and herbs are also introduced into the new kultrung to promote positive outcomes, welfare, and protection, and to keep away negative feelings and power in times of war and other calamities. Sometimes these protections are taken from the tops of hills, because there they receive the most powerful energy. Then the cover of the kultrung is laced with horsehide twine to the laurel-wood base. Herbs are put on the surface of the drum and made to move in a special dance called *purun*. If the herbs stay on the drum, the Machi will have beneficial strength and many healing abilities given to her or him by Ngünechen.

As the Machi's tongue is pierced, the kultrung-maker draws the design of the rainbow and the four parts of the world. A mixture of blue stones and mud taken from the hills creates a pigment called *külmawe*. Red, which is usually drawn using horse blood, represents the continuum of life and the strength of nature and people in communion with Ngünechen. The rainbow indicates the place of the best remedies and illuminates the Machi's mind as she or he communicates with the deities in trance. This spiritual state, called Adelwekemachi, prepares the new Machi to learn. The new Machi receives the spiritual energy to continue along the positive roads that will guide her or him in becoming a healer and a mediator between the people and Ngünechen.

—**María Catrileo (Mapuche) and Gloria Quidel (Mapuche)**

Mapuche *kultrung* (shaman's drum), ca. 1920. Chile. Horsehide, wood, horsehair, paint; 18 x 47 cm. Exchange with the Museo Nacional de História Natural during the Thea Heye Chile Expedition led by Samuel K. Lothrop. 17/7322

Selk´nam bow and arrows

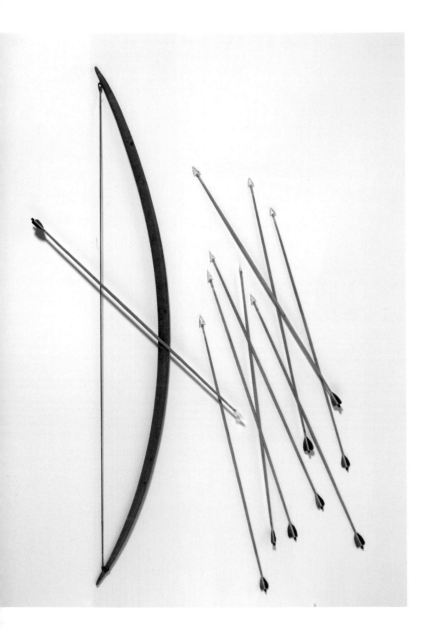

In the old days, there lived an evil and powerful woman named Táita. She controlled the whole area and was selfish, giving nobody any water to drink. Only she hunted in those days, sharing only a small part of her catch with others. Without her permission, no one was allowed to work or undertake anything; lacking weapons, nobody killed animals. Many of the people were weak, dying of hunger and thirst. Finally a wise and able young man named Táiyin killed Táita with his slingshot. He took the evil woman's bows and arrows and showed them to his people, for until that moment they had not known of such weapons. The men copied these weapons and made these bows and arrows for themselves and went hunting, successfully killing guanacos.

—Unidentified Selk´nam, ca. 1918

Selk´nam (Ona) bow and arrows, ca. 1900. Tierra del Fuego Province, Argentina. Beech wood, sinew, wood, glass, feathers; 145 x 24 cm (bow); 79 x 3.5 cm (arrows). Collected by Charles W. Furlong and Samuel K. Lothrop. 5/8568, 14/2402

Mapuche Machi's Rewe
(shaman's ladder)

The Mapuche medicine woman or man called Machi possesses ritual objects to carry out the ceremony for each medical treatment or pleading ritual. The Mapuche developed the art of stone and wood sculpture with the intention of establishing communication between Ngünechen (the deity that governs the world) and human beings. The new shaman provides her- or himself with a wooden pole called Kemukemu. This pole is transformed into a sacred Rewe (clean and pure space) when she or he is initiated into the realm of a devoted Machi in a ritual called Ngeykurewen.

The first Rewe of a Machi has four steps carved into its front, representing the four main sacred spaces. These steps end at the top of the pole with a carved head representing the human spirits involved in the pleading ceremony. The Rewe is placed to the right side in front of the Machi's home. The Rewe is a means of transportation used by the Machi to reach Wenu Mapu—or the blue space above, where the deities live—to maintain communication with the sacred spirits.

With time, the Machi acquires new power and skills to appeal for the blessings of Ngünechen and fight against the evil spirits. Each new spiritual power merits a new sacred step carved into the pole. This eight-step Rewe seems to have belonged to an experienced, accomplished Machi with sufficient knowledge and strength to propitiate communication with Ngünechen. This necessary spiritual mediation allows her or him to face the strongest evil spirits and bring back the right equilibrium for the community in times of danger or calamity.

—María Catrileo (Mapuche)

Mapuche Machi's Rewe (shaman's ladder), ca. 1920. Collico, Chile. Wood; 287 x 25 cm. Collected during the Thea Heye Chile Expedition led by Samuel K. Lothrop. 17/5773

Pachamama

"Mother earth and light of the sun"—Aymara

THE ANDEAN REGION OF SOUTH AMERICA is a mosaic. Distinct environments, many isolated by deserts or mountain spurs, gave birth to extremely divergent, but historically related, societies. These societies represent the culmination of the exchange of ideas and cultural patterns between settlers of diverse backgrounds over many thousands of years.[1] After AD 500, the central Andes, especially Peru, witnessed the rise of a series of great states and empires, including the Moche, Huari, Tiwanaku, Lambayeque, Chimú, and Inka. Substantial numbers of peoples also lived outside the central Andes. Many permanent village sites and towns have been discovered in Colombia, Ecuador, Bolivia, Argentina, and Chile. Although many of these peoples practiced agriculture and herding or fishing, their environments were unaccommodating—circumstances that often dictated lower population densities—and they moved their settlements within a certain zone every few years. These communities seemingly were more difficult to organize into large polities, and their cultural histories are less well understood.

The Andean artifacts in the museum collections—the material record of these societies—represent the outcomes of both short- and long-distance interactions over time. Rather than view these objects as products of local societies, we should recognize that their art and symbolism were constituted by interaction with other groups, representing dynamic historical relations among different peoples. What makes an object Muisca, Tairona, Otavalo, Inka, or Aymara is its origin in a shared space united by a shared identity and culture. Yet that place, at the time of the object's making, was a context for interactions that constantly re-created identity and culture.

Beginning no later than the 10th millennium BC, there were movements of various peoples between North and South America. Interregional contacts and exchanges later intensified as different groups settled into specific regions. Especially clear are long-distance contacts between Mesoamerica and the Andes and between the Andes and the Amazon basin in the first millennium BC. The major exchange at this time appears to have been the introduction of a few food crops from the tropical lowlands, and possibly from Mesoamerica, into the central Andes. There also are a number of similarities between Chavín, the first great Andean art style in Peru, and art styles from the Amazon and northern Andes. In later periods, metallurgy apparently diffused from northwestern South America to western Mexico. There is no doubt that considerable cultural interaction occurred among all of these areas throughout time, with much of this contact taking place along sea lanes and between river and mountain valleys. Within all Andean areas, there were local coastal and highland traditions and co-traditions. During certain periods, these traditions developed along independent lines. At other times, they were unified by the spread of cultures such as Chavín, Moche, Huari, Tiwanaku, Chimú, and Inka.[2]

Several formal concepts were developed and shared in the ancient art and artifacts of the Andes. One is symmetry and double images, as seen on a complicated Tiwanaku stone mirror showing two opposing camelids (see page 39), a Lambayeque effigy vessel characterized by two snakes (page 50), and a bronze plaque from Argentina defined by two balanced iconographic panels (page 39). Another is the idea of combining in one image the features of several animals

Muisca tunjo (offering), AD 1000–1500. Bogotá, Columbia. Gold alloy; 12 x 5 cm. Presented by Mrs. Thea Heye. 17/8022

37

Tiwanaku, a major center of political, economic, and religious life beginning ca. AD 500, 2008. Southern shore of Lake Titicaca, Bolivia.

or of animals and humans. In its simplest form—the substitution of the parts of one creature for the same parts of another—this is best represented on a large stone seat from Manabi, Ecuador (page 55), and a gold figure of a man from Colombia (page 36). A more complex expression of the concept is the substitution of one part of one kind of animal for another part of another animal. Feline and snake motifs, as well as the use of red pigments, are also typical of many regions and reflect shared symbolic and artistic expressions. The art of pottery-making throughout the Andes reflects both a detailed understanding and control of the clay medium and vessel form. Something of the ideological and social system of which the potters were a part finds expression in their work, as well.

Influences shared by different regions in contact can be seen in other areas of technology. The highly efficient agricultural system that appeared early in coastal Ecuador and in areas of the Andes had a marked influence on the agricultural developments underlying the later coastal and highland civilizations of Peru. As early as 200 BC, urbanism began to develop in the Andes. By AD 200, practically all techniques of weaving were known, and both cotton and the wool of the llama, vicuña, and alpaca were used extensively.

Metallurgy was also well developed during this period. Gold, silver, copper, bronze, and various alloys

Bronze plaque, AD 900–1500. Atacamas Desert, Argentina. Copper alloy; 20 x 15 cm. Purchased from the Maryland Historical Society. 20/8192

Tiwanaku mirror, AD 500–1100. Tiwanaku, Bolivia. Slate, hematite, paint; 19 x 9 cm. Purchased from Robert L. Stolper. 24/2500

Lambayeque gold discs, AD 750–
1375. Chan Chan, Peru. Gold alloy;
5 cm. Major Otto Holstein Collection. 15/7233

Nazca pendants, AD 100–600.
Nazca Valley, Ica, Peru. Gold alloy;
17 x 15 cm. José A. Gayoso Collection. 17/8847

were used. These metals functioned primarily for making ornaments, but they were used for other purposes, too. Gold objects are best represented in the collection by ornaments from Colombia and Peru. Pre-Columbian indigenous people used several techniques to work the metal, from beating it with stone hammers to casting it in clay molds. Often they mixed the gold with copper to create *tumbaga*, an alloy more workable than pure gold. Several objects in the collection were shaped by the repoussé method, the design punched from behind with a template. The lost-wax process—encasing a wax model in clay and then pouring in hot metal—could produce a solid or hollow object.

Perhaps the most skilled goldsmiths and jewelers were the Muisca (or Chibcha) of Colombia and the Moche, Lambayeque, Chimú, and Inka of Peru who used gold prudently, often blending it with precious stones. Turquoise, highly prized, appears as early as 1000 BC in ornaments of the Chavín culture. Blue lapis came from northern Chile; it was polished into round beads and made into pendants, alternating with gold. Bone, shell, and wood were inlaid: mirror-backs were decorated with an inlay of turquoise and shell; wood was encased with gold. When the materials came to them directly or by trade, jewelers used quartz, agate, carnelian, bloodstone, and serpentine. Emeralds came to the central Andes via trade routes with people in Ecuador and Colombia.

There are a number of shared stylistic components in gold-, silver-, copper-, and bronze-working, but their temporal, geographic, and sociological significance is uncertain. Some stylistic distinctions seem to have a technological basis, in part. The designs on the embossed gold discs from Lambayeque, embossed plaques of copper from Ecuador, and embossed plaques and discs of bronze from Argentina have a sinuous quality of human features and lines similar to the quality of designs painted on pottery and other materials from the same regions. These plaques and discs are infrequently found items in archaeological sites and thus probably represented symbols of elite authority and power throughout the Andes from Colombia to Chile and Argentina.

The Tairona people of Colombia's Santa Marta Mountains were traders among the people of the north coast, close to the Caribbean Sea. Clever engineers as well as merchants, the Tairona mastered their tropical mountain environment and its long rainy season by constructing circular terraces of stone with intricate drainage systems. On the terraces they built houses similar to those of the Kogi today—a contemporary Santa Marta people—and planted crops that included corn, manioc, and potatoes. With coastal peoples, they traded gilded copper jewelry, cotton blankets, and parrot feathers for salt and fish. In exchange for emeralds mined by the Muisca in the northern Andes, the Tairona offered highly polished beads of carnelian, agate, and quartz. Priests, warriors, and artisans interacted in a tight network of towns linked by stone stairways, roads, and bridges, and inhabited by nearly 30,000 people. Though socially cohesive, the Tairona towns maintained political autonomy, and an independence that halted Spanish incursions until the early 1600s, when the last Tairona chiefs were captured and their towns burned.

The Muisca of the highlands of Colombia had neither cotton nor wool. Their principal trade items were salt and emeralds.[3] The great diversity of the territories in Colombia and Ecuador occupied by different societies led them to adopt a pronounced specialization in techniques of resource exploitation: in the selection of plants suited to different altitudes and climates, but also in the development of the valley slopes through the construction of terraces, house platforms, and irrigation and drainage systems—technologies that presume an ability to mobilize large numbers of peoples. Statuary, goldsmith's work, and pottery also made spectacular progress.

We know that some of the earliest pottery-making took place in coastal Ecuador, and that Ecuadorian ceramics influenced—or even intruded into—the earliest pottery traditions of Colombia, Peru, and regions even farther south. In each case, technologically sophisticated and aesthetically advanced ceramics with a long history of development in Ecuador—starting with the Valdivia culture in the fourth and

Tairona bowl, AD 400–900. Caldas Department, Colombia. Clay, paint; 15 x 13 x 8 cm. Gift of David T. Abercrombie. 13/6161

Right: Muisca ceramic head, AD 1200–1600. Colombia. Clay, paint; 26 x 15 x 29 cm. Purchased from Julius Carlebach. 23/920

Aerial view of a large Nazca hummingbird geoglyph. Pampa de San José, Ica Desert, Peru.

fifth millennia BC, and in the Amazon basin probably slightly later—were accepted by peoples whose ceramic traditions were less sophisticated. The figurine tradition of Valdivia represents one of the earliest known appearances of this form of artistic expression in the Americas (page 54). Other great art styles following Valdivia include the Machalilla and Chorrera in Ecuador; Cupisnique, Chavín, and Paracas in Peru; and San Agustín and Calima in Colombia.

The most prominent Chavín ruins are situated in a high valley on the eastern slope of the Andes, on a tributary of the Maranon River. In the middle of the first millennium BC, the Chavín art style spread over a large part of Peru.[4] Characterized by extremely elaborate stylization and by stirrup-spout jars, Chavín style is the result of a long evolution of early societies and cultures blending through the exchange of ideas. Some scholars believe that the Machalilla, Cupisnique, Chavín, Chorrera, and Paracas art styles are based on the same religious system, cosmology, and origin myths. The divergent styles of their pottery, in particular, reflect the isolation of various regions cut off from one another by mountain ridges. Nonetheless, pottery techniques bear witness to a common historical source of inspiration. Stirrup-spout bottles have been found in all of these cultures, as well as in later Moche, Nazca, and Chimú styles and in several later styles in Bolivia

Paracas vessel, 200 BC–AD 1. Ica Region, Peru. Clay, paint; 37 x 30 cm. Exchange with Walter Randel. 23/5500

and Chile. This form was in vogue in the whole of the central Andes for more than 2,000 years (page 46).

The climate of the Peruvian coast—especially in the south—and in northern Chile is extremely dry, allowing the preservation of organic materials, including textiles and mummies. The Paracas and Nazca cultures flourished on the edge of the coastal deserts of southern Peru and in the Atacama area of Chile. Paracas and Nazca produced some of the most elaborate and technologically developed weaving techniques in the world at the time. Archaeologists have discovered a large number of tombs on the Paracas promontory that date from 350 BC to AD 200. These sepulchers contained textiles so well-preserved that they seem new. The textiles were generally found in the mummy bundles of the important dead. The shrouds found at Paracas are especially remarkable for their vivid colors—burgundy, brick red, orange, yellow, and red ochre. They display a surprisingly wide range of weaving techniques, including tapestry and embroidery. The result is a very complicated and somewhat conventionalized design. Human figures, deities, and mythological animals such as the jaguar and the serpent-dragon are depicted on a solid or checkered background. These weaving techniques were handed down to the later Peruvian civilizations: the Moche, Nazca, Tiwanaku, Chimú, Quechua, and Aymara.

From AD 300 to 700, the Moche culture was the great power of the north coast of Peru. Large adobe pyramids and large irrigation works were built throughout the region.[5] Subsistence was based on agriculture, with secondary emphasis on fishing and herding. The Moche art style was highly naturalistic—in contrast to the complex stylization in vogue at Chavín—and pottery is a major source of information about the culture. Designs generally represent imagery from everyday life. Portraits, caricatures, and erotic scenes decorate admirable polychrome pots

Nazca poncho (detail), AD 1000.
Peru. Camelid fiber, plant fiber.
102 x 149 cm. Purchase. 18/946

Moche stirrup-spout vessel, AD 200–400. Chicama, Peru. Clay; 13 x 8 x 17 cm. Presented by Dr. and Mrs. Arthur M. Sackler. 23/8958

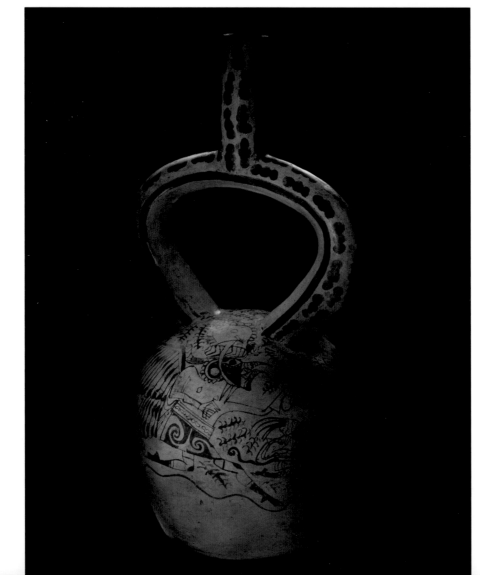

Moche stirrup-spout vessel, AD 400–700. Chimbote, Peru. Clay, paint; 35 x 16 cm. Purchase. 16/8980

Nazca bowl, AD 400–600. Nazca Valley, Peru. Clay, paint; 10 x 23 cm. Miguel V. Merino Schröder Collection. 11/2786

Ica figural vessel, AD 1400s. Nazca Region, Peru. Clay, paint; 18 x 13 cm. Exchange with John V. Carter. 20/7605

molded in forms that include figures, plants, animals, and weapons. It is apparent in the pottery that the Moche society was highly centralized, aristocratically structured, aggressively militaristic, and internally complex. The Moche culture is also remarkable for its architectural achievements. Moche techniques of gold-work also were highly developed. Moche goldsmiths executed high-quality works for religious and mortuary purposes. Many such ornaments were placed in the tombs of important dignitaries. Moche techniques in working gold—lost-wax casting, wire drawing, repoussé work, embossing, and soldering—were passed to the Lambayeque and Chimú cultures, which improved and widened the style of decoration and use.

The south coast of Peru and the highlands also saw the establishment of towns and agricultural

Chimú jar representing a squash, AD 1100–1400. Trujillo, Peru. Clay; 33 x 16 x 24 cm. Purchase. 14/4584

communities, as well as the development of a basically rural population, with groups of villages held together in shifting alliances.[6] The widest-spread cultures of the south—the Nazca, Ica, and Chincha—shared historical roots with the highland Huari culture. A style of pottery much less naturalistic than contemporaneous Moche ceramics developed between AD 350 and 850 south of Paracas in the Nazca region. Geometric stylization and economy of line resulted in an austere and elegant perfection. Nazca also has left colossal drawings traced on the ground (page 42). Like Moche, Nazca also represented a conquest society.

Between AD 500 and 1000, there appear to have been two major administrative and ceremonial centers and dual spheres of interaction. The military and commercial power known as Huari dominated the central and southern highlands and coast of Peru. Tiwanaku influenced the highlands of Bolivia and northern Chile. The early period, between AD 500 and 600, is marked by the spread of the Tiwanaku art style and religious symbolism. During the same period, the central Andes came under the control of Huari. Under Huari, the concept of planned compound architecture was carried to many regions. The great planned cities that followed on the north coast probably partly originated from Huari expansion and exchange of ideas. Tiwanaku and Huari were followed by the emergence of various polities and chiefdoms on the Peruvian coast from AD 1000 to 1460. Great urban centers were built by the Lambayeque and Chimú cultures in the north, the Chancay and Lima cultures on the central coast, and the Ica and Chincha cultures in the south.

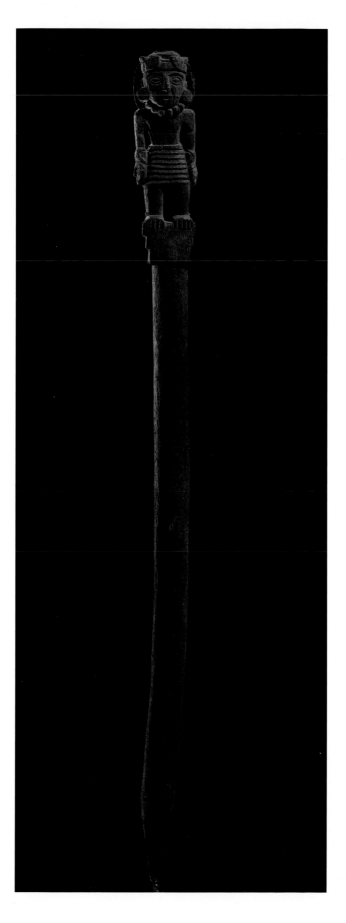

Chimú staff, AD 800–1400. Peru. Wood; 78 x 6 cm. Presented by
Dr. and Mrs. Arthur Sackler. 23/9244

Trade became somewhat more extensive than in the
previous period, facilitated by a network of roads.

The Chimú kingdom developed between AD 1100
and 1450. Its capital, Chan Chan, covered six square
miles of the Moche Valley and contained at least ten
large, walled compounds. The Chimú also built smaller
versions of Chan Chan in other north-coast valleys,
to serve as provincial centers. Chimú territory was,
in part, integrated by a system of trans-valley canals,
massive fortifications, and an extensive network of
roads that formed the basis of the later Inka highlands system. Chimú culture drew heavily on Moche
traditions. Achievements in the field of metallurgy
were particularly outstanding. An advanced-technol-
ogy metallurgical industry seems to have existed in
the Chimú capital, producing works of art remarkable
for their high quality and colossal dimensions. The
conquistadors described large gold and silver vessels.
Chimú metalwork—including death masks, sacrifi-
cial knives, jeweled ornaments, and pectorals—was
enveloped in myth by the Spaniards. The Chimú were
also masters at producing wooden staffs, textiles, and
other elaborate objects.

Less integration is seen in the rest of the Andes
during this same period. On the far north coast, the
Vicús culture developed towns and cities and a polychrome ceramic style that blended Ecuadorian and
Peruvian styles. Farther south on the north coast, the
Lambayeque culture is defined by massive pyramids,
large cities, elaborate gold objects, polished blackware
pottery, inlaid shell and wood, and other items. In the
central coast area there are cities similar in plan to
Lambayeque and Chimú cities, but generally smaller in
size. This area is mainly represented by the Chancay
culture, known for its elaborate human figurine vessels.

In creation stories, the early Inkas wandered from
their original homeland, Pacaritambo, and eventually reached the Cuzco Valley. According to histories

The Inka city of Machu Picchu, above the Urubamba Valley, Peru.

Lambayeque effigy vessel, AD 900–1300. La Libertad, Peru. Clay; 27 x 18 x 31 cm. Purchase. 24/6485

written soon after Spanish contact, the original Inkas, called Tambos, carried with them a golden staff that sank into the earth at the exact spot they were destined to settle. Cuzco was already home to at least two other groups, each more powerful than the Inkas. Only after many years of alliances, intermarriage, and warfare were the Inkas able to bring the peoples of Cuzco together and under their control. The earlier Cuzco groups were considered Inka even though they originally represented linguistically and ethnically separate groups from the Tambos.

The Inkas were the most expansionistic society in the Andes.[7] Nowhere was there another state capable of withstanding their ambitions, not even the powerful Chimú. At its height, the Inka Empire stretched north to southern Colombia and south to central Chile—2,500 miles along the Andes.

The empire was divided into four quarters (*tawantinsuyu*), each controlled by a governor (*apo*) stationed

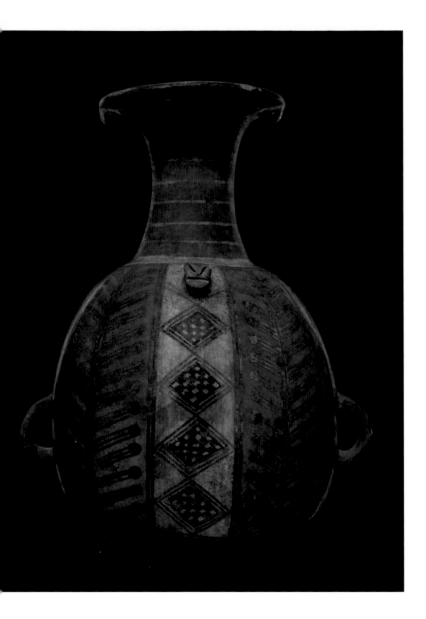

the Inkas took great measures to organize the peoples under them. Conquered populations were often relocated to other parts of the empire to reduce the possibility of uprisings. The conquerors typically demanded labor service from the subjugated peoples, as well as payment of formal tribute. The Inka Empire was the last of a long history of Andean polities, and in most aspects Inka government replicated the institutions and practices of its predecessors. Characteristically, all of the Andean empires permitted the inhabitants of their subjugated provinces to retain their own languages, ethnic identities, gods, and local rulers.

Master craftsmen, the Inkas also applied techniques that had already been devised by earlier peoples. They spread the use of bronze throughout the empire. Their greatest technological skills were in architecture, but they also elaborated weaving and pottery techniques. Stonemasonry was of such excellence that many Inka buildings have withstood the ravages of time, the Spanish, and earthquakes. The Inka believed in rewarding local people for their achievements and maintaining loyal clients among their followers by sponsoring elaborate feasts where excessive food and drink were consumed. The *qeros* in the museum's collection probably were used for the consumption of *chicha* (corn beer).

Without written language, but with a decimal system like ours, the Inkas developed an accounting system recorded in *khipus* to keep track of their empire. Khipus used series of colored and knotted strings to tabulate statistics: corn production, llama herds, enemy casualties, and taxes, among other data. *Quipu camayocs*, or keepers of the khipus, coded and decoded the information. They knew whether a yellow string signified gold or corn, and whether knots recorded farm boys recruited for war or counted minor gods.

in Cuzco. The four governors—usually close relatives of the emperor—formed a council of state. Each of the four quarters was divided into provinces (*waman*) that often corresponded to former conquered tribes or states. The system of roads begun by the Lambayeque and Chimú was expanded by the Inkas to connect all parts of the empire.

Early in their expansion, internal factions rose from the diverse groups who had only recently become Inka. Throughout the Andes, villages had been raided for tribute, but not for political consolidation. Later

Inka *khipu*, AD 1425–1532. Chulpaca, Peru. Cotton, dye; 72 x 39 cm. Exchange with the Universidad Nacional Mayor de San Marcos. 14/3866

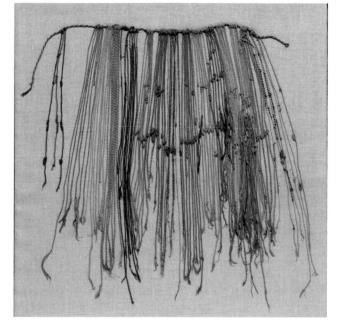

At the time of the Spanish conquest, the peoples of the Andes occupied different levels of sociopolitical integration. Whether groups experienced initial contact with the Spanish as liberation from the Inkas or traumatic defeat, contact brought widespread change to most Native cultures, and tragic declines in Native populations.

The strong unifying influence of the Inkas remains apparent in the Andes. Today most Andean people speak Quechua, the lingua franca of the Inkas. Yet families and communities also retain elements of their more ancient identities—in their belief systems, dress codes, and material culture. The people of the treeless altiplano of Bolivia and northern Chile and along the shore of Lake Titicaca have kept their Aymara language and much of their culture. The nearby Chipaya, who live on the isolated salt flats of southwestern Bolivia, have kept their native Uru language. The Quechua-speaking Otavalo of Ecuador, skilled

weavers in Inka times, have expanded their textile artistry into a lucrative worldwide business.

The indigenous peoples of the Andes have displayed remarkable cultural resilience in the face of catastrophic loss of populations after Spanish contact, loss of lands and local political autonomy, economic incursion and exploitation, and disrespectful treatment of their values and ways of life.[8] To the extent possible, Andean peoples have been selective about what aspects of the outside world they have incorporated into their cultures. But this process of blending has always characterized the history of these peoples, from the time of their first entry into the Andes to the current, global day.

—Tom Dillehay

Valdivia female figurines

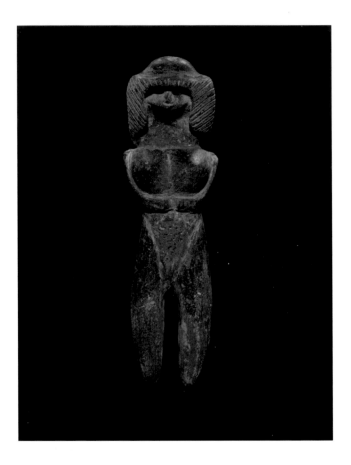

The ceramics of the Valdivia culture are the oldest known pottery in the Western Hemisphere, dating back to 3500 BC. Valdivia figurines appeared soon after the culture's emergence. The context in which the majority of these figurines are found suggests that they were associated with agricultural rituals and calling for rain. Since many are female, the figurines are also thought to have represented fertility, production, and agricultural development. Several figurines were intentionally broken by being thrown against a hard surface, a ritual that may have formed part of a ceremony.

Each figurine was individually modeled from a single block of clay. While many were polished in their natural color, some were painted completely with red slip and some are dichromatic, displaying red and the natural color of the clay. Between four and twenty centimeters in height, the majority are shown standing. Very few figurines are in a sitting position, though some appear to be resting on the ground.

Valdivia figurines are characterized by their straight standing pose; pronounced breasts, shoulders, and neck; and a raised head with a small face. The eyes and mouth are represented by simple lines cut into the clay, and the nose by a simple mark across the face or as an appliqué. Despite their simplicity, the figurines have vivid facial expressions. The makers also took care to highlight details of each figurine's hairstyle, their most distinguishing feature. The hair always appears to be flowing down the back of the figurines. Women in Valdivia culture may have kept their hair as a status symbol or as part of their belief system. This Andean custom continues into the 21st century.

—Ramiro Matos (Quechua)

Valdivia female figurines, ca. 3500 BC. Valdivia, Ecuador. Clay, paint; 4 x 3 x 4 cm to 3 x 2 x 10.5 cm. James Judge Collection, presented by Mrs. Alice K. Bache; purchased from Eugenia Rodriguez. 24/8403, 24/8404, 24/8728, 24/8730

Manteño seat

The museum houses a major collection of stone chairs from Cerro Jaboncillo and Cerro de Hojas, located along the coast of Mantas, Ecuador. These chairs are affiliated with the Manteño culture, which flourished from AD 500 to 1500. Several stone sculptures, stelae, monoliths, and chairs were excavated by Marshall H. Saville between 1906 and 1908, under the sponsorship of the Heye Foundation. There is a lack of archaeological data, however, that would define their context and associations. Scholars who study Manteño objects use ethnological analogy to hypothesize that stone chairs may have been used by spiritual leaders and were linked to astronomical observations, weather predictions, and public ceremonies conducted at certain times during the agricultural year. Spiritual leaders may have worked in pairs and larger groups, arranging the chairs to face east and west or to form a circle founded on the four directions.

The pedestal of this monolithic U-shaped seat is carved as a crouching figure with its legs drawn up under the body, forearms resting on the platform, and clenched fists facing forward. The figure's eyes and mouth were delicately

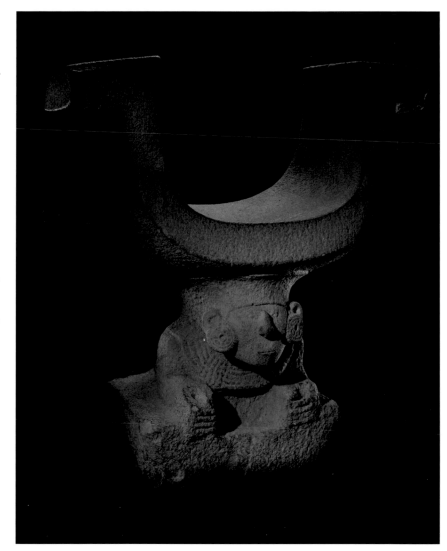

Manteño seat, AD 500–1500. Cerro Jaboncillo, Ecuador. Stone; 40 x 68 x 75 cm. Collected by George H. Pepper. 1/6380

engraved onto its face, which highlights its prominent nose and earspools. This anthropomorphic stone chair represents one of several Manteño styles; Manteño stonecarvers also created chairs with zoomorphic pedestals and without any sort of figurative representation. Manteño people crafted clay figurines with many of the same features seen on this stone chair. Some of these figurines are seated, and others are in a leaning position, which suggests that they represent spiritual leaders, shamans, or other high-status figures.

—Ramiro Matos (Quechua)

Inka terraced vessel

Inka terraced vessel, AD 1425–1532. Lima, Peru. Clay, paint; 31 x 18 x 26 cm. Purchased from Alan Lapiner. 24/1889

This beautiful Inka vessel, produced in the Provincial style along the south-central coast of Peru, bears Imperial Cusco influences. At first glance, the form appears to be a mountain effigy or a model of the great temple at Pachacamac, a settlement with a 1,500-year history, last occupied by the Inkas. Under the Inka, the temple was dedicated to the sun, also known as Inti, and housed the *rimac* (spirit who talks), or oracle. The vessel was made between AD 1470 and 1532 and formed part of an offering to this sacred site.

The three lower steps of the vessel's form represent *cocha*, or basins; the fourth is a platform; and the fifth comprises a cylindrical neck and expanded rim. The cocha—finely crafted, with slightly curved lower walls—resemble catchments in the arid mountains of the coast where water appears only during the rainy season. Similar cocha are found in the surrounding archaeological remains.

The vessel's front is decorated with small circles centered on dots, symbols for water. The lower part of the design displays an abstraction of agricultural terraces. The sides of the vessel are a metaphor for the arms and hands that sustain the cocha. Most likely created for ritual purposes, the vessel is painted according to the Andean cosmological tradition of *messa*, contrasting a light and a dark color. The top right side is white, which symbolizes snow and the male (*paña*), while the left side is dark, symbolizing Pachamama, or Mother Earth, and the female (*lloque*). The colors in the cocha alternate black-white-black on the *paña* side and white-black-white on the *lloque* side.

—Ramiro Matos (Quechua)

Inka qero

Gold and silver Inka drinking vessels were called *akilla*; wooden ones, *qeros*. The exteriors of wooden qeros were painted in multicolored, geometrical scenes, a technique learned in Pasto, in southern Colombia.

This qero bears a figurative scene divided by a central strip of *tokapu*—geometrical drawings whose meanings are not yet known. The scene shows the transportation of wooden beams from the warm valleys to the highlands of the Andes. Wooden beams were used in Colonial Inka construction projects, especially in the structure of the roofs of 17th-century temples, many of which can still be seen today. The mules below the tokapu band walk in one direction, those above in the other. In this way the artist conveyed the idea of an ascent from the lowlands of the east to the mountains.

The horsemen are either Spaniards or mestizos. One of the mules transports their baggage. The figures on foot are indigenous, as their style of dress indicates. The women offer qeros of *chicha*, a corn-based drink, to the travelers. Beside them are large, bicolored jugs with typical Inka designs. The painting is completed with an arrow pointing in an unclear direction, a palm orchard, and a mastiff dog.

Qeros were always made in pairs, one with masculine and the other with feminine connotations.

—Jorge A. Flores Ochoa (Quechua)

Inka qero, AD 1550–1800. Cuzco, Peru. Wood, paint, plant resin; 23 x 18 cm. Presented by Mrs. Thea Heye. 16/6132
Below: Rollout detail of the scene painted on the qero.

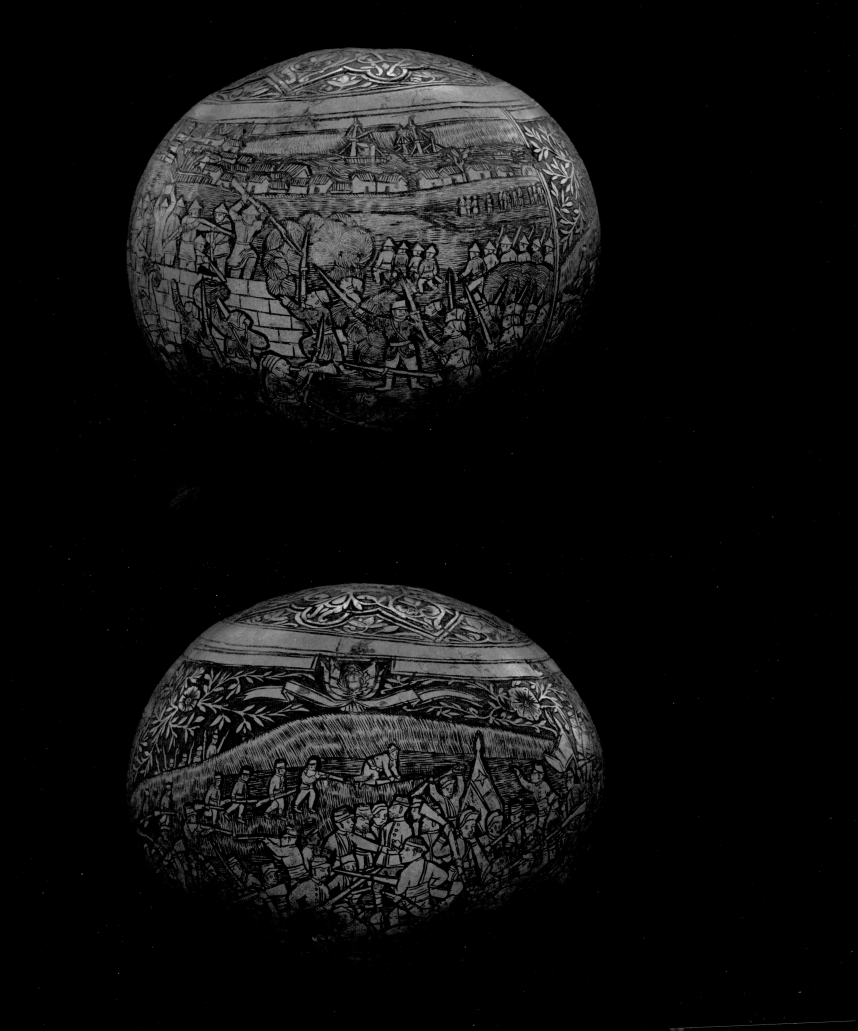

Mariano Flores Kananga (Quechua)

Carved gourd

We are confident that this engraved gourd—an Ayacucho-style sugar bowl—was crafted by Mariano Flores Kananga, a Quechua-speaking peasant from the village of San Mateo, at the top of Mayocc in Tayacaja Province, Peru. Flores is recognized as the best narrator of Peruvian customs, stories, and important events working in the medium, a traditional art of his time. In pieces made by Flores, we see information in even the smallest detail, so much so that people recognized each figure he depicted. This scene—the final encounter between Peruvian and Chilean forces at Arica on June 7, 1880—represents one of the culminating moments of the War of the Pacific (1879–1883), which weakened Peru's position as a continental power.

Flores's narrative blends maritime and Andean landscapes. From a wall or fort, Peruvian fighters—some shown wearing *lapichuco*, conical headgear typical of the Andean regions of Ayacucho and Andahuaylas—throw stones, mud bricks, and sticks at Chilean infantrymen, many of whom are dressed in the Zouave style adopted from the French army. The Peruvians are defending a mountain village, represented by a central plaza, churches, adobe houses with gabled roofs, and surrounding fields. Turning the gourd, we see the port of Arica, where the Chilean army surrounds the Peruvians, blocking their escape. The Chilean ships *Cochrane* and *Blanco Encalada* are shown in the background. In the final scene, on the hilltop where the battle ended, Colonel Francisco Bolognesi lies dying, aiming his revolver at his attackers, in fulfillment of his promise to fight until the last shots are fired. Another colonel, Roque Sáenz Peña, is being captured, while Commander Guillermo More falls lifeless at the feet of his brothers-in-arms. Peruvian sailors, survivors of the naval battle of Angamos, are shown trying to hold off the enemy with bayonets.

The understanding of property, citizenship, and civil rights among Quechua and Aymara-speaking Peruvians was worlds apart from the republican and constitutional ideas forced on them through conquest and colonialism. Indigenous Peruvians identified national government with Peru's ethnic tax. When the Chilean expeditionary army entered the highlands, however, indigenous Peruvians fought to maintain their dignity and way of life on lands the Quechua had inhabited for millennia. The Peruvian coat of arms that decorates the last scene of the Battle of Arica is a symbol of the people's love for their homeland.

Mariano Flores, who was nearly a century old when he died in 1949, would have been around thirty during the war. The details of his re-creation lead us to believe that he may have reproduced from memory an event he witnessed, perhaps even one in which he took part. Vivid stories might have provoked in his imagination and hands the capture of the hill and the failed naval campaign. But what are we to think about those Zouave-uniformed Chileans, whose appearance he is unlikely to have learned from books to which he could not have had access? Or the unusual headgear worn by the guerilla defenders of their country, about which the official history still has not given any account? Here ancestral art and vision are fused with personal and national history to create one of the most unique portrayals of war ever made, and a moment of indigenous Peruvian patriotism still relatively unknown.

— **Fernando Flores-Zuñiga, Percy Medina (Quechua), and Elizabeth Chanco (Quechua)**

Mariano Flores Kananga (Quechua, ca. 1850–1949), ca. 1925. Ayacucho, Peru. Gourd, pigment; 17 x 18 cm. Egbert P. Lott Collection. 15/9952

Households, villages, and waterways

IN THE AMAZON TODAY there are thousands of indigenous villages and hundreds of Native languages used in daily communication. Constitutional rights of indigenous peoples have been greatly increased since the 1980s, and the amount of legally demarcated territory under indigenous administration continues to expand. Indian presence, however, is not restricted to reservation enclaves; it is pervasive, and the Amazon's connection with its indigenous past goes much deeper than legally recognized peoples and territories. A vast Amazonian peasantry makes its living from river and forest resources and knows no other ancestry than its roots in the regional soil. The peoples of the Amazon—their cultivation techniques and subsistence crops, their preferred foods and specialized cuisine, healing techniques and diagnoses of illness, popular festivals and tales—represent elaborations of indigenous civilizations born in the area and its surrounding regions. Whether or not they identify as Indians, Amazonians enjoy their flavoring of *tucupi*, derived from the manioc tuber (*Manihot esculenta* L.); suffer from *panema* when hitting a tough streak of luck in hunting or fishing; and remain enthralled with the seductive menace that the *boto*, or freshwater dolphin, presents to unwary women.[1] The impositions of European colonialism; religious conversion; and the boom-and-bust rubber, mining, and logging industries have been part of a long history that has launched new identities and modes of interaction, but has also followed lines of continuity. It can be argued that these lines of continuity mark the Amazon as a region.

An overview of the Amazonian objects acquired by George Heye brings to the fore the role of material culture as an instrument of communication, at both the personal and intraregional level. The social life of Amazonians is built up through relations with nature and between different ethnicities (although the term "ethnicity" must be used advisedly, for in almost no instance are ethnic identities themselves the focus of ritual or even political activity). Most of the pieces shown on these pages were collected between 1910 and 1970 and represent peoples from far-flung areas within the large region. A striking commonality of experience emerges when considering historical contacts between European colonial powers and the peoples represented here. Although the Xingu region and the Jivaroan territories of Ecuador are exceptional in seeing consistent European contact only after the latter part of the 19th century, in all other areas indigenous independence was reasserted after initial colonial domination. These areas produced coalitions of different peoples that were successful in expelling Europeans for lengthy periods of time. The Spanish were banished from the central Selva area of Peru between 1742 and 1847 and from the Orinoco headwaters between 1776 and the early 20th century. In Brazil, transit along the Araguaia was halted between the 1730s and 1782 due to a royal edict designed to prevent gold smuggling; the river was only sparsely traveled for decades afterwards, the balance of forces remaining quite favorable to indigenous peoples. Thus the Amazon represents nations that gained significant experience in knitting together ties with other groups to resist missionaries, colonists, and agents of the state. During the respite from colonial control, significant consolidation of traditions and diplomacy

Shuar *akitiai* (ear ornaments), ca. 1930. Upper Amazon, Ecuador. Beetlewing covers, toucan feathers, plant fibers, glass beads; 27 x 11 cm. Collected by Dr. Victor Wolfgang von Hagen. 18/8740

occurred, and this shaped subsequent responses to the push by nation-states to assert control over the territories and activities of indigenous communities.

The Amazon region takes it name from the main channel of the world's most voluminous river. An immense natural catchment, the Amazon basin collects waters from the great Andean range as well as the massive plateau lands that flank it along the north and south. The portion of the channel called the Amazon swells from the combined waters of the Solimões and Purus rivers that join the great Rio Negro at the city of Manaus. The river continues east through the tropical forest heartland of Brazil, passing the Switzerland-sized island of Marajó at its mouth, before disgorging into the Atlantic. Breathtaking in its length, width, and sheer volume, the Amazon comprises the geographic centerpiece of the northern part of the South American continent.

Just above the Amazon watershed, the Orinoco River forms another drainage basin that extends over most of Venezuela and parts of Colombia. Beginning hard on the Venezuelan border along the western edge of the Brazilian state of Roraima, the Orinoco flows northwesterly and eventually traces the boundary between Venezuela and Colombia before circling back eastward to disgorge in the delta facing the Caribbean island of Trinidad. Part of the Orinoco's current meanders through the level Casiquiare Canal, where it joins the Rio Negro. The Amazon region thus encompasses the highlands dividing the two drainage basins, and ample examples of trade, transit, and cultural commonalities, as well as geography, make the upper and middle range of the Orinoco part of the greater Amazon. A number of nation-states have significant parts of their territory located in the Amazon; chief among these is, of course, Brazil, but also Colombia, Venezuela, Ecuador, Peru, Bolivia, French Guyana, Guyana, and Suriname.

Before the arrival of Europeans, the Amazon region had already been shaped by in-migration of peoples from other areas, the dissemination of crops and technology within the basin and its environs, and territories structured by patterns of conflict and trade.

For example, a large number of different strains of manioc and a number of ingenious devices for turning the often poisonous varieties into reliable and long-storing staples had turned most of Amazonia into an area of manioc (sometimes also referred to as cassava or yucca) cultivation.[2] Protein from either fish or game must be consumed as well, since manioc is deficient in key nutrients. Amazonian peoples have a highly developed knowledge of the habits of animals and many uses for wild plants that complement different manioc staple foods.

Marajoara culture
Widely distributed archaeological remains show the antiquity of the spread of manioc cultivation. Especially for inland areas, however, the archaeological record is quite sparse, and little is known about overland movements. It is certain that river travel promoted mobility and interaction over extensive distances. Despite this general understanding, however, there is much about the early period of human habitation in the Amazon that remains a mystery.

The magnificent ceramic vessels from the eastern portion of the Marajó Island, for example, constitute the flowering of a style that later declined and has no contemporary equal among Amazonian ceramicists. Pottery decoration often shows composite figures of anthropomorphized animals or combinations of different species in a single figure.[3] Its imagery, which likely relate to transformations of bodily form expressed in myth, places this pottery within a broad American tradition for which Mesoamerica and the Andes furnish the most developed examples.

The pieces shown here are ceremonial ware. The mounds in which they were found were used both for living and for elaborate funerary rites. In contrast to the observances of contemporary Amazonians, who tend to be more egalitarian, elaborate burial practices were reserved for only a few members of the community and indicate the presence of a society differentiated between elites and nonelites. Complex techniques are employed for ceremonial vessels and reveal standardization—they were sometimes produced in pairs,

Marajó bowl, AD 400–1300. Island of Marajó, State of Pará, Brazil. Clay, paint; 13 x 8 cm. Gorbiniano Villaca Collection. 14/6334

Marajó jar, AD 400–1300. Island of Marajó, Brazil. Clay, slip; 16 x 19 cm. Gift of the Mattatuck Historical Society. 24/1938

Marajó bowl, AD 400–1300. Rio Gurupi, State of Maranhão, Brazil. Clay, paint; 14 x 11 x 5 cm. Collected by Arthur H. Fisher. 14/9744

for example—that implies manufacture by ceramic specialists.[4] Other rare ceramic artifacts—such as stools, spoons, earplugs, figurines, and *tangas* (a female pubic covering that has entered into general language as the term for Brazilian bikini bottoms!)— also are not associated with domestic spaces.

The height of the Marajoara style occurred between AD 700 and 1100; afterward, the mound centers no longer were the focus of religious or domestic life.[5] Urns became less elaborate and styles more diversified, and the incidence of cremation after death increased.

Northwest Amazonia and the Guianan highlands

The present-day reality of European settlement in the Amazon is a poor guide to the past. By way of example, we can look at the Rio Negro region—which, although sparsely populated today, was an intermediary in a chain of trade that extended both toward the Andes to the west and the Guianan highlands to the east.[6] The contest between Portuguese and Spanish empires made this area the frontlines in border conflicts. Despite military defeats suffered by powerful groups and a good deal of migration and reshuffling of settlements, a macroregional sociopolitical system involving dozens of peoples of different languages and origins has always reconstituted itself over the centuries.[7] Marriages and the sharing of technology, ritual, foodstuffs, and raw materials extend over a wide area defined by the Rio Negro, the Içana, Uaupés, Guiania, and other, smaller rivers, and their interfluvial areas. Today the network sprawls through Venezuela, Brazil, and Colombia and involves a complex interlacing of alliances and traditional antagonisms.

If we start with a local group, we can begin to build up a picture of how material culture nurtures the fertility of the cosmos so that body, spirit, and intellect

Germano Teixeira (Wanano) using a ritual cigar-holder during a boy's naming ceremony, 1979. Rio Uaupés, Brazil.

may thrive. Each local settlement is composed of a group of brothers and their in-marrying wives, these women having been raised in communities speaking different first languages from those of their prospective husbands.[8] Groups sharing a common home language rank their respective communities oldest to youngest by the birth order of their founders. While each named group, such as Tukano, Desana, or Tuyuka, designates a distinct language composed of descendants from the same ancestor, material culture is shared throughout a regional network of kinship and alliances. The Tukano grouping has lent its name to the language family as a whole, and Tukano is used as a lingua franca throughout the network in both Spanish-speaking and Portuguese-speaking countries.[9] Each language family specializes in products required by others, which must, therefore, be acquired through trade, often at ceremonies called *po?oa* that involve reciprocal exchange between intermarrying communities and their allies.[10] Strict equivalencies of value are observed between items, so that Tukanos, who make wooden benches, exchange them for grater boards, strainers, and baskets at a fixed rate. The narratives and places cited in ritual performance encode the complexities of entanglements with colonial powers and emergent nation-states. The sounds produced by flutes and trumpets enable the chant-owner to travel to far-flung areas, tracing the historical geography of significant events that occurred in the different places named. Male and female initiation and curing are occasions when ritual chanting joins the imagery of destruction and upheaval with the agents of nurturing and healing, so that proper balance can be reestablished.[11]

The propagation and well-being of individual males and females, and of communities, requires extensive communication, and the displayed items can be understood as instruments of ritual action that make it possible for the society to tap into the flow of cosmic forces that provide fertility and make humans whole and healthy. Along with hallucinogenic substances, tobacco smoke, incense, and music function as means of communication necessary to sustain human life.

The shaman's stool represents the central connections between world layers in which distinct cosmological forces interact. The stool serves as a platform for communication. The striped diamonds on its sitting surface represent patterns on the skin of the anaconda-canoe, while the legs, seat, and seated person model an upward progression of layers, commencing with the female, uterine-level located bottommost. Women should never sit on such a bench. In the same way that a yellow-red-blue cosmic axis is aligned in the stool, a different arrangement of these complementary colors is presented in the headdress, which features red and yellow feathers and the blue-red tail feathers of the macaw.[12]

Ritual communication brings together kin and marriage partners as well. The unity of dispersed communities is commemorated as the myths of origin are enacted, confirming the association of numerous communities into a larger society without the coordination of a power center that issues edicts and maintains order. In a profound sense, each household, consisting of a number of extended families, is church, factory, and hospice, but also embassy, using diplomacy and knowledge to knit nature and society together and keep enemies at bay.

Although the regional system in the northwest Amazon was initially affected by border disputes between contending empires, strong resistance from the Ye´kuana and allied peoples allayed Spanish pressure from the north. The Ye´kuana initially welcomed the entrance of Spaniards during the mid-18th century into the upper reaches of the Orinoco. They relished the trading possibilities and accepted protection from their traditional enemies, the Kariña. But the relationship soon soured, and the Ye´kuana, in cooperation with other peoples of the region, rose up and forced the Spanish to abandon the string of forts they had set up to control the area. A coordinated uprising during a single evening in 1776 signaled the beginning of a century-and-a-half of relative freedom from Spanish intervention, although conflicts with indigenous Yanomami peoples grew in intensity.[13] Cut off from access to Spanish goods, the Ye´kuana soon sought

Tukanoan headring, ca. 1925. Rio Uaupés, State of Amazonas, Brazil. Macaw
feathers, orpendola feathers, toucan feathers, wood splints, plant fiber; 54
x 26 cm. Collected by Dr. Herbert S. Dickey. 16/375

Waiwái *pakára* (double basket), ca. 1910. Guyana. Mukru fiber, macaw feathers, cordage; 35 x 14 x 15 cm. Collected by A. Hyatt Verrill. 7/5021

new sources of iron manufactures. Eventually, a route was traced that led from the headwaters of the Orinoco, down through the territory of Brazil, and up the Essequibo River in Guiana to its mouth on the Caribbean, where trade with the Dutch (and later the British) could be established.[14]

The Orinoco watershed encompasses diverse environments, and within this area long distance trade is not unique to the Ye´kuana. Yde mentions the acquisition of Waiwái manioc graters from the savanna-dwelling Wapixana, while Guss refers to long-standing relations with the Makuxi that the Ye´kuana came to reject in their quest to deal directly with the Dutch.[15] Resources and manufactures from many different ecological regions are exchanged here, including salt, mussel pearl shell, stones for graters, pottery clay, and different plant products, including latex, plants needed to make arrow poison, bark for cigar wrappers, stools, hunting dogs, and talking parrots, as well as items of European manufacture, such as axe heads and machetes. In order to produce graters, the Waiwái themselves must undertake lengthy expeditions to gather necessary materials. Although every settlement is fiercely independent and maintains autonomy in its own affairs, each may be dependent on trade for even essentials. The Waiwái acquired the arrow reed they needed from the Mawayéna people, until they began to cultivate it themselves.[16]

The existence of long chains of trade networks meant that peoples of the interior received metal tools and other European goods—and, no doubt, Eurasian infectious diseases—long before they came face to face with colonial agents. At no time do there appear to be attempts by individuals to monopolize this trade in order to gain political leverage.[17] Nonetheless, evil is thought to have entered the world along with iron tools acquired through trade.[18]

Asháninka men formally dressed in cotton *kithaarentze*, body paint, and headdresses, 1964. Fernando Stahl mission village, Shahuaya, Upper Ucayali River, Peru.

Despite, or perhaps because of, the autonomy of individuals and settlements, there is a broad sharing of ideas across the enormous Guiana shield region of the northeastern Amazon. Thus the sort of weaving style seen in Ye´kuana *waja*, or circular serving trays, in which thin strips of different-colored cane are used to create designs, each with its own name and mythic referent, can also be seen in the Waiwái *pakára*. Among both peoples the double basket is used as storage for items associated with healing, such as packets of herbs, crystals, stones, and tobacco.[19] Many daily activities of a practical sort are accompanied by ritual and derive significance from their connection with mythic events. Technical mastery of basketry is associated with broad knowledge of the rituals associated with preparing raw materials and of the mythic events relating to the origin of the object being made.

The Andean montaña and adjacent lowlands

On the western side of the Amazon basin, the eastern foothills of the Andes extend from approximately 600 to 2,000 meters in elevation, separating the Andean highlands from the tropical forest of lower elevation.

Rainfall is higher in the foothills than on the basin floor, the height of the forest canopy is lower, and vegetation grows in denser stands.[20] The looming peaks of the highlands press against the tropical forest, and archaeological evidence for exchange between the regions goes back thousands of years. The profusion of languages reveals a complex history of settlement and interaction. Despite long-standing contact, the empires that rose and fell in the highlands were never able to extend their domination over the peoples of the forest in more than a cursory fashion. The sacred coca leaf used in highland culture was always in great demand, though, and the Inka used a variety of tactics, including conquest, trade, and resettlement, to maintain the desired supply from the lowland regions where coca was cultivated.[21]

Situated between the Andean highlands and the lowland tropical forests, the Asháninka (Campa) have long had contact with neighboring Arawak speakers—the Machiguenga, Nomatsiguenga, Amuesha and Piro—as well as with Indians from other linguistic backgrounds, such as the Shipibo and Conibo. All of these peoples have some version of the woven cotton

Asháninka
kithaarentze (tunic),
ca. 1925. Upper
Ucayali River, Peru.
Cotton, dye; 140 x
128 cm. Collected by
Wilhelm Schaeffler.
19/5956

Shipibo *chitonte* (woman's skirt), ca. 1925. Ucayali River, Peru. Cotton, paint; 64 x 66 cm. Collected by Wilhelm Schaeffler. 19/5940

Conibo jar, ca. 1910. State of Amazonas, Brazil. Clay, paint; 19 x 34 cm. Collected by Dr. William C. Farabee; exchange with University of Pennsylvania Museum. 18/1949

robe, or *kushma* (a Quechua word, the Asháninka is *kithaarentze*[22]). Asháninka women weave these garments with cotton they cultivate, spin, and dye with their own hands. Robes are sometimes used as trade items in male trading partnerships. New kushmas are reserved for formal occasions, such as visits to other communities. Once they have become soiled, they are dyed brown and used for everyday wear.[23]

In this area of the Amazon, diverse Indian peoples came together to push Europeans out of the region entirely. In the Peruvian central Selva, this transpired some two centuries after the initial Spanish conquest. Resistance centered around the so-called Cerro de la Sal (salt mountain). Although the mountain itself lay within territory used by the Amuesha (Yanesha)

Indians and neighboring groups of Asháninka, it attracted peoples from across the region in search of blocks of salt to extract and trade down river. Establishing his headquarters in this area, a mestizo rebel highlander, Juan Santos Atahualpa, directed a war to topple Spanish control. His use of the name Atahualpa, the Inka emperor executed by Pizarro, was emblematic of a struggle that sought to restore Indian rule. Juan Santos was never decisively vanquished, and until 1756 he continued to issue communiqués from his redoubt in the Gran Pajonal, the grasslands occupied by the Asháninka.[24]

The unity of highland and lowland Indians envisioned in the statements of Juan Santos was never consolidated, but the Asháninka were not the only lowland peoples to join his military campaign. His personal guard was composed of Piro Indians, and he distributed metal tools to different peoples, such as the Conibo, as a way of promulgating his leadership. Although a military thrust into the highlands was eventually repelled, the Spanish military, missionaries, and colonists did not return, and the eastern tropical forest region of Peru began a century-long hiatus from colonial administration.

Shipibo and Conibo

The lower portion of Asháninka territory lies above the winding Ucayali River. The Ucayali meanders through alluvial soils deposited from the Andes, turning back on itself and sometimes forming oxbow lakes. Along its banks, peoples such as the Shipibo and Conibo make use of the river's fish, aquatic mammal, and reptile resources to complement the gardens of corn, sweet manioc, and other staples they cultivate on the rich floodplain. These peoples are renowned for their dexterity in handling watercraft and make good use of the mobility afforded by their expertise. Since the 17th century, their position along a major waterway also has exposed them to incursions from missionaries. The Shipibo and Conibo have been part of a long and complex history involving relations with agents of Spanish colonialism, but also with pulses of warfare and raiding, particularly upon groups living in areas away from the major waterways. The Shipibo and Conibo have sometimes used their position along the river to gain access to metal tools and firearms, which yield advantages in contests with inland groups and one another. River travel enables the Shipibo to collect the resin, tempers, firewood and pebbles for polishing ceramics, these last located some 400 kilometers distant.[25]

Along with other ethnicities from the central lowlands of Peru, the Shipibo and Conibo were part of the coalition of peoples who took part in the uprising against the Spanish in 1742. Subsequent attempts by Jesuits to regain a foothold in this area were met by a generalized revolt in 1766. Only after 1790 was a missionary presence again a fact of life along the Ucayali.

After Peruvian independence in 1821, the region became engulfed in the rubber boom, and entire communities were forced to labor for rubber bosses. Indians became involved in the trade of other commercial products, such as sarsaparilla, turtle eggs, and manatee blubber, as well. During the 20th century, pressure from Ucayali mestizo elements brought the Shipibo and the Conibo together. Today they refer to one another as Jónibo (the people) or Jónicobo (the real people) in acknowledgment of a common identity.[26]

The geometrical designs echoing features of Shipibo–Conibo art have diffused up and down the Ucayali and Urubamba rivers and have engaged the imagination of artists of many different ethnicities. Shipibo–Conibo men make an array of items from wood, cane, bone, or stone, including the masterfully made canoes. And men are largely responsible for transmitting the oral heritage of myths, tales, and songs. However, with few exceptions,[27] only women artists execute the design patterns found both on their own creations—ceramics, beadwork, and cloth—and on objects made by men. In earlier times, the designs were ubiquitous, and any item of Shipibo–Conibo material culture, from house beams, to cooking utensils, to weaponry, might carry these complex patterns. The human body is also a canvas for the intricate motifs.[28] The

An Achuar man visiting a house on the Kapawi River, 1977. Ecuador.

appearance of the elaborate designs on such a diversity of media projected a powerful unified aesthetic. The style—which appears to be an amalgam of a cultural tradition that swept into the region around AD 500 and different indigenous and mestizo traditions within the multiethnic mission villages along the Ucayali—has retained its coherency since the 19th century.[29]

Shipibo-Conibo design—called *quënea* or *quené*—consists of explicit named elements and can be classified into rectilinear and curvilinear variants.[30] Working within an overall stylistic structure, women develop their individual styles by studying exemplary works of other artists, often traveling to see singular works. Libraries of designs may be stored in the private collections of avid potters. Creativity, complexity of form, and intricacy of the filler motifs are valued attributes of the aesthetic. Each design is original and copies are not made.

Shuar and Canelos Quichua of the Ecuadoran lowlands

The lands lying on the eastern side of the Andean range northward within Ecuador were also influenced by developments in the highlands, which have included the rise and fall of state societies over many hundreds of years. Such influences have seeped into the mythology and tales of Amazonians in this region. There is evidence of trade and conflict as well. The brightly colored feathers of birds from the lowlands—as well as the images of caymans, monkeys, snakes, and jaguars seen in the motifs and the stone artwork of the Chavín culture as early as 1000 BC—testify to the centrality of the Amazon in the imagination of highlanders.[31] Quichua, a variant of the Quechua language of the highlands, was widely spoken in the adjoining lowlands. It is probable that lowland Quichua developed from Quechua through a different route than the idiom spoken by the Inkas, whose dialect developed from a southern peripheral variant.[32]

The lowland areas lying southeast of Quito promised riches, but also presented considerable difficulties for the collection of cinnamon or gold, both of which were coveted by the Spanish. While missions were established, much of the region remained part of a largely unknown area within the enormous Oriente Province. Within the Oriente some territories were never missionized nor brought under any sort of administrative control until well into the 19th century. This was due, in part, to the area's daunting reputation, earned during an early rebellion in 1599, when Jivaroan-speaking peoples decisively beat back battalions of armed Spaniards.

Jivaroan peoples comprise an ethnolinguistic group composed of various subgroups that formerly raided and traded among themselves: the Shuar, Achuar, Shiwiar, Huambisa, and Aguaruna. The Shiwiar are located exclusively in Ecuador. Although the Shuar and Achuar primarily occupy territories located in Ecuador, they and the other subgroups have a presence in Peru as well. Anne Christine Taylor points out the centuries-old pattern whereby different Jivaroan groups maintain ongoing relations with non-Jivaroans peoples.[33] Formal trade relationships, similar to those seen among the Asháninka, exist here as well, permitting trade to continue even in the midst of conflict.

Trade is often a result of specialized skills associated with different groups. Finely crafted blowguns and *tawasap* (feathered headdresses), for example, are produced by the Achuar for a thriving intertribal trade, as are hunting dogs, curare poisons for hunting, and other items.[34] Intermarriage between peoples, the ability to speak both Quichua and Achuar or Shuar, and the exchange of goods and services—Canelos Quichua shamans may be consulted and they may also be the sources of power employed by Jivaroan shamans, for example—all point to repeated transactions between peoples. Taylor suggests a cultural convergence between peoples: "Jivaroans and Canelos share a lot that goes unremarked—similar bodily techniques, work habits, mythic narratives, diets, ways of using and understanding language, and manners of interacting."[35] Personal pedigrees of indigenous people in this region are full of allusions to ancestors of different ethnicities. Overall, the interaction taking place within the region can be called intercultural, because each of the existing peoples uses the cultural

traditions of others to understand its own configuration of belief and organization.

Although there have been recent changes in settlement patterns,[36] Shuar formerly lived in extended family households that were thinly dispersed across a wide territory in the eastern foothills of the Andes. Each household was a node in a network of people related by kinship and marriage, and committed to mutual help and mutual defense. There was no central authority and no kind of political hierarchy, although shamans, trading partners, and powerful men (*kakárum*) were recognized. The large, often fortified house was divided into a male and a female area, and women entered the male area to serve food and manioc beer to male residents and to guests. House layout was standardized: the sitting place and stool (*chimpui*) of the male head of the household, the placement of the wooden bench reserved for visitors (*kutank*), the sleeping places of a man and his wives, as well as those of the daughters and the daughters' husbands. Men faced the perils of the forests; women had to contend with the proclivity of manioc plants to suck the blood of human beings.[37] Both men and women made use of their ability to search for and interpret dreams and visions in order to understand the true nature of things and plot out the best course for human action.

All Shuar ceremonies are necessarily celebrated in households, with guests specially invited. It can take days of walking through the forest just to deliver the invitations. Visits between households are the occasion for heightened formality in which a defined protocol for behavior is observed; bodily decoration is applied; and beautiful ornaments, such as the beetle-wing ear ornaments and dance belts, are worn. Ceremonies involve dancing by men and women, the playing of drums, and the consumption of manioc

beer. A successful ceremony results in the consolidation of a man's place in a social network, and also in the strengthening of the supernatural power that ritual activities are designed to channel and make available to the ceremony sponsor.

Tapirapé, Karajá, Kayapó, and Xinguano societies of central Brazil

The Araguaia River of Brazil runs northward through the rolling savanna country and tropical forest before it joins the Tocantins. During much of the 18th century until 1782, the waterway between the southern colony of Brazil and the northern colony of Grão Pará was closed to travel in order to discourage contraband that would diminish tax revenue for the Crown. Historical records show that some 800 Karajás from two different groups were brought to São José de Mossamedes, an Indian settlement established by the

province of Goiás in 1781.[38] Non-Indian settlement in the province, however, tumbled with the decline of mining, and as late as 1903 a visiting priest traveling down the Araguaia remarked, "In sum, for most of its extent the Araguaia Valley is savage country: the left bank is occupied by Cayapós, Carajás, Chavantes, Tapirapés and other indigenous tribes and, during a stretch of 180 to 200 leagues, there is no sign of Christian inhabitants."[39]

Like the Shipibo–Conibo, the Karajá used their position along the main waterways to get access to trade goods from agents of colonial powers. But they have also sought trade relations with peoples such as the Xikrin–Kayapó, from whom they received vines and beeswax to fashion arrows, macaw tail-feathers, and macaw and parakeet hatchlings in return for beads, machetes, and axes.[40] Despite great linguistic differences between them, the Tapirapé and the Javaé, one of the three big Karajá groups, have long lived in proximity. The Javaé have been the source of metal tools for the Tapirapé as well, along with songs and, sadly, epidemic diseases. The Tapirapé share broadly similar mythic narratives with the Karajá.[41] While the Tapirapé have fought extensively against the Kayapó and the Karajá, there is ample evidence that they also have

Mebêngôkre burden basket, ca. 1920. State of Pará, Brazil. Cane, buriti fiber, cordage; 44 x 43 x 47 cm. Collected by Francis Gow-Smith. 13/6071

had a profound cultural influence on one another and have intermarried as well.[42] Both Tapirapé and Karajá relate that the theft of a mask led to the departure of the Tapirapé from Bananal Island, which they formerly shared with the Karajá.

Little wonder that similar masked figures would appear prominently in the rituals of the Xikrin and Tapirapé, as well as those of the presumed originators of this tradition, the Karajá. Although the masks represent different kinds of spirits among the different peoples—for the Tapirapé, anchunga; the Xikrin–Kayapó, bô; the Karajá, ijasò—in all cases the masks incarnate these spirits and make themselves visible.

The spirits among the Karajá are particularly associated with water animals, and most originate in the river bottom. Rituals bring these original beings into the congregation of living humans, in which the masks dance with women to the sounds of the spirit's own music. There are many kinds of spirits and many kinds of masks, all of which bear distinct names. With rare exceptions, the ijasò appear in pairs and are the only masks that wear feathered ornaments on their crown.[43] When not performing, masks are housed in the men's house, off limits to females and uninitiated boys. Women and girls, however, play an indispensible role in rituals, as performers, sponsors, and feeders of the masks.

Kayapó and Xingu peoples

Some 200 years ago, the Kayapó were one among a number of similar communities on the Brazilian savanna that built large circular villages around a cleared central plaza. Rivalries between different factions within the group resulted in schisms and the formation of new communities, some of which became enduring entities in their own right. The Xikrin originated in such a factional dispute.

Kayapó are masters of mobility and collective action. Burdened by neither hammocks nor pottery,

they were able to pack their belongings at a moment's notice and, traveling hard through the deep forest, live off the land for months at a time. A sleeping mat (rõnti-ô) can be fashioned from babassu palm leaves in less than ten minutes, a waterproof shelter with a thatched-palm roof in about twice the time. A toolkit can be produced with mollusk shells to use as scissors and tweezers, as well as a plane to smooth the wood of a war club (kô) or bow to the proper thickness.[44] Wild foods, such as Brazil nuts and cacao, can be collected, loaded into large baskets, and shared among the rest of the camp. Formerly, villages were occupied only part of the year, the other part being devoted to a trekking lifestyle that made hunting and collecting food more productive.

Young men and women and their older counterparts separate into groups to carry out different collective activities; raiding or work parties compete on a friendly basis to see who can best the other in accomplishment. While these age grades promote discipline and hard work, Kayapó also are expected to pursue their own development by seeking out elders with expertise from whom they might learn special songs, ritual knowledge, or abilities to heal. Some youngsters of both sexes are the recipients of great names and ritual privileges that contribute to the continuity of cultural knowledge, or kukradjà. Privileges include the right to wear certain ornaments, such as the mussel pearl shell necklace.[45] Other ornaments, such as the bandoliers decorated with the yellow feathers of the crested oropendula (arapê), may be worn by all participants in the collective dances. The transmission of names and privileges is ratified in a number of ceremonies that are joyfully celebrated by all as an occasion to experience the closeness of familial love and intimacy within the collective dances and feasts.[46] The beautiful ritual ornaments are on display by their owners at this time, and past generations who wore these ornaments, sang the songs, and danced the dances are thought to be literally present as well.

During the past two centuries, the different Kayapó subgroups have moved westward into forested savanna fringes and into the tropical forests proper in the states of Pará and Mato Grosso. Along the Xingu River, Kayapó repeatedly raided and visited the Juruna Indians—from whom they adopted the *kwor-kangô* (manioc liquid), a festival that has become a great name ceremony celebrated in all Kayapó villages.[47] Some groups moved as far west as the headwaters of the Xingu early in the 20th century.

This area had proved to be somewhat of a redoubt for indigenous people, protected by a treacherous stretch of rapids that delayed the first European incursion until 1884. During the preceding centuries, a unique society had arisen there that, despite persistent linguistic ethnocentrism, placed a premium on regional peace and joint defense against attacks from outside. Although the interconnected communities of this Xinguano society speak different languages, they intermarry, celebrate rituals in one another's villages, and share cultural styles and beliefs. Trade is an important part of the social convention governing relations between communities, with different communities maintaining monopolies over certain items that must be traded—a situation that recalls the exchanges between Tukanoan peoples.[48]

—William H. Fisher

A Xikrin boy, dressed by his mother in his ceremonial wealth and initiation attire, 1984. Bakajá Village, São José Porfírio Municipality, Pará, Brazil.

Mebêngôkre *ngâp* (ceremonial necklace)

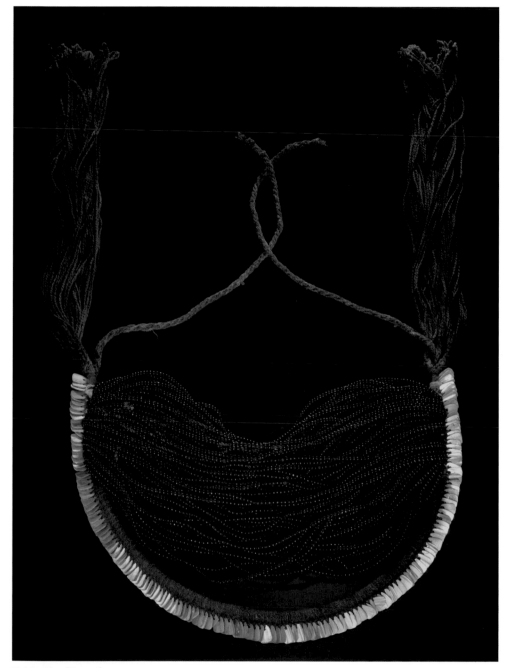

Mebêngôkre (Kayapó) *ngap*
(necklace), ca. 1960. State of
Pará, Brazil. Mother of pearl
from mussel shells, seeds,
cordage, paint or resin; 53 x 31
cm. Collected by George Love.
23/9438

Ngâp—ceremonial neck-
laces made by Kayapó
women from freshwa-
ter mussel shells, beads,
and cotton string (*kadjât
kunrâi*)—are worn by
adults and children in
rituals such as the Bemp,
Takâk, Kworokangô, and
Mebiok. These ceremonies
are the central focus of
social life in Kayapó communities. In them, people
receive new names, most
often from their grandparents. The ceremonies help
establish and confirm the
Kayapó identities of those
who receive names and celebrate the involvement of
the whole community.

The participation of
the entire community in
Kayapó ceremonies is very
important. The Kayapó
also seek to be beautiful
in their rituals. The value
of beauty (*mêtch*) and its
power (*prã*) are of major
importance to Kayapó
people.

—Piydjô Kayapó (Kayapó)

Tukanoan bench

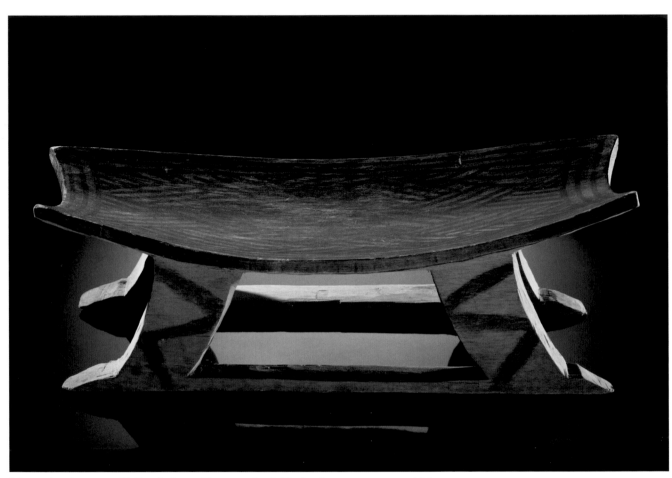

Tukanoan bench, ca. 1920. Rio Uaupés, State of Amazonas, Brazil. Wood, paint; 55 x 24 x 20 cm. 16/360

The Tukano make several types of ceremonial benches. The bench called *caapi* appeared when our ancestor emerged in human form. He was a *ʋhtãboho mahsɯ̃* (quartz stone being). His younger brother was a *taroʋhtã mahsɯ̃* (river stone being). The bench formed the pelvis of these Transforming Beings and, for this reason, was present during the transformation of humanity. Thus, these benches are considered to be seats of knowledge and of the life force of humans.

As the Transforming Beings journeyed through the houses of transformation, they sat on benches to converse, confer blessings, dance, sing, and drink ceremonial caapi, made from the *Banisteriopsis* vine. The designs on the bench represent different paths taken by the transformation canoe, up to the pelvis of the body of the God of Transformation of humanity. The feet of the bench are painted with designs of the *bayá*, leaders of ceremonial dance and chanting. Bayá designs are revealed during caapi ceremonies. The Transforming Beings had two sisters who, like their brothers, had their own life benches throughout the journey through the houses of transformation. The women had their own powers through the life bench, obtained through creation and transformation, as they accompanied the men.

The Tukano still view these benches as our ancestors viewed them, and our fathers continue to make benches for us to use in our homes, on ceremonial occasions, and in our houses of knowledge (traditional longhouses).

—Uremirĩ Aprigio Azevedo and Vilmar Azevedo (Tukano)

Achuar drinking horn (Canelos Quichua-made)

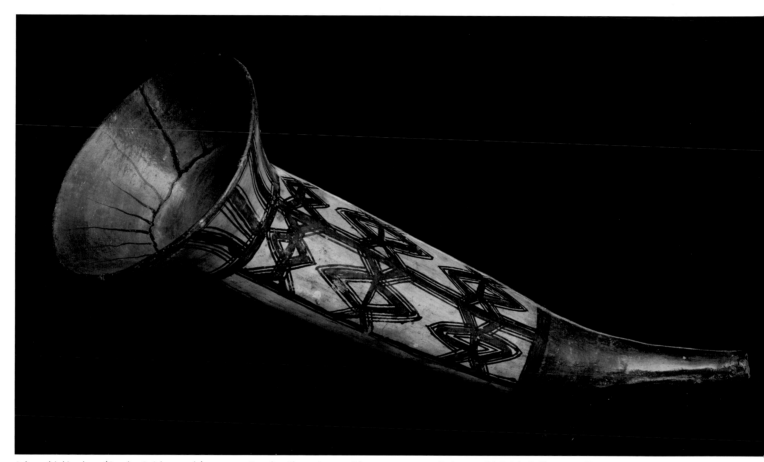

Achuar drinking horn (Canelos Quichua-made), ca. 1950. Ecuador. Clay, paint, varnish; 41 x 15 x 14 cm. Exchange with Ralph C. Altman. 22/8772

Shamanism is an important aspect of historical and present-day culture among the Shuar of the Amazon headwaters and the Achuar of the neighboring lowlands. In Shuar spiritual beliefs, *uwishin*, or shamans, are thought to possess magic and to be able to manipulate *tsentsak*—invisible, animate darts that will act when directed to.

By accumulating tsentsak, the Shuar believe they can protect themselves from, as well as attack, their enemies. The ability to control tsentsak can be attained by ingesting *natem* (typically *Banisteriopsis caapi*, a jungle vine of the family Malpighiaceae). Natem is used to prepare *ayahuasca*, a medicinal decoction and plant teacher whose use is still practiced as a religious sacrament among the Shuar. One takes ayahuasca in the presence of a shaman, from the shaman's hand or from a sacred cup.

Visions and dreams experienced during the sacrament are considered prophetic. For example, an adult male will typically rely on a vision to develop a hunting strategy and will look for corresponding omens throughout the hunt. There are several types of visions. *Kuntuknar* are positive visions of events that involve everyday things, such as the rainforest, family, waterfalls, animals, et cetera. *Mesekramprar* are visions designed to warn about impending disaster, such as disease, a raid by an enemy, or inclement weather—events that are believed to be inflicted by a shaman from an enemy tribe. During *penke karamprar*, the soul visits the soul of a deceased friend or relative. These visions can be positive or negative experiences, depending on whether the person died a peaceful or an unhappy death.

—Juan Carlos Jintiach and Richard Tsakimp (Shuar)

Shipibo *ainbo chomo* (water vessel in the form of a woman)

The intricate geometric designs are derived from the visions of murayá (shamans). Visions of these designs fill the murayá's mind's eye and are used by murayá for curing and for combating enemies.

—BAHUAN MËTSA

KNOWLEDGE KEEPER, SAN FRANCISCO DE YARINACOCHA

The Shipibo of the Ucayali River, a southern tributary of the Upper Amazon in Peru, produce some of the finest polychrome prefire slip-painted earthenware pottery in the world.[1] These ceramics, like the small water vessel (*ainbo chomo*) shown here, embody a unique tempering technology that took more than ten millennia to perfect. The process transforms their vessels' clay paste into a high tensile-strength composite material, allowing Shipibo ceramists to create the largest, thinnest, coil-built, complex-silhouette vessels in the Native Americas. The Shipibo are also notable in that they are one of the few indigenous groups in which the primary artists are women,[2] and whose principal rite of passage is a spectacular female, not male, puberty ceremony.[3] Shipibo women are also famous for cotton textiles woven in multiple colors, adorned with striking painted and embroidered designs.[4]

Shipibo art appears in multimedia covered with intricate, bilaterally symmetrical geometric designs in a baroque trilevel style.[5] The upper level, executed first, consists of broad formlines in rectilinear (*pontëquënëya*) and curvilinear (*mayaquënëya*) patterns; it is enhanced by secondary parallel finelines and tertiary intricate filler elements. Each design is unique, and insightful artistry is highly valued. The artist's inspiration is aided by covering her eyelids with the leaves of a colorfully veined *iponquënë*—named after a small but complexly patterned armor-headed catfish—in an effort to absorb their intricate tracery, as well as by dreams and visions. The designs originally derived from the hallucinogenic visions of male and rare post-menopausal female shamans using *ayahuasca* (or *nishi*), a psychotropic tea derived from the *Banisteriopsis caapi* vine, and strong tobacco (*romë rao*).[6]

In mythic times these patterns covered everything—the sky, trees, huts, people, animals, et cetera—in a continuous tissue of design. But due to the misdeeds of failed protohumans, this idyllic union ruptured and differentiated into floating, superimposed planes: Nëtë ŝhama (the sky world), Mai (the earth world), and Jënë ŝhama (the subaquatic underworld). Simultaneously, periodicity (day and night, or time), mortality, and speciation appeared.[7] And the geometric lineaments ruptured. Now they appear only on specific design fields, such as the upper parts of fineware pottery, people's faces, or the blades of war clubs. All these designs are preexistent; the artist has only to grasp and fix them in her mind (*shinan picotai*, "the thoughts emerge"), lay them over the design field, and cut where they match that field, letting the rest of the design fade back into invisibility. The visible design remains as a window into the vast reticulate intricacy of the universe.[8]

The people of the Upper Amazon today are under severe pressure from the surrounding Spanish-speaking *mestizo* population, commercial fishermen who have depleted the rivers and lakes of fish, turtles, and manatees, ruining the environment and destroying the Shipibo's subsistence base. The financial return from the tourist market,[9] largely the product of women's arts—textiles, jewelry, and pottery—is proving ever more crucial to buy the food, medicine, and access to Western education that will allow the Shipibo to survive in the modern world.[10] But their beautiful polychrome pots are more than a source of income: they are little portable versions of their triple-tiered universe.[11]

—Peter Roe and

Bahuan Mëtsa (Manuel Rengifo Barbaran, Shipibo)

Shipibo *ainbo chomo* (water vessel in the form of a woman), ca. 1965. San Francisco de Yarinacocha, Peru. Clay, paint; 23 x 28 cm. Collected by Mrs. Nicole H. Maxwell. 23/9608

Lords, cacicas, and the divine world

Maya archaeology

Between about AD 250 and 900, the Maya people maintained one of the most accomplished civilizations of world antiquity in the tropical lowlands of the Yucatán Peninsula and the mountains that form its broad base. Today that area—roughly half the size of Texas and divided among five nations—is home to some six million descendants of those ancient Maya. The Maya area comprises the eastern part of what we know as Mesoamerica, a land that stretches from the desert plateaus of north-central Mexico through Belize and Guatemala into the western reaches of Honduras and El Salvador. Its borders are imprecise, for they are defined not by politics, but rather by the similarity among the ways of the cultures and civilizations that occupied its highlands and lowlands beginning around 1500 BC.

The cultural practices that define Mesoamerica range from a subsistence pattern based largely on the cultivation of maize, to a religion based on a supernatural pantheon associated with nature and geography. Rituals and ceremonies included the sacred ball game and frequent sacrifices of both humans and animals. Mesoamericans excelled in astronomy and arithmetic and devised a complex calendar based on the cyclic movements of the sun, moon, and visible planets. This fundamental unity among cultures lasted for nearly 3,000 years, maintained by continual contact through commerce, occasional war and conquest, and political alliances that shifted over the passing centuries.

Olmec ceremonial axe, ca. 800–600 BC. State of Veracruz, Mexico. Granite; 31 x 17 x 12 cm. Leo Stein Collection; presented by Thea Heye. 16/3400

While cargo canoes plied the Atlantic and Pacific coastlines, human couriers walked a network of trails that crisscrossed the highlands and lowlands. Both carried pottery, textiles, obsidian, jade, shell, pigments, and dozens of other commodities for trade. The most important elements of this intercommunication, however, were the ideas that spread from one region to another in an unceasing exchange that unified cultures from the Olmec to the Mexica and beyond.

The Maya path to civilization began early in the first millennium BC, when the inhabitants of the Yucatán Peninsula adopted certain ideas of their neighbors and made them distinctly their own. These included the calendar and writing, as well as styles and motifs apparent in pottery, sculpture, and even architecture and city planning. This long-distance exchange is reflected in a Maya lidded vase (see page 105). Collected from Kaminaljuyú, a site within the suburbs of Guatemala City, it is stylistically identical to a class of elite ceramics common in the ancient metropolis of Teotihuacán, some 600 miles to the northwest. It dates to around AD 500, soon after powerful influences from that great city pervaded the Maya area. While the details regarding the nature of this cultural incursion are unclear, it played a key role in the formation of the early dynasties that ruled the city-states of the southern Maya lowlands.

During their cultural heyday, the Maya occupied more than 5,000 known settlements. Kings and queens—ruling in the name of the sun god and other ancestors, both real and mythical—held sway at such key centers as Caracol, Calakmul, Copán, Palenque, and Tikal. Following the abandonment of

Chupícuaro shell trumpet, AD 300–900. Chupícuaro, Mexico. Shell, stucco,
pigment; 11 x 15 x 24.5 cm. Exchange with Robert L. Stolper. 24/2892

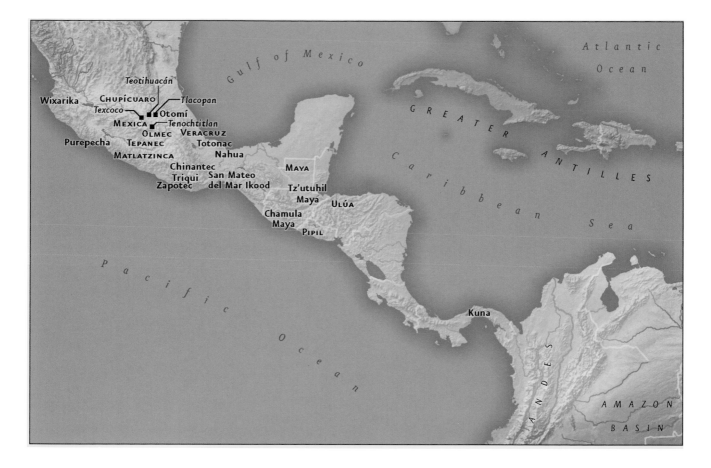

The Great Hieroglyphic Stairway.
Copán, Honduras.

Mexica Chicomecoatl (seven snakes), the maize goddess, AD 1325–1521. Probably Tenochtitlan, Mexico. Basalt; 70 x 30 x 15 cm. Fred Braun Collection. 8143

these and other cities by AD 900—a phenomenon still poorly understood—the Maya continued to flourish in Uxmal, Chichén Itzá, and other regional capitals in the highlands and lowlands until the Spanish appeared in their lands in the early 1500s.

Throughout the span of high civilization in the Maya area, various influences from distant Mesoamerican neighbors continue to show up in the surviving art and architecture and in smaller artifacts as well. The painted goggle-like pattern on the stone head from Uxmal, Yucatán, suggests that the subject of the portrait is in the guise of Tlaloc, the central Mexican god of rain and lightning, counterpart to the Maya Chaak (see page 104).[1]

The carefully chosen pieces shown here distill the essence of ancient Maya culture and civilization wrought by a society of elite nobility, warriors, traders, merchants, architects, sculptors, painters, and priests. Maya scribes, using the most sophisticated system of writing known in ancient America, recorded everything from simple tags of ownership, such as the short hieroglyphic text on a king's drinking cup (pages 92–93), to the sweeping grandeur of the history, both real and mythical, of their time and place. That record, deciphered only in recent decades, provides the living Maya, many of whom adhere to the beliefs and rituals of ancient tradition, with the knowledge of their long and distinguished history as one of the most accomplished cultures in the history of the world.

—George Stuart

The Mexica and the last Triple Alliance

Migrating from northern Mesoamerica, the Mexica and other Nahuatl-speaking peoples reached central Mexico in the 13th century AD. Upon their arrival, they found that many societies shared a common history strongly influenced by trade, war, and religion, in spite of ethnic, linguistic, and political differences. The Mexica's final destination was the Basin of Mexico, an area defined by five large lakes and the three societies already established there: The city of Colhuacan ruled the dominion that belonged to the Colhua ethnic

Teotihuacán mask, AD 200–600. Tlaltelolco, Mexico. Metamorphic greenstone; 28 x 28 cm. Conde de Penasco Collection. 2/6607

group, including the southern towns of Xochimilco and Cuitlahuac. Tetzcoco was the political capital of the Acolhua–Chichimeca, whose territory occupied the eastern strip. Azcapotzalco functioned as the capital of the Tepanec, who had settled in the western strip.

Given this intricate landscape, the Mexica had no choice but to found their capital city, Mexico-Tenochtitlan, on a small, uninhabited island in Lake Tetzcoco. As this was inside Tepanec territory, the Mexica became taxpayers to Azcapotzalco starting in 1325. But in the following century, things would change. In 1428 the Mexica militarily defeated their masters and established the last *excan tlatoloyan*, or Triple Alliance, comprising now the cities of Tenochtitlan, Tetzcoco, and Tlacopan.[1] Due to Mexico–Tenochtitlan's dominance, this alliance is wrongly referred to as the Mexica or Aztec empire. It is worth mentioning, as well, that the Mexica, after leaving their original homeland of Aztlan, never called themselves "Aztecs."

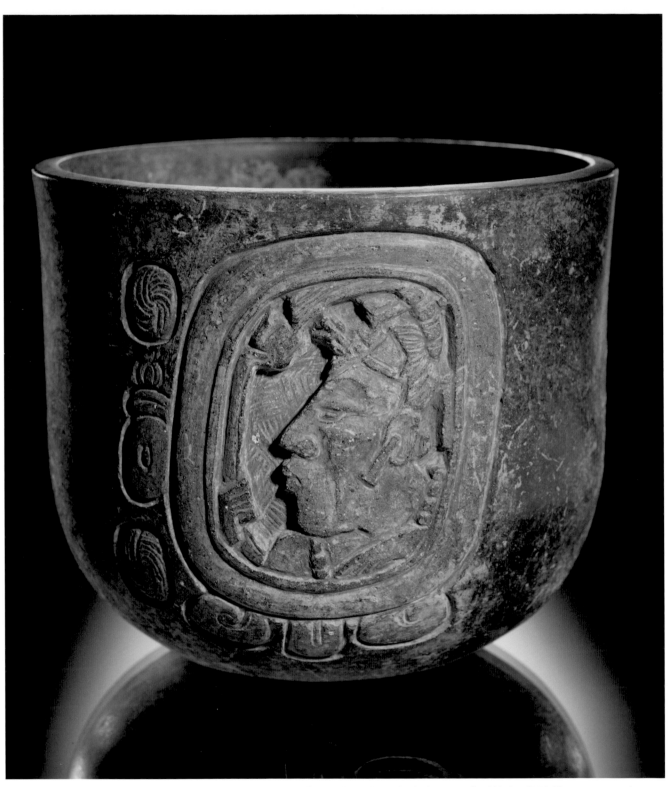

Maya slateware cup (front and back) bearing the hieroglyphic statement of ownership, "This is the drinking cup of K´ahk´ Uht K´inich [fire-countenanced sun god], King of Akankeh [modern Acanceh, Yucatán] and ball player," ca. AD 900. Chocolá, State of Campeche, Mexico. Clay, cinnabar; 11.5 x 13.5 cm. Exchange with James Economos. 24/8346

Infinity of Nations

Mexica Chinampanec Xipe Totec (our lord, the flayed one), war and harvest god, AD 1507. Tepepan, Federal District, Mexico. Basalt, pigment; 77.5 x 31 x 24 cm. Purchased in Paris. 16/3621

The excan tlatoloyan, a regional organization that transcended the state, was embedded in a setting of endemic warfare. Its main purpose was to resolve disputes between the different political entities that fell under its jurisdiction, although it also sought to look after the security of the region and absorb the states that resisted becoming part of the coalition. Under this pretext, its three capital cities led military expansion aimed at controlling the lake's basin and the large territory surrounding it.

To the west, in the Toluca and Ixtlahuaca valleys, other Chichimeca communities had reached important economic, cultural, and political heights. These groups formed an interesting linguistic confluence of peoples who spoke Otomian languages (Otomi, Mazahua, Matlatzinca, and Ocuilteca) and Nahuatl-speakers. When the Mexica began their expansionary period, the excan tlatoloyan conquered these neighboring groups, which by then had become highly divided. To the east, in the Puebla–Tlaxcala Valley, the Chichimeca had also established key centers of power. Among these, Tlaxcala, Cholula, Huexotzinco, and Tliliuhquitepec stand out as cities that joined forces to resist the constant hostility of the alliance, managing to maintain the region's independence. To the south, in the warm land of the Morelos Valley, lived other Nahuatl-speaking Chichimeca, specifically the Xochimilca and Tlahuica communities. The Mexica had long coveted the cotton and other tropical products these groups harvested, and they defeated the city of Cuauhnahuac after a protracted war. During this rapid expansion, the alliance annexed political entities made up of different ethnic groups with varying levels of development.

The imperial borders of the excan tlatoloyan stretched from the Gulf of Mexico to the Pacific Ocean and from the Purepecha (Tarascan) Empire down to today's border between Mexico and Guatemala. Yet the main goal of this hegemonic expansion was not

Infinity of Nations

Mexica Cihuateotl (goddess), AD 1325–1521. Probably Tenochtitlan, Mexico. Basalt; 33 x 36 x 66 cm. Purchase. 15/5597

territorial domination, but rather profits gained from taxation. Other goals included having exclusive access to certain natural resources, restructuring trade, and controlling key markets. In most cases, conquered cities paid duties, were forced to permit the unrestricted entry of merchants protected by the alliance, and had to provide troops and provisions to the armies of the conquerors. They kept their legal and political systems, however, as well as their deities. Still, they lived under the burdensome and unsettling conditions generated by the institutionalization of violence. In cases of extreme opposition, the excan tlatoloyan could impose a governor or, alternatively, destroy rebellious populations and occupy their territory with colonists.

At times, these tax-paying peoples not only had to hand over their locally produced goods, but they also had to pay their debt with goods acquired through trade with neighboring peoples. In this way, the

capital cities of the alliance acquired resources from regions well beyond its borders.

The *pochteca*—professional merchants from central Mexico who lived in the three capitals as well as the subjugated cities—took advantage of the huge territory controlled by the alliance. Although they enjoyed ample autonomy to trade, the pochteca were expected to serve their masters as ambassadors, spies, and, in rare cases, militiamen. The pochteca of the alliance jointly organized trade missions. Some pochteca of the Isthmus of Tehuantepec traded along the route to Anahuac Ayotlan on the Pacific Coast; others headed to Anahuac Xicalanco on the Gulf of Mexico. In their southern network, the pochteca controlled the region of Soconusco, a rich producer of cacao beans, an agricultural product that served as currency. In Xicalanco, the pochteca traded their goods with Zoque and Maya merchants, who in turn traded goods all the way to Honduras.

Tepanec Ehecatl, the wind god (detail), AD 1325–1521. San Miguel, Mexico. Basalt; 14 x 17 x 25 cm. H. H. Rice Collection; presented by James B. Ford. 9/2874

The museum's Mexica collection includes many remarkable stone sculptures distinguished by their aesthetic, cultural, and historic significance. They represent many of the deities of the peoples of the Triple Alliance and help us understand more fully their beliefs and history. The deities also appear in Native and European codices written shortly before and after Spanish conquest.

Chicomecoatl was the deity most revered by the farmers of central Mexico (page 90). Countless images of this maize goddess were produced, from the most humbly and crudely carved destined for family worship in rural communities, to more polished sculptures placed in the public temples of the capitals. This Mexica sculpture also has certain attributes of Chalchiuhtlicue, the goddess of ground water.

Xipe Totec, the god associated with fertility and war and patron saint of goldsmiths, was revered throughout Mesoamerica, especially by the Mexica and by the Yopi, who lived in the present-day state of Guerrero. Like Xipe, Mexica kings would wear the skins of sacrificed individuals when leading their armies on military campaigns. This Chinampanec image has the date 2-Reed on its back (see page 94).

Women who died giving birth to their first child became terrifying beings. Five days a year, they would come down from heaven to inflict paralysis upon children. The Mexica sculpture shown here represents the Cihuateotl who descended on 1-Eagle, one of those five days, as shown by the carving on her head (page 95). To avoid the Cihuateotl, mothers would prevent their children from leaving the house and would not bathe them.

As wind preceded rain, the faithful believed that Ehecatl "swept the path for the gods of water," bringing forth life and fertility. The most common feature of this god is his mouth-mask in the shape of a grebe's or duck's bill. The sculptor exemplified the inconstant and changing movement of the wind in the twisted body of this Tepanec sculpture, shown at left.

The sun god Tonatiuh is usually represented as a young, armed male, flying, surrounded by the solar disk. In this Mexica sculpture, he appears defeated, with an arrow piercing his mouth and his heart torn out (page 286). His curly hair symbolizes the sunset (Tlalchitonatiuh), since the deities of the earth and the underworld are depicted with this type of hair.

In the early 16th century, the excan tlatoloyan reached its greatest height, but its power did not endure. The political situation became highly unstable. Increasingly unhappy, many subjugated peoples saw in the arrival of the Spanish a unique opportunity to regain their freedom. In joining the Spanish, these nations paved the way for the process of conquest. Obviously, the end result did not match their initial expectations.

—Leonardo López Luján

Contemporary Mexico

There is a widely held belief in Mexico today that the society is divided into two ethnically distinct groups—indigenous people and people of mixed race, who are considered nonindigenous. The first group is a minority, both in numerical terms and politically, by virtue of its invisibility in public life. Mexico's indigenous peoples are often associated in the popular mind with stewardship of our past and our traditions, with geographically and culturally remote regions of the country, and—unfortunately—with poverty. Yet according to data collected by the National Institute of Statistics and Geography in 2000 and 2005, one-third of the speakers of indigenous languages in Mexico live in big cities; more than half live in cities of 50,000 to 500,000 inhabitants. The majority of indigenous Mexicans between the ages of five and twenty-five are urban dwellers. In other words, Mexico's Native people today live throughout the country.

Government policies in place for more than half a century have been explicit in the goal of bringing Mexico's Native population into contemporary society. At one time, these initiatives seemed to lead to the conclusion that indigenous people had two options: they could remain isolated from the national scene

Purepecha (Tarascan) gourd vessel,
1940–1950. State of Michoacán,
Mexico. Gourd, paint, wood;
29 x 35 cm. Presented by
Mr. J. A. L. Miller. 21/5680

Totonac Danza de los Ormegas
belt, ca. 1980. Wood, leather,
paint, copper, horsehair, glass;
25 x 14 x 33 cm (front) and
23 x 14 x 30 cm (back). Collected
and presented by Vera Neumann.
25/3163

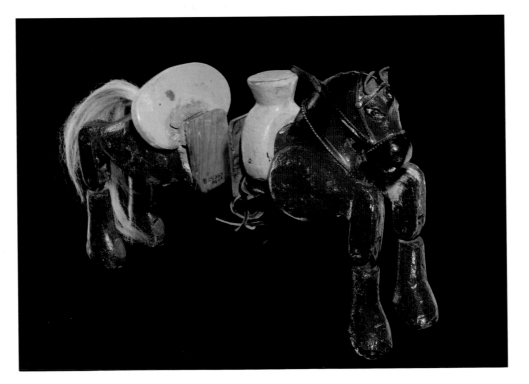

Nahua woman's belt, ca. 1925.
Milpa Alta, Federal District,
Mexico. Wool yarn, cotton yarn,
dye; 322 x 8 cm. 19/433

or assimilate into the modern world and abandon their languages, cultures, and, necessarily, identity. These policies did not, however, reduce the inequality of indigenous people. Furthermore, not only was indigenous culture not depleted over this period, it presented a creative form of resistance. By the 1970s, a group of participatory researchers, many associated with the National Indigenous Institute, developed a new critical discourse supporting the legitimacy of ethnic identity. Mexico began to see its multicultural, multiethnic population as a virtue and to reject earlier visions of cultural homogeneity.

During the 1980s, autonomous and independent associations emerged in certain indigenous regions seeking to become new social actors with a national presence. At the level of public policy, people began to explore concepts such as ethnic identity and sustainable development. Within universities, earlier models of anthropology were challenged by a new school of thought that seeks to involve indigenous people as the driving force of their own development.

Other factors that changed the structure of the relationship between the government and the indigenous communities of Mexico were the country's involvement in the 1989 Indigenous and Tribal Peoples Convention of the International Labor Organization and the 1992 amendment of the Fourth Article of the Constitution of Mexico, which defines the country as a multicultural society. One can't fail to mention that the signing of NAFTA and the emergence of the

Zapatista National Liberation Army challenged our understanding of a Mexico that doesn't exclude the indigenous population.

Within indigenous Mexican communities, secular affairs are largely the result of long historical processes and are expressed in different ways in each ethnic region. In all of the cultures in the country, however, there are similar elements that have a common pre-Columbian origin, subsequently mixed with elements of Christianity. Spiritual conquest was

A Wixarika *mara'akame* blesses villagers, 2002. San Andrés Cohamiata, Mexico. © 2002 Rachel Cobb.

Wixarika *mara'akame's* (shaman's) arrow, ca. 1930. Las Juntas, Mexico. Hawk feathers, parrot feathers, yarn, reed; 55 x 22 cm. Collected by Donald B. Cordry. 19/7866

the foundation of the great colonial endeavor, whose aim was to evangelize the lay indigenous people of the country. Violence and intolerance were essential elements in this endeavor, but they are not sufficient to explain the current state of religious belief among the country's indigenous people. For indigenous communities, divine power resides in things now related to Catholic imagery—the cross, the Virgin Mary, the saints—combined with sacred concepts and objects of pre-Columbian origin found in family altars or chapels, but also in hills, trees, caves, rivers, springs, and other ancient holy sites, both public and private.

The religiousness of indigenous communities is reflected largely in the annual cycle of holidays, which is closely related with the growth cycle of corn. This begins early in the year with the celebration of the New Year, the Three Kings, and the Virgin of Candelaria. On the last holiday, the blessing of seeds is followed by rituals calling for rain and the protection of the cornfields in the early stages of growth, and later by the celebrations of Carnival, Lent, Easter, and the Holy Cross. As crops are growing, the feasts of St. James the Apostle, the Assumption of the Virgin Mary, and St. Michael the Archangel are celebrated. Finally, the annual cycle of community religious holidays concludes with the celebration of the Day of the Dead, in late October and early November, which coincides with the corn harvest.

Shrines or places of ritual and festive importance are mostly located in sacred sites of pre-Columbian pilgrimage. Images of the Virgin, Christ, and the saints are worshiped in places that, in the indigenous belief system, embodied forces of nature such as the rain, sun, and soil, all of which are essential for growing corn.

Among Mexico's Native populations, a civil-religious hierarchy is predominant, with the primary aim of celebrating the holidays of the Catholic ritual calendar. Three levels of participation exist: The first level involves the entire community working on preparing the celebration of the patron saint's feast. The second is made up of stewards or principals who, on a rotating basis, pay most of the festival costs each year using family and personal resources. Those who act as stewards will later hold lifelong posts among the elders and heads of the community. These key advisers have a decisive voice in community relations and are considered to represent traditional authority. Unfortunately, in many ethnic communities the functions of government are carried out solely by men, while women's participation is limited to assisting roles. Finally, at the third level are stewardship roles for permanent specialists—band leader, director of dance, sexton, custodian of documents, traditional healer, and notary, among many others.

From the end of the last century and until the present, national life has become more democratic and political freedoms have expanded to all corners of the country. This process of democratization, not yet deep, has reached different indigenous communities unevenly. The most interesting case is the State of Oaxaca, where there is a majority of indigenous municipalities and where currently 420 out of 570 positions of municipal leadership are elected according to traditional practices and customs.

In economics, the production of crafts whose origin lies in the material culture of indigenous peoples has gained special significance, especially in light of the importance of tourism for Mexico. Together with migration to cities and to the United States in recent decades, craftwork has become the most important source of income for indigenous families in the countryside. Textiles, traditionally made by indigenous women, are a magnificent example of the enormous cultural diversity and resilience of the people of Mexico. Textiles reflect the history of a person's environment, both earthly and cosmic, and they represent animals and plants, myths and symbolic elements that transport humans to the divine world. The threads of textiles form a text where one can read the cosmogony, or origin stories, of a people, their way of life, and their history.

—Alejandro González Villarruel

The Taíno: People of the sea islands

The dynamic history of the Caribbean reflects the continually shifting interactions of widely diverse cultures, including the Taíno[1] of the Greater Antilles, the Lucayans of the Bahamas and the Turks and Caicos, and the Carib (Kalinago) of the Lesser Antilles, alongside the many others who settled in the region as early as 4000 BC. For these peoples of the *bagua cayos* (sea islands), the surrounding water was an aquatic highway linking island communities.

The ancestral roots of the Taíno can be traced back in the archaeological record to a sequence of rapid migrations by horticulturalists traveling up from the South American mainland through the Lesser Antilles to settle finally, by about 400 BC, in Puerto Rico and Hispaniola. The descendants of these voyagers prospered and quickly began to explore and settle other islands, so that by about AD 600, Cuba, Jamaica, and the Bahamas were colonized.[2] The following centuries, until the invasion of European powers, saw the expansion of settlements, the construction of monumental ball courts, an artistic florescence, and escalating sociopolitical complexity as *caciques* and *cacicas* rose to power. By the time Columbus arrived in the Bahamas on October 12, 1492, the densely inhabited Greater Antilles were home to distinct indigenous groups, many speaking mutually unintelligible languages. These were independent and self-sufficient communities, developing their own uniquely Caribbean lifeways in isolation from their mainland neighbors. Interaction between the peoples of the Greater Antilles and the mainland was not sustained enough to influence the trajectories of Caribbean cultures in any tangible way.[3]

Interaction within the insular Caribbean region during the centuries prior to European contact, on the other hand, included the expansion of larger Taíno polities to neighboring islands and the development of extensive inter-island trade networks. The sphere of cultural influence generating from Hispaniola and Puerto Rico reached well into the northern Lesser Antilles, and Taíno outposts may have reached as far as Saba in the Leeward Islands.[4] Taíno carvings have been found as far south as the Windward Islands, indicating that high-status objects, including *cohoba*[5]-related material, had a wide circulation. The distances

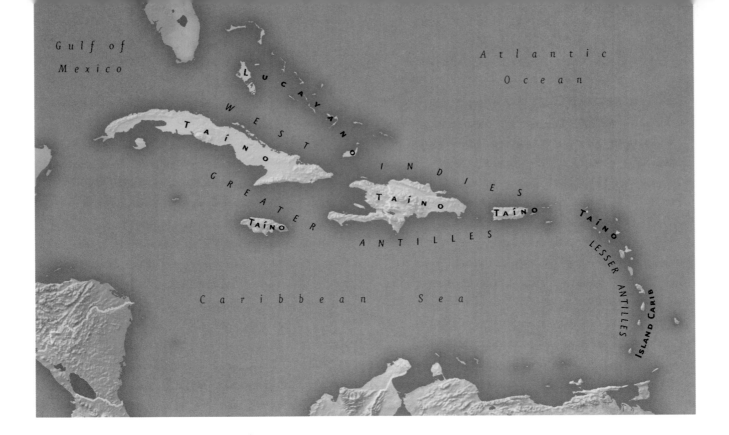

considerable—roughly 900 miles separates Hispaniola from the Grenadines—and trade on this scale was no small feat. The network must have been complex, especially considering the cultural diversity of the islands' inhabitants at the time, which raises intriguing questions about the histories of the traded items. Were they curiosities, or did they imply a political alliance or a kinship with the peoples to the north? Other island communities in closer proximity to the stylistics hubs of Puerto Rico and Hispaniola had greater access to these desirable artifacts, or may have reinterpreted them locally.[6]

Artisans traveled between the islands to use various local resources, likely with the permission and support of local caciques and cacicas. During the early colonial period, for example, the Spanish Royal Chronicler Peter Martyr D'Anghera mentions the presence of Carib canoe builders from St. Croix in southeastern Puerto Rico, taking advantage of the island's substantial trees.[7] Examples of specialists traveling to resource-rich islands to harvest materials and manufacture goods can be seen in other regions, stretching further back in time: at a site on Grand Turk dating to between AD 1000 and 1200, more than 7,000 shell beads in various stages of manufacture were recovered

alongside imported chert tools and ceramics, suggesting that Hispaniolan artisans were making a sea journey of some 140 miles specifically to work conch and chama shells.[8]

Relations were not always peaceful. By around AD 1300, the links between the people of the Windward Islands and those of the Leeward Islands and Puerto Rico may have grown hostile, perhaps accounting for the depopulation of many of the Leewards.[9] The history of warfare and raiding by the Carib on their Taíno neighbors was emphasized by early Spanish colonizers—though much for their own purposes, to justify enslavement and expansion. This interpretation has long overshadowed the mutually beneficial interactions that undoubtedly also occurred, and continued after colonization in some instances—from trade to political alliances to kin relationships binding different island communities together. Indeed, warriors from the Virgin Islands joined forces with the Taíno rebelling against the Spanish in the battles of 1513, while Taíno escaping the escalating violence on Puerto Rico in the early 16th century were given asylum as far south as Trinidad.[10]

The exchange of valued objects was in many ways at the core of bringing people together across these

Taíno *guaíza* mask, AD 1000–1500. Province of Guantánamo, Cuba. Conch shell; 14 x 15 x 3 cm. 4/6049

Lucayan *duho* (seat), high-back style, AD 1000–1500. Turks and Caicos Islands, Bahamas. Wood: 84 x 15 x 21 cm. Lady Edith Blake Collection. 5/9385

distances, whether in alliance, marriage, trade, or tribute. Among the most prestigious and politically binding of gifts were the ceremonial seats known as *duhos*,[11] such as the ones offered by the cacique Guacanagarí to Columbus in 1493[12] or the fourteen given by the cacica Anacaona to honor Bartolomé Columbus upon his visit to the *cacicazgo* of Xaraguá in late 1496 or early 1497.[13] It may well be within this context of political maneuvering that Taíno duhos have been found as far south as Dominica, and potentially St. Vincent.[14] It is also in the competitive jostling of caciques and cacicas that we can begin to explore the importance of duhos in the Bahamas and Turks and Caicos islands, where the elaboration of the form reached new heights.

Guaízas, or masks, were also important gifts for high-ranking individuals. In 1492, Guacanagarí presented Columbus with "masks with golden eyes and ears of gold."[15] During the admiral's second visit to the island, in 1493, a letter written by the expedition's medical officer, Diego Alvarez Chanca, states that two Taíno, arriving at Columbus's ship, again brought gold masks which Guacanagarí "sent as a present; one for the admiral and the other for a captain who had been with him on the previous voyage."[16] It is clear that the Taíno targeted such objects for those in positions

of power and authority. The significance of these exchanges likely had deep resonance for the Taíno: in interpreting Ramon Pané's manuscript on Taíno myths, José Arrom noted the link between the term for *goeíza*, or "living spirit or soul," and guaízas, and José Oliver has argued that the guaíza is the very core of a cacique's or cacica's personhood—his or her soul.[17] In this context, the giving of masks was not simply an exchange of objects, but one that may have intertwined people's personal identities and histories.

Underpinning these material exchanges were a series of less visible but more complex interactions involving the exchange of ideas and worldviews— the movements of people as individuals or marriage partners, entire communities settling new islands, or new communities arriving to intermingle with those already in residence. There are also the social biographies of these objects—the personal, intimate histories that mark people's relationships with them and the powers they represent. These objects, each resonant with its own unique history and meaning, are a window onto the Caribbean's past and the rich tapestry of connections between its peoples.

—Joanna Ostapkowicz

Maya portrait head

It is likely that this modeled stucco head from the Uxmal site is part of an architectural decoration and that it refers to a member of the ruling family or honors an ancestor. It is associated with the building known as the Governor's House, the main architectural theme of which is a series of overlapping figure heads carved in stone representing the god of rain, Chaak. In impressive temples and palaces, jutting sculptures were an important part of the architectural design, often representing mythological beings or rulers. Inscriptions, in addition to being decorative, also sent various messages to the observer.

Modeled stucco—lime-based plaster—is one of the great art forms developed in pre-Columbian times. Entire cities were covered with stucco. Architectural sculpture such as figure heads, free-standing sculpture, wall coatings, floors—all were made with stucco. The beautifully made face on this piece can be seen as an ancient portrait, with adornments such as ear ornaments and a headband, but the body paint stands out, probably indicating ceremonial activities. Unfortunately, due to its fragility, stucco art—especially on the exterior of structures—was the first to erode or be destroyed after buildings were abandoned. Because of this, stucco representations are not abundant in collections of Maya artifacts. This piece should be regarded as one of the most significant, because of its color and its creator's artistic skill.

—Edgar Suyuc (Kaqchikel Maya)

Maya portrait head, AD 300–900. Uxmal, Mexico. Stucco, paint; 25 x 26 x 28 cm. Collected by Thomas Gann; presented by James B. Ford. 8/1972

Maya tripod vessel

This orange ceramic jar with its castellated base and modeled cover exemplifies the artistry attained by Maya potters during the Classic period, ca. AD 250 to 900. The vessel's shape, design, color, and decoration date its production to the first part of this period, when Kaminaljuyú experienced a cultural transition. There is evidence that during this time the wider Maya region established closer ties with central Mexico. This jar and others like it are thought to be examples of such interaction, especially with the city of Teotihuacán.

The history of Kaminaljuyú, the largest city of the ancient Maya in the highlands of Guatemala, dates back to 2000 BC. The city was abandoned around AD 900. For nearly 3,000 years, the Maya leveraged the abundance of resources that were found nearby, especially such valuable stones as jade and obsidian. The figure decorating the lid wears the headdress of an *ahaw*, or noble, and a necklace and ear ornaments representing precious stones. These elements confirm the status of the owner. Such vessels were often used in funerary offerings.

—Edgar Suyuc (Kaqchikel Maya)

Maya tripod vessel with lid, AD 350–450. Kaminaljuyú, Guatemala. Clay; 27 x 11 cm. Purchased from Judy Small. 23/2217

Maya bas-relief depicting a ball player

The Mesoamerican ball game had several connotations. Chief among them was clearly the triumph of good over evil, although the game also had cosmological, ritual, and sporting aspects. The hero twins portrayed in the *Popol Vuh*—the K'iche' sacred book that was written after the arrival of the Spaniards, but whose scenes have been depicted in art since the origins of the civilization—succeeded in leaving the underworld after defeating the Lords of the Night at the ball game. Known ball courts are located in the civic–ceremonial areas of towns or cities, confirming the importance and sacred nature of the game.

—Edgar Suyuc (Kaqchikel Maya)

For fifteen centuries, from 600 BC to AD 900, the Maya civilization held sway over a vast area of tropical lowlands on the Yucatán peninsula, an area known today as the Petén. Other Maya groups lived and continue to live in the highlands of Guatemala and Chiapas and the arid lowlands of northern Yucatán. It was in the Petén, however, that the civilization of the Classic Maya achieved its apogee.

During the millennium between 200 BC and AD 800, the lowland Maya constructed dozens, if not hundreds, of monumental cities with royal palaces, temples, marketplaces, reservoirs, and ball courts. Inhabited by rulers, nobles, scribes, artists, merchants, farmers, warriors, and slaves—the spectrum of Maya society—these cities were also the canvas upon which the artistic eye of the lowland Maya delighted. Temples and palaces were covered in white plaster, sculpted into the visages of gods, and then painted vibrant colors. Buildings were also outfitted with lintels, stairways, and panels inscribed with hieroglyphic texts honoring the gods and extolling with great precision the reigns, wars, and families of the rulers.

The image on this panel is an "action shot" of a man kneeling in preparation to receive the bouncing rubber ball that formed an integral part of the ball game played throughout Mesoamerica. The two hieroglyphs in the upper right identify the subject as a ball player and possibly a jaguar deity. The ball is labeled with the numeral 9 and the hieroglyph *nahb*, thought to mean "hand-span." It seems that the ball was nine hand-spans in circumference—that is, about two feet in diameter.

This panel, believed to be from the ball court at La Corona, is one in a series that portray individuals in distinct ball-playing poses or contain hieroglyphic texts describing the events depicted. The texts suggest that these ball players were nobles, though not necessarily rulers. The texts identify the players with enigmatic and perhaps divine titles. It is possible that they were re-creating the sacred ball game between gods in the underworld at the time of the world's creation.

Dating to the 7th or 8th century AD, the panels were made at a time when the lowland Maya civilization was dominated by the imperial city of Calakmul, in modern Campeche. In fact, the historical record suggests that the Calakmul kings sojourned at La Corona on several occasions. It is very possible that while they were there, they played the ball game and performed in related rituals in the ball court. In the 8th century AD, Calakmul would be defeated by its rivals, and La Corona's fortunes would decline. By AD 900, much of lowland Maya civilization had collapsed, leaving abandoned sites like La Corona to be enshrouded by the rain forest for nearly a millennium.

—Marcello A. Canuto and Tomás Barrientos Q.

Maya bas-relief depicting a ball player, AD 600–750. La Corona, Department of el Petén, Guatemala. Limestone; 37 x 28.5 cm. 24/457

Tepanec Quetzalcoatl (feathered serpent)

and Tlaltecuhtli, goddess of the earth

This large volcanic-stone sculpture is carved in the shape of Quetzalcoatl, the creator and patron of humanity; god of Venus and the sunrise; inventor of the calendar; donor of corn, fire, time, and *pulque* (fermented maguey); and protector of trade. On the base, shown above, there is an image of a zoomorphic Tlaltecuhtli, goddess of the earth.

During the Post-Classical era (AD 900–1521), the rulers of different Mesoamerican groups exercised power delegated by Quetzalcoatl and at times personified him in order to accomplish their mission. In Colonial times, the Spanish had the head of this Quetzalcoatl sculpture cut off—disfigured—and its body drilled to create a base for a Christian cross raised in the cemetery of Coyoacán. The alteration represented—from a Colonial Spanish and Christian point of view—the destruction of an age of idolatry and the dawning of a new Christian era. This intention is explicit in a letter dated August 25, 1538, and addressed to Antonio de Mendoza, the first viceroy of New Spain, in which the Holy Roman Emperor Charles V decreed, "I command that you . . . would have thrown down and removed all the pyramids and temples for idols which were in this New Spain, . . . and you should provide that the stone from them is taken to build churches and monasteries."

The Coyoacán cross was dismantled sometime between 1850 and 1854, when the French painter Edouard Pingret bought the Quetzalcoatl sculpture and took it to Paris, where George Heye acquired it much later.

—**Leonardo López Luján**

Tepanec Quetzalcoatl (feathered serpent), god of life and creation, ca. 1325–1521. Coyoacán, Basin of Mexico, Mexico. Basalt, pigment; 32 x 78 cm. Purchased in Paris from the Collection of Dr. Louis Capitan. 17/5441

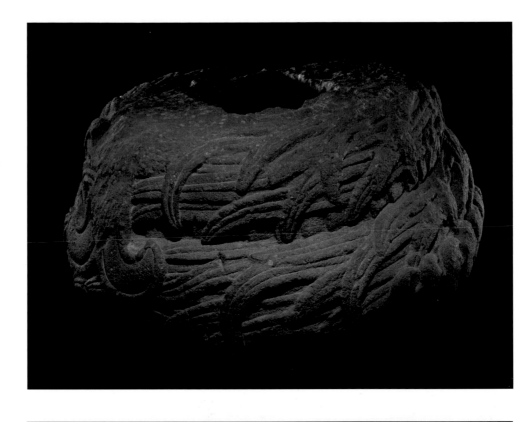

Taíno *zemí* of Itiba Cahubaba

Taíno *zemí* of Itiba Cahubaba, AD 1200–1500. Santiago de los Caballeros, Dominican Republic. Clay; 15 x 9 x 18 cm. Collected by Henry Hunt. 12/7442

Itiba Cahubaba, "Great Bleeding Mother," is a primary ancestor spirit among those respected deities the Taíno call *zemí*. Itiba succumbs in childbirth, begetting with her sacrifice the humanity and universe of the Taíno. Her four sons will be creators of the ocean and the land and will beget the living Mother Earth and her support of humanity.

Identified by Caribbean scholar José Juan Arrom, Itiba Cahubaba is notable for her oblong eyes, indicative of Taíno depictions of deities. Itiba's emaciated arms, always folded over her bulging belly, represent the suffering of her creation. Cosmic navigator, Itiba Cahubaba wears a headdress with four trapezoid incisions that appear to depict the Caribbean winter (short) and summer (long) solstices. According to Arrom, the curvature of her cap informs Taíno navigation.

In Cuba, Itiba Cahubaba is associated with pregnancy, labor, delivery, and—among the people of the eastern mountains— the Virgen de la Caridad del Cobre, the matron saint of the island. Many pregnant and post-natal women attend the Virgen's shrine in supplication and thanks. Taíno descendants from the Sagua–Baracoa Mountains still make offerings and burn tobacco for the Mother Earth spirit and attribute the success of their crops and the potency of their traditional herbal medicines to her benevolence.[1] The names of Caribbean Taíno cosmological personalities also continue to figure in the toponymy of the islands. There is a historic Río Cahobabo and a nearby village Playitas de Cahobabo in the easternmost part of Cuba. The local population from the region of Cahobabo sustains many Native herbal and culinary traditions.

—José Barreiro (Taíno)

Taíno *zemí* of Deminán Caracaracol

Taíno *zemí* of Deminán Caracaracol, AD 1200–1500. Andrés, Dominican Republic. Clay; 22 x 22 x 41 cm. Collected by Theodoor de Booy. 5/3753

Son of Itiba Cahubaba, Deminán is first among her quadruplets, leading his brothers in misadventures of creation throughout the Caribbean universe. To create the Caribbean Sea, its fish and its islands, its people and their procreation, the Sacred Four disturb the secrets of the YaYá, Original Spirit. Deminán and his nameless brothers capture fire, *casabe* (cassava bread), and tobacco for the use of the people. When, in the course of the creational journey, men and women are separated, the wandering men beseech the four brothers. Assisted by their mother's ally, Inriri Cahubabayael (woodpecker), they carve new women out of swimming creatures. Later, while requesting casabe (still traditional Taíno food), Deminán offends a grandfather spirit, who blows a wad of herbs and creative powders on Deminán's back. Deminán gestates a turtle, which his brothers deliver by cutting into his flesh. Before plants and food for humans, there must be earth. Thus Caguama, Creator Turtle, is brought forth by the quadruple powers, who care for her, the living Earth, and upon her build their house, the Taíno *bohio*.

The important figure of Deminán is found in many forms in the Taíno Caribbean. In this thin-walled ceramic, collected in Quisqueya (the Dominican Republic), Deminán's wide face and contemplative forehead convey an expression of deep thought, as befitting the creation of the earth and humanity. The turtle is clearly visible on his arched and ailing back. The figure depicts Deminán in the lineage of suffering creators, his very thin arms the result of an extended fast. His oblong eyes and cosmic navigator's cap follow in the style of his mother.

—José Barreiro (Taíno)

Tlu te inti ya

"Where the grass comes together"—Mescalero Apache

FROM MOUNTAIN PEAKS to rugged canyons and desert basins, all of the Southwest is dry. Tree rings document periods of severe drought. In this environment marginal for agriculture, American Indians successfully farmed maize, squash, and beans for thousands of years. These peoples developed a variety of techniques to cultivate the soil and conserve moisture. They built spectacular cliff dwellings and the enormous adobe town of Casas Grandes in Chihuahua, Mexico.[1]

The major archaeological traditions of the Southwest are the Ancestral Puebloan, Hohokam, and Mogollon, and the less clear Patayan. The traditions, defined by similarities in material culture, do not refer to language or ethnic groups, or to political entities such as tribes. Nevertheless, the modern Pueblo Indians of New Mexico and the Hopi of Arizona are descendants of both the Ancestral Puebloan and Mogollon traditions. The Rarámuri (Tarahumara) and Tepehuan of northern Mexico also are seen as Mogollon descendants, and the modern O'odham and Yumans of Arizona as descendants of the Hohokam and the Patayan.[2]

Cultural exchange of ideas, rituals, beliefs, and goods, and movements of people linked communities of the Southwest with one another and with others throughout North and Central America. Archaeology provides access to the material evidence of interactions—for example, the movement of marine shell, turquoise, copper, and feathers. Archaeologists also recognize shared symbols such as parrots, lightning, and terraced clouds, and can trace some symbols to present-day art and ritual. We have only shadowy ideas of how these items and symbols functioned in the world of the past or what they meant to those who created and used them.[3]

Some of the earliest remains of the Ancestral Puebloan tradition, made by foragers who first planted corn in the northern Southwest between about 2000 BC and AD 500, have been found at Grand Gulch, in the rugged mountains of southeastern Utah. Dry rock shelters that were used as habitations, for storage, and as places to bury the dead preserved finely made coiled baskets; twined yucca-fiber bags, sandals, tumplines, and sashes; and blankets made of strips of rabbit fur held in twined cordage.[4]

Early Ancestral Puebloans made elaborate hunting nets of yucca fiber and human hair, and cordage snares and traps to capture small game. They used shaped wooden sticks to dispatch rabbits and hunted larger game using spears thrown with a spear-thrower, or atlatl. They kept dogs and may have used them for hunting. The people were mobile, moving among rock shelters and small pithouses (houses with excavated floors) seasonally. By about AD 500, Ancestral Puebloans began making pottery containers and bows and arrows for hunting. They also developed more productive forms of maize. They soon built surface structures, first for storage and then as dwellings. Eventually they made above-ground dwellings of masonry, and their pithouses became more elaborate and like kivas, ceremonial rooms used in modern Pueblo Indian villages. An abundance of beads made of Gulf of California and Pacific Coast shell, and of course, the presence of maize and squash, which were domesticated in central Mexico, reflect long-distance movement and exchange.[5]

Chaco Canyon preserves magnificent ruins of multistory stone buildings, called great houses, built by Ancestral Puebloan people between about AD 900 and

Ancestral Pueblo jars, AD 900–1130. Pueblo Bonito, Chaco Canyon, New Mexico. Clay, paint; 15 x 14 x 25 cm, 25 x 11.5 cm. Collected by George H. Pepper. Mrs. Thea Heye Collection. 5/2116, 5/2109

Pueblo Bonito, Chaco Canyon, New Mexico.

Casas Grandes (also called Paquimé), Chihuahua, Mexico.

Infinity of Nations

Ancestral Hopi bowl, AD 1300s.
Homol´ovi, Navajo County,
Arizona. Clay, paint; 16 x 31 cm.
Purchase. 5/609

Ancestral Pueblo mug, ca. AD 1200. Cliff Palace, Mesa Verde, Colorado. Clay, paint; 13 x 9.5 x 10 cm. Herbert Bra Me Collection. 6/7156

Hohokam scoop, AD 450–1150. Maricopa County, Arizona. Clay, paint; 18 x 13 x 8.5 cm. 22/753

Acoma polychrome jar, ca. 1900–1920. Acoma Pueblo, New Mexico. Clay, paint; 28 x 30 cm. William M. Fitzhugh Collection. 19/4330

Infinity of Nations

AD 1150. Pueblo Bonito, the most famous of these, was among the earliest. The great houses were planned, formal structures—less like dwellings than public architecture, although they probably functioned as both throughout their long use. From the AD 1000s to the middle AD 1100s, between seventy-five and one hundred similarly formal great houses were constructed throughout the San Juan basin and adjacent uplands. Chaco Canyon has the densest concentration of great houses and other elaborate features and is therefore understood to have been the major regional center. More than 200,000 roof beams were carried on foot into the canyon from higher elevations some fifty miles away, as were thousands of pottery vessels. Elaborate irrigation systems channeled run-off from the cliffs into prepared fields below. Stairways were chipped into the sandstone cliff walls, and hundreds of miles of causeway roads were built within the canyon and connecting the canyon to other Chacoan communities. Imports from Mexico included copper bells, cacao, and macaw parrots. Chaco also imported great quantities of turquoise, which its people worked into thousands of beads and ornaments.[6]

There is continuing debate among researchers about the nature of Chacoan society and the size of the Chacoan polity.[7] The amount of material moved and the great formality of Chaco suggest that the Chacoan regional system was tightly integrated, powerful, and probably hierarchically organized. After AD 1150 the Chaco regional system, whatever it had been, changed dramatically. In the wake of widespread drought, people left small farming communities throughout the region. Many people moved to better-watered, higher elevations, and the great center at Chaco Canyon was no longer sustained.

Before about AD 900, Mogollon people living along the Mimbres River in southwestern New Mexico occupied large pithouse settlements. They made burnished redware pottery or brownware painted with red designs. They traded extensively with their Hohokam neighbors to the west and probably also with neighbors in Mexico, receiving copper bells, parrots, pendants, and shell bracelets, perhaps in exchange for

game and upland products. Mimbres people farmed the river floodplain and built agricultural terraces and irrigation canals where appropriate. By about AD 1000 Mimbres settlements reorganized into above-ground pueblos. The people began making spectacular black-on-white pottery with geometric and figurative designs, including naturalistic representations of animals, birds, insects, fish, and human beings, sometimes shown in scenes of ceremony or daily life. This pottery was used in everyday life and included in burials.[8] Classic Mimbres pottery continues to inspire pottery design, especially among their Pueblo Indian descendants at Acoma Pueblo.

About AD 1150, the Mimbres way of life changed dramatically. Large pueblos were no longer occupied. Some people moved north or south, out of the region altogether. Others remained but lived in much smaller, dispersed settlements. After about fifty years, Mimbres people no longer made their magnificent pottery.[9]

Compared to Chaco Canyon, the environment of the Mesa Verde region is relatively lush. Ancestral Puebloans began settling there in numbers from about AD 600. They farmed the rich loessic soils of the mesa tops, cultivating corn, beans, and squash. At times of population increase, they also farmed side canyons, where they built agricultural terraces, series of check dams in arroyos, and reservoirs that may have provided water for domestic use. Ancestral Puebloans of Mesa Verde also made distinctive decorated pottery, painted with heavy black-line elements on a polished white-slipped background, of which mugs are a hallmark form.

At first the people of Mesa Verde lived in large pithouses, some with antechambers and wing walls that divided interior space for different activities. Between about AD 750 and AD 900, they built very large villages consisting of long arcs of contiguous surface rooms with associated pithouses. One of these housed an estimated 500 people, although it may not have been occupied for more than a generation.[10] Archaeologists view these large villages as models for some of the great houses built in Chaco Canyon, and indeed there appears to have been movement of people from Mesa

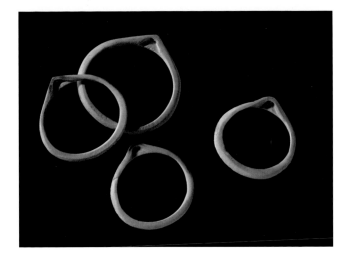

Hohokam bracelets, AD 450–1150. Gila County, Arizona. *Glycymeris* shell; 7 cm (average diameter). James E. Sullivan Collection. 23/1968

Verde into Chaco Canyon around AD 900.[11] During the ascendancy of Chaco in the AD 1000s, a number of Chaco great houses were built in the Mesa Verde region, among them Lowry Ruin and Chimney Rock Pueblo.

The environment of Mesa Verde made it an attractive location during the droughts of the early AD 1100s, and many Ancestral Puebloans who had left small farming communities in the San Juan basin converged there. The Mesa Verde region experienced its greatest population from the late AD 1100s through the mid AD 1200s. At this time the spectacular cliff houses were built. Cliff Palace, the most famous of these, with 141 rooms, was only one of hundreds of such dwellings.[12] Every part of the region that could be farmed probably was. There is increased evidence of interpersonal violence and warfare. Some villages were burned.

By the mid AD 1200s, people began leaving the Mesa Verde region, and by AD 1300 there is no evidence that people lived there on a permanent basis. Severe drought, shorter growing seasons, overpopulation, warfare, and disease are all implicated as causes. What is clear is that the people of Mesa Verde did not disappear. The oral histories of many of today's Pueblo Indians speak of ancestral migrations from the Mesa Verde region.[13]

Hohokam farmers occupied some of the most extreme deserts of North America. Their heartland was the middle Gila and Salt River drainages, where they constructed more than 500 miles of canals and planted an estimated 700,000 acres of irrigated fields. The Hohokam depended on corn, beans, squash, and local crops they brought into cultivation. Cotton and agave were grown for food and fibers.[14]

Hohokam domestic architecture consisted of separate round or square houses grouped around courtyards or central plazas. Between about AD 450 and AD 1150, Hohokam settlements began to reflect a flowering in the arts, public architecture, commerce, and rituals linking them to cultures in West Mexico and Mesoamerica. Among thousands of Hohokam villages, about 225 had ballcourts—oval, bowl-shaped areas, some 230 feet long and 100 feet wide, with earthen embankments. Thought to have been used for ritual ball games similar to those played throughout Mesoamerica, Central America, and the Caribbean, the courts were public architecture. Objects having parallels in West Mexico include caches of clay figurines, carved stone palettes, and stone censers.[15]

In addition to making unpainted ware for cooking and storage, the Hohokam produced pottery decorated with intricate geometric figures—often incorporating birds, lizards, and humans—painted in red on buff backgrounds. Vessel shapes—including scoops, plates, censers, tripod and rectangular vessels, animal effigies, and jars—are more diverse than those found among other contemporary southwestern peoples. Larger vessels were built by coiling thin ropes of clay and then paddling the coils against a smooth anvil held inside the pot, leaving a slightly dimpled interior. The Hohokam carved and etched shell to make beads, bracelets, rings, and geometric forms. Shell was obtained from both the Pacific and the Gulf of California, and finished shell objects were distributed throughout the Southwest. The ubiquity of Hohokam

bracelets crafted of *Glycymeris* from the gulf, coupled with the observation that they come in various sizes, suggests that they were worn by everyone from young children to adults. The Hohokam also made small stone objects, including pyrite mirrors like those from West Mexico.[16]

Around AD 1150, the Hohokam ballcourt-based system ended, and new ideologies and routes of commerce transformed the society. Population and irrigation systems increased, craft items lost detail (pottery) or stopped being made (palettes). No new ballcourts were built. The function of massive earthen platform mounds constructed by the Hohokam changed between about AD 1250 and 1325, when elite residences were built on their summits and villages became walled compounds.[17]

There is no evidence of Hohokam towns being inhabited into the 16th century. In the AD 1600s, the Phoenix basin O'odham, who show much continuity with the Hohokam, numbered about 3,000; their population is estimated to have been between 30,000 and 60,000 in AD 1300. There is little agreement about what happened, although there is evidence that canals were breached by floods initiated by heavy rainfall at higher elevations. Some Hohokam were probably drawn to Casas Grandes in Chihuahua.[18]

A center of population, commerce, ritual, and power, the great town of Casas Grandes (also called Paquimé) flourished from about AD 1280 to AD 1450. Much of Casas Grandes resembles Ancestral Puebloan communities, although on a much larger scale, with multistoried blocks of adobe rooms surrounding courtyards and plazas. Beyond the cellular configuration of the pueblo, the architecture reflects Mesoamerican elements, including great plazas, platform and effigy mounds, macaw breeding pens, I- and T-shaped ballcourts, and a walk-in well. The pottery of this period resembles Ancestral Puebloan pottery of the same period but is remarkably standardized, suggesting production by specialists. Figurative representations on ceramics include parrots, humans, and many forms of serpents—most dramatically, the plumed serpent, an icon throughout western North America. Diverse effigy vessels represent animals and humans, some with iconic features indicating various roles in society.[19]

Eventually Casas Grandes was not maintained, and parts of it were burned. Charles C. Di Peso, who directed major excavations at the site, believes that it was destroyed during an internal revolt, with the survivors moving north, where they joined Ancestral Puebloans.[20] Much 15th-century pottery of the Ancestral Pueblo region reflects these journeys or other kinds of regional interaction.

The production of striking polychrome pottery decorated with representations of stylized birds, especially parrots, are among the symbols that united pottery traditions and people across the Southwest. Ancient pottery has served as inspiration for the modern revival Pueblo pottery, especially at Hopi, on the southern edge of Black Mesa, Arizona. The ancestors of today's Hopi people came from several groups of villages across the region—places like Homol'ovi, a cluster of seven large villages and many small settlements on the Little Colorado River about fifty miles south of Hopi, settled between about AD 1240 and 1400.

Today, descendants of the original inhabitants of the Southwest live in portions of their traditional territories. Yet despite incursions of Western Europeans, epidemics, warfare, religious persecution, cultural prejudice, and periods of forced acculturation, much of Native culture remains intact. Native languages are spoken, religious customs observed, artistic traditions flourish, and value systems are maintained.

—Linda Cordell

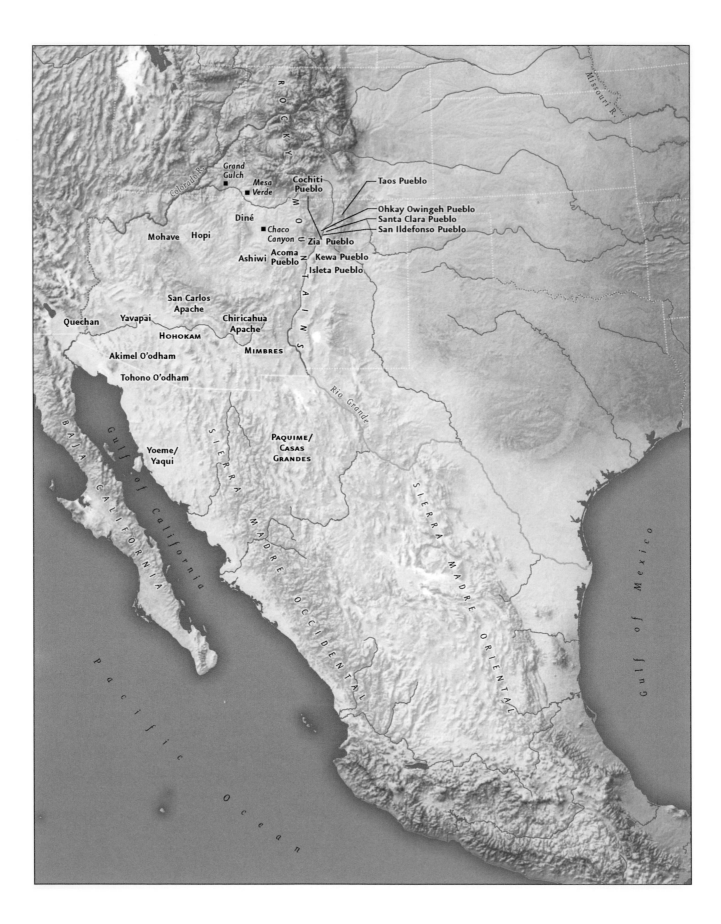

Grand
Gulch

Mesa
Verde

Cochiti
Pueblo

Taos Pueblo

Ohkay Owingeh Pueblo
Santa Clara Pueblo
San Ildefonso Pueblo

Diné

Chaco
Canyon

Zia Pueblo

Mohave   Hopi

Ashiwi   Acoma
              Pueblo

Kewa Pueblo

Isleta Pueblo

San Carlos
Apache

Quechan   Yavapai

Chiricahua
Apache

Hohokam

Akimel O'odham

MIMBRES

Tohono O'odham

Colorado R.

ROCKY

MOUNTAINS

Missouri R.

Rio Grande

Paquime/
Casas
Grandes

Yoeme/
Yaqui

BAJA CALIFORNIA

Gulf of California

SIERRA

MADRE

OCCIDENTAL

SIERRA

MADRE

ORIENTAL

Gulf of Mexico

Pacific Ocean

The historic Southwest

By the 14th century, trade networks extending from Mesoamerica linked all areas of the Southwest. Trade routes also extended eastward into modern Oklahoma, Kansas, Missouri, Arkansas, and Texas. The peoples in the Southwest region traded items such as shell, turquoise, obsidian, agate, petrified wood, a wide range of pottery, maize, cotton cloth, piñon nuts, and perhaps tobacco in exchange for bison and deer hides, bison meat, Osage orange bow wood, freshwater shell, Gulf Coast marine shell, and alibates flint, as well as elbow ceramic pipes and Caddoan pottery.[1] Contacts among the Native peoples of the Southwest and between the Southwest and Plains regions were facilitated by trade fairs held at Taos, Picuris, and Pecos. Other influences included trading-and-raiding by the Diné (Navajo) and Apache tribes for slaves, food, and livestock.

During the 1540s, when Spanish expeditions following trails that connected these centuries-old trade networks entered the Southwest, they found small, inhabited adobe villages scattered throughout the Rio Grande Valley. The configuration of these settlements—multiroom attached dwellings surrounding internal plazas—reminded the Spanish of their own villages, and they called them *pueblos* (the Spanish word for "village") and their inhabitants, Pueblo Indians. Spain formally claimed possession of the Southwest region in 1598 and established a capital at Yungeh Oweenge (Mockingbird Place), near present-day Ohkay Owingeh, formerly known as San Juan Pueblo.[2] The Spanish named this settlement San Gabriel, and missionaries set about Christianizing the Puebloans and exploiting them as slaves under the *encomienda* system.[3] After some eighty years of brutal treatment, the pueblos united and revolted against the Spanish in 1680. The Puebloans were successful in expelling the Spanish and kept them out of New Mexico for the next twelve years.

Trade among the western and Rio Grande pueblos was ongoing both before and after the Pueblo Revolt, and it can be assumed that the Puebloans used their pottery for barter with the Spaniards as well.[4] Spanish trade goods included metal jewelry in the form of buttons, buckles, pendants, crosses, and various ornaments for horsegear.

Although the arrival of the Spanish and later European-Americans was a catalyst for rapid change, the Native peoples of the Southwest continue to live on their original lands to some extent. Their distinct cultures have survived because of a strong sense of place and individual tribal identity based on their arts, language, architecture, and religious practices. Puebloans living in the Southwest today include the Hopi in western Arizona; the Acoma, Laguna, and Zuni of western New Mexico; and the Taos, Picuris, Ohkay Owingeh (San Juan), Santa Clara, San Ildefonso, Pojoaque, Nambé, Tesuque, Cochiti, Jemez, Zia, Santa Ana, Kewa (Santo Domingo), San Felipe, Sandia, and Isleta who occupy villages in northern New Mexico and along the Rio Grande. Other Native peoples of the region are the Diné (Navajo) and the Chiricahua, Mescalero, Jicarilla, and White Mountain Apaches (Indé) in Arizona and New Mexico; the O´odham (Akimel and Tohono), Yumans (Maricopa, Cocopah, Quechan, and Mohave), and Pais (Hualapai, Yavapai, and Havasupai) in Arizona; and the Rarámuri (Tarahumara) and Tepehuan in northern Mexico.

As European-Americans moved into the Southwest at the close of the Mexican-American War in 1848, new forces of change were inevitable. The Cocopahs became involved in the navigation of steamships up the lower Colorado River until the late 1800s.[5] The transcontinental railroad cutting across the heart of the Southwest in the 1880s thrust the pueblos squarely into European-American-dominated territorial life in New Mexico. The expanded system of trading posts introduced a new cash economy to pueblos such as Laguna and Acoma, which benefitted economically by their close proximity to the tracks.

Pueblo pottery sold at the train stops also served various functions within Pueblo households, such as storage, cooking, and serving food, or carrying and storing water. Pottery-making continued to flourish during the mid-to-late 1800s. Broken pots were

Nampeyo with one of her large,
Sikyatki-inspired vessels, ca. 1910.
Hopi, Arizona. P007128

Nampeyo with one of her large, Sikyatki-inspired vessels, ca. 1910. Hopi, Arizona. P007128

repaired and reused or recycled as chimneys on the tops of pueblo homes. In the late 19th century, pottery could still be identified by pueblo, based on specific design elements that had been passed down from one generation to the next. Many of the designs used on Acoma, Laguna, and Zuni pottery bear a strong resemblance to the fine-line hatching designs found on ancestral pottery from Mesa Verde and Chaco Canyon. As more commercially made goods became available, however, the utilitarian uses for pottery diminished, and the focus turned to production for tourist and collector markets.

By the early 1900s, it appeared that the art was dying out. A handful of women are credited with revitalizing pottery-making in their villages. Born about 1860, the Hopi–Tewa potter Nampeyo started making pottery for household use—utilitarian vessels covered with a thick, cream-colored slip and painted with Hopi katsina images or motifs adapted from Zuni pottery. By the early 1890s, Nampeyo had taken the lead role in a bold movement to revitalize Hopi pottery. She had exceptional skills and a special gift for understanding space and layout on the surface of a pot. Eventually she abandoned the current use of design and white slip

Joseph Head (Akimel O'odham) recounting history recorded on a calendar stick to Henry Soatikee, 1921. Gila River Reservation, Arizona. N24596

Ute man wearing a Diné first phase chief blanket, 1874. Los Pinos, Colorado. P00426

in favor of the unslipped, polished surfaces she found on ancient examples of Sikyatki wares. By 1900 she had developed the shapes and painted motifs that are today hallmarks of her family. San Ildefonso potter Maria Martinez led a pottery revival in the early 20th century and is one of a few Native American artists to achieve worldwide recognition.[6] As Richard Spivey observed, Maria "set the standard of excellence that made her not only the most famous Indian potter but one of the great potters of the world."[7] The work of Rosalia Medina Toribio of Zia Pueblo is a wonderful example of the continuation of centuries-old traditions of hand-built matte-paint pottery. Margaret Tafoya learned the art of pottery-making from her mother, Sarafina. In the 1920s elaborately carved pottery became popular at Santa Clara. This may have been in response to a change in the clay that required a thicker-walled vessel after Santa Clara's traditional clay source was lost in a landslide.[8] Today, Santa Clara has become known for its carved redware and blackware as well as incised and sgraffito decoration.

The weaving arts have a much longer tradition than pottery in the Southwest. Examples of textiles, sandals, and basketry have survived for millennia. The Navajo continue to weave wool rugs and blankets today, and the Pueblos their handwoven cotton and embroidered mantas, kilts, and sashes. The Man-in-the-Maze design applied to Akimel O'odham (Pima) baskets has been commercialized by European-Americans and applied to any number of things for decades, despite the tribe's intellectual property rights. O'odham basketry designs may have their roots in early Hohokam pottery designs, as well as in elements found in nature. Tohono O'odham artist Terrol Johnson has taken the art to a new level, using materials such as gourds and bronze to complement his basketry.

Diné first phase chief blanket

For countless generations, Ute and Navajo communities have bordered one another in what we now call the Four Corners region. Expert weavers, the Navajo possessed a remarkable herding economy that included hundreds of thousands of sheep, while the Utes combined hunting and seasonal gathering with a migratory equestrian lifestyle within their beloved Colorado Rocky Mountain homelands. It is not surprising that one of the earliest-known Navajo trade blankets was acquired among the Navajo's Ute neighbors during a U.S. government expedition through Arizona in 1851.

In September of that year, Captain Lorenzo Sitgreaves, with a small crew of topographers and an escort of thirty infantrymen, set out from the Zuni Pueblo with instructions to explore and map the Zuni and Colorado rivers and evaluate their navigability in light of the possibility of war with the Mormons in Utah. Prepared for both war and research, early U.S. expeditions in the Southwest were charged with the collection and documentation of countless natural and ethnographic elements, including the presence of trade goods in Indian communities. Spanish governors in New Mexico had traded cloth and other wares to Ute delegations beginning in the 1600s, and the presence in Ute society of European-American trade goods, as well as goods produced by other Indian tribes, was commonplace by the end of the U.S.–Mexican War in 1848. This blanket dates to a time before reservations and wars confined the peoples of the Southwest, an under-recognized period of Indian autonomy and exchange in American history.

—Ned Blackhawk (Western Shoshone)

Diné (Navajo) first phase chief blanket, ca. 1840–1850. New Mexico. Wool, dye; 179 x 13 cm. Presented by S. W. Woodhouse, Jr. 11/8280

Akimel O´odham Oos:hikbina (calendar stick)

Akimel O´odham Oos:hikbina
(calendar stick), ca. 1833–1921.
Gila Crossing, Arizona. Saguaro
cactus wood, paint; 91 x 3 x 2 cm.
Collected by Edward H. Davis.
10/4878

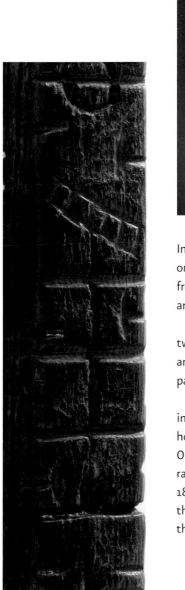

In the absence of a formal written language, the O´odham of southern Arizona relied on oral tradition for memorializing significant events. The Oos:hikbina—translated literally from O´odham as "stick cuts upon"—was one way that the Akimel O´odham (River People) annotated oral history. The other manner of revitalizing human memory is through songs.

Most often, an Oos:hikbina was made by trimming a dry saguaro cactus rib flat on one or two sides to enable the recorder and keeper to etch dots, small notches, V-shaped grooves, and deep, straight-line cuts across the stick representing years. The symbols were often painted with natural pigments of blue soot and red clay.

This Oos:hikbina, kept by Mr. Joseph Head and acquired by the collector Edward H. Davis in 1921, records events beginning in 1833. The Gila River Indian Community, the keeper's homeland, was established by executive order in 1859. Several battles in which the Akimel O´odham and Piipaash (Maricopa) joined forces against enemy tribes are recorded. Natural phenomena and European influence—including the coming of the railroads in 1878 and 1886—are revealed with etched symbolism. The Oos:hikbina does not record every event that affected the lives of the Akimel O´odham and Piipaash, but it does provide insight into the inevitable progression of new beginnings.

—Barnaby Lewis (Akimel O´odham)

128

The Pueblo, O´odham, and Yuman peoples for the most part continue to live where the Spanish found them; unlike many tribes they were not forcibly removed from their homelands. A cradleboard made around 1910 illustrates the continuity of Quechan culture. Cradleboards made with a hooped frame and a mattress of soft bark and woven hood were carried by women and rocked back and forth on the lap. Often times they were set upright against a wall or tree for the baby to watch the activities of the household. Cradleboards were specific to girls and boys based on the color scheme of the hood and the items attached to it.[9] The red cloth, which was introduced by Mexicans, and the stitched white lines with the attached feathers suggest that this cradleboard was more than likely made for a boy.

The history of the Navajo and Apache was much different. Between 1800 and 1850 Navajo women were known for weaving beautiful wool blankets that were traded to Plains tribes as far north as the Blackfeet, where they were worn by chiefs and their wives. The ways of life of the Navajo and Mescalero Apache were disrupted in 1864 when the U.S. military rounded them up and forcibly removed them from their homes. They were marched on foot over hundreds of miles to be incarcerated at Bosque Redondo, an internment camp at Fort Sumner in New Mexico. One of the greatest tragedies in American history, this is referred to as "The Long Walk" by the Navajo. They barely survived incarceration. After their release in 1868, the Navajo returned home to find that the U.S. military had destroyed their homes, orchards, and herds of churro sheep. The merinos that were given to them provided wool of lesser quality.[10] This presented new challenges for Navajo weavers, who turned to commercial yarns for their blankets and rugs.

Other Apache groups also suffered under the U.S. military during the 1870s and 1880s. Like all Indian people dealing with the encroachment of immigrants into their homeland, the Apaches were viewed as obstacles to European-American settlement, industry, and progress.[11] New settlers in the Arizona Territory complained bitterly to the U.S. government and demanded that something be done to stop the Apache raids on their homes. The U.S. Army acted swiftly, recruiting Western Apache as scouts to assist in rounding up the "hostile Indians," in particular the Chiricahuas, who opposed the Indian Bureau's attempts to concentrate all Apaches on the San Carlos Reservation. The Apache scouts wore deer hide shirts to distinguish them from other Apaches and from regular army officers.[12]

Naiche was among the Chiricahuas who escaped with Geronimo and their relatives as they were being brought back to the San Carlos Reservation from Mexico by General George Crook in May 1886, only to surrender in September that year. Many Chiricahua and Warm Springs Apaches surrendered and were taken to Fort Marion in Florida. Held in crowded and unsanitary conditions, twenty percent of the Chiricahua prisoners died there. After eight long years' imprisonment, the Chiricahuas were transferred to Fort Sill, Oklahoma. It wasn't until 1913 that they were finally given full freedom to leave or stay at Fort Sill.[13] It is amazing that their culture survived. The girls' puberty ceremony (na hi es) Naiche painted on deer hide continues to be an important rite of passage for Apache girls (see page 136).

The Native peoples of the Southwest have endured ongoing environmental, cultural, artistic, and political change for millennia. Their arts will continue to change and grow with the annual Santa Fe Indian Market, as well as the ongoing and potential new markets held at museums across the country annually. A legacy of change and interactions with others has helped the Native peoples of the Southwest to shape and sustain a strong identity in both their arts and culture, and they will no doubt continue to maintain a strong cultural identity and sense of place within the larger global community of the 21st century.

—Shelby Tisdale

Margaret Tafoya (Santa Clara,
1904–2001), vase, 1962. Santa
Clara Pueblo, New Mexico. Clay;
25 x 22 cm. Purchased from Mrs.
Kathleen Peters. 24/3736

Facing: Rosalia Medina Toribio
(Zia, 1858–1950), polychrome
jar, ca. 1920–1929. Zia Pueblo,
New Mexico. Clay, paint; 58 x 45
cm. Collected by John L. Nelson.
16/5780

Ancestral Pueblo stone jar

For the A:shiwi (Zuni) people, Pueblo Bonito is important for playing an innermost role in our emergence and migration story. Different groups of people who emerged from the underworlds had a destiny and a purpose regarding their migration. For the A:shiwi, it was about finding the middle place at the time of emergence. In terms of how people came into this particular area, since the creation of time, our people have identified certain terrain—arroyos, buttes, plateaus, and mountains and how they connect to generate significant trails. People marked monuments in line with the sun or with points in the night sky. Within the vast valley in all directions, even on the sheer walls of the mountains, they made different types of inscriptions. To this day our songs talk about thunder beings or the four-footed animals that link and identify trails leading from Zuni to the Chaco area and to Pueblo Bonito (Innodekwe) in particular.

The richness of the spiritual life people had there still remains within our culture. The circular room blocks served as kivas, or ceremonial chambers, some probably for medicine societies, rain priest societies, or other men's society groups. The men who earned the right to keep the rituals were the backbone of the villages. I keep reflecting on the emergence and the migration. A lot of those people carried sacred bundles to continue building on the creation. The ceremonial chambers were where everything the people brought up from the underworlds was refined. Otherwise, the practice of the societies and the songs that exist today in Zuni would no longer be here. When the people left Chaco, they carried everything they could on their journey. That is how all these different sites are connected to the heart of the Pueblo of Zuni. Our ceremonialism and spirituality connect us to these places.

The creation of this vessel was very significant to a certain membership of people. The vessel must have had a designated caretaker who had the honor to find the right soft stone to create it and apply the design. The design represents the thunder beings and their relation to the formation of clouds. The lifelines painted with red hematite connect the different directions and the journeys of the different groups of people. The vessel was probably used for making some type of medicinal powder, or as a way of containing something for ceremonial use. The pigments used in the design are azurite, which is the blue, and red hematite, probably mixed with another clay to make sure the design held the stone's surface. The black portion is also clay. We use quite an abundance of that black clay pigment for our prayer sticks and some for body paint.

It is evident that there was prayer and spiritual process put into this vessel. It was probably kept in a cool area. It must have had some form of traditional curation away from a lot of light to have kept its color. Sensitive and significant objects were always kept inside another confinement; maybe this vessel was kept in a larger pottery jar with a lid, or maybe a special box was made for it. Somebody put a lot of care into it as it still remains pristine and delicate.

People probably carried this vessel from one place to another until eventually it ended up at Pueblo Bonito. Some kind of event must have occurred for it to be left behind. After I came back from the museum, I put more thought to it. That was my conclusion, the more I studied the work applied to the vessel and the kind of pigments used on it, especially the black pigment, which is really very significant in Pueblo country. The vessel is a special gift. It must have had someone to take care of it, as is practiced to this day in the heart of the A:shiwi people.

—Arden Kucate (A:shiwi)
Tribal councilman, Pueblo of Zuni

Ancestral Pueblo stone jar, ca. AD 1000. Pueblo Bonito, Chaco Canyon, New Mexico. Sandstone, pigment; 20 x 13 cm. Collected by George H. Pepper. 5/1364

Ancestral A:shiwi plate and candlestick

Ancestral A:shiwi (Zuni) plate and candlestick, ca. 1629–1680. Hawikku, New Mexico. Clay; 6 x 20.5 cm (plate), 16 x 7 cm (candlestick). Hendricks–Hodge Expedition. 8/6825, 9/6974

Hawikku, one of several ancestral villages of the A:shiwi (Zuni), served as a regional crossroad for trade and knowledge. Hawikku is also popularly known as the site of first contact between nonindigenous and indigenous peoples in North America and has had its share of conjecture and debate. At Hawikku, the story goes, in 1539 a Moorish slave named Estevan, scouting ahead of a Spanish group, met A:shiwi. Interestingly, it seems the first nonindigenous contact with the peoples of North America was actually made by an African. It wasn't until a year later that Coronado finally led his expedition to Hawikku.

During the Spanish occupancy, which lasted roughly 140 years, many new things were introduced to our people, including ceramic styles that met the cultural and religious needs of the missionaries. This candleholder and plate obviously do not follow the traditions of A:shiwi ceramic-making before the Spaniards' arrival or after their departure. That said, the plate in particular is revealing because the painted designs represent a definite continuity of A:shiwi artistic and cultural sensibilities, even through the disruption of the Spanish period.

Our people resisted attempts at cultural and political domination. The brutality of the missionaries resulted in the Pueblo Revolt of 1680 and the killing of Catholic priests and burning of mission churches. Hawikku, today a rocky and nondescript hill overlooking cornfields, reminds us that, like our handmade creations, our culture may sometimes adapt to external influences, but it will always remain deeply A:shiwi.

—Jim Enote (A:shiwi)

Nampeyo (Hopi–Tewa) polychrome jar

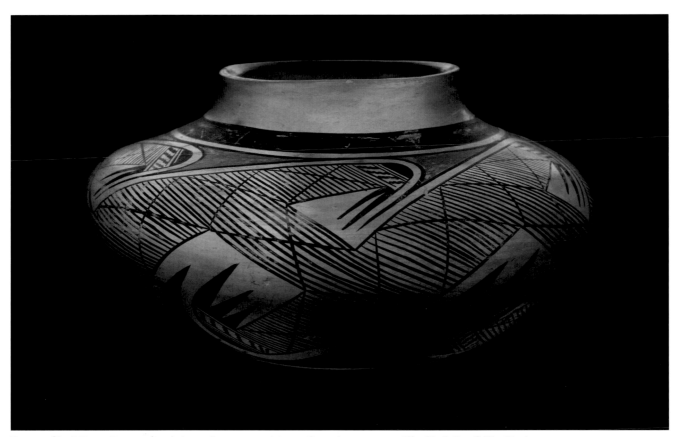

Nampeyo (Hopi–Tewa, 1859–1942), polychrome jar, ca. 1930s. Arizona. Clay, paint; 13 x 21 cm. Gift of R. E. Mansfield. 26/4462

When I first began to paint, I used to go to the ancient village and pick up pieces of pottery and copy the designs. That is how I learned to paint. But now I just close my eyes and see designs and I paint them.

—NAMPEYO, 1920S

Nampeyo's art was a gift she used to express the life of her ancestors. The design she painted on this jar is commonly called the migration pattern, a symbolic portrayal of the migration of the Hopi. Abstract bird wings create a never-ending pattern of movement that envelops the vessel. The design also alludes to waves of water, which speaks of the migrations of people through the seas.

When this pot was created, probably in the early 1930s, Nampeyo was in her mid-seventies. Her eyesight was fading, and her daughters often assisted in her work. Before this time, she had traveled to the Grand Canyon to demonstrate and display her pottery. In 1910, her art took her to an exhibit in Chicago, a rare journey for a Native artist at that time.

Like Pueblo ancestors, this jar itself has experienced a migration. The vessel began its journey in Hopi lands. All the places it has seen since then are unclear, though one clue is written in pencil on the bottom of the vessel—"7/29/34 C. M. Armack," presumably the date of first "collection" and the collector's name. After being acquired by the National Museum of the American Indian in 2005, the jar sits here, eager to share the history of its own migration as well as the journeys of Nampeyo and her people.

—Les Namingha (Zuni/Tewa–Hopi)

Naiche (Chiricahua Apache) painting of a girl's puberty ceremony

All we want is to be freed and be released as prisoners, given land and homes that we can call our own. That is all we think about. We have learned to work. That is generally the way when they take anybody to learn. After they have taught them for a while they will look at them and think well now these people have learned enough I guess. I will give them some kind of work. . . . Are we going to work here for you as long as we can move our hands, work until we are so old we can't work anymore?

—NAICHE, 1911
SPEAKING TO U.S. ARMY OFFICIALS
AT FORT SILL, OKLAHOMA

As I look at this painting by Naiche, the last hereditary leader of the Chokonen band of Chiricahuas, I can only think that a story is being told by a leader, a person, a prisoner—how the gáhé danced at a girl's puberty ceremony among the birds, insects, and plant life; under the stars; in front of the Creator and the people. Where did it happen? Was the ceremony held in Mexico, where Chiricahuas fled from the United States Army? Arizona, where they were confined to a reservation? In the East—Florida, Alabama, or Oklahoma—where Chiricahuas were held as prisoners of war for twenty-seven long years? Or here, in Mescalero, where some agreed to go when they were released? Most important, I think that the people, Indé, carry the story on, as told on the hide.

—Oliver Enjady (Mescalero Apache)

Naiche (Chiricahua Apache, 1857–1921), painting of a girl's puberty ceremony, ca. 1907. Fort Sill, Oklahoma. Chamois skin, paint; 78 x 67 cm. Collected by Mark R. Harrington. 2/1417

Julian Martinez (San Ildefonso) *Buffalo Dancers*

*Julian was a good man, and he was head of some
ceremony, and he became governor. Sometimes they
re-elect[ed] him to take care of his people. At a
ceremony, in [the] Indian way, he was very good.
He helped me. He helped me with everything.*

—MARIA MARTINEZ, 1977
SPEAKING ABOUT HER HUSBAND, JULIAN

Julian Martinez is perhaps best known for his collabo-
rations with his wife, Maria, the Pueblo potter. Yet
in the 1920s and late 1930s, Martinez distinguished
himself as an easel painter, a member of what became
known as the San Ildefonso School. In 1932, he was
one of four artists and eight students who painted the
first murals at the Santa Fe Indian School and founded
the Mural Guild.

Martinez's paintings, in which he often combined
the figurative and abstract, influenced generations of
Native American artists. Dorothy Dunn, the founder of
the Studio at the Santa Fe Indian School, recognized
him as an innovator and credited him with introducing
an improvised *avanyu*, or water serpent, and the eques-
trian figure to watercolor painting. The former is a classic pottery motif, while the latter is a
Pueblo adaptation of the Plains Warrior, according to Dunn.

The Buffalo Dance is held during the winter months, though parts of the dance may
be performed in summer. Martinez and his contemporaries often painted Pueblo ceremonial dances. What makes this work unusual within Martinez's larger oeuvre is its deer hide
ground. Most of his paintings are on paper or, in the case of his murals, canvas.

—Michelle McGeough (Métis)

Julian Martinez (San Ildefonso,
1884–1943), *Buffalo Dancers*, ca.
1930s. San Ildefonso Pueblo, New
Mexico. Hide, paint; 79 x 61 cm.
Henry Craig Fleming Collection.
22/8644

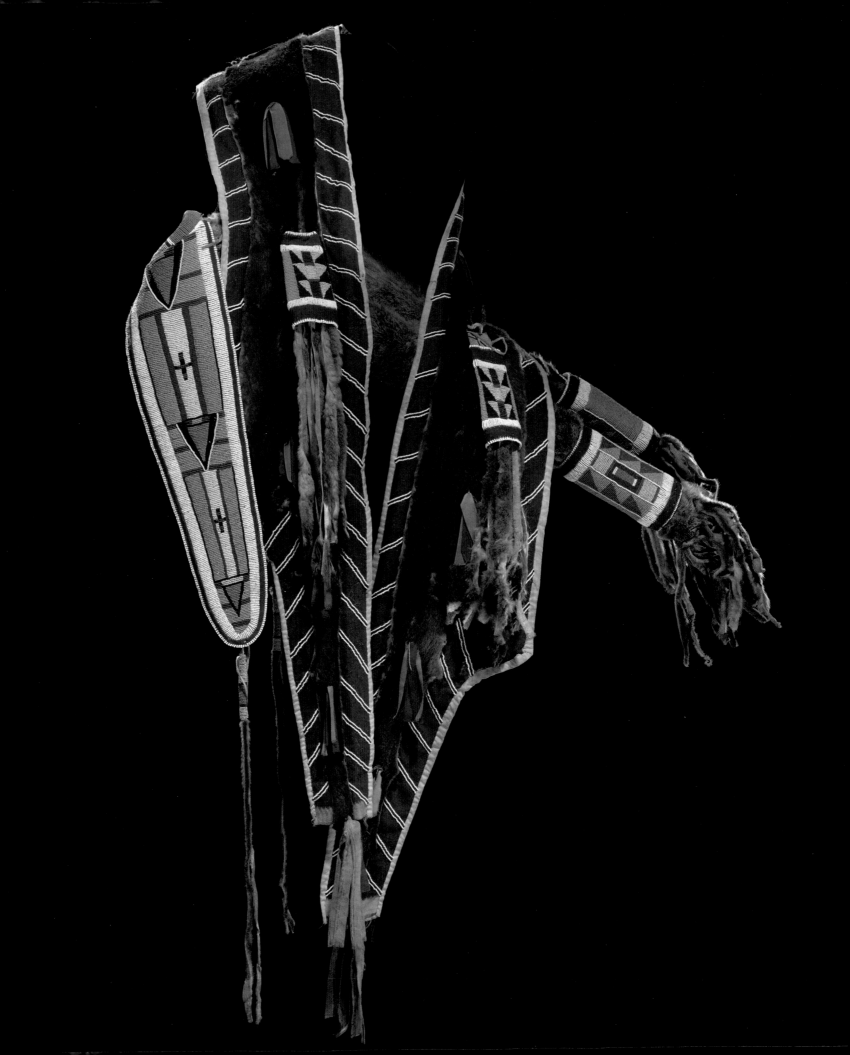

Personal histories

THE MAJORITY OF OBJECTS from the Great Plains and Plateau in museums today—and the National Museum of the American Indian is no exception—were acquired between 1850 and 1925. First collected by explorers, traders, and military men, these objects reflect a preoccupation with American Indian leaders variously characterized as natural aristocrats or warlike savages.[1] Collectors sought clothing, horse-trappings, drawing books, and other belongings of men they sometimes recognized as akin to themselves: men who engaged in the dynamic history of their nations in negotiation and in warfare.[2] The Plains and Plateau collections at the National Museum of the American Indian—among the strongest in the museum—document interactions among the indigenous nations of those regions, but they also move beyond this to highlight national and global contacts.

"Interaction" is an inexact word, encompassing events from alliance and exchange to warfare and genocide. Interaction may involve five men sitting around a campfire recalling their exploits in battle and horse-capture as they pass around a book that depicts these events. It includes the sharing of personal religious visions by publicly depicting them on shields and drums, or the spread of new religious movements across the entire sweep of the West. When individuals from different cultures meet, they come away changed, and that change is reflected in the objects they wear and use in daily life. Contact is also reflected in what non-Native people collected as mementos. Through all of these cultural transactions, art can be a vivid record of diplomacy, adversity, bravery, treachery, or hope.

The vast region of the Great Plains stretches west from the Mississippi River to the Rockies, and from

Assiniboine rifle case, ca. 1890. Saskatchewan, Canada. Deer hide, glass beads; 101 x 5.5 cm. Edward Borein Collection. 20/7685

present-day Texas north into Canada. More than two dozen Native nations inhabit this prairie once rich in animal life and crossed by vectors of intercultural trade, both anciently and in the historic period. It is also where some of the most egregious events of 19th century U.S. Indian policy transpired. Many objects under consideration here reflect this complicated cultural background. Moreover, as objects made principally by peoples who were nomadic, those examined in this chapter are carriers of deep and complicated personal history. All across the West, clothing and accessories were rich sources of information about the wearer. In 1832 the artist George Catlin (1796–1872) arrived at Fort Clark, in what is today North Dakota, intent upon documenting the peoples of the Plains who

Nimíipuu (Nez Perce) quiver, ca. 1890. Idaho. Otter fur, hide, wool, muslin, glass beads, silk ribbon; 157 x 44 cm. Purchase. 1/4369   **139**

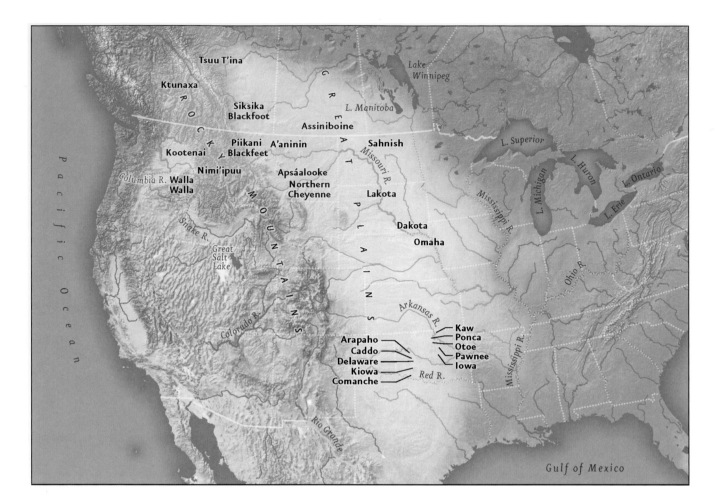

were still unfamiliar to anyone but traders and military men. Catlin painted a full-length portrait of the Mandan chief Mato-Tope, whom he described as "free, generous, elegant, and gentlemanly in his deportment—handsome, brave, and valiant; wearing a robe on his back with the history of his battles emblazoned on it which would fill a book themselves, if properly translated."[3] In his letters, Catlin explained the meaning of the clothing Mato-Tope wore for his formal portrait. His shirt, made of mountain sheep skins, was ornamented with porcupine quill embroidery done by his female relatives and hairlocks from enemies slain in battle. It bears drawings of combat, amplified on the buffalo skin robe he wore. Catlin described the headdress of eagle feathers and ermine skins as "the most costly part of an Indian's dress in all of this country." Of the split buffalo horns at the front of his headdress, Catlin remarked that only those "whose exceeding

valour, worth, and power [is] admitted by all the nation" wore such emblems of power.

When Mato-Tope came to Catlin's tipi to pose for his portrait, he was wearing many other accoutrements that Catlin omitted for simplicity's sake, including a bear claw necklace, a painted shield, a bow and quiver of arrows, a pipe and tobacco bag, a belt holding his tomahawk and scalping knife, a beaver skin medicine bag, and a war club. This would be the Plains equivalent of a four-star general dressed in his full military regalia, with his medals, epaulettes, ribbons, and stars. Each item is an emblem of the Mandan chief's rank and status.

Catlin's inventory of the meaning of Mato-Tope's finery reminds us that when we look at an individual man's shirt in a museum context, we are seeing only the merest glimpse of the history he meant to convey in his clothing.[4] To Mato-Tope, the most important

accoutrement was the feathered, steel-tipped lance he holds. It had belonged to an enemy who killed Mato-Tope's brother and left it stuck in his body. Mato-Tope took it, swearing to avenge his brother's death. Four years later, he traveled to the Arikara enemy village, entered the tipi of the sleeping chief, and drove the lance through its previous owner's body. Mato-Tope then scalped him, and returned home with both lance and scalp. Since stories of military bravery were told and retold around campfires, all who saw Mato-Tope in his ceremonial splendor would recall his exploits by viewing him with these things.

When Karl Bodmer and Prince Maximilian traveled up the Missouri River in 1833 and 1834, very few non-Indians had seen the Northern Plains. Nonetheless, the results of nearly a century of exchange with non-Natives—fur traders and the small numbers of militiamen who manned the forts—were already in evidence. At Fort McKenzie in August 1833, the Prince was surely astonished that one of the gifts given to

Ponca(?) parfleche bag, ca. 1830. Oklahoma. Buffalo hide, beads, sinew; 46 x 41 x 9 cm. Collected by T. R. Roddy. 6/4077

Piikani Blackfeet (Northern Piegan) mirror board and pouch, ca. 1860. Piikani Reserve, Alberta, Canada. Wood, coyote fur, hide, glass beads, brass tacks, pigment; 59 x 22 cm. Collected by Donald Cadzow. 14/9556

him by a Blackfeet chief was a British officer's scarlet coat, acquired in an earlier encounter with French or British traders who came down the rivers from New France (Canada). In his diary, Maximilian recorded his distress at seeing such European overcoats and top hats worn as finery.[5] During those same years, an essential element in every trader's pack—alongside beads and mirrors, metal awls and sewing needles—were packets

George Catlin (1796–1872), *Máh-to-tóh-pa, Fours Bears, Second Chief in Full Dress*, 1832. Oil on canvas. 73.7 x 60.9 cm.

of Chinese vermilion. This pigment provides an example of the scope of global mercantilism evident in the American West. It was mined in southwest China, packaged there in papers stamped with the address of the merchants who sold it, shipped across the Pacific, and traded through ancient marketplaces across the Plateau and Plains. These examples demonstrate that there was no "pristine," untouched Indian America. Embedded in even the oldest objects are trade networks that had crossed the continent from north to south and east to west since antiquity.

The museum is fortunate to have the remarkable early war shirt of the Brulé Lakota chief Spotted Tail (Sinte Gleska, 1823–1881), who played a crucial role in negotiations with the U. S. government during the 1870s.[6] In the 19th century, each Lakota band was led by a small number of *wakikonza*, or shirt-wearers, who were responsible for governing and protecting the people.[7] In 1855 Spotted Tail and three other ranking Brulé warriors turned themselves in at Fort Laramie, Wyoming, to prevent retaliation on the Lakota for the killing of some whites. Although they feared they

would be executed, they gave themselves up to ensure the safety of their people. This was likely the very war shirt that Spotted Tail wore when he surrendered at Fort Laramie, as described by George Hyde:

> On October 18 the troops and a large body of Sioux were assembled at Fort Laramie when Spotted Tail and his companions appeared, mounted on fine ponies and wearing handsome war costumes. As they advanced slowly, the men were singing their death songs.[8]

Second Lieutenant Charles Sawtelle obtained this shirt from Spotted Tail at the fort—whether by purchase, gift, or theft we do not know.[9] From Fort Laramie, the prisoners were taken to the much larger Fort Leavenworth, Kansas. Again, Hyde provides a vivid picture of the "education" that Spotted Tail gained along the route:

> "[The road toward Kansas] was swarming with whites, thousands of white men, women, and children in camps or on the road, moving in a steady stream westward to the Pacific Coast. There were also settlements in Kansas, towns of wooden houses. . . . Spotted Tail must have realized what fate had in store for his own tribe. Sooner or later, the Brulés would have to give up their wandering life of hunting and fighting and learn to live like white people.[10]

This realization about the size and strength of the white population was reinforced when Spotted Tail traveled to Washington in 1870 as part of a delegation to demand from President Ulysses S. Grant land and buffalo hunting rights for his people. The delegation visited Philadelphia, New York, and Chicago before returning to Dakota Territory.[11] Spotted Tail later became one of the leading advocates for peace with the U.S. military and government, for everything he had seen in his adult life and in his travels convinced him that war against the U.S. military was futile.

In 1879, Spotted Tail let himself be persuaded to send four of his sons and two grandchildren to the newly opened Carlisle Indian School in Pennsylvania, believing that mastery of the white man's language was essential for the next generation to maneuver successfully in the larger world. At the end of Carlisle's first school year, a delegation of chiefs was invited to witness the "success" of this new educational venture. But what Spotted Tail found enraged him: his sons, deeply unhappy, were being trained in manual labor, not reading and writing. Spotted Tail tried to take all 34 of the children from the Rosebud Reservation home, but was prevented from taking any but his own.[12] Murdered by another Sioux in the following year, Spotted Tail did not live to see education come to Rosebud. His name lives on at Sinte Gleska University, founded at Rosebud in 1970.[13]

Tsuu T´ina (Sarcee) coat, ca. 1890.
Saskatchewan, Canada. Deer
hide, cotton cloth, otter fur,
glass beads, ochre; 73 x 118 cm.
Mrs. Edwin C. Ward Collection.
11/4236

Unlike the many shirts painted with battle scenes, or the quilled and beaded shirt worn by his uncle, Spotted Tail, the shirt catalogued as belonging to the Oglala leader Crazy Horse (Tashunca-uitco, ca. 1842–1877) is a relatively modest garment. In his youthful vision quest, Crazy Horse had learned he was not to wear the fine accoutrements of war to which other successful warriors and headmen were entitled.

Legendary in his bravery and modesty, Crazy Horse has been a figure of deep respect and admiration among Native and non-Native people alike.[14] He fought in many battles, most notably the battles of the Rosebud and the Little Big Horn in 1876. He didn't participate in peace treaties and never went to Washington. He was fierce in his determination that the Lakota should continue their traditional way of life,

unhampered by white men and their restrictive laws. Like Spotted Tail, Crazy Horse was a shirt-wearer, responsible for the welfare of his people. In May 1877, after a winter of bitter cold and deprivation, he brought his followers—some 900 people and 2,000 horses—into Fort Robinson, Nebraska, to surrender and to live at Spotted Tail's Agency. Four months later, Crazy Horse was killed during his arrest, either by his friend Little Big Man or by a white soldier.

Whether or not this shirt ever belonged to Crazy Horse—Donovin Sprague raises his doubts on page 155—its history is tied to his life. The man who obtained it, Captain John Gregory Bourke (1846–1896), spent much of the 1870s involved in military campaigns in the West.[15] Bourke, who met Crazy Horse shortly after his surrender, wrote of his death, "The United States will never again be forced to cope with an aborigine who is a match in the field for the whole miserable skeleton called its army and in the council for the shrewdest men civilization could pit against him."[16]

Like other military men, Bourke collected numerous mementos of his combat days, but he made a unique transformation from soldier to ethnologist by the late 1870s, exhibiting great empathy for Indian peoples and their diverse histories.[17] In June 1881, five years after Bourke fought the Lakota—including Crazy Horse—at the Battle of the Rosebud, he was a guest at the great Sun Dance held at Pine Ridge. He took voluminous notes, with his former foe Little Big Man by his side. This is likely when Bourke obtained Crazy Horse's shirt from Little Big Man, for he never returned to Pine Ridge.[18]

A history somewhat different from that of these men is told in the beaded clothing of Plateau and Plains women.[19] Beaded baby carriers, too, were lovingly crafted by women. The virtuoso work on the Kootenai cradle includes materials from around the world: cowrie and dentalium shells, elk teeth, brass beads, basket beads, and faceted beads, as well as delicate silk

and sturdy woolens. The ultramodern woman who created it in the late 19th century not only used a sewing machine to stitch the trade cloth, she machine-pieced the hide itself, a labor-saving effort that allowed her to spend more time on her bold floral beadwork. Green silk edges the head of the cradleboard; the serrated black and white beadwork and vivid floral patterns against a rusty orange background would all serve to accentuate and frame the face of the honored baby carried within. In many tribes, it has long been customary for female relatives to make such elaborate gifts.

Cecile Gravelle, a Kootenai woman, probably no longer wore traditional dress on a daily basis in the 1920s, yet it should come as no surprise that her twin girls Elizabeth and Mary had fine and individualistic cradleboards. This artform continues in some Plateau and Plains families today. Acclaimed Kiowa beadworker Vanessa Paukeigope Jennings has beaded more

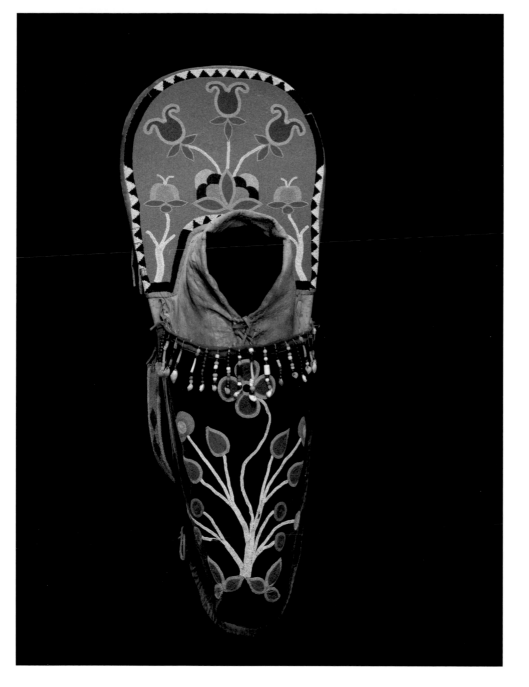

than two dozen cradleboards in the last twenty years, including one for her grandson in 1999.[20]

The life of Susette La Flesche (Inshata Theumba, 1854–1903) was worlds apart from those of the men discussed earlier (see page 157). The daughter of an Omaha chief of mixed Native and non-Native heritage, and a member of what has been called "an emerging reservation elite,"[21] La Flesche graduated from the Elizabeth Institute in Elizabeth, New Jersey in 1875. A famous advocate for Indian rights, La Flesche and her husband, Thomas Tibbles, were present as war correspondents at Wounded Knee in 1890; indeed, Tibbles was the first to send out an account of the disaster.[22]

As befitted a cosmopolitan woman who had dined with poet Henry Wadsworth Longfellow and President Rutherford B. Hayes, Susette La Flesche's wedding dress was of the latest style. A "princess dress" (named for Princess Alexandra of Great Britain),[23] it is a far

Cecile Gravelle (Kootenai) with her twin daughters, Elizabeth and Mary, in beaded cradleboards, ca. 1920.

military exploits gave way to a much smaller format. Personal histories were inscribed in drawing books or lined account ledgers, giving rise to the term "ledger art." Such drawings were sometimes carried into battle, and were used as *aides-memoire* to recall feats of bravery. In the second half of the 19th century on the Great Plains and Plateau it is almost impossible to extricate the personal history of Native warriors and leaders from U.S. military history. Two drawing books in the museum are excellent examples of that.

The double trophy roster described by Gordon Yellowman on page 154 is a fine example of the complexities of ownership and usage of Native objects. Its name refers to the fact that it was a trophy on both sides of the Indian wars. Although little is known of its owner, High Bull (ca. 1848–1876), he almost certainly participated in the Battle of Little Big Horn. The small memorandum book in which he drew scenes of Cheyenne warrior history had belonged to 1st Sargeant Brown of G Troop of the 7th Cavalry, who died in that battle on June 25, 1876. High Bull probably took it from Brown's body as one of the spoils of war.[25]

Sargeant Brown's use of the book had been brief: April 19 to June 24. He recorded marksmanship records, lists of horse equipment, and other small traces of the daily life of a soldier. His last entry reads, "McEgan lost his carbine on the march while on duty with pack train, June 24, 1876." The next day, these men would lose their lives in the last great military victory for Cheyenne and Lakota warriors, who killed Custer and all of his troops. Over the next five months, High Bull and his comrades inscribed their history over Brown's mundane lists and rosters. The book was recaptured by white soldiers during the raid on Dull Knife's village on November 26, 1876, in which many Cheyenne were killed. The wholesale destruction—burning some two hundred tipis and their contents, destroying all of the food caches, and slaughtering hundreds of horses—left the survivors unprepared for the harsh winter of the Northern Plains. In the village, the soldiers found much evidence of this band's participation in the Battle of Little Big Horn: Army

cry from the traditional Indian clothing customarily collected by museums. Yet it is just as important in representing the reality of Native life in the 19th century. As an Omaha, La Flesche was part of the Plains cultural sphere, but acculturation to white ways came earlier to those of mixed Native–white heritage, like La Flesche, reminding us that there were many ways of being Indian in the 19th-century American West.[24]

With increasing contact with outsiders, and as buffalo grew more scarce after 1875 due to the depredations of white hunters, the painted hide robe depicting horse gear, horses with U.S. brands, flags, clothes, wallets full of money, and letters stamped and ready to be sent back east.[26]

Old Bear, an elderly Cheyenne to whom the historian and naturalist George Bird Grinnell showed this ledger book in 1898, identified it as belonging to High Bull. Some twenty-two drawings illustrating battles against the Crow and Shoshone remain in the book today. Many pages were removed between High Bull's use of it and its return visit to the Cheyenne in 1898, for Grinnell reported that Old Bear "recognized the book as soon as it was handed to him, and professed great indignation that many of the pictures had been taken out of it."[27] Today, the life of this drawing book in a Native-run national museum adds one more chapter to the complex history of a truly intercultural object.

The second drawing book belonged to a man named Red Dog who was the leader of the Oyuhpe Band of the Northern Oglala in the 1860s and '70s (see page 158). In 1867 he had a following of "over 100 tipis," more than any other band leader, including the illustrious and far better known Red Cloud.[28] Red Dog was part of the 1870 delegation to Washington to discuss Lakota dissatisfaction with the Fort Laramie Treaty of 1868. Since the *itancan* was responsible for the welfare of his people, including the fair distribution of goods and foodstuff, Red Dog was concerned about the graft and corruption that led to the denial of rations promised by earlier treaties and councils.[29]

Red Dog's ledger book records portraits of several men in his band, among them Low Dog, Red Crow, Respects Nothing, White Cow Chief, and a dozen others.[30] Unlike many such books, this one does not reveal the heroic actions of these men in their many battles to save their people and their land from domination by the U. S. military. Instead, we see simple portraits of the men, mostly

Iromagaja (Rain-in-the-Face, Hunkpapa Lakota, ca. 1835–1905), drawing. Standing Rock Reservation, North Dakota, ca. 1885. Paper, colored pencil; 18 x 11.5 cm. Bequest of De Cost Smith. 20/1626

on horseback. In the Plains artistic tradition, a man's identity was revealed through his clothing, the imagery on his shield, and the idiosyncratic painting of his horse, rather than by physiognomic accuracy. Within the Oyuhpe, such a book would have been passed around a camp circle, while men narrated their brave deeds. Many, including Red Dog himself, had fought at the Battle of Little Bighorn.[31]

Names of about half of the men depicted in Red Dog's drawing book appear in *The Crazy Horse Surrender Ledger*, a roster of those at the Red Cloud Agency in 1876 and 1877, including the 217 men and their families under Crazy Horse who surrendered there in May of 1877. While their names and deeds crop up occasionally in white narratives of the time, it is thrilling to see their self-portraits as free men, astride their horses, before they were confined to the poverty of reservation life.

There may have been good reason why the Oglala men who drew in this book presented simple self-portraits rather than more complex scenes of fighting. The book was collected around 1884 by Valentine McGillycuddy, who was the agent at the former Red Cloud Agency—renamed Pine Ridge in 1878—from 1879 to 1886.[32] This was less than a decade after the resounding defeat of Custer and his men, and it probably was too soon for these warriors to reveal their participation in events that had undermined white America's blithe confidence during the centennial summer. Later, however, many of these men did tell white historians the details of their bravery, while others recorded these scenes in their drawing books.[33]

The drawings were made in a lined notebook with a leather cover stamped with "Department of the Interior. U.S. Indian Service," and it is likely that McGillycuddy commissioned the drawings, perhaps as a gift for William Techumseh Sherman, the commanding general of the Army during the Indian wars, whose own bookplate ("W. T. Sherman, General") is glued in the back of the book. One of the sad realities behind many of the objects that came into museums through the hands of military men is that soldiers collected such items as mementos of the people whom they sought to exterminate. Sherman (1820–1891) was an implacable and ruthless foe of Indians.[34] Despite having welcomed Spotted Tail into his home in 1878 when the Brulé delegation came to Washington, Sherman sought to wipe out the Sioux on the Great Plains.

But men like Spotted Tail, Crazy Horse, and Sitting Bull had their own otherworldly means of protection against the forces of military might. Used in conjunction with their formidable fighting skills, objects of spiritual power were important when Native people confronted their white oppressors. The museum houses several objects that reflect the spiritual experiences of 19th century Native leaders of the West. Spiritual encounters on the Great Plains and Plateau can never be divorced from military ones, for many warriors had visions that influenced their actions in war. Personal visions were painted on tipis, shields, drums, shirts, and other objects.

Arapoosh, (also known as Sore Belly or Rotten Belly, ca. 1795–1834) was chief of the River Crow in the first decades of the 19th century. Both a war leader and a medicine man, he is remembered by the Crow Nation for his steadfast refusal to be party to the treaty of August 4, 1825, signed by the Mountain Crow, the Mandan, and the Hidatsa. It is said that he was so angered by this treaty that he used his medicine power to cause a tremendously destructive rain to fall.[35] Other stories have been passed down about his power to cause hailstorms against his enemies, and numerous early accounts mention his leadership.[36] Prince Maximilian met him during his first season on the Upper Missouri in 1833, and stories were still being told about him when anthropologist Robert Lowie embarked upon his fieldwork on the Crow Reservation in 1907.[37]

Edwin Denig, a fur trader on the Upper Missouri from 1833 to 1856, described the River Crow chief as one who "made no show of his medicine, no parade of sacrifices or smokings, no songs or ceremonies, but silently and alone he prayed to the thunder for assistance. . . . His great superiority over others consisted in decision,

Shield associated with Chief Arapoosh (Sore Belly, Apsáalooke [Crow], ca. 1795–1834), ca. 1825. Montana. Buffalo hide, deer hide, bird head, feathers, pigment, brass tacks, wool cloth, horsehair; 67 x 62 x 10 cm. Collected by William Wildschut. 11/7680

Iowa drop, ca. 1890. Oklahoma. Otter fur, hide, silk, wool cloth, glass beads; 122 x 14 cm. Dr. W. C. Barnard Collection. 16/9178

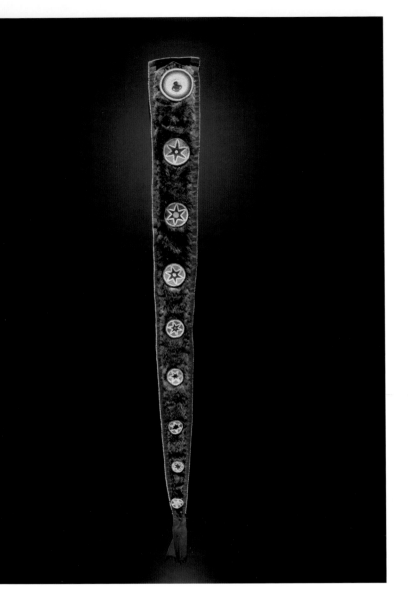

Most prominent is the dried head and neck of a sandhill crane. Red trade cloth is wrapped around some of these elements. By 1830, people on the Northern Plains had long relied on cloth made in the mills of Stroud, England, which came to them in the packs of fur traders.[40] The late Smithsonian anthropologist John Ewers described Arapoosh's shield as "undoubtedly the most famous of all Crow Indian war medicines."[41] While shields were the personal medicine of particular individuals, they were often handed down through families. This one stayed in Crow hands for generations, until it was purchased from Mrs. Bull Tongue, who had inherited it from her husband, sometime between 1918 and 1923 by William Wildschut, who was acting on behalf of George Heye's Museum of the American Indian. It is one of the museum's great treasures.[42]

In the NMAI collection is an unusual square drum. On the front is the face of a Thunder Being whose horns are echoed by actual buffalo horns affixed to the drum itself—an important object even if its association with Sitting Bull (1831–1890, Tatanka Iyotanka, in Lakota) is in question. On the drum, the yellow face is featureless, except for the bright red orbs of the eyes. The horned head, with its strokes of hair across the top, rising as if in static electricity, occurs in other images of Thunder Beings as well.[43] Many descriptions emphasize the powerful, glowing eyes; Black Elk called the eyes "bright as stars," while George Bushotter said that Thunder Beings "do not open their eyes except when they make lightning." One can imagine this drum being struck with a stick during ceremonial songs, the sound ringing out like the thunder itself.

The Plains and Plateau collections at NMAI contain an infinity of personal stories. Not all of them reflect the national and international reach of indigenous cultures as acutely as the objects highlighted for discussion here. Yet in each one of them we sense a world of possible histories.

—Janet Catherine Berlo

action, and an utter disregard for the safety of his own person."[38] His power came from the thunder, and his shield depicts a Thunder Being. All across the Northern Plains, Thunder Beings have revealed themselves to human beings in vision quests.[39] These powerful supernaturals bring summer's dramatic electrical storms—indeed, they *are* the thunder, the lightning, the wind, and the hail.

The composition of his shield indicates that Arapoosh relied not only on the powers of the Thunder Beings, but also on animals from the realms of both sky and earth. Affixed to his shield are eagle, crow, and hawk feathers, and the tail of a black-tailed deer.

Lakota square hand drum

Lakota square hand drum, ca. 1860–1870. North Dakota(?). Hide, horn, wood, paint; 59 x 49 x 7 cm. Gift of John S. Williams. 23/2202.

Museum catalogue information states that this drum was given to Elisha Slocum, an agent of the Adams Express Company in North Dakota, by John Crawford. According to Slocum, the drum belonged to Sitting Bull, the Hunkpapa Lakota medicine man.

While I question that association, the drum is similar to a square drum said to be Assiniboine or Yanktonai Lakota from the Fort Peck Reservation in Montana. The two drums are so close in design that the same person could have painted them. Both show a yellow face with red eyes and no mouth, with black painted buffalo horns protruding from the face. Both drums also have two similar circular designs above the face.

Only the "Sitting Bull" has actual horns. The use and depiction of painted buffalo horns on these images likely represents power. The color black could represent the buffalo—night and death for the buffalo if the hunt was successful. This drum could have been used for calling buffalo to ensure a successful hunt and the well-being of the tribe.

I believe this drum is from the Assiniboine or Yanktonai Lakota. Following the 1862 Minnesota conflict known as the Dakota War, the Yanktonai made treaties with the United States. Many of those called Lower Yanktonai settled at Fort Peck, home today to the Assiniboine and Sioux. Those called Upper Yanktonai settled mostly at Standing Rock Reservation, where Sitting Bull and his people also lived.

—Donovin Sprague (Minnicoujou Lakota)

High Bull (Northern Cheyenne)

Double trophy roster book drawings

High Bull (Northern Cheyenne, ca. 1848–1876), double trophy roster book drawings, 1876. Montana. Paper, graphite; 12.5 x 19 cm. Presented by Grace Hoffman White. 10/8725

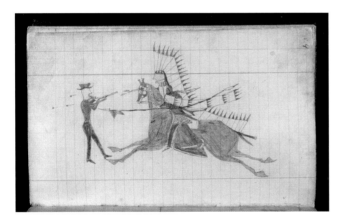

High Bull and other warriors recorded events reflecting their lives—including courtships, marriages, and war exploits—in this ledger book, captured at the Little Big Horn. The book was retaken six months later, after High Bull was killed in battle.

High Bull's encounters with George Armstrong Custer—or Yellow Hair, as the Cheyenne called him—began with brief skirmishes. In 1869 a traditional council of Cheyenne chiefs, including High Bull and the Cheyenne Arrow Keeper Stone Forehead, met to settle a peace agreement. The chiefs informed Lieutenant Colonel Custer that by smoking the red pipe, he had agreed to all the terms they had discussed. From that day forward, Custer promised, "I will no longer attack or kill a Cheyenne." Before Custer left the tipi, the Arrow Keeper took the ceremonial pipe and emptied the tobacco on Custer's boots, saying that if Custer broke his promise he would turn into those ashes.

High Bull, a decorated warrior, fought to protect all Cheyenne and fulfill his role as a chief. His legacy and spirit continue through this astonishing book.

—Gordon Yellowman (Southern Cheyenne)

Shirt associated with Tashunca-uitco
(Crazy Horse, Oglala Lakota)

Shirt associated with Tashunca-uitco (Crazy Horse, Oglala Lakota, 1849–1877), ca. 1870s. South Dakota. Hide, horsehair, human hair, quill, pigment, woodpecker feathers, arrowhead, cocoon; 87 x 142 cm. Major John G. Bourke Collection. Presented by Mrs. Alexander H. Richardson and Mrs. Alexander W. Maish. 16/1351

My land is where my dead lie buried.

—CRAZY HORSE, 1877

Captain John Bourke, an aide to General George Crook, commander of the Department of the Platte, recorded that this Lakota war shirt was presented to him by Little Big Man, who led him to believe that it had once belonged to Crazy Horse, or that it had at least been worn by him. According to family history, the shirt cannot have belonged to the great Lakota chief, who never kept scalps he took in war but instead left them upon the ground.

Crazy Horse fought throughout his life to resist U.S. military incursions into Lakota territory. Little Big Man had been a Lakota headman along with Crazy Horse. In May 1877, however, after their surrender at Camp Robinson, Little Big Man became a scout. Little Big Man was involved in Crazy Horse's death that September. Through a chain of events that remain tangled, Crook ordered Crazy Horse's arrest. Crazy Horse resisted being locked in a guardhouse, produced a knife, and in the scuffle cut Little Big Man deeply on the wrist. A few minutes later, Crazy Horse was mortally stabbed with a bayonet while under surrender.

The red circular design on the chest of this shirt may represent the sun. The red streaked lines may represent thunder beings (lightning). Yellow may be associated with growth and the summer season. The blue may represent the sky, heavens, and water, an essential element of life. Feathers adorning the arms of the shirt are a symbol of honors earned by the owner.

—Donovin Sprague (Minnicoujou Lakota)

Moccasins associated with Peo Peo T'olikt

(Bird Alighting, Nimi'ipuu)

After the soldiers left, we returned to our ruined homes. Several teepees had been burned or otherwise ruined. Much had been carried away and many objects destroyed or badly damaged. Brass buckets always carefully kept by the women, lay battered, smashed. . . . Growing gardens trampled and destroyed. Nearly all our horses were taken and every hoof of cattle driven away.

—PEO PEO T'OLIKT,
THE ATTACK ON THE CAMP AT CLEAR CREEK

Moccasins associated with Peo Peo T'olikt (Bird Alighting, Nimi'ipuu, b.?–1935), ca. 1880. Idaho. Deer hide, glass beads, cotton thread; 27 x 12 x 8 cm. Purchased from the Mabton Museum shop. 22/9590

Peo Peo T'olikt was a grandson of Ni Mii Puu leader Xa xac ilpilp (Red Grizzly Bear), who met and counseled explorers Lewis and Clark in 1805 and 1806. Shortly after the outbreak of the 1877 war with the United States, Peo Peo T'olikt was camped at Clear Creek near Kooskia, Idaho. Chief Looking Glass had declared that he wanted peace and had moved his band to Clear Creek on the Lapwai Reservation. Although the camp raised a white flag, on July 1 it was attacked and destroyed by angry soldiers and volunteer militiamen.

The band joined the fight at the Clearwater River and continued on the war trail all the way to Canada, covering nearly 1,300 miles in four months. Peo Peo T'olikt was involved in heavy, sometimes hand-to-hand, fighting. He also served as an outrider to protect the hard-traveling Nez Perce. He lost a wife and young son in the war, but his exploits were many, among them capturing the cannon and 2,000 rounds of cartridges at Big Hole, stealing Gen. Oliver Howard's mules and horses at Camas Meadows, and protecting the camp at Bear Paw.

In June 1878, after staying with the Sioux of Chief Sitting Bull, a few Nez Perce decided to return to the United States. They reached the Lapwai Indian Agency, where some were allowed to remain. Others were sent to the Oklahoma Territory. Peo Peo T'olikt was eventually allotted land on the reservation. He passed away in 1935 on his ranch near Lenore, Idaho.

These moccasins are beaded with seed beads of the late 1800s, which the Ni Mii Puu people readily adopted and used in the floral and geometric designs.

—Allen Pinkham, Sr. (Ni Mii Puu)

Wedding dress worn by Inshata-Theumba
(Susette La Flesche, Omaha)

Wedding dress worn by Inshata-Theumba (Susette La Flesche or Bright Eyes, Omaha, 1854–1903), ca. 1881. Nebraska. Wool; 76 x 101 cm (blouse), 112 x 88 cm (skirt). Gift of Mrs. Vivian K. Barris and Dr. Joan B. La Noue. 25/2192

When the Indian, being a man and not a child or thing, or merely an animal, as some of the would-be civilizers have termed him, fights for his property, liberty, and life, they call him a savage. When the first settlers in this country fought for their property, liberty, and lives, they were called heroes. When the Indian in fighting this great nation wins a battle, it is called a massacre; when this great nation in fighting the Indian wins, it is called a victory.

—SUSETTE LA FLESCHE

Susette La Flesche was born south of present-day Omaha, Nebraska, into a family descended from significant tribal leaders on both sides. As a child she lived in a traditional earthlodge, though she also attended a mission school and later a school on the East Coast, returning to work as a teacher in her Omaha community.

In 1877 La Flesche witnessed the expulsion of the Ponca from Nebraska to Indian Territory and the subsequent imprisonment of Standing Bear and other Poncas who attempted to return to their homeland. These events launched her career as an activist arguing against the involuntary removal of Native people and for Indian citizenship rights. La Flesche performed in eastern cities to great effect. Wearing an Omaha deerskin dress, she enlightened Boston and New York audiences on the suffering of tribal communities and American injustice and called for a new direction in federal Indian policy.

La Flesche found a soulmate in Thomas Tibbles, a reporter for the *Omaha Herald*. Both La Flesche and Tibbles played major roles in the 1879 civil rights decision that ended the Ponca imprisonment and led to the historic ruling, "An Indian is a person within the meaning of the law of the United States." Bicultural and bilingual, schooled in Western ways and Omaha culture, La Flesche wore this elegant skirt and jacket trimmed in hand-stitched silk, satin, and lace when she married Tibbles on July 23, 1881. The wedding was held on restored Ponca land.

—Brenda J. Child (Red Lake Ojibwe)

Sunka Luta (Red Dog, Oglala Lakota)

Ledger book drawings

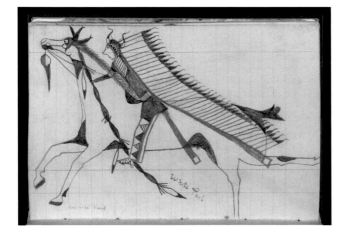

Sunka Luta (Red Dog, Oglala Lakota, ca. 1848– d.?), ledger book drawings, ca. 1884. Pine Ridge Reservation, South Dakota. Paper, leather, graphite, ink, colored pencil; 20 x 14 cm. Presented by Eleanor Sherman Fitch. 20/6230

I have but few words to say to you, my friends. When the good spirit raised us, he raised us with good men for counsels and he raised you with good men for counsels. But yours are all the time getting bad, while ours remain good.

—RED DOG, JUNE 16, 1870

Red Dog, an *itancan* (leader) of the Oglala Oyuhpe band, lived during a time of great transition, when many Lakota, Dakota, and Nakota people first witnessed the arrival of non-Indians. He was the brother-in-law of the well-known Chief Red Cloud and by many accounts was called upon by Red Cloud to be his spokesman.

Around 1884 Red Dog created fifty-two crayon drawings. Similar pictographs in rock art most often recount events of war against an enemy or horse raiding against other tribes. Lakota men also painted their exploits in this manner on their tipi dwellings.

The drawings of White Tail and White Feather Tail show warriors dressed in fine Lakota regalia complete with headdresses, one horse's tail tied up to prepare for action. Drawings often show a favorite spear, bow and arrows, rifle, or handgun, or maybe just a rope or coup stick. A rope would find its way around a loose horse, and a coup stick would be used to touch the enemy. It was more honorable to touch the enemy and get away with his possessions than to kill him. In Lakota values, being a warrior is an important aspect of bravery. Entering an enemy camp to take a prized horse or perhaps a herd of horses, often at high risk, was also a skillful act of bravery and chance. One eagle feather could be presented to a warrior for an outstanding deed. The riders in these drawings proudly display feathers they earned from previous encounters with the enemy.

—Donovin Sprague (Minnicoujou Lakota)

Tomahawk associated with Mee-nah-tsee–us
(White Swan, Apsáalooke)

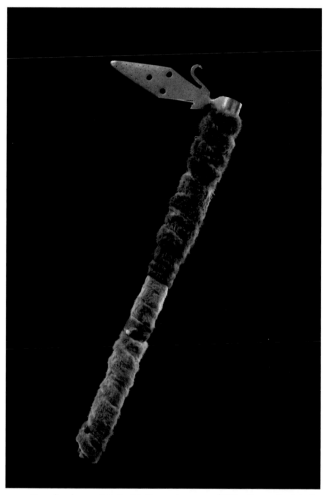

Tomahawk associated with Mee-nah-tsee-us (White Swan, Apsáalooke [Crow], ca. 1851–1904), ca. 1890. Montana. Wood, iron, otter fur, paint; 60 x 23 cm. Collected by William Wildschut. 12/640

White Swan grew up in the traditional manner of young Crow males, maturing into a warrior probably by the age of thirteen. In 1876 he enlisted as a scout for the U.S. Army, first with the 7th Infantry, later on detachment to the 7th Cavalry under George Armstrong Custer. On the morning of June 25, 1876, White Swan and several other Crow scouts ascended what is now known as the Crow's Nest, where they spotted the large Sioux and Cheyenne encampment in the Little Big Horn Valley. He accompanied the Army's attack on the south end of the camp later that afternoon. Severely wounded, he was transported to the steamer *The Far West* on the Big Horn River for medical care. In 1897 he applied for and received a pension of $17 a month for his loyal service as a scout.

White Swan was noted for his artwork and craftsmanship, evident in his paintings and in his personal attire, such as this tomahawk. The tomahawk in Northern Plains warrior culture evolved from being a weapon or tool to possessing spiritual significance. Army scouts like White Swan carried tomahawks for counting coup, or spiritual purposes. Early non-Indian visitors believed that most warriors adorned themselves and their weapons merely for decoration. In fact, the weapons' décor represented war deeds or instructions received from a vision or a medicine man. White Swan, the noted warrior, scout, and artist, is interred at the Custer Battlefield National Cemetery.

—Alden Big Man (Apsáalooke)

Nishkû´ntu (John Wilson, Caddo/Delaware)

Peyote rattle

Keep your mind on peyote and don't think anything about the people around you or anything outside. Look at peyote and the fire all the time and think of it. Sit quiet and do not move around or be uneasy. Then you will not get sick or see visions. Visions and nausea are signs of bad self-adjustment to the proper religious attitude.

—JOHN WILSON'S
INSTRUCTIONS TO HIS
NEPHEW GEORGE
ANDERSON ON HOW TO
FIND THE PEYOTE WAY

Nishkû´ntu (John Wilson or Moonhead, Caddo/Delaware, ca. 1845–1901), peyote rattle, ca. 1885. Oklahoma. Gourd, wood, hide, glass beads, brass bells, feathers; 80 x 10 x 9 cm. Collected by Mark R. Harrington. 6/1651

While the rattle has always played significant roles in American Indian ceremonial life, it is particularly important in the Native American Church, used with the water drum to accompany the songs performed during the all-night peyote ceremony.

John Wilson, or Moonhead, a Caddo member, was a very early adherent to the ceremony, which was newly popular in Oklahoma in the late 1800s. Borrowed over many generations from Indian peoples on the Mexican border, the ceremony came to Wilson via the Comanche peyote leader Quanah Parker. Wilson redefined the church through an appropriation of the Europeans' Jesus as a key figure in what was nevertheless conceived of as a traditional Indian ritual. The ceremony was, thus, not yet Christian; rather, Wilson's use of Jesus was an attempt to appropriate the spiritual power of the colonizer.

Like Parker, who made the ceremony Comanche in many respects, Wilson modified it to reflect traditional Caddo ceremonial life. His most striking innovation was to change the altar from Parker's half-moon or crescent to what is known as the cross-fire altar. This shift, rooted in the Caddo symbolic world, represented the four directions—a symbol common in a great many indigenous American communities. Only decades later did the altar come to be seen as representing the cross of crucifixion. While this is certainly a violation of Wilson's intention, the Christian interpretation of the cross-fire altar has become firmly entrenched in an important segment of the church, among Indian adherents who seek to reconcile traditional Indian practices with missionary Christianity.

—George E. "Tink" Tinker (wazhazhe, Osage Nation)

Comanche peyote fan, ca. 1890. Oklahoma. Wood, feathers, glass beads, hide, metal beads; 57 x 9 cm. Gift of Don E. Meyer. 22/9197

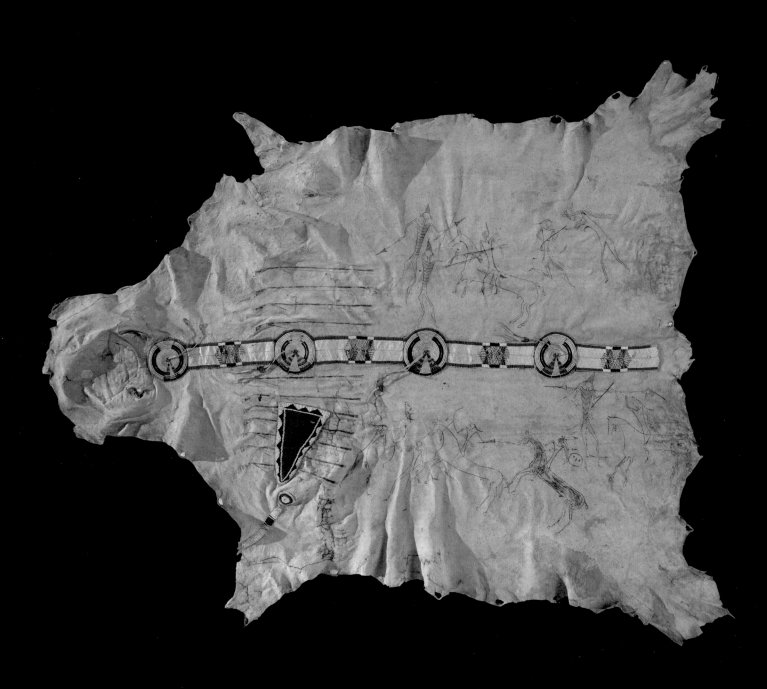

Apsáalooke warrior's exploit robe, ca. 1850. Fort Benton, Montana. Buffalo hide,
pigment, red wool trade cloth, beads, porcupine quill, horsehair; 224 x 193 cm.
Collected by William H. Schieffelin. Presented by William de la Montagne Cary. 1/2558

Apsáalooke warrior's exploit robe

This magnificent buffalo robe was acquired from a Blackfoot[1] at Fort Benton in 1861 by William H. Schieffelin, the son of a prominent New York family.[2] Located on the Missouri River at the furthest point navigable by steamboats, Fort Benton was at that time a major trading post of the American Fur Company.[3] The river in this area was a natural, although contested, boundary between the Blackfoot in the north and their enemies the Apsáalooke, or Crow Indians, to the south. The Blackfoot and Apsáalooke journeyed to Fort Benton to trade for beads, steel knives, and copper pots, but most of all for guns, powder, and lead. Both nations knew that whoever controlled the arms trade and had horses reliably available would control the hunting territories. The trade system that developed along the Missouri concentrated the competition between the Blackfoot and Apsáalooke and increased the level of violence when the two groups met.[4]

The images on this robe—with their elongated graceful forms, quillwork strip, and triangular patch representing a horse's head—are typical Apsáalooke.[5] How the robe came into the possession of a Blackfoot is now pure speculation. It could have been a war trophy. It could just as likely have been received in trade or as a gift during moments of peace between these two mighty foes.

Apsáalooke social and political structure was intimately tied to the military prowess of individuals. Leaders did not inherit their position, nor were they elected or appointed. Male status was based on a man's martial accomplishments. Although other qualities were admired, without warrior credentials a man had no standing.[6] The first step to becoming a person of eminence, a chief, was by achieving the four requisite war honors: to strike a live enemy in battle either with the hand or an object held in the hand, capture the picketed horse of an enemy, take an enemy's weapons in battle, and lead a successful war party. Many other war honors, though not counted toward chiefly status, were also deemed important.[7]

Personal war records were communicated through public orations at major gatherings and visual representations on personal possessions. Biographic warrior art, termed *chiwaálaatuua* (narrative writing) in Apsáalooke, gave public notice of an individual's accomplishments. Even with variations in imagery within and between tribes, biographic art was easily read by friend or enemy.[8] Contemporary Apsáalooke people, apparently like their ancestors, generally read narrative writing from right to left. Complex images, such as this robe would have been read from top to bottom and then right to left, as the vignettes would have been visible when the robe was worn. Within individual warfare scenes, the aggressor or victor was usually placed on the right, the enemy or vanquished on the left.

Six vignettes present the impressive military record of the robe's original Apsáalooke owner. The first shows the victor—with face paint and Apsáalooke upright bangs and flowing long hair—running to seize the gun of a wounded enemy. In the second, the Apsáalooke warrior touches the live enemy with his lance; two stripes on the hind end of his horse indicate that he already had two war honors at the time. The third vignette shows the hero engaged in an intense firefight with two enemies; he is wounded by one and kills the other. The fourth has the Apsáalooke successfully counting coup on a fleeing enemy who has dispatched two arrows to slow his pursuer. The fifth is an elegant, though simple presentation of the hero taking a bow from an enemy. The sixth and last presents eleven trade guns secured from the enemy.

We often remark what stories objects from the past could tell if they only spoke. Well, this one does, and it says:

Uuwatbalaxxiim bulutchik—I took a gun.
Baláxxiikaashim bulutchik—I took a bow.
Daákse dúhpaa baalichik—I struck live enemies twice.
Biskoochíia biiúuk Hawátam baappeék—I was wounded by the enemy, I killed one.
Uuwatbalaxxiia axpáwatim bahkuulaawóok—I brought back eleven guns.

—Patrick J. Hill (Takes The Lead, Apsáalooke)
and Timothy P. McCleary

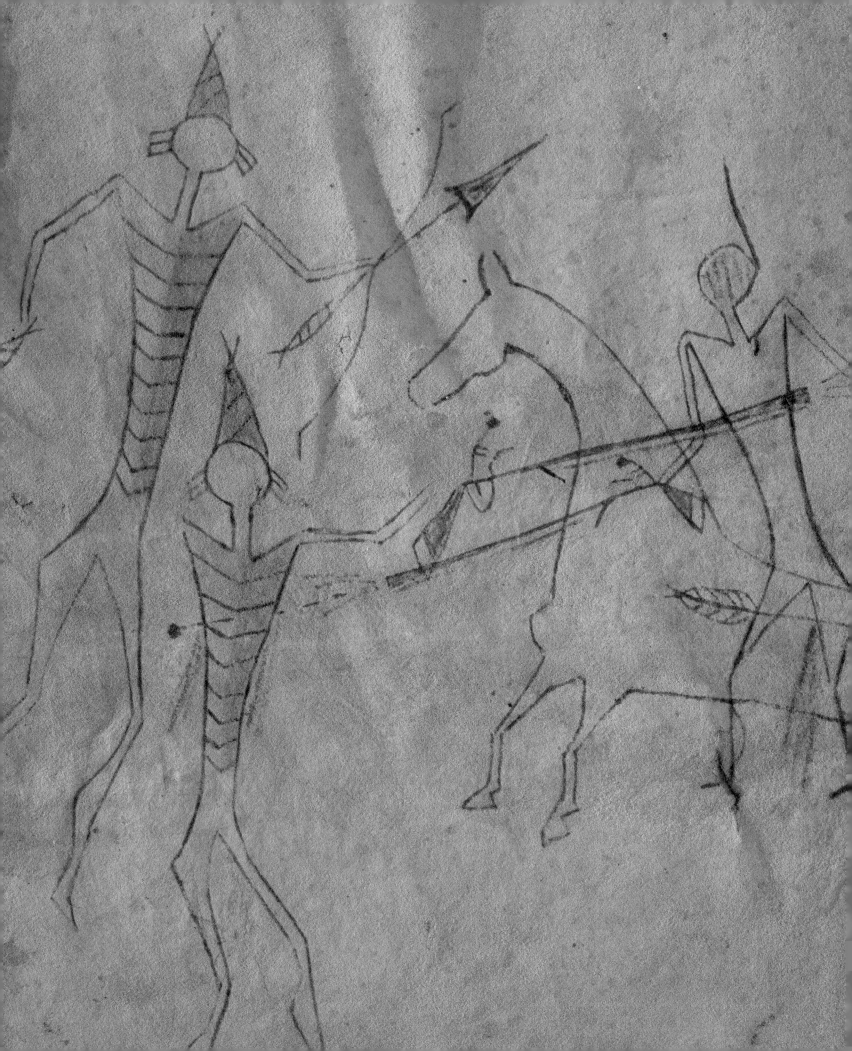

Sauk bowl, ca. 1850. Oklahoma. Wood, brass tacks; 24 x 44 cm.
Collected by Mark R. Harrington. 2/6544

Indigenous terrain

THE HAUDENOSAUNEE (IROQUOIS) TWINS fought over what form the earth would take. The elder twin, Sapling, made it soft, yielding, and fertile. His brother, Flint, made hard, craggy places and sharp mountains. When they came to blows, Sapling shattered splinters of rock from Flint's body, which became outcrops of precious varieties of stone. Flint's defeated body lies as mountains to the west.[1] Similarly, Gloscap, protagonist of Naskapi stories of origin, battled his stone-monster brother whose body became the mountains of the Gaspe Peninsula.[2] In the Great Lakes region, Anishinaabe (Ojibwe) stories tell how Nanabozo created the land upon which we live from grains of sand retrieved by Muskrat, who dove down through the Flood to bring earth to its watery surface. The Anishinaabe geography of the Great Lakes is marked by subsequent stories of Nanabozo's activities: the outcrop of flint that is his own brother's battered body on the bluffs overlooking Grand Traverse Bay in Michigan; the globs of mud he hurled after Beaver, which became the Apostle Islands along the southern Lake Superior shore; or the barbed elk antler harpoon he discarded, which is now Manitoulin Island on the northern edge of Georgian Bay.[3]

The vast "wilderness" of the North American Woodlands imagined by Europeans was in fact the discursive space of countless generations: a terrain interwoven with words and stories. The geographic etymologies of eastern North America are filled with Native names of places, the few that survive of the countless lost.[4] Every feature of North America—its mountains, rock, streams, and lakes, its trees, shrubs, herbs, and animals, its flyways, spawning grounds, sugar bush, and sacred places—had all resided in the deep, local knowledge of indigenous peoples for many thousands of years.

Histories of these relationships between people and terrain are etched upon the surface of the land and in things produced from it. Some of the earliest archeological signs of cultural activity are tied to technologies of stone: its technical and spiritual properties, its physical and semiotic attributes, and its settings in particular locations. During the period of the late Pleistocene more than 11,000 years ago, modestly scaled paleoindian bands circulated south of the retreating glaciers across the broad savannas not yet forested with the hickory and oak to come. Band territories from east to west were oriented, in varying degrees, toward access to significant sources of high-quality cryptocrystalline stone, used to make lance blades for hunting large game.[5] Over the past two decades, advances of archaeometric techniques have allowed more detailed and accurate sourcing of the raw materials for stone artifacts, leading to the conclusion that sources for stone were far more instrumental in the organization of paleoindian regional territories and their ethnic boundaries than previously imagined.[6] All these stone sources remained active with increasing intensity up until recent centuries.

No doubt all the great quarry locations, valuable and necessary in the lives of thousands of generations, had their own stories of origin and significance. Few such stories have survived. A link between oral tradition, location, and distinctive and sacred stone is commemorated today as the Pipestone National Monument located in southwest Minnesota. This is the source of a red, metamorphic claystone called catlinite, quarried

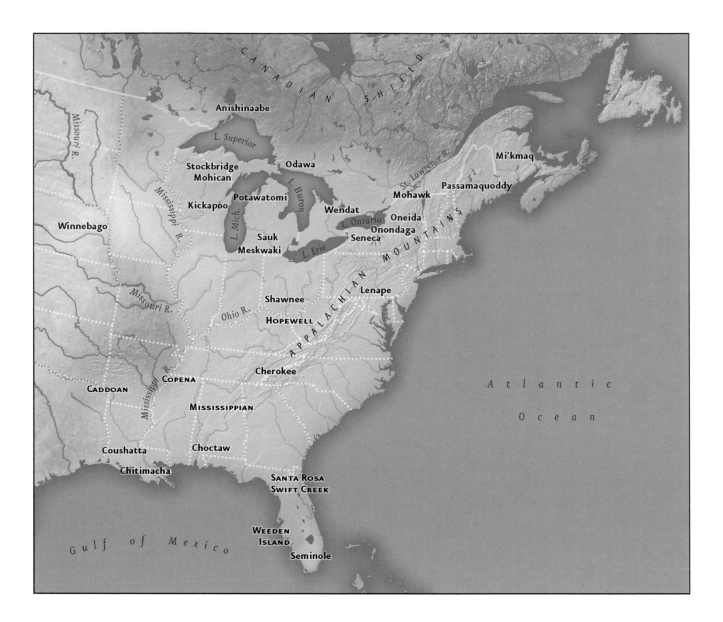

for thousands of years to create smoking pipes, pendants, and ornaments distributed broadly among the many nations of the Woodlands and Plains.[7] Pipe carvers of several different nations quarried stone from the site during more recent centuries: Yankton, Dakota, Iowa, Pawnee, Sauk, and tribes of the "Upper Missouri" are mentioned in historical accounts.[8] All nations evidently approached the quarries with deference, conducting ritual fasts and other preparations prior to removing stone.

The significance of catlinite stems in part from its technical attributes—its ability to absorb heat without shattering when used for smoking pipes—and its visual characteristics—its deep red color and the significance of red as a semantic category. While archaeological research has tended to privilege technical considerations in its analyses of stone artifacts from eastern North America, it is becoming increasingly clear that considerations of color, texture, luster, and figuration in indigenous stone choices are linked to historically deep cultural metaphors.

The privileged nature of implements, ornaments, and other objects made of copper is a case in point. Inter-regional exchange and privileged access to copper objects are clearly visible in the archaeological record as early as 3000 BC. The term "Old Copper tradition" refers to the practice of creating a wide range of copper blades and implements during the Late Archaic period (3000–1000 BC) along the Upper Great Lakes. Contrary to presumptions about copper metallurgy as a stage of technological "progress," these cold-hammered and cut copper implements offer no practical advantage over their stone equivalents, which appear at the same sites in comparable numbers and are considerably less labor intensive to produce.[9]

The choice of copper was motivated evidently by its semantic and symbolic attributes, an idea very much supported by a long-standing link between copper and religious ideologies in eastern North America.[10] Copper is rich in metaphorical associations. It is the antler of the horned serpent struck from its head during a vision quest and preserved in a sacred bundle. The underwater panther, Michipissi, is said to be sheathed in scales of copper. Copper is linked to water, the Underworld, and the powers of Underworld serpents and monsters.

Copper was quarried from deposits in the Keewinaw peninsula on southern Lake Superior during the Late Archaic,[11] but more frequently collected in later eras as chunks of float copper brought south in glacial till. The Holocene mantle of glacially deposited sand, cobbles, and boulders contains limitless treasure of exotic hardstone transported from sources in the Precambrian Canadian Shield to the rolling moraines of New England, New York, Ohio, Michigan, Indiana, Illinois, and Wisconsin. Beginning as early as 5000 BC, residents of this glaciated terrain sought out erratic chunks and cobbles of green hardstones, olivine gabbros, and diorites for use as axes, celts, and other varieties of ground-stone implements.

Of special consideration, however, are erratic boulders of a distinctive gray, banded slate torn from beds of Precambrian stone in north-central Quebec. A concentration of such banded slate erratics, very likely the broken fragments of a large piece tumbled in glacial till, is located in Richland County of north-central Ohio.[12] This and presumably other locations like it

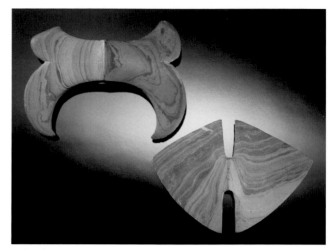

Archaic bannerstones, 6000–3000 BC. Noble County, Indiana; Momence, Kankakee County, Illinois. Slate; each 14 x 10 cm. Albert L. Addis Collection; purchase. 4/6786, 13/9478

became the quarry sources for banded slate in central North America. Archaic period artists shaped tabular gorgets, pendants, and atlatl weights from this hard and brittle material with percussive pecking, and then ground and polished their surfaces to bring out the stone's figurative qualities. Preference for banded slate to create an astounding number and variety of gorgets, pendants, and atlatl weights is visible in more than 5,000 years of the archaeological record in the Midwest, from the Middle Archaic (5000 BC) to the Middle Woodland (ending AD 400), and encompassing in addition a geographic expanse ranging from the region of the Ohio–Mississippi confluence east to New York and Pennsylvania. Through the circulation of objects and ideas across regional and ethnic boundaries, the cultural significance of banded slate and its artifact forms demonstrated remarkable durability. Unlike copper, however, the links between banded slate and cultural thought and practice did not endure.

Speckled granite, banded claystones, porphyries with large phenocrysts, diorite, mottled chlorite, rose quartz, steatite, jasper, colorful pipe stones, and many other varieties of colored and figured rock, polished to a glossy luster, with their links to qualities of the earth and particular sites or locations where they can be found, all functioned as symbolic ties between human beings and the environments they inhabited

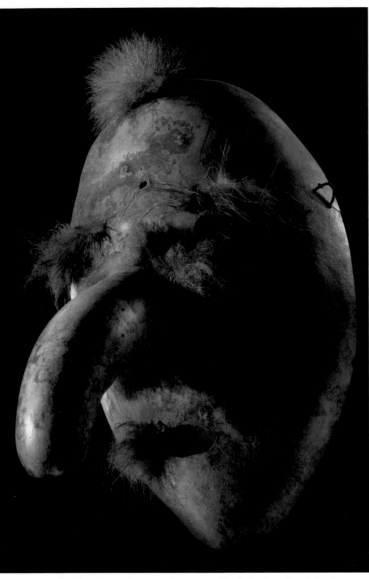

Cherokee Booger Dance mask, ca. 1910. North Carolina. Gourd, fox fur, cordage; 29 x 17 x 17 cm. Exchange with John White. 23/7839

world comprised of grandmothers, grandfathers, aunts and uncles, sisters and brothers of other-than-human kinds of man-beings."[14] Whereas Enlightenment philosophy contrasts the realms of culture and nature, the social relations of indigenous North Americans were not limited to just human beings, but extended to animals, plants, geography, and unseen worlds (not always) beyond human perception. Expressions of social relationship such as grandfather and grandmother, uncle and aunt, brother and sister, or cousin could refer to a human being, an animal, an object, a place, or a spirit.

A "New World" arrived in the form of ships from Europe. In stories repeated in several locations, New England Algonkians saw the ships at first as floating islands, their masts as trees and sails as clouds.[15] This new world offered opportunities for new and novel social relations. The visitors from Europe often remarked upon the reverence expressed by the North Americans for their person or for the seemingly miraculous possessions they brought with them. The delegations they encountered rubbed their foreheads with tobacco; blew tobacco smoke over their axes, guns, and swords of iron and steel; and called them spirits, or manitous. The Europeans interpreted such expressions of respect and awe as superstition—they could not recognize the initial steps necessary to create social relations with such unfamiliar beings, materials, and things.

The history of Native North American and European diplomacy is replete with the affinal and metaphorical creations of social ties. Consider the famous but failed gambit of Powhatan, the Virginia paramount chief and reluctant host to England's Jamestown colony. In an attempt to maneuver the formal adoption of John Smith into his community, he staged the intercession of one of his daughters, Pocahontas.[16] Intermarriage established the innumerable alliances, indispensable to centuries of the fur trade, between Native women with their extended families and European men and their companies. The formal language of negotiation and treaty-making employed the terms Father, Uncle, Brother, and Cousin, not simply as rhetorical

through their transformation into expressive and meaningful objects. In their analyses of archaeological evidence, interpreters of North America's past have been increasingly led to see the indigenous geography of North America as "kinship-based structuring of sacred space."[13] As scholar George Hamell put it, human beings "did not inhabit a *natural world* comprised of inorganic, astronomical, meteorological, and geological phenomena, and plants and animals. Rather, they inhabited and maintained through ritual a *social*

flourishes, but instead to give structure to the relations between disparate peoples.

Similarly, when evaluating the novel things and materials brought by Europeans, their reality was made sensible by socializing processes of analogy and metaphor. Firearms linked to thunder, brass kettles to water and the underworld; iron and steel possessed analogues among the vast geological resources of North America, albeit with profoundly increased potencies. Color and luster were powerful ordering devices. Preferences for certain types of cloth, glass beads, and other ornamental trade items often corresponded to values expressed through their color: red for the animating forces of life; or white, sky blue, the transparency and reflective qualities of crystal, glass, and silver signifying peace, spiritual purity, and prophetic clarity.[17] The "baubles" and "trifles"—colored cloth, glass beads, silver ornaments—dismissively offered for furs in early encounters between Europeans and Native peoples possessed value because of the semantic qualities of their material. On the other side of the ledger, a Montaignais (coastal Algonkian) man gloated to a Jesuit missionary in 1634, "The beaver does everything perfectly well, it makes kettles, hatchets, swords, knives, and bread; and in short it makes everything."[18]

The appeal of "red caps . . . tin bells . . . silver rings, and glass beads" among a host of further media for fashion, in addition to more utilitarian iron axes, steel knives, and firearms in fur trade transactions, does not align necessarily with the values of European materialism. Rather, in North America, these goods joined a broad range of materialist expressions of connection to spiritual structures and forces, in particular those rooted in Native traditions of dress and ornament. Through clothing, ornament, body-painting, and tattoo, the body becomes a discursive site where the relations between the individual and the greater social and spiritual cosmos can be inscribed. Natchez men tattooed symbols of their war honors, their public biographies, on their chests, arms, and thighs.[19] The Huron and Ottawa of the 17th century tattooed and painted their bodies with images of manitous and signs of their clans.[20] Colorful cloth, printed cottons, silk

Wendat (Huron) leggings, ca. 1830. Ontario, Canada. Wool, leather, silk, quill, moose hair, metal, horse hair, cotton thread; 73 x 31.5 cm. Purchased in London. Presented by Mrs. Thea Heye. 17/6320

Sauk breechcloth, ca. 1880. Oklahoma. Wool cloth, cotton trim, glass beads; 134 x 44 cm. Collected by Mark R. Harrington. 2/6428

Clockwise from top left:
Delaware bandolier bag, ca. 1850.
Oklahoma. Hide, cotton cloth,
silk ribbon, glass beads, wool
yarn, metal cones; 68 x 47 cm.
Purchase. 21/3358

Seminole councilor coat, ca. 1900.
Florida. Cotton; 95 x 167 cm.
Collected by Mark R. Harrington.
1/8274

Kickapoo hair ornament, ca. 1900.
Oklahoma. Cotton cloth, silk
ribbon, glass beads, mother
of pearl buttons; 55 x 16 cm.
Collected by Mark R. Harrington.
2/5237

Wendat (Huron) moccasins, ca.
1800. Canada. Hide, porcupine
quill, metal cones, horsehair, dye.
28 x 8.5 x 7 cm. Purchase. 19/6362

Gilbert Stuart (1755–1828),
Joseph Brant, 1786. Oil on canvas.
59.7 x 61 cm.

ribbon, glass beads, and silver brooches added semantic richness to these long-standing traditions.

In this light, it is interesting to consider sets of objects preserved from the distant past, collected by European, Colonial, and American soldiers, priests, officials, and travelers and now housed in museums: a precious small number of sleeve bags for fire-starting equipment or for pipes and tobacco; shot pouches; folded wallets or belt pouches; and a few rare sets of garments and mats, all made of deerskin and embroidered with porcupine quills, some with white glass beads or cone-shaped tin pendants. The few preserved from the Great Lakes region during the 17th and 18th centuries are the oldest to survive. On many, porcupine quill embroidery traces out the shapes of thunderbirds, underwater panthers, equal-armed crosses signifying the four directions, and other animals, figures, and sacred symbols. These are images of mythic beings, but also metaphors for the larger structure of a sacred cosmos: the dome of the sky, the watery

Effigy pipe associated with Thayendanegea
(Joseph Brant, Mohawk)

Among us we have no prisons, we have no pompous parade of courts, we have no written laws, and yet judges are as highly revered among us as they are among you, and their decisions are as highly regarded. . . . We have among us no splendid villains above the control of our laws. Daring wickedness is never suffered to triumph over helpless innocence. The estates of widows and orphans are never devoured by enterprising sharpers. In a word, we have no robbery under color of law.

—JOSEPH BRANT, LETTER TO AN
UNKNOWN CORRESPONDENT, 1807

Effigy pipe associated with Thayendanegea (Joseph Brant, Mohawk, ca. 1742–1807), ca. 1785. New York. Wood, slate, porcupine quill, dye, silver; 79 x 7 x 6 cm. Presented by Joseph Keppler. 18/6071

When Joseph Brant presented a carved pipe to Dr. Caleb Benton sometime in the early 1790s, he was carrying on an ancient Haudenosaunee (Six Nations Iroquois) practice. Pipes were exchanged at meetings with visiting dignitaries and used to conclude treaties. Between individuals, the gift of a pipe and tobacco affirmed friendship and gratitude for an act of generosity or kindness.

After the Revolution, Britain's Haudenosaunee allies were left vulnerable, their lands open to expropriation. Brant, a commissioned officer for the Crown, led many displaced Mohawks to a new homeland on the Grand River in Upper Canada (now Ontario). He also sought compensation for Mohawk territorial losses from New York state and from the federal government in Philadelphia.

Brant may have received or purchased the Benton pipe during a visit to the capital in 1790. He travelled throughout Haudenosaunee territory shortly afterward in an effort to create a united front against U.S. intrusions. He also tried to form a confederation of Native nations in the Midwest to oppose American expansion. On one of those trips, he fell gravely ill and rested in a private residence near Seneca Lake. This may have been the home of Dr. Benton, who had built a tavern on the western shore of Seneca Lake, the traditional territory of the Cayuga Nation.

Brant would have known of Benton's involvement in the Genesee Land Company, which used bribery and intimidation to buy and sell Native lands, often at enormous profits. But a personal friendship with one of the non-Native leaders of western New York would have been important to Brant's strategy. The pipe may also have been Brant's way of expressing his gratitude for Dr. Benton's medical assistance.

—Doug George-Kanentiio (Akwesasne Mohawk)

Armbands associated with John Quinney

(Stockbridge Mohican)

Armbands associated with John Quinney (Stockbridge Mohican [Mahican], 1797–1855), 1793 or 1813. Brotherton, Wisconsin. Silver; 5.5 x 8.5 cm. 24/1108

These armbands belonged to the Mohican sachem John W. Quinney, one of the leading political figures of the Stockbridge Nation from 1822 to 1855. Quinney represented his tribe at numerous treaty sessions and in lobbying state governments and the United States to ratify treaties and enact laws for the tribe's benefit. Beginning in 1830, Quinney made at least nine diplomatic missions to Washington, ultimately spending more than five years away from home representing his tribe. Amazingly, in 1846 he convinced Congress to repeal the 1843 law that had dissolved the Stockbridge Nation.

In 1837 Quinney wrote the tribe's first constitution, which provided for executive, legislative, and judicial branches. The constitution also required that elected leaders be Christians and males. This is not surprising since missionaries had been living with the Stockbridge from 1736 onward, in Massachusetts, upstate New York, and the Wisconsin Territory. Quinney's constitution was controversial in several other ways, however, and was replaced in 1857. A stamp in the silver of these armbands indicates that they were made in 1793 or 1813 by Crispin Fuller, an English silversmith. They may have been given to Quinney by an older Mohican leader who had received them from British officials. A stylized engraving of the Royal Coat of Arms strongly suggests that they were a diplomatic gift. England, France, Spain, and the United States distributed gifts as "sovereignty tokens." These governments assumed that the Indian leaders who accepted them recognized the sovereignty of the donor country, as indeed tribal leaders expected their nations to be recognized as sovereign.

It is curious, the history of my tribe, in its decline, during the last two centuries and a half. Nothing that deserved the name of purchase was ever made. From various causes, they were induced to abandon their territory at intervals, and retire further to the inland. Deeds were given, indifferently to the Government, or to individuals, for which little or no consideration was paid. The Indian was informed, in many instances, that he was selling one parcel, while the conveyance described other, and much larger limits. Should a particular band, for purposes of hunting or fishing, desert, for a time, its usual place of residence the land was said to be abandoned, and the Indian claim extinguished. To legalize and confirm titles thus acquired, laws and edicts were subsequently passed, and these laws were said then, and are now called, justice! Oh! What a mockery to confound justice with law.

— JOHN W. QUINNEY, JULY 4, 1854,
SPEAKING IN REIDSVILLE, NEW YORK

—Robert J. Miller (Eastern Shawnee Tribe of Oklahoma)

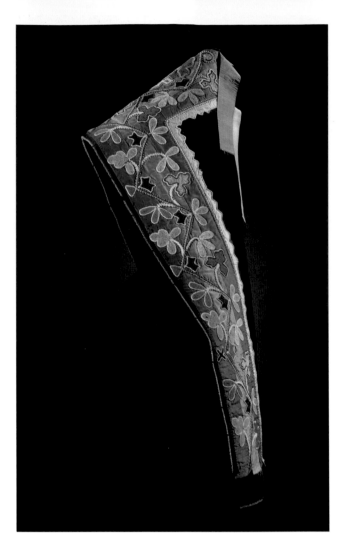

underworld beneath the earth, the terrestrial world that stretches out in the four cardinal directions. Combined, these constellations of symbols describe the dimensions of a cosmos where "I stand in the center," to quote the often-repeated Anishinaabe concept. When these symbols are displayed on the body, almost always in combination with one another, they express this relation between self and the sacred.

The new media of imported cloth, glass beads, wool yarns, silk ribbon, and other products of the emerging industry of consumer goods in Europe offered Native North Americans opportunities to expand and transform traditions of dress and ornament. These media were adapted to ancient techniques of manufacture, such as fingerweaving (braiding), twining, and appliqué, or inspired new techniques, such as bead-weaving with heddles and box looms. Traditions of design expanded, building upon the accepted metaphors by creating symbolic ornaments of increasing complexity. Native North American artists also absorbed and repurposed designs and images of European origin, the floral and textile patterns printed on imported

Anishinaabe hood, ca. 1860–1880. Canada. Wool cloth, silk ribbons, glass beads; 69 x 28 cm. Purchase. 13/5898

From left to right:
Chitimacha basket, ca. 1920. Louisiana. Cane, dye; 21 x 11 x 13.7 cm. Purchase. 11/8264

Chitimacha basket, ca. 1900. Louisiana. Cane, dye; 18 x 18 x 10 cm. Joseph Keppler Collection. 9558

Chitimacha basket, ca. 1890. Louisiana. Cane, dye; 13 x 13 x 14 cm. Gift of Dr. Margaret J. Sharpe. 22/5207

cotton cloth, and the pictorial traditions of European decorative and fine arts. Relations with the newcomers created new opportunities for market arts—baskets, decorated boxes, beaded "whimsies," purses, and slippers—where the skills and labor of artists supported traditional, family-based economies.

The histories of conflict and accommodation that characterize European and Native North American relations are dominated by the unrelenting and ongoing reduction of Native North American land and language. The two are closely intertwined. Language, as the expression of experience, is the means by which the land is socialized. Land is where the individual and community are situated, not just geographically, but mythically, poetically, economically, and spiritually. Visual culture, material expression, or art, whatever we wish to call it, materializes these relations in durable and persisting things, preserved from the past or renewed today in acts of artistic creation. As language and land-based knowledge are painstakingly recovered and restored in initiatives increasingly common throughout North America today, objects preserved from the past emerge from the mute silence of museum storerooms to speak of their metaphors of origin and experience once again. And artists today strive to fill the void left by centuries of destruction and loss by creating new metaphors, alluding to new experiences of today's world and its promises and challenges.

It is difficult to say, when reflecting upon such broad trajectories of history, whether a tide has begun to ebb, restoring a possibility of indigenous culture in the contemporary world, or even whether it has begun to slow from an unrelenting movement of an all-devouring globalism. Our lifetimes may be too brief to tell. But these objects, these stories, these diverse and locally rooted human relationships with the earth, insist upon that potentiality.

—David W. Penney

Anishinaabe birchbark house, ca. 1885–1910. Upper Great Lakes. Birchbark, porcupine quill, dye; 28 x 20 x 22 cm. Purchase. 21/1979

Mary Agosa Mixamung quilling a birchbark box, ca. 1940.

Undiscovered America

THE VAST TERRITORY from the Gulf Coast to the northern edge of the Great Lakes and from the Atlantic Coast to the Great Plains has had a long history of cultural experimentation that led to the establishment of town-sized communities of agriculturalists in the Midwest and the Southeast before suffering from the destabilization attendant on the climate deterioration of the Little Ice Age beginning around AD 1300.

The artistic achievements of these pre-Columbian Woodlands cultures have yet to claim their rightful attention. The aesthetic principles embodied in the best examples of their arts stand up to comparison with the singular pieces of other civilizations. Objects of chipped and ground stone, ceramic, and marine shell shown here reveal some of the diversity in excellent craftwork and decoration. The rich archaeology of each time period can barely be hinted at in this survey, but readers are treated to some exquisite creations of human handiwork.

The earliest known cultural period, about 13,000 years ago, is represented in the museum's collections by Clovis fluted points that tipped spears intended for hunting game as large as mammoths and mastodons. Ground-stone pieces include a kind of atlatl weight particularly well known in the Late Archaic period, 5,000 to 3,000 years ago. These presented a puzzle for many years. Collectors called them by their shapes—bannerstones, bar weights, birdstones, boatstones, et cetera. Now archaeologists are confident that they are hyperelaborate weights for stabilizing spear-throwers. The same basic form persists far later into the Woodlands period, roughly 1000 BC to AD 1000.

The largest atlatl weights and the large double-tapered chipped-stone biface represent an elaboration of design that draws attention to their functional impracticality. It seems problematic whether they were ever employed functionally. Does distorting their shape and rendering them in less suitable material imply a contradiction between form and function? Yes, but in an important way. By making a symbolic weapon or weapon-part, the fabricator is creating a means to exhibit distinction and prestige. The fabricators clearly had the technical ability to convert particularly attractive stones into objects of uncommon beauty. Notice the manner in which the grain and colors in the lithic material are used to enhance the final product. This is no accident, and it was presumably a quality eagerly sought.

Were these things merely highly decorated or highly elaborate versions of workaday tools and instruments? Or did their aesthetics single them out? Did their detail place them in the category of hypertrophic artifacts—too elaborate or delicate to perform the functions their shapes would more commonly dictate? Mississippian period (AD 1000–1550) axes produced from a single block of stone and ax heads of copper or elongated green stones belong to this category as well—all show little mechanical use and indeed would shatter if used with any kind of force. They take the sense of usage from its mechanical purpose, or "toolness," and confer a ritual meaning.

It would be a mistake to take from this chapter an impression that only technological expertise was at work in early cultures. In the precontact past, art concerned itself with spiritual matters and not with the mundane existence of everyday life. Conceptions of one's place in the world were rendered concrete in cosmological design. Basic conceptions of the universe

Mississippian long-nosed gods maskettes, AD 1100–1500. Illinois. Marine shell, probably lightning whelk; 6 x 5 x 5.5 cm. Collected by Eugene and Paul Wright. 24/3506, 24/3507, 24/3508

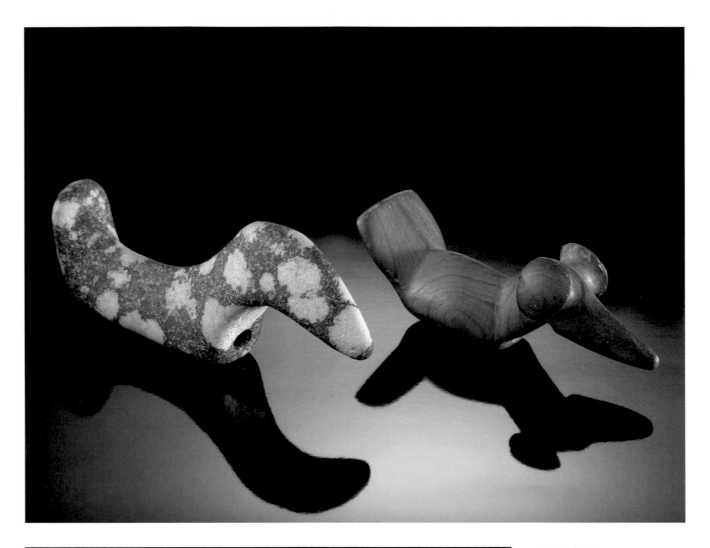

Archaic birdstones, 3000–1000 BC. Schenectady, Schenectady County, New York; Watertown, Jefferson County, New York. Porphyry; 11 x 4 x 2 cm. Slate; 9 x 2.5 x 3.5 cm. Collected by I. McGirk Mitchell and E. M. Jackson. 7/4409, 5/4385

Archaic bannerstones, 3000–1000 BC. Pike County, Missouri; Williamston County, Illinois. Porphyry; 7 x 6 x 3 cm. Rose quartz; 7.5 x 6 x 2 cm. Collected by I. McGirk Mitchell. Presented by Harmon W. Hendricks. 14/6179, 6/1563

Right: Caddoan blade, ca. AD 1100. Foster Place, Lafayette County, Arkansas. Flint; 34.5 x 6.5 cm. Clarence B. Moore Collection. 17/442

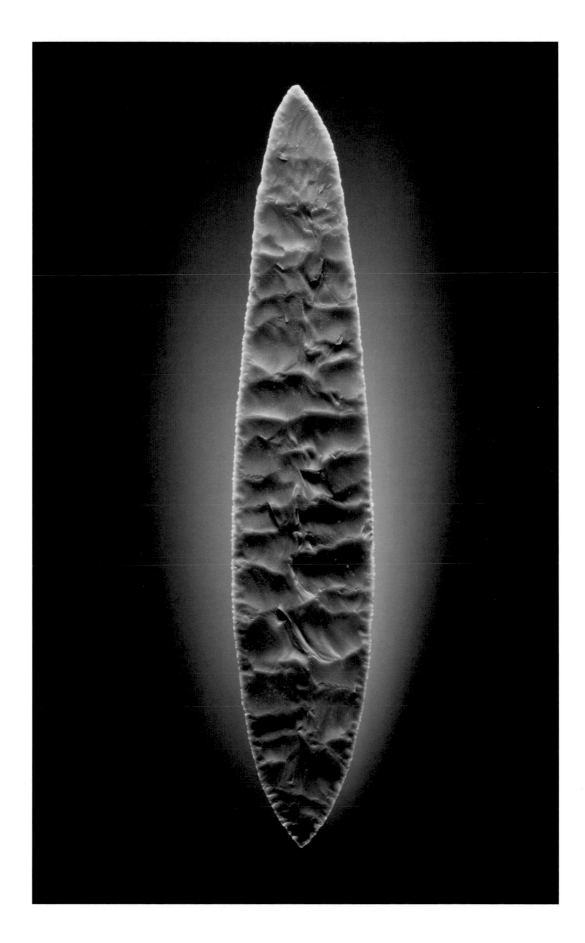

Mississippian Piasa effigy pipe,
AD 1300–1500. Moundville,
Hale County, Alabama. Glendon
limestone; 14 x 7 x 11 cm. Clarence
B. Moore Collection. 17/893

and its origin were expressed verbally in legend and song, but particular images, motifs, and designs were a physical form of expression. Nonmaterial and material forms were dual modes of expression, rather than isolated aspects of culture. The cosmology was predicated on the division between a Middle World of human life and other worlds. The Upper World was situated above the daytime sky, and the Beneath World lay beneath the living surface, to which it was connected by underlying waters.

Among all the different visions and priorities current at different times and places, certain ones were selected for artistic expression. The potter, engraver of shell, or maker of some other object was not governed by whims or trends of the day. A choice was always on the table, but the kinds of choices taken

were connected with some sort of meaning. I am not referring to a specific message, one that we only need to crack in order to read the object. Rather we should think in terms of a connection between the decoration, its location on the pot, say, and its effect on the observer. Decoration cannot be divorced from some generalized notion of function—the intended use for the pot, and for pots in general. In some Muskogean languages, the pot represents a metaphor for the world on which we live. The rim delineates the edge of that world. Following the implications of this conception, the decorative modification of the rim and lip—the form that modification takes—is potentially an extension of the pot metaphor through the ways in which the edge is treated.

Caddoan bottle, ca. AD 1300.
Haley Place, Miller County,
Arkansas. Clay, paint; 18 x 11 cm.
Clarence B. Moore Collection.
17/4658

The decoration we see here had concrete meanings to the creators and others in their social world. Those meanings were likely not to refer to any one thing, but engaged a complex of interconnected associations, invoking different aspects of that complex depending upon the time, place, and situation. A vessel from a site on the banks of the Arkansas River displays the scalplock motif that can be seen worn on the belt of the birdman figure depicted on the famous Castalian Springs gorget (see page 188). In this engraved figure, then, we have the referencing of an important symbol that we know elsewhere as a tangible artifact. Another such artifact is the club or mace brandished in the upraised hand of the warrior figure, a reference that exists as a hypertrophic example in chipped stone from the Spiro Mound site.

The birdman figure exemplifies action that might appear to be counterintuitive, but nonetheless illustrates the insight that comparative iconographic research has gone far to advance our understanding of the religious aspects of life in the Mississippian period. Kent Reilly and members of the Iconographic Workshop he has convened for the past ten years at Texas State University have developed useful perspectives to this figure and other spirits.[1] In this instance the birdman stands for the rebirth of humanity. The image appears to represent Morning Star's recovery of his father's head after defeating an emissary of death in the form of the scalplock. Birdman's identity is revealed by a tablet-shaped power bundle mounted on the forehead, a sacred life-conferring instrument in the form of a bilobed arrow carried upright in the hair, as Tom Evans notes, and a long hair braid suspended on the right side of the head. The latter two in particular are diagnostic features of this spirit.

Mississippian statuary is justly famous for its frequent monumentality. Judging by postcontact testimony, southeastern mortuary shrines contained one or a pair of such figures. In this context they assumed some of the properties of life-controlling deities. The large examples are carved from rocks of different color—white marble, dark stone, red claystone, grey sandstone, and white limestone. More modest-sized

ones are often produced in pottery form. Color has importance, although at this point we cannot go beyond this obvious statement. The figures sculpted belong to distinct spirits, the earthmother being a common one, birdman being another. Others have been proposed as well. I should add that earthmother is not reducible to a female figure. What is important about these images is that they are not drawn from ordinary individuals. Rather, earthmother and birdman are deities belonging to the spiritual world, even though they were evidently visualized in material forms familiar to the artist. These figural images and the more abstract images refer to and may even invoke that spiritual world.

When pre-Columbian art and artifacts were mere appendages to the study of postcontact tribal arts, the historical time-depth in the Eastern Woodlands was little appreciated. All of the specialized arts, and even the commonplace practice of erecting mounds, were regarded as having an origin in the hearth of civilization in Mesoamerica. This old idea has been seriously upended by the results of fresh investigations using advanced techniques, including more refined dating. For one, the erection by Woodland cultures of mounds in precise geometric alignments can be placed earlier than in Mesoamerica based upon present information. These advances in knowledge are sufficient on their own to shake the foundations of the old idea that all fresh cultural conceptions reached the Woodlands long after they were perfected in more advanced areas to the south. This one-way diffusion of innovation has become seriously undermined. The relationship of the East with the lands to the south is likely to have been complex and the source of cultural innovations not so one-sided.

In the past, so unfamiliar were scholars and collectors with pre-Columbian artifacts that, as examples came to light, they were attributed to Mesoamerican inspiration, if not direct importation. The appearance of hawk and serpent imagery, and the appearance of severed heads and weaponry, cemented this Mesoamerican connection, particularly since certain styles featured very realistic representations. True, footgear typical of Eastern Woodlands moccasins substituted for

Hopewell platform pipe, 200 BC–AD 400. Franklin, Warren County, Ohio. Steatite; 11.5 x 3.5 x 5 cm. Purchase. 1/1014

Mesoamerican sandals in these images. But despite the difference in fauna represented and in articles of dress and clothing, the sophisticated depiction of humans and animals has repeatedly invoked Mesoamerican influences.

A persistent issue raised by those who have difficulty in visualizing the civilized aspect to the culture of the Mississippian period at its high point in the 14th century is that they do not see a connection between the refined arts of that period or earlier ones and the relatively unrefined figural representations of later centuries. Here I am focusing on the handling of the complete figure, particularly the face.

The difficulty has a long history. In the early 19th century, it achieved form as the Mound Builder myth, which attributed mounds and sophisticated artwork to peoples from Mesoamerica who were forced out of the Eastern Woodlands by the ancestors of the tribes encountered by Europeans.[2] This myth encapsulated the distinction between civilized Indians from the south and savage Indians occupying lands north of the border. Contemporary Indians in this very biased

scenario were no longer treated as the heirs of those who constructed the mounds and created the art. All archaeological evidence has pointed to undisturbed continuity of culture.

Early writers were impressed by the excellence displayed by selected pieces. The human and animal effigy pipes of the Hopewellian period (AD 1–200) caught scholars' attention in the 1840s. In their 1848 publication, Squier and Davis drew upon their favorable impression to place the arts of that period on a par with those from the Andean and Mexican civilizations.[3]

The first pieces of high art for the Mississippian period were not recovered until the 1880s. First the Etowah site in northwestern Georgia was discovered. Soon afterward the town site of Moundville, in south-central Alabama, was explored as well. By the time that the main mound at the Spiro site in eastern Oklahoma opened up, the scholarly world was becoming comfortable with the idea that the sophisticated art of the Mississippian period was not a fluke of trade, but represented something important about indigenous history in the Southeast.

Mississippian jar depicting a frog, AD 1200–1400. Blytheville, Mississippi County, Arkansas. Clay; 24 x 18 x 19 cm. Mrs. Thea Heye Collection. 5/6528

It has taken advances in our knowledge to appreciate more fully what that amounted to. It is safe to state that the weaknesses of our knowledge about that period were based on an almost total reliance on the formal aspects of art and the assemblages of artifacts. This was a natural science approach that eschewed interpretation about meaning in favor of facts about shape, manufacture, and material. Objects were treated as something akin to items to be found in a prehistoric version of the Sears Roebuck catalogue. Knowledge of the past depended on finding the catalogue most relevant in time and place. After determining the proper catalogue, the objects would become the telltale evidences of long-gone technologies and some indication of cultural priorities. These objects fell into well-known categories—weapons, figures, and where preservation has permitted, baskets, blankets, et cetera. Almost all of these are domestic objects or objects of everyday use.

An unfortunate consequence of preferring Mesoamerican authorship, no matter how indirect it may be conceived to be, is to deny the peoples of the Eastern Woodlands their rightful place as creators of a unique artistic world. An oft-implied stumbling block to restoring Indian heritage is the disjunction between the sophisticated rendering of the human body during the Hopewellian and Mississippian periods. Nothing like these ways of drafting the human body is found immediately before or after European contact. But archaeological investigations have demonstrated that populations had declined severely even before European diseases had taken their toll. In light of this fact, it is expectable that artistic sophistication would have declined as well. Archaeologists have argued that the social and economic support systems for schools of artists had withered, and as a consequence artists spent significantly less time sharpening their skills. The connection between skill level and support systems has now been generally acknowledged.[4] The years of training and practice to master aesthetics and technique could be achieved through the patronage of key individuals in a stable maize-based economy, but would find haphazard support in unstable economies.

This brings us to the deliberately broken condition of many items. An exhibit such as this portrays objects of the Eastern Woodlands as objective creations. But they often had an intentional ending to their social use life: a ritually imbued pot is broken and the pieces piled together with a few crucial sherds missing, never to be recovered. Hopewellian pots that Squier and Davis meticulously restored in nicely engraved images are represented by less than a third of the original. The pattern is so commonplace in ritual deposits associated with mounds that it has to be regarded as intentional.

This condition alerts us to the disjunction between the intended use life of many of the artifacts on display and our contemporary museum approach. David Penney expressed it well when he wrote,

This indigenous aesthetic system, then, is one in which the formal properties of an object, those that we may admire as art or sculpture, seem inexorably tied to exclusive knowledge, privilege, and access to power. This represents a kind of Pandora's box for archaeology: if an objective of archaeological research is greater insight to the cultural meanings of artifacts and an understanding of the cultural values they represent, then what is the price of such knowledge? Assertive Native American voices have been saying for some time that when these objects were consigned to the earth with elaborate and necessary ritual, they were intended to stay there. After excavation, the social lives of these things resumed, albeit in the very different contexts of museum collections, exhibitions, and academic research.[5]

—James A. Brown

Mississippian gorget

Mississippian gorget, AD 1250–1350. Castalian Springs, Sumner County, Tennessee. Whelk shell; 10 cm. William E. Myer Collection. 15/853

Long ago along the Gulf Coast, a large mollusk, probably a lightning whelk, washed ashore. This gift from the Underworld was passed from hand to hand and community to community along long-since-forgotten trails. Far from where it was found, an artist of great skill carved a glimpse of his world. Much knowledge has been lost with the passage of time and the violent interruption of our ways. Yet some held onto the basics of the old ways until about a hundred years ago, when much of it was recorded for our enlightenment.

We have given the name Mississippian to the people who produced this shell gorget and call their religion the Southeastern Ceremonial Complex. In much of the Woodlands, the Morning Star was equated with masculinity—the ultimate warrior, hunter, protector, and defender, as well as conqueror and destroyer.

This gorget depicts a young warrior dancing in imitation of the Morning Star. The severed head held in the dancer's right hand is proof of that successful imitation. In life, his roached hair would have been painted red like the crest of the woodpecker, an earthly symbol of the red planet that is the Morning Star. The copper ornament pinned through the hair at the back of his head symbolizes the spear-thrower and spear, a weapon that had fallen out of use centuries earlier with the advent of the bow. The eye pattern seen on the dancer's face is thought to suggest the pattern found on the faces of certain hawks who symbolize swift pursuit and unerring aim in striking an enemy. The flint mace in the dancer's left hand often was painted half red for the Morning Star and half white for the corresponding female deity, the Evening Star.

—Tom Evans (Skidi Pawnee)

Peace medal

Peace medal, 1676. Massachusetts Bay Colony. Copper alloy; 14 x 10 cm. Purchase. 23/9269

The General Court of Massachusetts Bay granted this medal during the 17th-century conflict known as the War with the Indians of New England, later called King Philip's War. The English were losing to this indigenous alliance against colonial expansion until they pursued a full-scale effort to recruit Christian Indian scouts from a forced internment camp the English had established on Deer Island in Boston Harbor. While some Indians from the Praying Town of Natick and the Mohegan nation had assisted the English from the beginning, large-scale recruitment of men from Deer Island did not occur until the spring of 1676, when the English faced "frequent and violent" raids and every expedition to locate the encampments of the resistance had failed. As the missionary Daniel Gookin observed, "After our Indians went out, the balance turned of the English side."

This medal was most likely given to the eighty men who formed an Indian company based in Charlestown under Captain Samuel Hunting. Officers of this company included Andrew Pittimee (of Natick), James Quanapohit (of Nashaway and Natick), John Magus (of Natick), Job Kattenanit (of Hassanamesit), and James Speen (of Natick), all of whom had been interned on Deer Island. Some of the Native men who served the English lost their lives in the war, but many returned to their Praying Towns. They petitioned to prevent the execution and enslavement of their relations who were falsely declared enemy combatants by the colony. Some were instrumental in securing land rights and in negotiating with the English after the war. Many of their descendants continue to serve as leaders in the Nipmuc communities in the state of Massachusetts today.

The image on the medal is based on the Massachusetts seal, which was part of a marketing campaign to draw English settlers to the new colony. In the original seal, the Indian figure is portrayed saying, "Come over and help us," a reference to the missionary project. Ironically, it was the English who often required help, whether in navigating an unknown territory, learning to subsist upon native foods, or winning a war.

—Lisa Brooks (Abenaki)

Anishinaabe outfit collected by Andrew Foster, ca. 1790. Fort Michilimackinac, Michigan. Birchbark, cotton, linen, wool, feathers, silk, silver brooches, porcupine quills, horsehair, hide, sinew. The Andrew Foster Collection. Exchange with George Terasaki. 24/2000, 24/2001, 24/2002, 24/2003, 24/2004, 24/2006, 24/2012, 24/2016, 24/2022, 24/2034

Anishinaabe outfit collected by Andrew Foster

The Anishinaabe and eastern Plains clothing and ceremonial items acquired by Lieutenant Andrew Foster during his military service in North America represent one of a handful of 18th-century collections that have come down to us relatively intact and that can be documented to a specific region and time period. In their diversity, the items in the Foster collection speak eloquently of the mingling of many different nations in the central Great Lakes between the Revolutionary War and the War of 1812. The leggings, shirt, trade-silver ornaments, otter-skin Midewiwin bag, and cradleboard with its porcupine-quilled ornaments are probably Anishinaabe, while the moccasins ornamented with loom-woven quillwork may have been made by a woman from the Huron–Wendat community living near Detroit. The pipe stems, quiver, shield, shield cover, and crooked knife with a handle carved in the form of a horse are in the style of the eastern Sioux, while the powder horn, cartridge holder and belt, and two pairs of worn, undecorated moccasins would have been the gear of a frontier soldier.

Nearly all military officers and colonial officials who served in eastern North America during the mid-18th and early-19th centuries eagerly sought out finely crafted wares made for the curio market.[1] This magnificent outfit suggests a different history. It most closely resembles an outfit presented to Lieutenant John Caldwell on the occasion of his adoption by Anishinaabeg in the Ohio Territory in 1780.[2]

Between 1763 and 1796, Foster's regiment was posted to frontier forts at the Miami Rapids near Detroit and Michilimackinac, in the heart of the Great Lakes region.[3] Family traditions hold that Foster was "taken prisoner by some Red Indians" and "made a chief."[4] Similar romantic notions go back to the 18th century, but they may nevertheless have some basis in fact. Mrs. Simcoe, the wife of the first governor of Upper Canada, described Anishinaabeg she met "from near Lake Huron" around 1795 as wearing almost identical garments.[5] Anishinaabe makers would have acquired the luxury goods used to make the outfit, in combination with traditional materials of hide, eagle feathers, and porcupine quills, either through the fur trade or as presents given by the European powers to seal alliances.

Although it is impossible to know exactly how Andrew Foster acquired his outfit, it seems likely that it was presented to him as a gift. In this way the ogimaag, or chiefs, of the Anishinaabeg signaled their ability to provide for their British allies, while simultaneously recognizing their important political status.[6] Such gestures were an integral part of the practice of ritual adoption. Anishinaabe peoples recognized two categories of being—meyaagizid and inawemaagen, foreigner and relative.[7] By accepting their gift, Foster would have recognized his kinship with the Anishinaabeg. Equally important, the status conveyed by the outfit would have identified Foster as a leader. Ritual adoption was designed to compel British officers to mobilize all of the power at their disposal to protect and serve the interests of their new relatives.

It would be a mistake, however, to interpret the adoption of British soldiers as a sign of political dependence. The Americans sent armed forces into the Ohio Valley twice in 1790 and 1791, intent on breaking up an alliance of Native peoples that included Great Lakes Indians such as Anishinaabeg and Huron–Wendat. Both expeditions ended in defeat for the American forces, adding strength to the Native alliance, but also raising the stakes for the U.S. government.[8] During the late 18th century, the Anishinaabeg constituted a demographic majority in the Lake Superior region. The United States would be forced to come to terms with their power again when it lost posts at Detroit and Mackinac to warriors fighting as British allies in the War of 1812.

Anishinaabe diplomacy resulted in social relationships with diverse Native peoples—the Dakota at the edge of the Great Plains, the Cree peoples of the northern boreal forests and the coast of Hudson Bay, and the Huron–Wendat at Detroit and in the Ohio River valley. No matter how Foster acquired his outfit, in their design and in combining material artifacts from other important Native peoples, these garments reflect the power and political aspirations of the Anishinaabeg.

—Ruth B. Phillips and Michael Witgen (Ojibwe)

Pipe tomahawk presented to Chief Tecumseh
(Shawnee, 1768–1813)

Pipe tomahawk presented to Chief Tecumseh (Shawnee, 1768–1813), ca. 1812. Canada. Wood, iron, lead; 66 x 22.5 cm. Gift of Sarah Russell Imhof and Joseph A. Imhof. 17/6249

This ceremonial pipe-tomahawk, a gift from Colonel Henry Procter to Tecumseh, probably was presented to the Shawnee war chief at Fort Malden, in Amherstburg, Ontario, late in the autumn of 1812. During that summer, when the War of 1812 officially started, Tecumseh led Native American warriors against the Americans on the Detroit frontier. In mid-August he joined with British forces led by General Isaac Brock to capture Detroit from General William Hull and an American army.

Tecumseh admired Brock's decision to prosecute the war against the Americans vigorously, and Tecumseh and Brock became good friends. After Brock was killed on October 13, 1812, the British command passed to Procter. More cautious than Brock, Procter was reluctant to attack American positions in Ohio, and Tecumseh soon lost patience with his hesitancy. In response, Procter met repeatedly with Tecumseh and other Native Americans, attempting to maintain their loyalty and support for the Crown. At these meetings the British often awarded tomahawks and other gifts of weapons to tribal leaders.

This tomahawk is typical of such a weapon and bears the inscription "To Chief Tecumseh / From Col. Proctor / MDCCCXII." (The inscription, with its alternate spelling, can be seen in the detail image on page 19.) The tomahawk was probably made in France. The gift did little to mend the rift between Tecumseh and Procter. Less than a year later, on October 5, 1813, when the Americans attacked at the Battle of the Thames, Procter and the British fled from the field. Tecumseh and his warriors stood and fought, but Tecumseh was killed, and Native American armed resistance subsequently disintegrated.

—R. David Edmunds (Cherokee)

Garters associated with Osceola

(Seminole, 1804–1838)

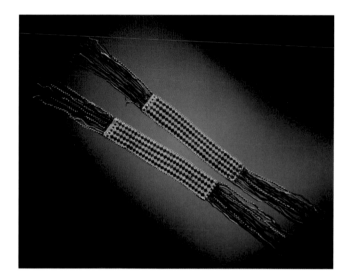

My Brothers! When the Great Spirit tells me to go with the white man, I go, but he tells me not to go. The white man says I shall go, and he will send people to make me go, but I have a rifle, and I have some powder and some lead. I say, we must not leave our homes and lands. If any of our people want to go west we won't let them, and I tell them they are our enemies, and we will treat them so, for the Great Spirit will protect us.

—OSCEOLA, 1834

Garters associated with Osceola (Seminole, 1804–1838), ca. 1835. Florida. Wool yarn, glass beads; 84 x 7 cm. Dr. George Jackson Fisher Collection. 22/9751

These leg garters likely belonged to the Seminole leader Osceola. Born in 1804 to Polly Coppinger, a part Muscogee Creek woman, Osceola was the most famous of several Seminole leaders who rose to prominence during the Second Seminole War, from 1835 to 1842. Osceola, whose name means Black Drink Singer, was also strong in medicine and was known for his ability to consume the black drink made from yaupon holly.

Osceola's great strength as a leader in war was his ability to plan and supervise multiple attacks. He was involved in more than a dozen battles and skirmishes and led Seminole warriors and their Creek and African-American allies against the U.S. Army and Florida militia and volunteers from 1835 until 1837, when illness led him to surrender.

Osceola enjoyed the stature and recognition that he had earned. George Catlin produced two paintings of Osceola. In each of them the war leader wears clothes of Seminole tradition. These finger-woven wool garters, which have beads woven into the pattern, are very similar to the garters Osceola wore in Catlin's full-length portrait, painted in 1838, shortly before the Seminole leader's death while he was imprisoned at Fort Moultrie, South Carolina. The image became widely known through a lithograph published by Catlin.

—**Donald L. Fixico (Shawnee/Sac and Fox/Muscogee Creek/Seminole)**

Peace medal presented to Kiyo´kaga

(Chief Keokuk, Sac and Fox)

Peace medal presented to Kiyo´kaga (Chief Keokuk, Sac and Fox, ca. 1780–1848), 1845. Franklin County, Kansas. Silver, hide, glass beads; 13.5 cm. Purchase. 24/1074

Following the Black Hawk War of 1832 and Black Hawk's imprisonment, the Sauk and Fox looked for new leadership to guide their negotiations with the United States. Keokuk (He Who Moves About), who had advocated peace, emerged as the leader of both groups as they became known as the Sac and Fox. Using strategies of accommodation, delay, and persuasion, Keokuk secured a new homeland for his people.

Awarding peace medals was U.S. government protocol for acknowledging distinguished Native leaders who posed no threat to the U.S. interests and served to maintain U.S.–tribal relations. From 1792 to 1892, the United States gave numerous silver or silver-plated peace medals of various sizes and oval or circular shape to Indian leaders. The government bestowed this medal on the articulate Indian statesman in 1847 after several negotiations that led to the removal of his people farther west to Indian Territory. The medal, a bust of James Polk on one side and two hands shaking on the other, symbolizes "peace and friendship," the most common sentiment in U.S.–Indian treaties from 1778 through the last treaty, negotiated in 1868.

—Donald L. Fixico (Shawnee/Sac and Fox/Muscogee Creek/Seminole)

Burden strap associated with Tekahionwake
(E. Pauline Johnson, Mohawk)

Burden strap associated with Tekahionwake (E. Pauline Johnson, Mohawk, 1861–1913), 1760–1800. New York. Hemp, moose hair, glass beads; 503 x 6 cm. Collected and donated by E. Pauline Johnson. 2/5326

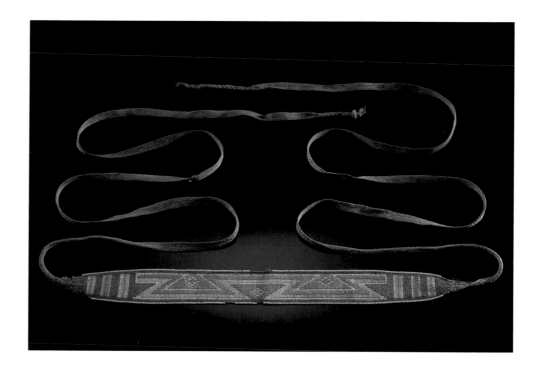

Oh, why have your people forced on me the name of Pauline Johnson? Was not my Indian name good enough? Do you think you help us by bidding us forget our blood?

——TEKAHIONWAKE

Like most Native American objects, the burden strap—*gas-ha´-ah* in Kanyenkeha´ka, the Mohawk language—is utilitarian, yet decorated to distinguish its nation and other affiliations. Primarily finger woven of cured basswood strips, Indian hemp, or elm, burden straps help carry heavy loads by distributing the weight over the back. At first glance, it appears as though it should be worn like a headband. In fact, it is designed to rest along the hairline. Today people use burden straps to portage canoes.

Emily Pauline Johnson was born and raised at Chiefswood, her family's estate on the Six Nations of the Grand River Territory. She was the daughter of a Mohawk hereditary chief and an English lady. She gained fame in the late 19th century by composing and performing her original poetry in Canada, the United States, and England.

When the Six Nations left New York state after the American Revolution, Pauline's paternal grandmother wrapped a silver communion service in rags and carried it the whole distance to Canada using a burden strap. One of the soldiers escorting the family actually speared through the bundle in a bid to get the old grandma to move faster. To this day a piece of the set, which was given to the Mohawks by Queen Anne, has a mark where the bayonet scratched the silver.

—Paula Whitlow (Mohawk)

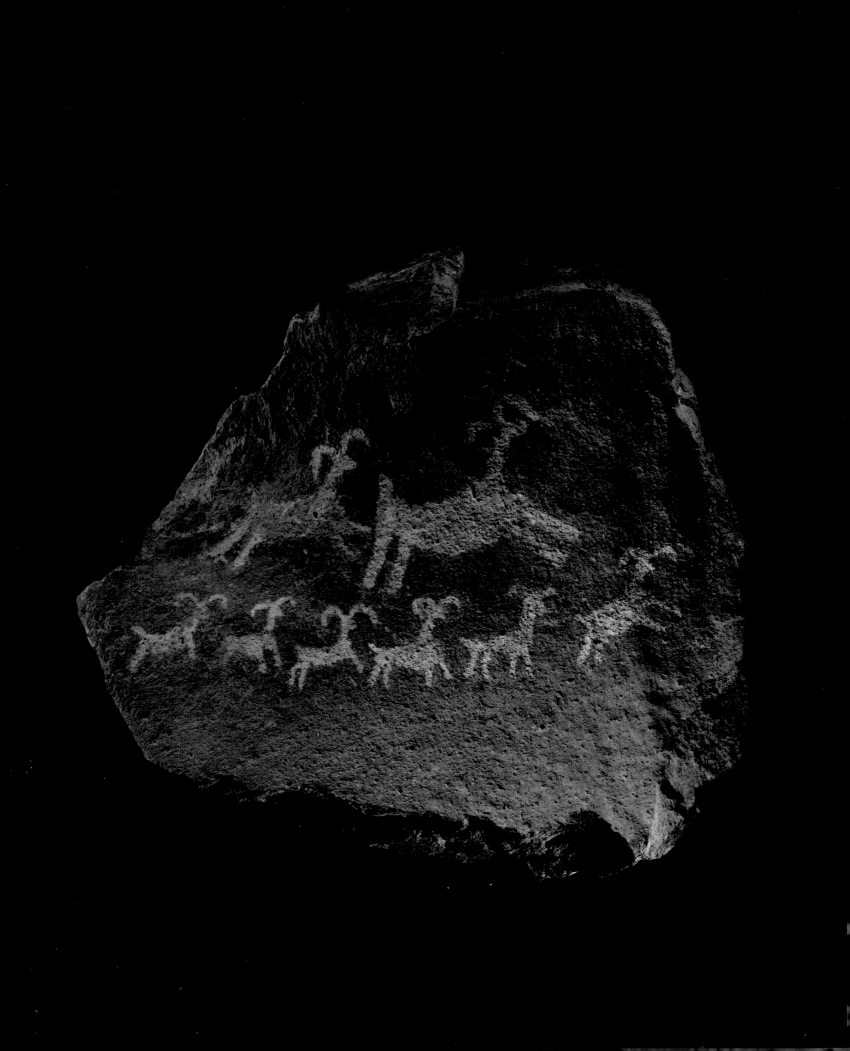

Paba hanokwaetu

"A vast, rugged place"—Northern Paiute

NATIVE CALIFORNIA REPRESENTS one of the most culturally and linguistically diverse regions on earth. Equally diverse is its broader environment, a land encompassing vast deserts, fertile valleys, snow-capped mountains, and hundreds of miles of changing coastline. Still, for many individuals today, general understanding of the state's numerous and varied Native cultures—those who have for millennia called California home—remains locked within a construct defined by views and perceptions that have changed little over the past one hundred years and more.

The creation of California the state, for many, also required the creation of the state's history—much of it based upon little more than conjecture. That history not only lauded the achievements of its conquering citizens, white Americans, but somewhat surprisingly perhaps, also spoke to the histories and cultures of the state's original inhabitants—its Native peoples. Yet this region, which had at one time been part of New Spain's vast northernmost frontier, by the American period came to have very distinct and set borders. In reality, California's superimposed *political* boundaries, then as now, abide little to the *cultural* boundaries along the borders of its three neighboring territories and eventual states—Arizona, Nevada, and Oregon. The same can be said for California's international border shared with Mexico.

Too often, according to strict, often doctrinaire interpretations and assumptions, our understanding of cultures has been influenced, and in California's case defined, by those who sought to better understand the past by collecting in the present. That is to say, many of the objects present in the museum's collection and in similar collections throughout the nation—most

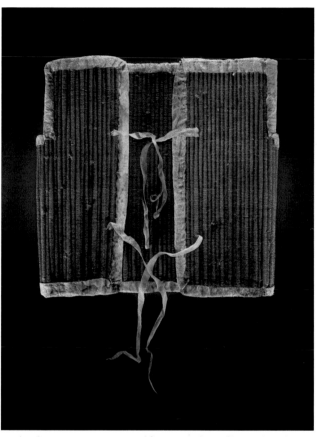

Karuk rod-armor vest, ca. 1900. California. Wood, iris, fiber cord, leather; 57 x 59 cm. Collected by Grace Nicholson. 5/2365

particularly objects from California—were collected in the hopes of preserving a record of a dying indigenous past uncorrupted by the intrusions of white culture and society. Many of the individuals who collected these and other objects naively assumed they could capture pieces of an "unaltered" period in time, seemingly forgetting that the material cultures they sought to record were, much like their own, fluid, not static; constantly changing, adapting, and accommodating, as all peoples and their cultures tend to do.

Petroglyph depicting mountain sheep, AD 600–1300. Sand Tank, Inyo County, California. Basalt; 20 x 47 x 50 cm. Purchase. 20/3884

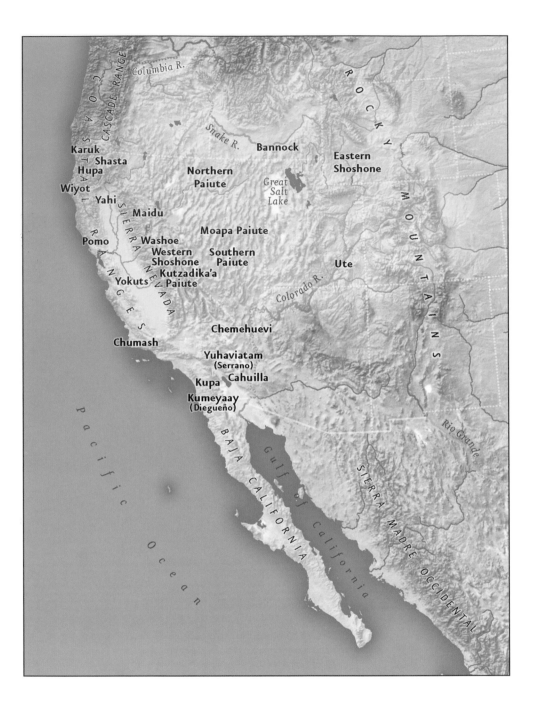

Native California's material culture is as diverse as the people who create it. The pieces shown here represent only a handful of the numerous and diverse peoples who traditionally called this region home. These limited examples, nevertheless, afford us the opportunity to better understand certain aspects of Native California. Some pieces are sometimes interpreted as "truly Californian," viewed as unique to the peoples who made them, speaking little to any cultural influences or introductions beyond that of their own inhabited geographic region. With other pieces, though, these narrowly defined parameters become far more fluid, enabling us to see how some California regions were unquestionably influenced by Native peoples more closely associated today with other regions of the American West, such as the Southwest, the Pacific Northwest Coast, and even the Great Plains.

Northern Paiute moccasins, ca. 1900. Fort Bidwell, Modoc County, California. Beads, hide; 26 x 11 x 13.5 cm. 16/5387

Cultural links between Native California and sometimes-distant parts of North America are not difficult to identify. These links are easily expressed by a pair of finely beaded Northern Paiute moccasins, reminiscent of the Plains or Upper Plateau cultures that undoubtedly inspired them. The moccasins were collected by Edward H. Davis—a contract field collector for the Museum of the American Indian responsible for obtaining many of the museum's California items—probably before 1930 at the Fort Bidwell Indian Reservation in the Surprise Valley. In the state's far northeastern corner, adjacent to both southeastern Oregon and northwestern Nevada, basketmaking is a lesser-known artistic expression. Then as today, women at Fort Bidwell were just as likely to identify with nearby equine cultures, learning instead the arts of brain-tanning deer hide and beading, known to generation upon generation of women throughout the Great Plains and Plateau. Today, while beading still abounds, brain-tanning in some regions is on the wane. The old methods that use deer brain for the tanning process have fallen off as more and more deer hunters choose to keep trophy heads. Tanners first turned to cow brain as an alternative, but with the onset of mad cow disease, that practice is now illegal. Increasingly, tanners have begun to use pig brain, and many believe the higher fat content actually lends a better, more supple hide. Making necessary accommodations, artists continue to practice this traditional skill.

A similar history can be attributed to the braided horsehair belt catalogued as having been made by the Shasta Indians, also of northwestern California. Despite the increasing number of horses seen throughout Alta California during the Mexican era's Rancho culture—made possible by huge Spanish land grants—or the horses that surely arrived with the throngs of wealth-seekers during the Gold Rush, it is uncommon to see material culture derived from horses, even among Mission Indians of Southern California who incorporated the horse into their cultural orientation earlier than most groups within the state. The Shasta belt is clearly an exception. Adorned with both shell and brass buttons, trade beads, sewing thimbles, and even a watch gear, the belt is a highly personalized piece, enhanced in a somewhat whimsical fashion

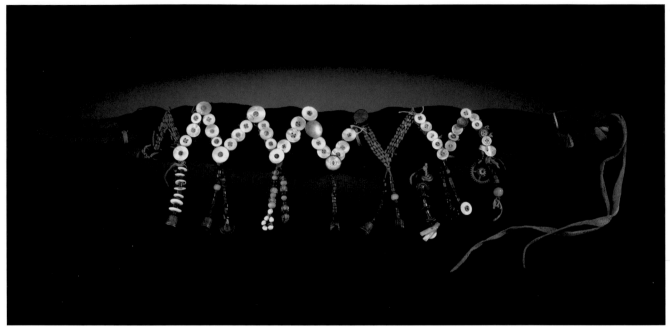

Shasta belt, ca. 1860–1890. California. Horsehair, leather, wool cloth, buttons and thimbles, cotton string; 82 x 9 cm. Purchase. 3/9299

perhaps even by the female wearer who may also have been the maker. Similar braided horsehair belts can be found in the Southwest Museum of the American Indian, Autry National Center collection in Los Angeles—one there, like this one, is attributed to the Shasta, the other to their immediate western neighbors, the Karuk people.

Of course, outside influences found within Native California's great diversity of material cultures cannot be attributed solely to other Indian peoples. European-Americans, the imposers of new boundaries, unwittingly obscured Native cultural distinctions they so often sought to identify. An excellent example of this is seen in the yucca fiber saddle blanket collected from Cupeño Indians at the village of Agua Caliente—not to be mistaken for the Agua Caliente Band of Cahuilla Indians who have long lived in the Palm Springs area. In the era of sustained contact, beginning in 1769, among the Spanish and then Alta California's numerous coastally oriented cultures, the Cupeño and their ancestors lived for millennia in and around the area of what is today northeast San Diego County's Lake Henshaw Valley. Over time the Cupeño came within the sphere of influence of Mission San Luis Rey de

Francia, established in 1798, near today's coastal town of Oceanside and the sprawling Camp Pendleton Marine Corp Base, and its *asistencia*—a sister mission without a resident priest—San Antonia de Pala, some thirty miles inland from the ocean. By the late Spanish period, Mission San Luis Rey came to be the largest and most prosperous of all the California missions.

Despite the often slave-like conditions the Franciscan missionaries perpetrated on the Indians to achieve this prosperous state, the Native peoples adopted numerous elements of broader Hispanic culture. One was their participation in the pastoral economy, based upon the sometimes enormous sheep and cattle herds that helped to sustain the missions. Indian labor was integral to these vast herds' maintenance. Along with this essential labor came the Indians' mastery of the horse as a tool of the trade. From the end of the Spanish era, to Mexico's expropriation of mission lands and the imposition of the Rancho system, and well into the Anglo-American era, the Indian *vaquero*, or horseman, became synonymous with the state's cattle industry. Part of every vaquero's riding gear would surely have been a saddle blanket. Indian saddle blankets, generally associated with the fine weaves produced by the

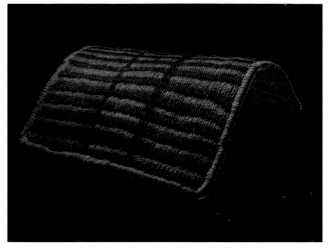

Kupangaxwichem (Cupeño) saddle blanket, ca. 1875–1900. Agua Caliente, San Diego County, California. Yucca fiber; 81 x 65 cm. Collected by Edward H. Davis. 6/5900

Kupangaxwichem (Cupeño) Indians spinning yucca, ca. 1895 to 1923.

Diné (Navajo) from sheep's wool, were different in much of southern California. Although they served the same purpose—protecting both horse and rider—these saddle blankets were made from the region's ubiquitous yucca plant. Known to most whites for its beautiful, nonperennial bloom, the yucca plant's fibrous leaves or shoots are strong and durable, traditionally used by Native peoples in creating a host of utilitarian items such as sandals and cordage. Unlike baskets, though, which were woven almost exclusively by women, items made with yucca fiber tended to be processed and made by men. Yucca shoots were stripped apart to create fine individual fibers. Like the Diné, who spun their own raw wool, California Indians spun the fibers together on a similar-style spinning wheel to create a fibrous yarn. Once enough yarn was spun, it was woven into a mat, often with intricate design patterns or even color schemes. Even where wool was available, the Cupeño and other regional groups chose to use traditional materials to create a nontraditional item readily incorporated into their own culture.

A similar example is the trio of lidded baskets made by the Wiyot basket-weaver Elizabeth Hickox. Hickox's work represents, for many people then as today, the very finest of California Indian basketry. Ironically,

perhaps, her signature lidded baskets were decidedly nontraditional in shape, influenced by the tastes of eager white basket dealers and collectors during the first two decades of the 1900s. Yet Hickox strayed little from the traditional basketmaking resources of her region: beargrass, black fern, and willow or hazel sticks for weaving; yellow tree moss for dying porcupine quills. Her designs—including "frog's foot," "cut wood," and "long worm"—speak to a deep understanding of the age-old stories, beliefs, and conventions of the Lower Klamath River region that continue to shape her people's culture today (see page 229).

In many respects, Hickox's experience as a 20th-century basket-weaver is no different from that of any other American Indian artist, past or present. As Native peoples have understood for millennia, the movement and introduction of new materials, methods, designs, and applications is as old as culture itself. Without these phenomena we would not see new and compelling directions in either traditional or innovative expression among Native artists in California and throughout Indian Country. The nontraditional, over time, comes to be the traditional, the foundation of living culture.

—Steven M. Karr

The Great Basin

The vast semiarid interior of western North America, from roughly the Sierra Nevada on the west to the Rocky Mountains on the east, and from the Snake River plain on the north to the Colorado River drainage on the south, is generally referred to as the Great Basin. The 19th-century explorer John Charles Frémont named the region based on his observation of a major geographic feature: its streams and rivers drain to the interior rather than to the sea. Although something of a misnomer—the landscape is not one basin, but many—Frémont's characterization has colored impressions of the region's Native peoples as relatively isolated and focused inward, rather than as interconnected to groups in other regions and thus also focused outward. Although the Native peoples of the Great Basin do have cultural traditions and linguistic features that are uniquely theirs, they also share many practices with neighbors on their borders and beyond.

The Great Basin is the homeland of nations and tribes whose ancestors through many generations developed ingenious solutions to living in this seemingly harsh land. The region appears uninviting to the unfamiliar, as it is characteristically dry (precipitation in the valleys ranges from 2.5 to 10 inches annually), in some areas extremely hot in summer (Death Valley routinely reaches 120°F), and very cold in winter (the Rocky Mountains and Sierra Nevada can be –20°F). But to those who know it well, these conditions are not and were not impediments to living, and the region is a life-sustaining place, a source of profound spiritual strength, and a true homeland.

Prior to disruption by European-Americans, the people here made a good living by hunting, gathering, and, where possible, fishing and a little farming. They developed a wide variety of specialized tools—such as nets, traps, decoys, and unique bows and arrows for hunting and fishing—as well as a suite of baskets and grinding implements for collecting and processing plant foods. They followed a seasonal round within their territories that took them from valley floors to mountain ranges to coincide with the movement of game animals, birds, and fish, and the ripening of plant foods. They lived in cool brush-, mat-, or skin-covered structures in the hot summers and more substantial and better-insulated houses in the cold winters. Although their populations were low in some areas, as food resources could be scattered and scarce, they were linked through intermarriage to areas with more to offer. They could always call on kinship connections in times of need.

Nor have its Native peoples experienced the Great Basin as an isolating or insulating place. Its broad valleys and intervening mountain ranges were interlaced with trails and pathways that were minor and major corridors for travel in all directions. Materials, ideas, and people moved in and out of the region. Great Basin peoples visited the Pacific Ocean, the Columbia River, the bison-hunting grounds east of the Rockies, the pueblos of the Southwest, and more. They journeyed for certain foods, to exchange tools, for entertainment, and for ceremonies. And they welcomed people from those and other areas who reciprocated. People today do the same, visiting each other's regional harvest festivals, such as the annual Pinenut Festival in September at the Walker River Reservation in Nevada, the Shoshone–Bannock powwow in August at the Fort Hall Indian Reservation in Idaho, and the annual Bear Dance in the spring on the Southern Ute Reservation in Colorado. There are also frequent sports events and other activities that keep the people closely connected to their relatives and friends throughout the region and beyond.

The Great Basin has one of the longest records of human occupation in the whole of Native North America: 14,000 years in dry caves in what is today southeastern Oregon, 10,000 to 12,000 years in similar places in several other locations. Although living today is certainly easier in many ways than it was at various times in the distant past, present-day tribes and communities face many of the same overall issues as did their ancestors. These include locating and preserving access to resources, especially water; securing economic stability; and promoting individual and tribal identity by sustaining indigenous languages and cultures. Although the ways of accomplishing them have changed through time, the overall goals of the peoples of the Great Basin remain remarkably the same. The objects in the museum's collections illustrate some of their achievements.

Resources: water

The Great Basin is basically a desert with cold winters in the north and a hotter, and even drier, desert in the south. Fluctuations in temperature within a single day can be fifty to sixty degrees Fahrenheit or more, as can the difference between summer temperatures and winter ones. Such conditions strain plants, animals, and people, who need to find food and, above all, water. Fortunately, another important geographical feature of the Great Basin—the many relatively high mountain ranges and intervening basins—creates many small springs, seeps, and rock tanks or potholes that hold long- and short-term water supplies. A number of permanent and ephemeral streams and a few rivers offer additional water, and food plants and animals are found near them all. Nearly all permanent and ephemeral water sources are also archaeological sites; the remains of hunting weapons, camp debris, and rock art mark their sustained use over millennia. Great Basin languages and songs catalogue hundreds of names for these resources. Finding them and then remembering their exact locations often meant the difference between life and death.

Through the centuries people also carried water with them, using the dried paunches of animals or basketry water carriers. Water bottles tend to be tribally and regionally distinctive, and these fine-woven, pitch-coated, and watertight containers were active items of trade in and beyond the region. For example, the Southern Paiute people traded their pitch water bottles to the Hopi people of the Southwest, as did the Southern Ute to the Jicarilla Apache. The Owens Valley Paiute traded theirs to the Yokuts people of south-central California, as did the Northern Paiute to the Achomawi and other groups in northern California. Sturdier coiled water carriers made by the Northern and Southern Ute were favored in the early and mid-1800s by the horse-using Wind River and Snake River Shoshone people, who soon learned the technique of making them. Older people today still talk about how well these baskets kept water cool and how they gave it real flavor.

Today many Great Basin tribes, along with other Native peoples in the dry western United States, are fighting vigorously in the courts to protect their springs, streams, and water rights for future generations. In September 2008, the Pyramid Lake Paiute Tribe of western Nevada signed the Truckee River Operating Agreement, part of the larger Truckee River Negotiated Settlement, which goes a long way toward settling a lengthy case by providing an equitable division of the river's waters among urban, rural, and tribal users in California and Nevada. The Fallon Paiute–Shoshone Tribe is also involved in these negotiations, as well as others affecting the division of the waters of the Carson River. And the Southern Ute Tribe of southwestern Colorado has recently negotiated a solution to water storage and irrigation issues involving the Animas River, which flows through portions of their reservation. Water remains key to life in the region.

Economic security

From the distant past, Great Basin peoples have also developed ingenious ways of collecting and processing food supplies. Tule duck decoys lured waterfowl to local marshes, while gill nets and dip nets caught fish, waterfowl, and land birds. Fish spears and harpoons landed large species of fish, and basketry fish traps helped take both large and small fish. Specialized bows, made of bighorn sheep horn carefully steamed, bent, and carved into shape, improved the power and effectiveness of hunters and were a highly prized trade item to surrounding regions. Specially designed arrows made hunting rabbits, birds, and large game easier. Tactical measures—constructing surrounds; driving

Northern Paiute water bottle basket, ca. 1880–1900. Nevada. Plant fiber, pitch; 28 x 32 x 44 cm. Presented by Jay Noble Emley. 18/2189

Southern Paiute water bottle baskets, ca. 1880–1920. Arizona. Plant fiber, pitch, hair; 31 29 x 33 cm, 11 x 13 x 18 cm. M. F. Savage Collection; Frederick W. Skiff Collection. 7004, 15/6554

Northern Paiute duck decoy and fishing net, ca. 1920. Stillwater Reservation, Nevada. Tule rush, duck pelt, feathers, cordage; 37 x 15 x 18 cm, 42 x 28 cm. Collected by Mark R. Harrington. 13/4190, 13/4186

Pyramid Lake Northern Paiute fishing net and spear, ca. 1920. Pyramid Lake Reservation, Nevada. Dogbane or Indian hemp, wood, bone, cordage, pitch; 44 x 13 cm, 66 x 4 cm. Collected by Mark R. Harrington. 13/3835, 13/4096

Walker River Northern Paiute fish trap, ca. 1920. Walker River Reservation, Nevada. Willow shoots, cloth; 58 x 30 x 30 cm. Collected by Mark R. Harrington. 13/3789

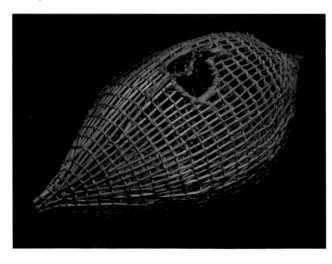

animals into nets or other impounds or traps, sometimes with fire; and the use of snares of many types—improved the abilities of hunters (usually men) to feed their families.

Women made many kinds of baskets for specific jobs in collecting and processing plant and animal foods. These were often distinctive to each tribe, but some styles were similar to those in California. Large conical baskets served as containers for collecting and storing seeds and nuts, especially those from the pinyon pine, a regional plant and important staff of life. Flat winnowing and parching trays allowed the sifting of seeds and nuts from chaff, as well as their preliminary cooking by hot coals. Women knocked seeds from plants with basketry seed beaters, also efficient tools. And watertight boiling baskets served to cook foods, including mushes and stews, by stone boiling.

Today, some families throughout the region still hunt game animals, rabbits, and waterfowl, though not for total subsistence and usually with modern equipment. People also collect some plant foods, including roots, spring greens, berries, and occasionally seeds. Families actively collect pine nuts in good harvest years more than any other vegetable food. In recent times, prices for pine nuts have escalated due to scarcity, federal control of many of the best picking areas (Nevada is 87 percent federal or tribal land), and the spread of beetles that are killing the trees. Several tribes and individuals are fighting back to save these important resources, including on federal lands over which they still feel keen stewardship.

In addition, tribes are building into legal settlements rights and protections for food resources. The Truckee River Operating Agreement provides the Pyramid Lake Paiute Tribe sufficient river flow to maintain fish species that have long sustained their people, including the threatened Lahontan cutthroat trout and the endangered cui-ui sucker. Litigation by the Fallon Paiute–Shoshone over the Carson River seeks to preserve both Stillwater Marsh—home to thousands of migrating waterfowl and part of the tribe's original lands—and the tribe's water rights for irrigation. Other Great Basin tribes are not afraid to use the courts to acquire environmental justice for natural resources.

In the early years of the 20th century, many Great Basin Native women worked toward economic security for their families through the development of their basketmaking skills and sales of their basketry to

Northern Paiute burden basket, ca. 1910. Arizona. Willow, horsehair, wood splints; 76 x 71 cm. Frederick W. Skiff Collection. 15/6547

Northern Paiute winnowing basket, ca. 1920. Klamath Reservation, Oregon. Willow; 64 x 52 x 15 cm. Collected by Edward H. Davis. 16/5391

Above, clockwise beginning on the left:
Washoe basket, ca. 1900–1905. Nevada. Willow. 12 x 15 cm. Presented by Archer M. Huntington. 9/169

Washoe or Northern Paiute basket, ca. 1940s. Western Nevada. Willow, glass beads; 17 x 16 cm. Transferred from Indian Arts and Crafts Board, Department of the Interior. 26/1393

Sandra Eagle (Pyramid Lake Paiute/Shoshone), miniature basket, ca. 2000. Pyramid Lake Reservation, Washoe County, Nevada. Willow, shell beads, glass beads; 2 x 3.5 cm. Gift of R. E. Mansfield. 26/4076

Left: Sue Coleman (Washoe), making a large burden basket. The tradition of basketmaking as fine art continues among the Washoe today.

the emerging arts and crafts market. Throughout the region, where opportunities existed, women developed unique basket shapes and fine weaves that are today seen as fine art. Weavers were sometimes inspired by the shapes and designs created by fine basket-weavers from other areas, especially California. The tradition of basketry as fine art continues in the Great Basin, and includes the unique beaded baskets made in the region. Intertribal trade in baskets also continues in, for example, the wedding baskets made by Southern Paiute and Southern Ute weavers for the Diné people of the Southwest.

Ute shirt, ca. 1870–1880.
Colorado or Utah. Wool cloth,
hide, glass beads; 69 x 162 cm.
Purchase. 21/1222

Identity

Many objects here speak to the unique identity of
Great Basin tribes and individuals. Others speak to
shared ideas and identities with surrounding regions
and demonstrate long periods of exchange. On the eastern side of the Great Basin, Ute and Shoshone peoples
who took to horses and many aspects of Plains life
late in the 17th or early in the 18th century adopted
similar styles of decorative art in quillwork and glass
beads. Floral patterns originating to the north and
east among the Métis and Algonkian-speaking peoples
are seen on many beaded items of clothing and horse
gear among the Wind River and Northern Shoshone
people and the Northern Ute. While Great Basin bead-
workers developed distinctive interpretations of these
styles, often blending them with their own aesthetics
in color and pattern, they were nonetheless creating
designs within a more widespread tradition. The Wind
River and Northern Shoshone also adopted aspects
of the transmontane style, especially after the 1830s,
when glass seed beads became available to them. The

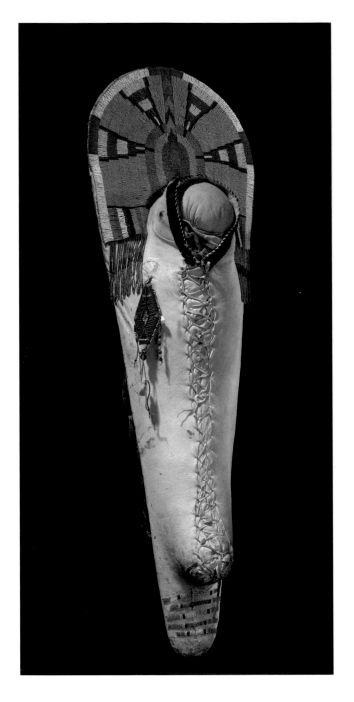

Bannock cradleboard, ca. 1900–1920. Fort Hall Reservation, Idaho. Wood, hide, glass beads, cotton thread, brass sequins and jingles, cowrie shells, velveteen, bone beads; 121 x 37 x 15 cm. Collected by William Wildschut. 15/2400

Shoshone shared these patterns with the Crow people of the Plains and the Nimi´ipuu (Nez Perce) and other groups of the Columbia Plateau. Although some of these styles have been modified today, their patterns still remain in the lively beadwork traditions practiced by the Fort Hall Shoshone–Bannock, the Shoshone people on the Wind River Reservation, and families on the Ute reservations in Utah and Colorado.

Today tribes and individuals still work hard to maintain their identity in their art and culture, yet they also acknowledge and preserve those things that are shared regionally and beyond. Great Basin people value their unique languages—all but the Washoe people speak dialects of languages affiliated with the Numic Branch of the widespread Uto–Aztecan linguistic family—and several have programs for language learning. Most have participated in the indigenous Great Basin Native Languages Conference, since 1996 held annually to semiannually as an intertribal exchange of ideas and formats for language instruction. Recently representatives of the Comanche of Oklahoma, who also speak a Numic language, have attended, and they and others have hosted a broader Uto–Aztecan language conference. Groups attending these and many other gatherings in the region share their unique foods, dances, songs, and other aspects of their cultures, while at the same time looking to common themes and values. The Great Basin Native Basket Weavers Association has met jointly with the California Indian Basketweavers Association on at least three occasions in the recent past, and members of both also attend meetings of similar organizations in Arizona and the Northwest.

—Catherine S. Fowler

Mary and William Benson (Pomo)
Willow basket

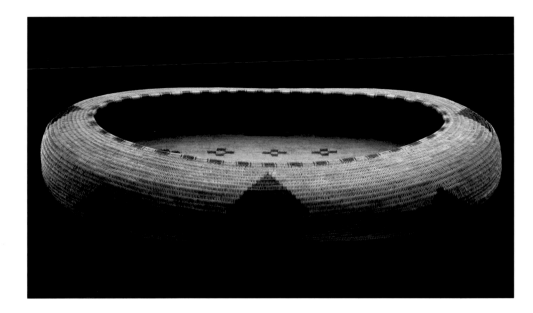

Mary Knight Benson (Pomo, ca. 1876–1930) and William Benson (Pomo, 1862–1937), basket, 1929–1931. Yokayo Rancheria, Mendocino County, California. Sedge, gray willow, bulrush; 58 x 34 x 10 cm. Collected by Grace Nicholson. Purchased from Mrs. Thyra Maxwell. 24/2118

This elegant basket sits at the center of a complex web of relationships. Two of the world's most gifted weavers—Mary Knight Benson and her husband, William Benson—created it for Grace Nicholson, a Pasadena-based dealer in American Indian art. For nearly thirty years, Nicholson provided the Bensons with a regular, modest stipend and assisted them during various adversities. This allowed William and Mary to devote much of their time to creating some of the finest baskets ever woven, and it provided Grace with a regular supply of superb material to sell.

In the early summer of 1930, William wrote Nicholson to tell her of Mary's death, leaving this basket unfinished. Nicholson asked William to complete it, something virtually unthinkable. Among Pomoan communities at that time, the deceased's personal possessions—particularly pieces of handiwork—were destroyed, a practice that embodied the family's deep grief.

William Benson profoundly mourned Mary's passing and he resisted Nicholson's plea. But Nicholson learned about ethnographic work Benson was engaged in with linguist Jaime de Angulo. "Now other parties have had the benefit of your work," she fumed, ". . . and I will not even be mentioned for all my work in the matter even though I have furnished the funds all these years to make it possible to preserve the legends, etc." Primarily, I believe, to mend the rupture in their relationship, William Benson agreed to finish the basket Mary began. He sent it to Nicholson late in 1931, noting, "This is the Hardes[t] job . . . This is the Best I could do on it." Only one more letter exists between him and Nicholson, written in 1932.

—Sherrie Smith-Ferri (Dry Creek Pomo/Bodega Bay Miwok descent)

I am Getting along Allright But One Thing I can not Forget That Is Mary, I Can See Her Face Ever Now and Then.

—WILLIAM BENSON,
LETTER TO
GRACE NICHOLSON,
DECEMBER 1, 1930

Juana Basilia Sitmelelene (Chumash, 1782-1838), basket, ca. 1815–1822. Mission San Buenaventura, California. Sumac, *juncus textilis*, mud dye; 9 x 48 cm. Gift of Mrs. Willis Rice in memory of Dr. Arthur Horton Cleveland. 23/132

Juana Basilia Sitmelelene (Chumash)

Coin basket

The Chumash are a group of related Native peoples of coastal southern California, centered around Santa Barbara and the Northern Channel Islands. For thousands of years, Chumash women made baskets for domestic use. There were trays, basins, and deep bowls for food preparation; large burden baskets; globular storage baskets; and jar-shaped baskets for keeping valuables. Women's basketry hats served as a standard measure when trading acorns and other seeds. Cooking baskets, used for stone-boiling mush, were so tightly woven that they held water.

Skilled weavers that they were, Chumash women were accustomed to making baskets for sale or trade to other Native people, within their own villages or beyond. So when Spanish explorers and missionaries made their way into Chumash territory in the late 18th century, weavers were able to adapt their techniques to meet requests from the outsiders. They created oval and rectangular sewing baskets with lids, added pedestal bases to traditional bowls, and fashioned at least one basket in the shape of a padre's hat. New design patterns included pictorial elements and inscriptions. These were all executed using their traditional weaving techniques and plant materials—juncus (basket rush) or deer grass foundations sewn with split juncus and sumac—and largely following the traditional design layout with a border band.

The pinnacle of Chumash art was achieved in baskets into which they wove designs identical to those on Spanish colonial coins in circulation during the Mission Period. Sometimes called "presentation baskets" because one of them features an inscription indicating it was intended as a gift, these baskets are some of the finest ever made anywhere in the world. The skill involved in creating the intricate patterns is truly unparalleled.

Only six of these heraldic design baskets are known to exist today. Three of them are inscribed with words in Spanish that had been written out for the weavers to copy as they wove. These inscriptions include the weavers' names—Juana Basilia, María Marta, and María Sebastiana. Traditionally, weavers did not sign their baskets. That these women were asked to do so shows the high regard in which their art was held. Although this basket does not bear her name, its weaving technique and design layout are nearly identical to another presentation basket known to have been woven by Juana Basilia Sitmelelene.

—Jan Timbrook

When I first met this remarkable basket, it was like meeting an old friend, because we have almost the exact basket on display at the Santa Barbara Museum of Natural History, made by the same weaver. In studying this basket, I was perplexed by the date 1711, woven around the edge of the central design, about a century earlier than it was thought to have been made. After discussing it, we concluded that Juana Basilia had copied the year from the coin she used for the design.

I appreciate the beauty, intricacy, and hard work in making a basket of this quality. It is hard on the mind, as well as the hands. Your spirit needs to be in a good place in order to create such beauty.

Although they are sometimes called "presentation baskets," they were not necessarily woven as gifts, but rather served as a means of supplementing the weaver's income and supporting her family. Perhaps in developing her artistry, Sitmelelene was able to be relieved of her daily mission work. Also, continuing her craft as a weaver would have allowed her to return to traditional gathering places and practice traditional rituals.

— Ernestine Ygnacio-De Soto (Barbareño Chumash)

The survival of sacramental registers allows us to reconstruct details of Sitmelelene's life. She was born about 1782 in the ranchería (village) of Sumuawawa. The exact site and territory of this ranchería has not been determined with any certainty, but it may have been located in one of the inland valleys of the Santa Monica Mountains near the current city of Thousand Oaks. Her father had moved to Sumuawawa from Loxostox´ni, a Lulapin (Ventureño Chumash) town on the coast between Malibu and Point Mugu. Sitmelelene was born in her mother's ranchería, reflecting the matrilocal postmarital residence pattern that was practiced by most families in the Chumash region. The year of her birth was a momentous one: In 1782 three Spanish settlements—the Pueblo of Los Angeles, the Mission of San Buenaventura, and the Presidio of Santa Bárbara—were founded within one or two days' travel from her home territory. So during the years that Sitmelelene grew up, these colonial establishments were also developing.

While living in her Native ranchería, Sitmelelene learned the art of basketweaving, probably from her mother. Reaching adulthood, Sitmelelene married Chitchacuaha, a man from Kimishax, in the Santa Monica Mountains. Their newborn daughter Chuastimenahuan was baptized as Filotea María at Mission San Buenaventura on February 11, 1804. Two years later, in February 1806, Sitmelelene and Chitchacuaha were themselves baptized there and given the Christian names Juana Basilia and Gabriel de Jesús. By that time, the number of Ventureño Chumash affiliated with the mission had reached more than 1,150 people. After 1810, the only Chumash peoples who had not resettled at missions were those who resided on the Channel Islands and in the interior mountains of the Coast Ranges.

The dedication woven around the rim of one of Juana Basilia's Spanish coin baskets indicates that it was presented by the Spanish governor of California to a friend in Mexico. A letter survives transferring certain items made by Chumash women to the governor in 1817, so it is possible that the basket was created by then. The preceding year, the mission had attained its highest Chumash population—more than 1,300 individuals—with the addition of families who had migrated from Santa Cruz Island.

Juana Basilia's daughter Filotea María married in 1818, but none of Filotea María's seven children reached adulthood. Throughout the Mission Period, the death rate remained high, especially among the very young. In 1824, Juana Basilia's husband died at about age 50. The following year, she married Juan Mariano Sulupcucagele, a widower about her own age whom she had known her entire life, as he too had come from Sumuawawa. He died ten years later. In 1837, Filotea María died from complications resulting from childbirth. Having outlived all the other members of her family, Juana Basilia Sitmelelene passed away soon thereafter.

The Ventureño Chumash community continued to flourish in the years following the mission's secularization, and the basketmaking tradition in which Juana Basilia Sitmelelene excelled was maintained by a group of skilled weavers in the city of Ventura that grew up around the former mission. The baskets made by these talented women—Candelaria Valenzuela, Petra Pico, and others—are today exhibited in museums in many parts of the country.

— John R. Johnson

I am fortunate to have been in the presence of this basket more than once. Each time I am taken by a detail that makes me think I am viewing it again for the first time. As an aspiring weaver, I am struck by the symmetry of the design elements and the perfection of its execution. The basket's beauty is visually arresting. The construction's strength has protected it through centuries for us.

I can only imagine the circumstances Sitmelelene lived and worked in. I cry for her family, living in the midst of irreversible destruction. Her extraordinary work is a window into a legacy interrupted by forces of both nature and man. In the catastrophic wake of contact, her life and her genius endured. She remained true to herself as an artist perpetuating a glorious tradition.

Sitmelelene sings to me a song of resilience through her basket. She lives.

—Nicolasa I. Sandoval (Santa Ynez Band of Chumash Indians)

Duck decoys

Northern Paiute duck decoy, ca. 1920. Stillwater Reservation, Nevada.
Tule rush, duck pelt, feathers; 37 x 15 x 18 cm.
Collected by Mark R. Harrington. 13/4190

Duck decoys, ca. 400 BC–AD 100. Lovelock Cave, Humboldt County,
Nevada. Tule rush, feathers, cordage, paint; 31 x 12 cm.
Collected by Mark R. Harrington. 13/4512, 13/4513

Envision a hunter crouched low amidst the tule marsh of centuries ago. The survival of his band depended on his skills as a hunter. In the early morning sky, flocks of ducks and geese fly by. His arrows cannot fly high enough into the sky to reach the flocks passing by, so he sets his best creative weapon on the water, the tule duck decoy. This is an ancient hunting tool used by his people from time immemorial. The floating tule duck brings the flock within reach, and his people survive another day.

The art of making this clever hunting tool is a tradition that has been passed down from hunter to hunter throughout the centuries. Duck skins from earlier kills were stretched over the decoys, making them very lifelike. In even earlier times, the waterfowl's feathers were woven onto the decoy and tied on with hemp strings. The heads and necks of some were painted to match the colors of the duck species. In doing this, the hunter made the duck decoy appear very real, and the waterfowl would then fly into the zone within reach of his bow and arrow.

The tule duck decoy is still being made and used today by Native hunters, especially at the Stillwater Marsh in western Nevada.

—**Lois George-Kane (Fallon Paiute–Shoshone) and Vicki Kane (Paiute–Shoshone)**

Dat so la lee (Dabuda or Louisa Keyser, Washoe)
Degikup baskets

Dat so la lee (Dabuda or Louisa Keyser, Washoe, ca. 1835–1925), *degikup* baskets, ca. 1895. Nevada. Willow; 12 x 17 cm; 10 x 16 cm. Presented by Archer M. Huntington. Purchase. 9/167, 11/8261

Traditionally, Washoe utilitarian baskets, or *degikup*, were round, watertight baskets made to hold such things as acorn mush, pine nut soup, and a drink made from wild rhubarb. Degikup were also important in Washoe ceremonies. During the Washoe girls' dance, food was put in degikup and given to singers in thanks for their singing; another degikup was thrown out to the dancers as a gift. These baskets were relatively simple in form and design—as were Dat so la lee's first baskets. However, Dat so la lee transformed the shape and design of degikup, making truly aesthetic, sculptured baskets.

The basket with the hourglass design, somewhat unusual for a Dat so la lee basket because of its widely flared mouth, was made with willow foundation rods and thread. The hourglass design is woven with dyed bracken root, and the interior bear paw motif is woven with redbud. Willows were found along the main watercourses in Washoe country, especially along the Carson River where Dat so la lee lived. The red branches (western redbud) used for the bear paw motif were found in traditional Washoe lands along the hillsides in Woodfords Canyon and Lake Tahoe, and in Miwok country and other places along the western border of the California Sierras. The bracken fern root used for the hourglass had to be dug up and dyed in dark mud before being woven in the basket design.

The basket with the fern bracken root woven into vertical columns is more typical of Dat so la lee's work. It incorporates a more traditional design repeated around the basket.

—Jo Ann Nevers (Washoe)

Hupa *naʹwehch* (Jump Dance basket)

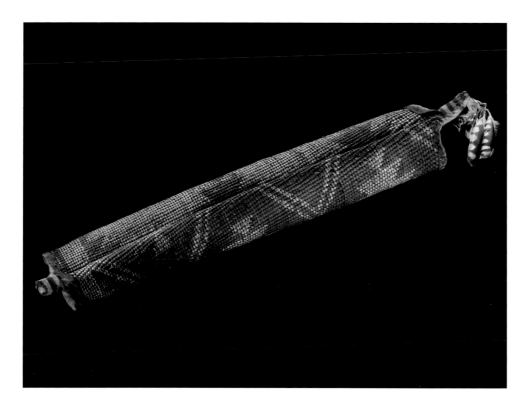

Hupa *naʹwehch* (Jump Dance basket), ca. 1880. California. Yew wood, maidenhair fern, bear grass, spruce root, hide, woodpecker feather, sinew, paint; 65 x 10 x 7 cm. Collected by Alexander Brizard. 2182

The Xay-chʹidilye (Jump Dance) is completed every two years by people from the Hoopa Tribe of northern California. The ceremony is conducted only in the fall and is one part of three ceremonies held in three sections to bring balance back into the world. The first ceremony is called the Xonsil-chʹidilye (White Deerskin Dance) and lasts for ten days. This dance is believed to remove evil or bad from the people preparing for the second ceremony, the Taːʹaltul (Boat Dance). The Boat Dance is conducted toward the last days of the White Deerskin Dance as a way for the people to gather prayer from the past, present, and future. After a ten-day resting period, the Hupa people begin the Jump Dance. The Jump Dance is a time for re-creation of the world or putting the world back into balance. This third ceremony is believed to bring the entire world back into order.

The *naʹwehch* (Jump Dance basket) serves a vital role in the completion of this ceremony. With each stitch of the basket the weaver breathes life into its creation and makes way for the basket to take its place as a living part of the community. An active participant in the ceremony, the basket is responsible for the important task of removing evil or bad from the world and putting good back into it. The dancer holds that basket in his right hand. Keeping time with the song and other dancers, he lifts the basket high in the air and then returns it to his stomach area. With a loud stomp of his foot, the evil or bad is stomped into the ground. The basket is then lifted again high in the air, releasing good back into the world. This action is considered a way of replacing evil or bad in the world with good.

—Bradley Marshall (Hoopa)

Ishi (Yahi)

Arrows

*Live like the white people from now on. I want to stay where I am.
I will grow old here, and die in this house.*

—ISHI, 1911, TURNING DOWN AN OFFER TO LEAVE
THE MUSEUM OF ANTHROPOLOGY AND RETURN ALONE
TO NORTHERN CALIFORNIA

Ishi (Yahi, b.?–1915), arrows,
1911–1916. California. Wood,
stone, feathers, sinew; 80 x 5 cm.
Collected by Saxton Pope from
Ishi. Gift of Dr. Charles Grayson.
23/2535, 23/2536

Ishi was a Yahi Indian, believed to be that last survivor of his people. Adhering to Yahi tradition, Ishi never uttered his own name, and so we do not know it. Ishi—"man" in his native language—was the name given to him by the anthropologist Alfred L. Kroeber. Beginning with his emergence from the "wilds" of California in 1911 and his entrance into the public imagination, until his death from tuberculosis five years later, Ishi lived at the Museum of Anthropology at the University of California, San Francisco. During the last short years of his life, he served as a flesh-and-blood memorial to America's past and confirmation, in the popular imagination, of the "vanishing Indian."

Ishi's arrows represent the hyper-real—objects of ethnographic interest reproduced within the walls of the museum. One of the stories we might read from them is that they are authentic objects made by the last of the Yahi Indians, something salvaged from Yahi material culture. A counternarrative might be that having Ishi make items he knew would be used only for exhibition introduced performance art to the ethnographic museum. Alternatively, it may be that Ishi expressed the power of his identity by producing something no one else could—or that with no way to resist being a sideshow, he made his position clear through the creation of implements of war and survival.

Ultimately, these objects can be understood as telling a story of control and compromise or strategic accommodation—or a combination of both. In opening a door for other Native peoples to work inside the museum, Ishi was not the last of his kind, but the first.

—John N. Low (Pokagon Potawatomi)

Elizabeth Hickox (Wiyot/Karuk)

Lidded baskets

Elizabeth Hickox (Wiyot/Karuk, 1875–1947) baskets, ca. 1920. California. Maidenhair fern, spruce root, hazel shoots, porcupine quill; 13 x 11 cm, 21 x 20 cm, 12.5 x 15 cm. Bequest of Mary H. Davis; gift of Mrs. Marcella Klein Wasson; purchased from Mrs. Thyra Maxwell. 22/1927, 25/3, 24/4103

I have a black and white basket half made now And I shall send it to you as soon as I've finished it. . . . I was over to the Indian dance but I dident get to see any pretty baskets over there so did not get any. I am as ever Your Friend. Mrs. Luther Hickox.

—ELIZABETH CONRAD HICKOX,
LETTER TO GRACE NICHOLSON, OCTOBER 3, 1911

Elizabeth Hickox is considered one of the finest basket-weavers of her time. She lived along the Salmon River in Northern California and wove with her daughter, Louisa. The creation of a basket was a yearlong process not limited to weaving. Each material would be gathered at a specific time, then prepared and sorted for later incorporation into a basket. Elizabeth wove only with materials with which she could produce the finest product. She favored the dark contrast of five-fingered fern (*Adiantum aleuticum*) with the porcupine quills dyed bright yellow with wolf lichen (*Letharia vulpina*). From 1911 to 1934, Elizabeth wove about five baskets a year.

Most of the baskets Elizabeth produced were not for functional use—cooking and ceremony—but as objects of art meant for display. These would be sold to dealers and local tourists to generate income. While utilitarian baskets carried only simple design elements and traditional forms, baskets marketed for sale possessed elaborate designs and innovative forms in order to attract buyers. Unlike many of the basket-weavers of the time who wove for local sale, Elizabeth sold her works to Grace Nicholson, a dealer in Pasadena who marketed the baskets to wealthy collectors across the country.

Elizabeth continued to weave gift baskets even after the market for baskets dwindled. This, along with the care she put into each piece, reflects the love she felt for her art.

—Erin Rentz (Karuk)

Xanˊs olaḱala ik awiˊnakola

"Our beautiful land"—Kwakˊwala

IN 1929, THE COLLECTOR and museum founder George Heye purchased in Paris a rare and distinctive Alaskan Native hat, a replica in split spruce root of the cloth hats worn in the 19th century by the English, French, and Russian sailors who served as crew on numerous voyages to the Alaskan coast (see page 234). We do not know the name of the Tlingit woman who made it, nor why she was moved to such a masterful endeavor. Was it commissioned by a sea captain to take home as a souvenir? Did she find a technical or artistic challenge in creating such an unusual example of the basket-maker's art, a departure from weaving the gathering and storage containers so essential for domestic life? Had she created it as an innovative piece of ceremonial regalia for a high-ranking *hit saati* (house owner) who later exchanged it for a gun or some lengths of blue and scarlet English woolen cloth? All we know today is that its presence in a Paris shop marks one of countless similar encounters in the past two centuries, a period during which prodigious numbers of objects from the North Pacific were acquired by sailors, missionaries, museum agents, government officials, and tourists. Together these objects represent one of the world's great art traditions—a tradition that has been compared to the classic arts of Egypt and medieval Europe.[1] It was created by what has been described as "a handful of sea hunters living in tiny communities"[2] along a coastal region that stretches some 1,200 miles, from Yakutat Bay in the Alaska panhandle to the Columbia River valley in Washington state.[3]

This rare example of Native artistry took its place as part of the Northwest Coast collection of what is now the National Museum of the American Indian, an assemblage of more than 25,000 objects that include tiny ivory carvings and giant totem poles, exquisitely carved feast spoons and serving dishes, ceremonial masks, fishing gear and spindle whorls, Chilkat dancing robes, boxes and baskets, and contemporary silk screen prints. Most of the pieces shown here date from the 19th century, a period that began during the early incursions of European-American explorers and closed with much of traditional life transformed by Western economies, churches, schools, and forms of governance. Throughout this turbulent hundred years, people managed to preserve traditional values and to express them in new ways, often with new materials.

What is commonly referred to as the Northwest Coast is a land of spectacular beauty, with wooded islands and deep, narrow inlets; snow-capped mountains marked by glaciers; dense forests of cedar and spruce; rivers running to the sea; and an abundance of animal life, particularly salmon and other fish. The inhabitants are a mosaic of tribes—the Tlingit of the Alaska panhandle; the Tsimshian, Nisgaˊa, and Gitxsan around the Nass and Skeena rivers; the Haida of the Queen Charlotte Islands; the Haisla, Heiltsuk (Bella Bella), and Nuxalk (Bella Coola) of the central British Columbian coast. To the south are the Kwakwaka̲ˊwakw, on Vancouver Island and the adjoining mainland, and the two whale-hunting tribes—the Nuu-chah-nulth on the west coast of Vancouver Island and the Makah on the Olympic Peninsula of western Washington. Nearby are the numerous Salish peoples of the coast and interior. These nations speak many languages but are connected through trade, intermarriage, and history, and by common ways of life in fishing and wood-carving technologies, economy, social organization, art, and ceremony.

Da.axiigang (Charles Edenshaw, Haida, 1839–1920), Bear Mother carving, ca. 1900. Queen Charlotte Islands, British Columbia. Argillite; 6 x 7 x 8 cm. Purchase. 19/6253

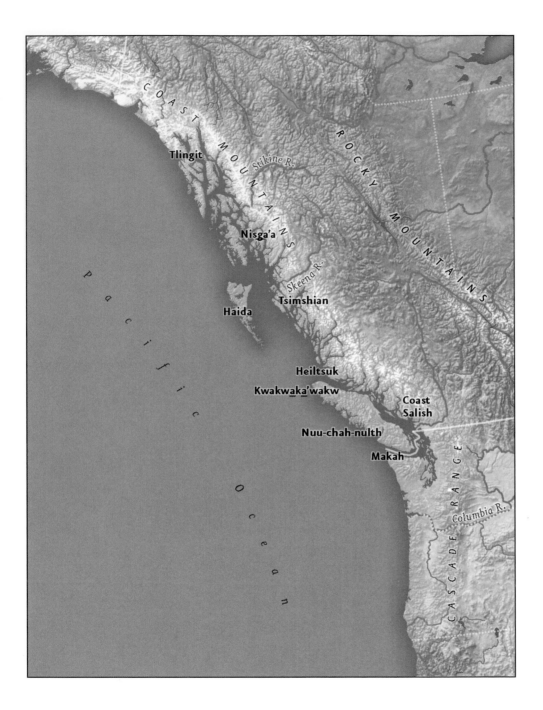

Archaeological and linguistic evidence indicates that these ways of life are both very old and widely connected to a world beyond the immediate region. Archaeological sites in coastal British Columbia reveal exotic goods brought from distant places, such as amber from Alaska, dentalium shell from Vancouver Island, and copper from interior Alaska. One archaeological site contained rods of copper sheathed with cedar bark, which may be forerunners of the rod armor observed by 18th-century visitors—and which, claim some scholars, is related to the Chinese and Japanese armor in use since the Bronze Age.[4]

There are also hints from oral histories of widely ranging connections between local communities and distant, sometimes very distant, realms. Stories about Raven, the Creator–Trickster who brought light to the world, are told around campfires not only throughout the Northwest Coast and Alaska, but as far west as Siberia and as far east as Canada's Mackenzie River.[5]

The clans and family groups who once lived in enormous wooden houses in villages along the shore trace their ancestry to the remote past and their origins to encounters between an ancestor and a supernatural being. Clans are distinguished by crests—symbolic representations of ancestral figures such as Raven, Bear, Eagle, or Killer Whale. The richest and most dramatic arts are created as accoutrements of social and ceremonial life. Major ceremonies highlighted by oratory, dance performance, telling of ancestral histories, and distribution of gifts to invited guests mark memorials for the dead, marriages, secret society initiations, and other significant events. These complex events are often lumped together as "potlatches," a word coined in English from a Chinook term meaning "to give away." These large public gatherings allowed for the display of great wealth through feasting, lavish gifts, and the wearing of regalia that incorporated costly materials acquired through trade routes in use long before white men came.

Because resources, although locally abundant, vary greatly from one place to another, trade and competition for scarce and specialized commodities existed from ancient times. European and Yankee voyagers to the Northwest Coast in the 18th century observed Native people paddling hundreds of miles to trade, raid for and capture slaves, and make war on traditional enemies. The enormous dugout canoes laden with goods, which traveled the coast through narrow channels and open seas, were made by the Haida from the giant red cedars of Haida Gwaii (the Queen Charlotte Islands). Traded all along the coast, the canoes were painted with clan designs or otherwise marked by local artists with insignia of the owner. A Tlingit purchaser, for example, might add a canoe prow figure carved in the form of a shaman who would guide the way and warn of the approach of enemy combatants.

Each tribe had resources that could be exchanged for other commodities. The Haida had opercula shell, highly valued for inlay decoration on feast dishes and

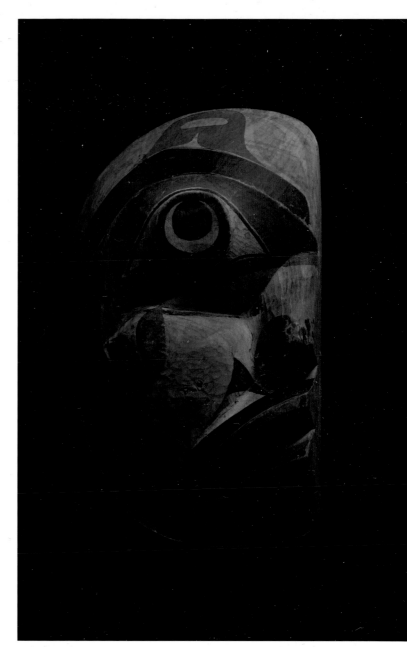

Heiltsuk mask, ca. 1880. Vancouver Island, British Columbia. Wood, paint; 20 x 10 x 29 cm. D. F. Tozier Collection. 6/8833

bowls. The Tlingit provided goods acquired from their Athapaskan trading partners in the interior—copper from the Copper River; moose, caribou, and marmot skins; and porcupine quillwork. They also traded spruce root baskets as well as Chilkat blankets. These chiefly robes, which originated with the Tsimshian, were made from mountain sheep wool and cedar bark, and were prized as far south as Kwakwaka'wakw country.

Coast Salish robe, ca. 1860. Yale, British Columbia. Mountain goat and sheep wool; 117 x 114 cm. Presented by Harmon W. Hendricks. 14/4864

Another inland resource was mountain sheep horn for making large serving ladles and small feast bowls.

The Tsimshian also made large canoes as well as finely carved Raven rattles and headdresses, and processed red ochre for use in painting. The Nuxalk, who were known for their ability to hunt mountain goats, provided goat tallow, dried meat, and the goat horn to make small, exquisitely carved feast spoons. The Nuu-chah-nulth offered sharks' teeth and the dentalium shells everywhere prized as ornaments; dentalium was also highly valued among the Yurok of northern California, who used the shells as money. The Kwakwaka'wakw had yellow cedar bark, useful in making ropes and clothing, while the Coast Salish offered blankets woven of mountain goat and sheep wool, and sometimes dog hair, as well as dressed elk hides acquired at the Dalles, the great aboriginal

trading center on the Columbia River.[6] It was there that the Salish supplied their neighbors in the Plateau with the much-desired dentalium shells, and it was from there that the shells were traded eastward from tribe to tribe, some ultimately traveling as far east as the Great Lakes.

The greatest Native trading event along the northern Northwest Coast took place at the mouth of the Nass River during the early spring run of the oolichan, or candlefish, so called because its rich quantity of oil allowed it to burn like a candle. Each year Tlingit, Haida, Gitxsan, Nisga'a, Tsimshian, and others converged, carrying goods to trade for the rich and highly desired oolichan oil, which is still used today as a special feast food. Oolichan oil was also carried along land routes that became known as grease trails. One grease trail, on Vancouver Island, marked trade between the

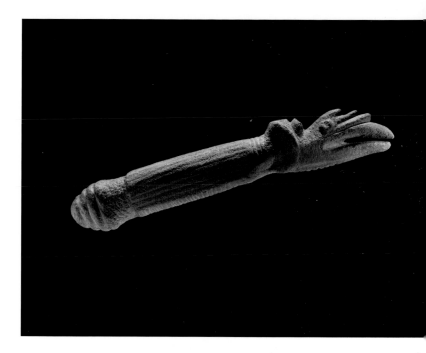

Nuu-chah-nulth and the Kwakwaka´wakw; others led
across the mountains into the interior.

Trade routes on the mainland from the coast eastward to the interior were often claimed by specific
family groups. One Sitka Tlingit clan owned the right
to trade for copper with the Athapaskan groups on the
Copper River and became rich and powerful through
that monopoly. Similarly, the Taku Tlingit claimed
the Taku River, and the Chilkat Tlingit dominated
the trails to the interior along the Chilkat River. The
Wrangell clans at the mouth of the Stikine River held
all trading rights with the Tahltans at the Stikine's
headwaters far inland. Coastal Russian traders had to
arrange with the Wrangell Tlingit leaders, a succes-
sion of chiefs named Shakes, to carry tobacco, brick
tea, flour, kettles, and firearms up the Stikine River
to trade with the Tahltan. The Tlingit exchanged the
goods for furs, carried the furs back down the river,
and sold them to the Russians at a handsome markup.
Such rights were jealously guarded and vigorously
defended. Yankee traders who tried to use the trails
were also turned back and had to negotiate trade with
the interior people through Tlingit middlemen.

Nor were the Tlingit the only masters of monopoly.
The Hudson's Bay Company, which had been expanding westward across Canada building forts as trading
posts, encountered similar opposition from the Native
defenders of trading rights. At Fort Simpson in British
Columbia the powerful Tsimshian chief Ligeex held all
rights to trade with the Gitxsan of the upper Skeena
River. The Hudson's Bay Company was forced to pay
Ligeex for the privilege of trading with the Gitxsan.
Payment was not always a solution. When, in 1854, the
company built the trading post of Fort Selkirk on the

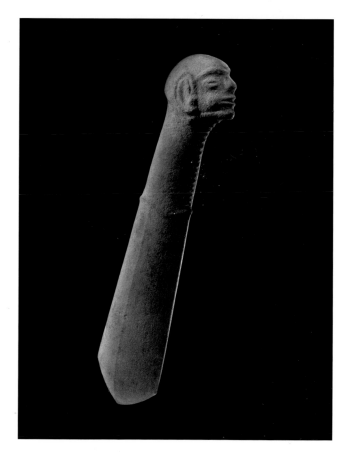

Yukon River two hundred miles inland from the coast, the Chilkat sent a war party to destroy it. It was forty years before the company ventured to rebuild there.

Many clan origin stories speak of epic journeys over great distances, sometimes crossing glaciers by sled or on foot. One Tlingit odyssey tells of young men who trekked across the St. Elias mountain range to the Copper River and brought back the first ivory and metal to fashion a fearsome war knife, the kind of weapon valued by warriors until the early 19th century.[7] The people of a Yakutat Tlingit lineage that claims descent from Athapaskans from the interior still wear dance shirts in Athapaskan style, made of ermine fur or caribou skin decorated with porcupine quills, materials traditionally acquired from Athapaskan trading partners.

The first waves of globalization broke on the coastal shores in the 18th century—the Russians in 1741, the Spanish in 1774, the English in 1778, the French in 1786, and eventually the Yankee sea captains who were called "Boston Men." When the early arrivals discovered that the dark, thick fur of the sea otter could be sold in China for incredibly high prices, a marine-based "gold rush" brought great and sudden riches to Native clan leaders who were able to control the trading—Maquinna on Vancouver Island, Ligeex on the lower Skeena, Shakes at the Stikine, Cuneah of Haida Gwaii, Tatoosh of the Makah, Kotlean of the Sitka Tlingits, and others who are named in

Yakutat Tlingit wearing ceremonial clothing, photographed at Sitka Potlatch, 1904, Sitka, Alaska.

ships' logs. From roughly 1792 to 1812, during the boom period of the sea otter fur market (otter pelts were in fact called "soft gold"), hundreds of ships visited the coast bringing metal, guns and ammunition, tobacco and rum, woolen blankets, copper sheets, knives and axes—new goods to exchange for furs. The Native people traded with great skill and enthusiasm, playing one trader against another and forcing higher and higher prices as sea otters became scarcer.

Organized as the Russian–American Company, the Russians tried to plant a permanent foothold in Alaska. Having established colonies in Kodiak and Unalaska, they moved south in the 1790s, building forts at Yakutat Bay and Archangel, near present-day Sitka. They brought with them priests of the Russian Orthodox Church whose mission was to baptize Tlingit leaders and convert the populace to Christianity. Tensions persisted, however. Led by Kotlean, warriors in sixty canoes burned the fort at Archangel in 1802. The Russians rebuilt at a new location—the modern city of Sitka, originally called New Archangel—and in 1804 a Russian warship, assisted by other vessels, pounded the Native people into submission. Perhaps in retaliation, the outpost at Yakutat was destroyed in 1805 and never rebuilt. The Russian presence in Alaska was established, centered in Sitka; St. Michael's Cathedral was consecrated in 1848 and, having been once destroyed and rebuilt, still exists today.[8]

Yakutat Tlingit pipe, ca. 1820–1850. Alaska. Wood, brass; 25 x 9.5 x 6.5 cm. Collected by Lieutenant George Thornton Emmons. 9207

Throughout the 19th century and later, individuals with entrepreneurial and political skills and talented artists managed to ride the rough waves of foreign intrusion and emerge with success. By the 1820s the sea otter had been overhunted and was close to extinction, but furs were still available inland—marten, fox, lynx, and especially beaver, which had become fashionable for hats in the European markets. The coastal peoples continued inland trade with their Athapaskan neighbors—the Ahtna, Sekani, Chilcotin, and Tahltan, among others—and throughout the 19th century the Hudson's Bay Company increased its presence. After 1867, the year the United States purchased Alaska, the Russian trading posts were taken over by the Alaska Commercial Company.

The Haida, with no access to mainland furs, turned to other money-making pursuits. Some Haida men crewed on Yankee ships and traveled to Hawaiʻi and other Pacific ports in the China trade. The Haida also learned to grow potatoes and began using their giant canoes to carry them to markets where they were much in demand. Sitka, for example, was perpetually short of supplies and welcomed the goods. In addition, by the 1820s Haida carvers had begun to create a unique form of souvenir art—carvings from the black shale known as argillite that originates in the Queen Charlotte Islands. Carvings of pipes, platters, animal figures, and flutes were popular with the sailors who wintered over at Masset and Skidegate.[9] The earliest pipes borrowed freely from scrimshaw designs and the carved motifs on ships. Later on, miniature carvings of totem poles became popular; small, easily transported, and exotic, they made ideal souvenirs.

One of the most successful and renowned of the Haida carvers was Charles Edenshaw (1839–1920), who excelled not only in stone-carving, but also in wood-carving and the making of silver bracelets. He became one of the first Native artists whose name was known to the outside world. He and his wife, Isabella (1858–1920), who was a gifted basket-weaver, traveled to towns from Juneau to Victoria in the summers, selling his carvings and her baskets while Isabella also worked in the canneries. In addition to his carving

Haida flute, ca. 1850. Queen Charlotte Islands, British Columbia. Argillite, silver inlay; 16.3 x 1 cm. Collected by Lady Franklin. 2/9790

skills, Edenshaw was a talented painter and created the designs on some thirty-one finely woven spruce root hats made by Isabella. Each hat was finished with a four-point red and black star painted on the crown, usually considered to be his signature (see page 237).

During the 1880s a lively tourist market developed, with steamship routes along the inland waterway from Seattle to Glacier Bay marked by stops at numerous ports for souvenir shopping. Silver bracelets made from hammered coins were hawked on the streets of Juneau and Sitka, as were goat horn and wooden spoons, beadwork, and miniature carvings. One successful Sitka entrepreneur, Princess Thom (Qadjmt), acquired Tlingit baskets from her Yakutat relatives and brought them south in her own canoe to sell to the tourists in Sitka, becoming wealthy in the process. Baskets were highly favored by collectors, and Nuu-chah-nulth and Makah basket-weavers became known for small, exquisite

trinket baskets, many of them adorned with motifs of hunters in pursuit of whales.

By the late 19th century, the original Northwest Coast peoples had become inundated with newcomers—Chinese workers come to man the newly established salmon canneries, missionaries intent on wiping out pagan (non-Christian) ways of life, gold miners with hopes of finding a fortune, farmers and sheep ranchers in lower British Columbia, as well as the aforementioned tourists. Each group left its mark. Some unwittingly brought diseases; smallpox and measles devastated whole communities. Missionaries such as Thomas Crosby, William Duncan, and Sheldon Jackson labored to bring Native people to Christianity, in one case going so far as to move an entire community to a new location built along Anglo lines.

There were many pressures to change Native cultures into Western models. In 1884 the Canadian government outlawed the potlatch as a wasteful and profligate practice. The Kwakwaka'wakw responded by continuing to practice their ceremonies in remote places far from the interference of government and church authorities. As late as 1921, Royal Canadian Mounted Police interrupted a huge potlatch at Village Island in British Columbia, arrested the participants, and forced them to surrender their ceremonial masks and other regalia. Ironically, the wealth given away at what became known as Dan Cranmer's potlatch included not only traditional goods such as blankets, bracelets, and twenty-four canoes, but pool tables, sewing machines, gramophones, and guitars, the purchase of which probably served as a stimulus to the local Canadian economy.

Xi´xa´niyus (Bob Harris) in Hama̓tsa dress, 1904. Louisiana Purchase Exposition, St. Louis Fair.

Native people not only produced exotic objects for an outside market, but in some cases offered themselves as entertainment for a profit. Perhaps one of the most influential of these enterprises was a group of Nuxalk men who, in 1885 and '86, toured cities in Germany as a dance troupe. They caught the attention of a young anthropologist named Franz Boas, newly returned to Berlin from a year of research among the central Inuit, and so captivated him that he devoted the rest of his life and his long academic career to the Northwest Coast.

The world's fairs and expositions of the late 19th and early 20th centuries offered other opportunities for Northwest Coast people to interact with the wider world. Both the Chicago World's Fair of 1893 and the St. Louis Universal Exposition of 1904 featured groups of Kwakwaka̱´wakw men and women, and, in Chicago, several Nuu-chah-nulth as well. These arts entrepreneurs

Xiʹxaʹniyus (Bob Harris, Kwakwa̲kaʹwakw)
K̲umuk̲wa̲mł (Chief of the undersea mask)

This mask is carved from western red cedar and is painted in green, red, and black natural pigment paints and two shades of blue made from Reckitt's laundry whitener. The mask represents K̲umugweʹ (Wealthy), the Chief of the undersea kingdom. The eyes are inlayed with round blue trade beads that created a sparkling reflection from the firelight as the dancer slowly moved around the fire on the dance floor. The eyebrows are thick and represent those of a male, supporting the belief that this is K̲umugweʹ and not his wife. Between the eyebrows there is an overhanging cluster of red frown lines, a signature of the artist; the symbolism of this feature is unknown.

The U-shaped designs on much of the face represent scaling like that of fish or supernatural beings from the sea. Two stylized salmon-trout heads are further representation of the fishlike qualities K̲umugweʹ possesses. These ovoid appendages are part of the composition of some character that was originally mounted on top of the head. A large hole drilled through the top of the mask would have allowed the lost prop to twist from side to side or spin around. There is a smaller hole where a string was threaded through to manipulate the object on top. The prop could have been one of many creatures associated with K̲umugweʹ—a starfish, various fishes or sea mammals, sea birds such as seagulls, or diving birds like loons, messengers between the upper world and the undersea. Scales or gills around the outside rim of the mask are made from a different type of wood. Their artwork does not match the quality of the facial design, and the blue and red shades do not match. This mask has been repaired and made more elaborate than it originally was, most likely by another artist not familiar with the style of the master carver who created it.

There appears to have been a bundle of hair nailed on top of the mask behind the left trout head. The presence of hair suggests that this is a mask for the Dłuwala̲xa (Returned from Heaven Ceremony), now called Tła̕sa̲la (Peace Dances) by the Kwakwa̲kaʹwakw. These dances are considered less sacred than the Tseka̲ (Sacred Red Cedar Bark Ceremonies), which are only performed in the winter season.

All ceremonial Kwakwa̲kaʹwakw masks depict characters from family histories or supernatural encounters. All details on masks have a story and are intentional. Another name for K̲umugweʹ is Tła̲kwagila (Copper-Maker), as he is the greatest source of the most prized cultural wealth, copper. His house is made of copper, and his wealth is often sought after by legendary heroes in hope of gaining cultural riches. Various sea monsters guard his home under the ocean, and the doorway of his supernatural house is a mouth of one of these fabulous creatures that is constantly opening and snapping shut. In many stories, certain ancestors were able to safely encounter K̲umugweʹ and enter his house. After befriending the supernatural being, some young men were permitted to marry one of his daughters and receive his riches as dowry. The killer whales are the warriors of K̲umugweʹ, and the sea lions are his messengers; seals are his pets and are considered his dogs. All the fishes and supernatural beings from the sea reside in his house and belong to him.

This mask is made by the famous Da̕naxda̕xw (New Vancouver Tribe) carver Bob Harris. Bob's everyday or summer name was Xiʹxaʹniyus (Always Giving Away All His Blankets). He was an initiated Hama̕tsa (Cannibal Dancer), and his winter dance or secret society name was Baxwbakwalanukw (Man-Eater). He was a Hereditary Chief belonging to the K̲amk̲amta̲lał (Song Makers Clan) of the Aʹwa̕etłala (Knight Inlet Tribe), amalgamated with the Da̕naxda̕xw in recent times and now considered one tribe. Today, Xiʹxaʹniyus Bob Harris is considered among the Kwakwa̲kaʹwakw to be one of the greatest master carvers of all time.

—**William Wasden Jr. (Hiłamas, Kwakwa̲kaʹwakw)**

K̲umuk̲wa̲mł (Chief of the undersea mask), ca. 1900. Vancouver Island, British Columbia, Canada. Wood, paint; 35.5 x 40.5 cm. Purchase. 14/9624

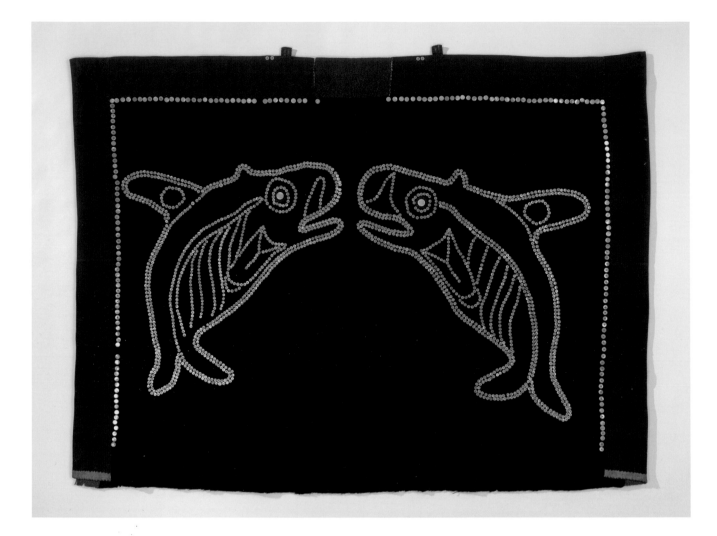

performed dances and also made carvings and weavings for a monthly salary. One of the St. Louis performers, the artist Bob Harris, was a participant in one of the most sensational and horrifying events of the fair—the supposed killing and eating of a so-called Pygmy man (actually a dummy made of cooked mutton). The power and theatricality of Kwakwaka'wakw ceremonies lost nothing in their relocation to foreign soil and the presence of a foreign audience.

Throughout the 19th century and beyond, the original people of the Pacific Northwest Coast have displayed a remarkable ability to confront devastating outside forces—disease, foreign invasions, cultural pressures, economic hardships—and not only to adapt but to prevail, showing creativity and pragmatism in that adaptation. On the just a single level, that of

material culture, there are numerous examples of such "creative encounter" here. One is a type of ceremonial blanket created in the 19th century entirely from foreign wares—dark blue broadcloth imported from the Stroud Valley in England; red flannel from textile mills in Manchester and Massachusetts; and pearl buttons, some made in China and the rest from American and European sources. From this sewing chest full of imported goods was born the glorious garment known as the button blanket, proudly displaying the family crest of the owner. The earliest-known button blankets appear in a drawing by a Russian artist in 1844 of a Tlingit funeral in Sitka. Button blankets are still made and worn today, and at large tribal gatherings hundreds of people of all ages come together to proclaim pride in their heritage and identity.

Facing: Button blanket associated with Chief George Kyan (Tlingit, 1857–1955), ca. 1920–1930. Ketchikan, Alaska. Wool, mother of pearl and abalone shell buttons, glass buttons; 133 x 175 cm. Exchange with George Terasaki. 23/6180

Tlingit pipe, ca. 1820–1860. Lituya Bay, Alaska. Wood, copper, abalone shell; 25 x 7.5 x 13 cm. Collected by Lieutenant George Thornton Emmons. 9205

Today, two centuries removed from the encounters that are remembered in songs still sung, epic tales still told, and journals written by voyagers, explorers, and traders, the people of this region still cherish and carry on their ancient traditions. The forms in which they are expressed have expanded to include tribal museums and cultural centers, teaching programs to salvage endangered languages, and new forms of traditional arts. A present-day example of creativity and pragmatism can be found in the work of Haida artist Robert Davidson, great-grandson of Charles Edenshaw. When Davidson received a commission in the 1980s to carve three totem poles for the sculpture garden at Pepsico World Headquarters in Purchase, New York, he was exhorted to "make this the best work you've ever done." Davidson's tongue-in-cheek working title for his creation was *The Pepsi Challenge*, a reference to a highly successful advertising campaign of the time. Like his ancestors, Davidson has the wit to best non-Native traders at their own game.

But we began this chapter with an object that embodies the rich cultural history recorded in the museum's Northwest Coast collections. I'd like to end there, as well, with a pipe made from European materials recycled into a new purpose. During the early years of the fur trade, leaf tobacco became available along the Pacific Northwest Coast for the first time, a replacement for a cultivated Native chewing tobacco.

Smoking became both a ceremonial and a recreational pastime, and carved wooden pipe bowls decorated with crest designs and events from Native history were produced in great numbers. Many pipes were carved of walnut salvaged from the butts of discarded muskets, with a section of brass or iron musket barrel inserted into the carved bowl to hold the tobacco.

This pipe, carved by a Tlingit artist some time in the early 19th century, depicts Lituya Bay in southeastern Alaska. According to Tlingit legend, the bay was guarded by a froglike sea monster and his slave, a bear, who periodically shook the surface of the water and caused great waves to drown unwary travelers. The two brass-covered ridges on the pipe are waves that have engulfed a canoe and its occupants.

When Lieutenant G. T. Emmons acquired the pipe in 1888, he was told that a century earlier the people of Lituya Bay had seen two boatloads of white men drowned in the waves. This incident from Tlingit oral history is also recorded in the journals of the French explorer Jean Francois de Galaup (1741–ca. 1788), comte de La Perouse, who wrote that in 1786, while exploring the bay, two of his boats capsized in enormous tidal waves with great loss of life. These corroborating accounts provide insight into the layers of meaning embedded in objects that may be seen by outsiders merely as beautiful works of art.

—Mary Jane Lenz

Tlingit basketry hat

Tlingit basketry hat, ca. 1820.
Alaska. Spruce root, jointed grass;
12 x 40 cm. Purchase. 16/5272

A sailor's hat, woven of spruce root and grass—using what you have to remember what you saw. . . .

When explorers came upon the coast of Alaska, their uniforms must have looked strange to the Tlingit living along the glaciers and fjords. The need to trade for fresh water and supplies would have brought foreigners and locals together as the anchor hit bottom. Long-distance mariners themselves, the Tlingit understood well the needs of travelers. As more *glei kwaan* (people from across the water) arrived, so did the trade wool to make hats. A window of time closed, and this lovely sailor's hat became a "collector's item," rather than a prestigious clan object. Similar stories play out over and over on the shelves of museums around the world.

The weaver's use of negative spaces in the design on the band, and the abundance of roots needed to weave a piece this large, lead me to speculate that she lived near Yakutat, Alaska. Only in Yakutat and Sitka did the Tlingit turn the tide of invasion. In 1802 the Tlingit drove the Russians from Sitka, only to lose it again in 1804. In Yakutat the Tlingit homeland was secured after a battle in 1805; the Russians never did rebuild the settlement there.

Sailor hats made of wool felt are worn today in Tlingit dance regalia. Sitka's dancers wear them when they perform a group of songs called the Aleut Series, recognizing not only the Russians, but also the unfortunate Aleutics who accompanied them in hunting and battle as slaves. The historic voices are silent now, except for one very outspoken Tlingit hat.

—Ch´ais-koowu-tla´a T´ak dein taan, Ta´ax̱´ hit
(Teri Rofkar, Tlingit Raven Clan, Snail House)

Knife and sheath associated with Chief Shakes VI (Tlingit)

Knife and sheath associated with Chief Shakes VI (Tlingit b.?–1916), ca. 1840–1890. Etolin Island, Alaska. Iron, brass, ivory, abalone, caribou hide, wool cloth, cotton cloth, glass beads, dentalium shell; 75 x 12 cm (sheath), 46 x 5 cm (knife). The Judge Nathan Bijur Collection. 23/5601

This knife and sheath belonged to Chief Shakes VI. His names were Sheiyksh, Ltusháax̱´w, and Gúshtlein. His wife was from the Ḵaach.ádi clan. The father of Chief Shakes was a man named Sk´aawulyeil. His uncle was Chief Shakes V (X´adaneik), whose mother was Aanshaa-wasnook, sister of Chief Shakes IV, whose other names were Xwaakeil and Keishíshk´. Before Chief Shakes VI died in 1916, he was ordered to will his property to his widow and not his maternal nephew, contrary to Tlingit inheritance laws. Afterward, all of his property wound up outside his clan.

A dagger is called gwálaa, literally "it strikes" or "it hits." Referred to as x´aan.át, it is something used in battle and kept close at hand. The figure of the man in the Raven's beak, done in ivory and inlaid with abalone shell, is classic Tlingit formline design. This and the brass overlay on the hilt covered with leather show the skill of the dagger's creator. The dagger dates from the 19th century. The sheath's beadwork is classic Taal taan (Tahltan) in style. Much beadwork of this style has been found among the Shx´at ḵwaan (Stikine people) of Wrangell. The beaded sheath and the valuable táx´xee (dentalium shell), obtained in trade as well, complement the craftsmanship of the dagger and the history of the Tlingit.

—Harold Jacobs (Ghooch Shaayí, Hít Tlein [Big House] of the T´aakhu khwaan)

Da.axiigang (Charles Edenshaw, Haida)
Bear Mother carving

My father started carving one winter when he was sick. When he was fourteen he was sick all winter long. He was in bed, but he got some argillite and started carving a totem pole. After that he carved his first bracelet, out of silver-dollar pieces melted together.

—FLORENCE EDENSHAW DAVIDSON, CHARLES AND ISABELLA'S DAUGHTER, 1982

Da.axiigang (Charles Edenshaw, Haida, 1839–1920), Bear Mother carving, ca. 1900. Queen Charlotte Islands, British Columbia. Argillite; 6 x 7 x 8 cm. Purchase. 19/6253

This unique freestanding sculpture carved by Charles Edenshaw illustrates one of his favorite stories—the Bear Mother and her two cubs. Its uniqueness is that there are only a few carvings done in red argillite, and the two cubs are shown as one in the human state and the other in the animal state. Most illustrations of this myth show both cubs in the animal state. Charles had the ability to capture an expression of caring in the face of the Bear Mother that has a haunting feeling. He pushed the boundaries of Haida art in many of his creations, and this carving is one in which he truly succeeds in capturing a moment in the story.

—Robert Davidson (Haida)

Kwii.aang and Da.axiigang

(Isabella and Charles Edenshaw, Haida)

Spruce-root hat

*My mother used to weave
baskets and hats all winter
long. When she was going
to start her weaving she
soaked the roots overnight,
so they'd be easy to work.
She'd get up early in the
morning and cook and,
after everyone was finished
eating, she'd go to work
splitting the roots again
and weaving them into a
hat or basket. She worked
all day long, day after day.
. . . It was just like having
a business. When she fin-
ished a hat she put it in a
dark place and then my dad
would paint a design on it.*

—FLORENCE EDENSHAW
DAVIDSON, 1982

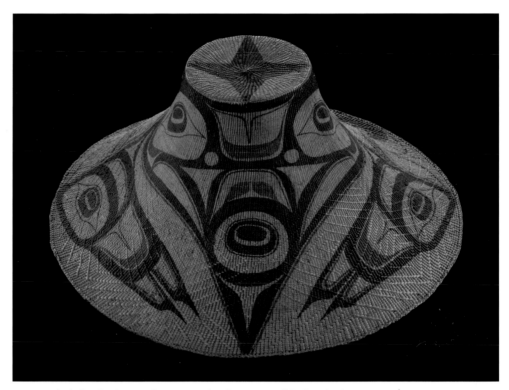

Kwii.aang (Isabella Edenshaw, Haida, 1858–1926) and Da.axiigang (Charles Edenshaw,
Haida, 1839–1920), spruce-root hat, ca. 1900. Queen Charlotte Islands, British
Columbia. Cedar bark, spruce root, paint; 21 x 43 cm. E. M. Brodhurst Collection.
19/6110

This spruce root hat woven by Isabella Edenshaw demonstrates great knowledge and craftsmanship that was developed over the centuries. There are multiple layers of creativity hap-
pening here: first, to gather the roots, which can be found only in sandy areas; second, the
labor-intensive preparation of the roots; third, creating the shape of the hat; and fourth, the
pattern created within the weaving.

The beautiful Raven painting done by Isabella's husband, Charles, adds dimension to the
shape. It is always exciting to examine her subtle creativity woven into her hats, baskets,
and mats. Her mastery and attention to detail are absolutely flawless and inspiring to the
viewer.

—Robert Davidson (Haida)

Hiłamas (Willie Seaweed or Smoky Top, ´Nak´waxda´xw Kwakw<u>a</u>ka´wakw, 1873–1967), *gikiwe´* (chief's headdress), ca. 1949.
Vancouver Island, British Columbia. Cedar wood, paint, velveteen; 50 x 22 cm. Purchased from Wilhelm Helmer. 23/8252

Hiłamas (Willie Seaweed, Kwakwaka´wakw)

gikiwe´ (chief's headdress)

Willie Seaweed, Smoky Top, was born about 1873 and was 94 years old when he passed away. He came from Blunden Harbour, a very isolated Kwakwaka´wakw village. This allowed his tribe to be very cultural and traditional.

As well as being a high-ranking chief, he was unquestionably one of the best Kwakwaka´wakw carvers ever. Chief Seaweed gave life to his masks by making them fit so beautifully to the faces of people who wore and danced them. For example, the distance between each eye would be measured to match the dancer's face. He created perfect circles with a compass and drew straight lines with a straightedge.[1] He would sand down a finished form and paint it white, then add other colors like black and red to create a clean and exact product. His legacy is still seen everywhere on totem poles, masks, and other paraphernalia. It is fitting then that one of his masterpieces is this chief's headdress he made for himself of a killer whale and two ravens.

I did not know Chief Smoky Top well, for he was already sixty-six years old when I was born. But I danced one of the masks in the Atlakim forest kingdom legend. This is one of the most striking sets of dance masks ever created, carved by Willie Seaweed. The fit was perfect, the vision clear, the style profound. It was inspirational. I would for the brief moment become the figure I represented, to transcend to another consciousness, to play out in some small way the meaning, purpose, intent, and value of Kwakwaka´wakw cosmology and worldview.

—**Chief Robert Joseph** (Kwakwaka´wakw)

The period spanning Willie Seaweed's lifetime brought innumerable changes to the Kwakwaka´wakw world. By the late 1870s, various settlers in British Columbia—including missionaries, Indian agents, teachers, and cannery owners—joined forces to convince Canada that the potlatch, with its dramatic dances and lavish distribution of wealth, was an impediment to the conversion and assimilation of the province's First Nations. In 1884, the revised Indian Act officially prohibited the ceremony and its accompanying festivities. By the mid-1920s, the potlatch had been forced underground.[2]

Yet some Kwakwaka´wakw chiefs—including Willie Seaweed—kept their traditions alive, in part by modifying artistic and ceremonial practice in order to evade the letter of the law. They kept carving masks and other regalia. By selling a good number of carvings on the curio market or to museums, families may have displaced attention from the fact that they were also passing hereditary rights to the next generation via the objects that make those rights manifest. They also kept dancing, but they adapted the hereditary prerogatives to public demonstrations of "cultural heritage" that were allowed—even encouraged—by the authorities. In 1951, the potlatch prohibition was dropped, and Kwakwaka´wakw families slowly brought the potlatch back into the light of day, much to the astonishment of anthropologists and government officials. Around the same time, large new museum exhibitions and catalogues in British Columbia began featuring Seaweed's distinctive artwork, which quickly gained a prominent reputation in the emerging Northwest Coast art world and helped redefine the canon of Kwakwaka´wakw art in the 20th century.

Through his leadership as a hereditary chief, his flexibility in the face of colonial restriction, and his singular vision and creativity as an artist, Willie Seaweed was central to the survival of Kwakwaka´wakw culture. Like the two ravens on his headdress, he looked back to the Kwakwaka´wakw past and at the same time forward to an intercultural future in British Columbia. His efforts helped establish some of the conditions for 21st-century cultural and political sovereignty movements in Canada.

—**Aaron Glass**

Tuktuyaaqtuuq

"Where the Caribou cross"—Inuvialuktun

In the very earliest time,
when both people and animals lived on earth,
a person could become an animal if he wanted to
and an animal could become a human being.
Sometimes they were people
and sometimes animals
and there was no difference.
All spoke the same language.
That was the time when words were like magic.
The human mind had mysterious powers.
A word spoken by chance
might have strange consequences.
It would suddenly come alive
and what people wanted to happen could happen—
all you had to do was say it.
Nobody could explain this:
That's the way it was.

—Nalungiaq (Netsilingmiut Inuit)

From the ice-bordered fjords of Greenland, across the stormy North Atlantic waters to Labrador, and all across the Canadian Arctic and the Canadian Shield to the Rocky Mountains and beyond to Alaska and the arch of the Aleutian Islands, the New World's northern tier is a place of extraordinary diversity, beauty, and mystery. For many thousands of years it lay buried beneath a blanket of glacial ice that held time in abeyance. Ironically, while the Arctic and Subarctic landscapes of North America are among the youngest on the planet, having evolved in the lee of the ice that ended around 7,000 years ago, the rocks that are its bones are among the oldest in the world. Around 20,000 years ago the ice began its retreat, exposing

new ice-sculpted lands and the maze of waterways that would become one of its defining features. Intrepid populations of ancestral Native Americans and Inuit came in the wake of the ice, following the bounty of birds and animals adapted to the rigors of the new lands. Only after the disappearance of the continental ice sheets could the vast expanse of boreal forest and arctic tundra evolve.

While the northern forests and tundra might seem intimidating and ominously barren, ancestral Indian, Aleut, and Inuit people quickly perfected a wide array of social and technological strategies that adapted to the seasonal abundance of migratory waterfowl, fish returning to the rivers to spawn, caribou herds, and the wealth of marine mammals and other species that thrived in the cold ocean waters bordering both sides of the continent. The northern lands are a place of extremes in darkness and light, temperatures, resource abundance alternating with scarcity. The many indigenous peoples who live in the frozen north—Greenlanders, Inuits, Iñupiat, Yupiit, Aleuts, and their Athapaskan and Algonkian Indian neighbors—are among the last practitioners of humanity's common hunting and gathering heritage. These cultures share an extraordinary legacy predicated on an intimacy with the land and animals that harkens back to social relationships at the very heart of what it means to be a human being. Today across the North, northern Native American, Inuit, and Aleut peoples recognize the gifts of the ancestors—language, oral history, customary law—and the beautiful things—archaeological remains and ethnographic objects—as sources for pride and inspiration that erode the boundaries of time.[1]

Iñupiaq man's parka, ca. 1900. Cape Nome, Alaska. Caribou, fox and wolf skins, wool, sinew; 134 x 131 cm. Purchased from the Fred Harvey Company. 6/3308

Yup'ik mask, ca. 1910. Good
News Bay, Alaska. Driftwood,
baleen, feathers, paint, cotton
twine. 49 x 39 cm. Purchase.
12/910

The Arctic and Subarctic are no longer an inaccessible extreme. The mechanized onslaught of resource extraction—the North American Arctic contains immense deposits of oil and minerals, hydroelectric potential, lumber, and other natural resources—coupled with the North's increasing geopolitical significance and a global information infrastructure, has fractured even these last safeholds of cultural and ecological diversity.

Political autonomy and economic authority have begun to provide northern Native leaders with the means to confront challenges of climate change and social, political, and economic pressures even more foreboding than those confronted by their pioneering ancestors, whose footsteps were guided by shamans and the animal masters—the spirit overlords seen to control the coming and going of all living things.

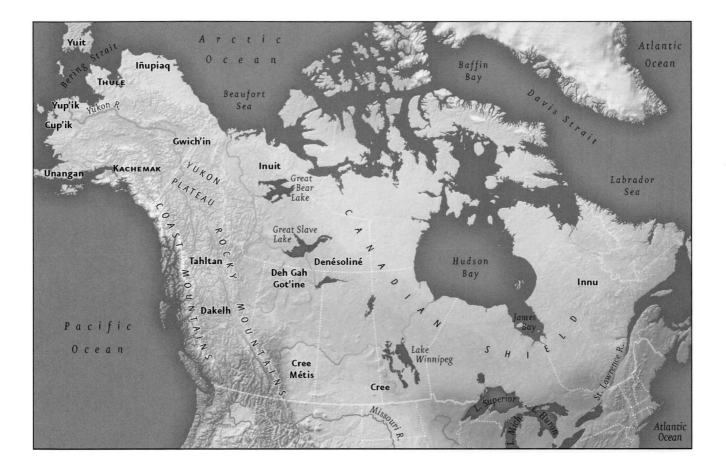

Kachemak lamp, ca. AD 500–
1100. Cook Inlet, Alaska. Stone;
42 x 37 x 15 cm. Collected by
Anderson Ankehl. 4/9236

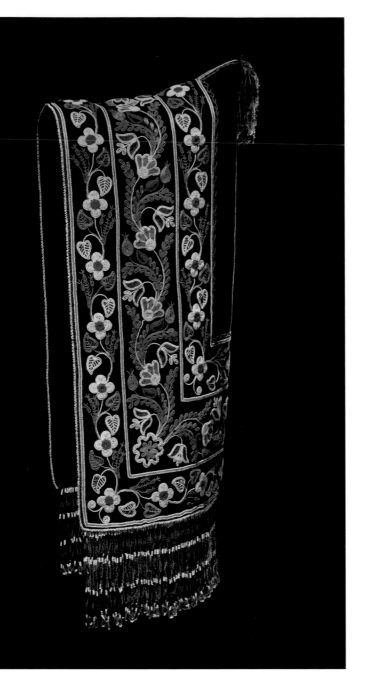

James Bay Cree hood, ca. 1840. James Bay, Canada. Wool, velvet, glass beads; 66 x 29 cm. Presented by Florence C. Quinby. 20/8126

Since time immemorial the rigors imposed by northern lands have shaped Native culture and identity. The ability to flourish in the periglacial environments of the late Pleistocene is evidence that the earliest peoples in the New World must have arrived with a sophisticated technology that included not only the weapons and tools used to hunt large Ice Age mammals like mammoths and giant ground sloths, but also watercraft, snowshoes, and toboggans. Ancestral Native Americans moved into northern lands almost immediately after the glaciers receded. Oral traditions of disappearing crystal mountains, catastrophic floods, and strange monsters attest to Pleistocene landscapes and animals that disappeared 10,000 years ago. Distinctive stone tools of varying traditions indicate that several different groups of hunters out of Asia crossed over the land-bridge between Asia and North America around 14,000 years ago and rapidly spread throughout the northern and southern hemispheres.[2]

Although the trail of these earliest peoples can be glimpsed for the most part only in collections of lost and abandoned stone tools and a few faint hearths, the challenges of high latitudes, including extremes of darkness and cold, would have necessitated ingenious housing and clothing as well. It has been said that northern Native peoples "wear their houses on their backs," an allusion to the importance from the beginning of tailored clothing. Clothing not only afforded shelter from the austerities of the boreal climate, but was also a medium by which a person's relationship to the spiritual world could be displayed and affirmed. Clothing figured significantly in the success of the hunter whose "luck" was predicated on currying the favor of the animal masters. Beautiful and carefully crafted clothing, a hallmark of northern Native peoples, signaled a basic tenet of life in the boreal forest and arctic tundra: that all living things had souls, and that one honored and respected the spirits of the animals whose lives had

Cree Métis coat, ca. 1874. Upper Missouri River. Hide, mother of pearl buttons, silk ribbon, porcupine quill, dyes; 116 x 97 cm. Purchase. 19/1253

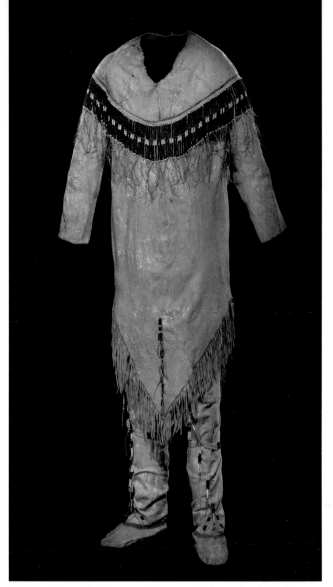

Gwich´in shirt and leggings, ca. 1860–1890. Alaska. Caribou hide, glass beads, pigment, sinew; 126 x 127 cm (shirt), 128 x 60 cm (leggings). William M. Fitzhugh Collection. 19/3265

been given so that human beings could feed and clothe themselves. One way of honoring this intimate relationship was by making beautiful things. It can be argued that the needle was the critical artifact that made life in the North possible—the needle and the ingenuity of northern Native seamstresses who could craft waterproof parkas out of seal intestines and fish skins; make parkas, pants, mittens, and boots that stood up to the harshest winter conditions from polar bear fur and the hides of bearded seals, moose, and caribou; sew lightweight parkas of bird skins; weave moisture-wicking socks from grass; and create baskets and containers from animal bladders and fish and bird skins, as well as grasses and birchbark.[3]

The museum's collections include an outstanding array of clothing from across the Arctic. These pieces reflect regional differences in their designs and materials but share many common features dictated by the practicalities of life in the North. Decoration is ubiquitous and includes a wide spectrum of painted, beaded, sewn, and appliquéd designs that are fabulous examples of the skill and care Native women brought to bear in their creation. This Arctic and Subarctic clothing epitomizes the character of the museum's collections in that it includes both rare early examples—a late-18th- to early-19th-century Cree painted caribou skin coat (see page 260) and the extraordinary Netsilik woman's beaded parka (amauti or tuilli, page 258)—as well as mid-20th-century blouses and skirts made of brightly printed manufactured cotton textiles. There are items of clothing that have obviously seen much wear and others that appear never to have been worn and were doubtless made for sale to tourists or anthropologists. The museum also has a remarkable number of small beaded items, including headbands and garters, medallions and charms, of which some were meant to adorn the bodies of men, women, and children, others to be attached to clothing, but which all share a common function: to serve as conduits

for the display of personal spirituality by showing respect to the animal spirits.

So-called "primitive" wood, bone, and stone manufactures belie an astonishingly sophisticated set of technologies that facilitated, in addition to housing and clothing needs, an impressive array of hunting devices and strategies. These technologies include traps and snares, harpoons and floats, fishing tackle, bows and arrows, fire-making equipment, and the means to facilitate travel over land, snow, and ice by sleds, snowshoes, and boats. Before the advent of travel by

Iñupiaq bow drill, ca. 1880–1920. Kotzebue Sound, Alaska. Ivory, paint; 43 x 1.5 cm. Purchase. 19/1629

Innu family on the Crooked River portage trail, east of the Naskapi River, 1921. Labrador, Canada.

Infinity of Nations

air, roads, and railroads, northern Native peoples journeyed overland by canoe and on foot, with snowshoes and toboggans. Intrepid and self-reliant, northern peoples perfected the skills and ability to travel far, light, and fast. Mobility has been a key strategy for survival among the small bands of northern Athapaskans—including the Gwich´in, Sahtú, and Tłįchǫ—and their Algonkian neighbors, the Cree and Innu.[4] Small family hunting bands frequently crisscrossed the maze of waterways, traveling hundreds of miles to visit relatives and pursue resources. This has always been so. Before the arrival of Europeans, materials like birch bark, caribou skins, and the stone for making tools—including copper for needles, awls, knives, and axes; steatite for cooking vessels; obsidian and beautiful cherts for flaked stone tools—have been found hundreds of miles from their sources, evidence of far-flung trade and interaction networks.[5]

One such example is Ramah chert, a beautiful translucent stone with exceptional flaking qualities whose source is a small quarry site in extreme northern Labrador, in the rugged Torngat Mountains. Soon after Ramah chert was "discovered" by "Maritime Archaic Indians" around 7,000 years ago, it was carried throughout the Canadian Maritimes and, eventually, to neighboring peoples as far away as the Great Lakes,

New England, and the Chesapeake Bay region. Such was its beauty and desirability. No one now can tell for sure the stories the Ramah chert artifacts carried with them, but the fact that it was shaped into exceptionally large sword-like blades and was found in ceremonial deposits, including ancient graves and caches, is dramatic testimony to the interconnected web of social relations that has always been a basic feature of northern Native peoples.

Once pioneering populations reached North America, they quickly adapted to the challenges imposed by northern lands. In comparison to more temperate and tropical climes, the North has less biological diversity. The incredible density and abundance of certain animals during certain seasons, however, more than compensated for the comparatively smaller numbers of species. Even today, after centuries of commercial hunting and fishing by non-Native industrial enterprises, the Arctic fishery is among the most productive on earth, and the herds of caribou are still the largest ungulate population on the planet. It is hard today to realize the tremendous concentrations of whales and seals that once inhabited the Arctic coastlines on both sides of the continent, or the numbers of caribou, birds, salmon, and cod that were available to northern peoples.

Hand-colored lantern slide of Uliggaq (Ella Pavil, Yup´ik), dressed in a seal-gut parka and standing next to a dip net full of tomcod, 1935. Kwigillingok, Alaska. L02290

Some indication of this vanished wealth is apparent in the traces left behind by Early Maritime Archaic cultures of the coastal Northeast who, around 8,000 years ago, had become adept marine mammal hunters and deep-water fishermen. The Maritime Archaic people of northern Newfoundland and Labrador traveled in ocean-going dugout canoes, lived in large communal houses, and practiced an elaborate mortuary ritual that included the construction of stone-capped burial mounds.[6] In the far north, in Greenland, by about 4,800 years ago, small bands of paleoeskimos using fossil driftwood and hunting musk ox entered that most distant land, effectively completing the peopling of the world. Except for a few scattered islands in the South Pacific and the frozen continent of Antarctica, the world had become inhabited.

Archaeological research has confirmed oral histories that speak of epic migrations throughout the North in response to social pressures and environmental and climatic change. A global warming event a thousand years ago diminished the amount of ice cover in the Arctic Ocean and enabled Alaskan whale-hunters, the ancestors of the Inuit, to pursue prey species across the Canadian Arctic from Alaska to Greenland. At the same time, spectacular volcanic eruptions in the St. Elias Mountains along the Alaska–Yukon border may have precipitated the migration of small bands of northern Athapaskan-speaking peoples—the ancestors of the Navajos, Apaches, and Pacific Athapaskans—into the American Southwest. Mobility and flexibility were central tenets of the essentially egalitarian small-band societies of the North, where cooperation and interdependence characterized group social organization. Seasonal aggregations coincided with resource abundance at fish runs that brought ocean species into their home rivers to spawn, caribou crossings, and places where seals and walrus were concentrated. Non-Native observers have often characterized northern peoples as impoverished, not realizing that their modest material culture masked a vibrant and complex cosmology and spoke of an intricate web of relationships between human beings, their northern homeland, the animals, and the animal masters.

Gifts for the animal masters

In spite of the diversity of Arctic and Subarctic cultures, the peoples of the North shared a profound set of core values that recognized the fundamental spiritual and economic relationships that linked human beings with animals. This intimate spiritual relationship is expressed in a rich reservoir of oral traditions and knowledge. It was, after all, animals who made life possible with the gift of their lives. Animal souls, like human souls, were pervasive and an essential component of the traditional way of life and language.[7]

For the Yupiit of Alaska and the Innu of northern Labrador, as for all the Indian and Inuit communities between, life itself has always been predicated on observing the proper practices in showing respect for the animals, whose gift of their lives enabled human beings to survive. To live as a proper human being, one needs to be aware of both the natural and supernatural worlds. A host of practices and behaviors, including "shaking tent" ceremonies, drumming, the reading of bones, the interpretation of dreams, and the celebration of the *mokoshan*—an Innu communal bone-marrow feast of thanksgiving—situated human beings in relationships with the spiritual world of animals and the animal masters, the "deities," for want of a clearer word, that controlled the coming and going of their wards, the animals on earth.

The pervasiveness of the deep spiritual underpinnings of the lives of northern Indian and Inuit hunters and their families is readily apparent in their material culture. The museum's collections contain a large number of propitiatory items, including charms made from bird skins, duck beaks, otter feet, and skeletal offerings (skulls of bears and porcupines) that signify and sanctify respect for the animals and the animal masters. There is a large collection of ceremonial carrying straps (*nimaban*) used by hunters when transporting

Right: Cree bag, ca. 1850. East of Red River, Canada. Hide,
quill, beads, sinew; 76 x 18 cm. Purchase. 12/7176

Below: Tahltan bag, ca. 1880–1890. British Columbia, Canada.
Wool, silk, cotton, glass beads, semi-tanned hide; 76 x 20 cm.
Collected by Lieutenant George Thornton Emmons. 9371

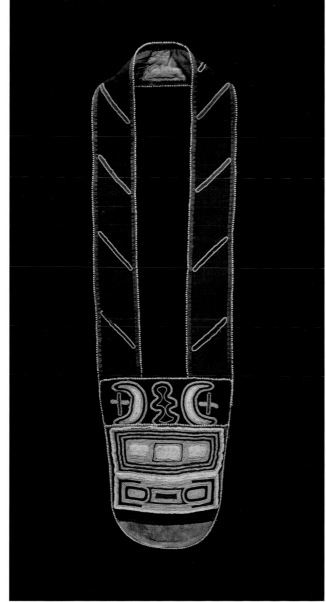

Iñupiaq model *qasgiq* (men's house), ca. 1900. Point Barrow, Alaska. Wood, ivory; 37 x 30 x 18 cm. Collected by Frank Wood. 5/3662

animals back to the camp. Many of the game bags, as well as the pouches for holding cartridges and other tools that hunters used, are elaborately decorated with dream-inspired designs emblematic of the hunter's relationship with the prey animals.[8]

We do not have far to look to find this rich spiritual overlay, apparent in symbolic practices and decorations that are attributes of even the seemingly most mundane objects. Animals who gave themselves to the hunter needed to be afforded respect, an acknowledgment of the spiritual agency that culminated in the hunter's success. Respect was evident in the selection of special tools for handling animals and for the presentation of the animal gifts: food, fat, and fur. With some classes of material culture—birch-bark meat-serving trays, for example, painted wooden grease ladles used during celebratory feasts, or snowshoes that regularly incorporate tufts of colored yarn and painted designs to ensure success in the hunt—it is nearly impossible to separate their function from their intrinsic symbolic—we might call it ceremonial—nature.

Neighbors and strangers

While the Arctic and Subarctic peoples were among the first North Americans to experience European and Asian contact—in the eastern Arctic by Norse adventurers around AD 1000 and later by 16th century Elizabethan explorers; and in the North Pacific by Russian fur traders (*promyshlenik*) in the mid-18th century—they were among the last to surrender their lands. In a region of the continent that held few inducements to European settlement, North America's northern Native peoples long retained a high degree of social and political autonomy and a traditional subsistence economy based on hunting, trapping, and fishing. Until quite recently, northern Native peoples spent most of the year at isolated hunting, fishing, and trapping camps. Leadership in the highly mobile family bands was traditionally fluid and flexible, predicated on the consent and wisdom of elders, hunters, and spiritual leaders. Today in most northern communities, elected band councils are the basic level of village authority.

It is only with the advent of modern technology and a global economy that threats to Native homelands

and land tenure have come in the guise of economic development. Throughout the 19th and 20th centuries, northern Native peoples only gradually shifted their alliances toward different posts and mission stations as groups came to recognize and appreciate the advantages of increasingly reliable trading relations. Only in the last forty years or so have socioeconomic factors— including health, education, and social-service initiatives and other government policies—encouraged a shift from camp life to village dwelling. And although people are drawn to village life, it is the land and waterways, and the environmentally based skills, heritage, and traditions that still define Indian, Aleut, and Inuit social and spiritual identity in the North. Many Indian and Inuit families still spend significant time in the country at fishing and hunting camps where the continuity between the past and the present is visibly affirmed. Northern Native peoples have never lost their intimate bond to the forest, tundra, and ice, to the land and its animals, whose very existence is intimately linked to their own.

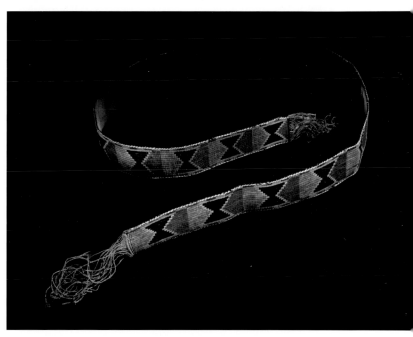

Recognition that northern Native cultures possessed a unique relationship to the land has been at the heart of anthropological work in the region for more than a century. One facet of this research and respect has been the active collecting of northern Native material culture for the uniquely Native perceptions, stories, and insight objects carry, provided we have the wisdom to look and listen.

The heyday of museum collecting in North American Indian and Inuit communities began around 1880. The relentless "tides of progress" had swept many Native North American peoples from their lands, destroyed their means of livelihood, and usurped

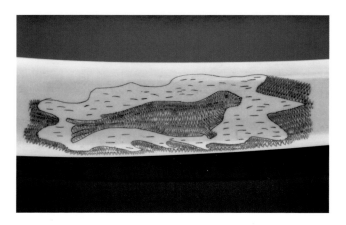

Dakelh (Carrier) box, ca. 1880. Skeena River, British Columbia, Canada. Birchbark, spruce root; 27 x 21 cm. From the Academy of Natural Sciences of Philadelphia. 16/7092

Facing: Innu ceremonial robe, attributed to Kowkachish (Manakanet), wife of Mestawapeo (Sam Rich), ca. 1920. Labrador, Newfoundland, Canada. Caribou skin, paint; 133 x 152 cm. Collected by Dr. Frank G. Speck. 17/6575

indigenous religions, governments, and traditions. In the eyes of most European-Americans it appeared that Native American cultures were likely to vanish beneath expanding commercial and political interests. It is with this notion of the "disappearing Indian" that the acquisition of the vast collections in anthropological museums worldwide was justified. So-called "salvage" anthropology sought to acquire and preserve whatever traces of "traditional" Indian culture could be "saved." And while the Native peoples of the North escaped many of the conflicts that characterized European-American and Native American relations elsewhere, the accelerated pace of economic development, government intervention, and missionary activity threatened to change northern lifestyles inalterably.

As a collector, George Heye was an inspired genius whose passion for Native American objects and artifacts was inexhaustible, if not insatiable. His collecting was organized like a military campaign as he sent his lieutenants—collectors, dealers, fur traders, archaeologists, and anthropologists—across the northern reaches of Canada, Greenland, and Alaska to acquire Native objects both mundane and of extraordinary beauty. The vast majority of Heye's northern Native Alaskan, Aleut, Inuit, Athapaskan, and Algonkian artifacts were collected by a cadre of perhaps a half-dozen noted individuals or acquired through exchanges with other museums, notably the Danish National Museum. Heye's largesse was a godsend to a number of prominent anthropologists whose fieldwork was supported by research funds he provided with the sole proviso that they bring back objects for his collection. Cécile Ganteaume reviews the scope of Heye's collecting in a separate essay (see page 275), but a few collectors important to the Arctic and Subarctic merit additional mention here.

The prominent Innu and Montagnais collections Heye amassed were the results of the acumen of Frank G. Speck and William Stiles; between them they account for more than 96 percent of the museum's northeastern Algonkian collection of more than 2,500 objects. Speck's association with George Heye, in particular, was a boon to both. The doyen of northeastern anthropologists, Speck (1881–1950) collected widely for the Museum of the American Indian–Heye Foundation, visiting most of the Cree and Innu communities in Québec and Labrador. He befriended the Newfoundland trapper and fur trader Richard White, who had established a trading post for the Inuit and Innu near Nain, Labrador, following World War I. Under Speck's direction, Heye acquired a large collection of Innu material culture from White, who had a close intimacy with the Barrenground Innu (the Mushuau-innu).

Alaska was also an important collecting field for Heye.[9] He had the tremendous good fortune to enlist the skills of a pair of inveterate collectors there: Adams Hollis Twitchell and George Emmons. Twitchell (1872–1949) was drawn to the Alaskan goldfields in the 1890s. In 1903 he settled near Bethel, established a trading post, and raised a family. A self-taught naturalist, he provided biological and cultural specimens to several universities and museums, including Heye's. Twitchell sent more than 300 superb Yup´ik objects to Heye in 1919, including an astonishing 55 masks. George Emmons (1852–1945) served in the U.S. Navy, stationed in Alaska between 1882 and 1889, after which he worked as an agent for the U.S. government.

He became deeply interested in the Native peoples of Alaska, especially the Indians of the Northwest Coast, among whom he traveled and collected extensively. Between 1891 and 1893 he was the organizer of the Alaskan display at the World's Columbian Exposition in Chicago. His intimacy with and appreciation of Native cultures allowed him to amass remarkable collections, and he sent many thousands of objects from Alaska to the Heye Museum and to the Smithsonian, the Field Museum in Chicago, and the American Museum of Natural History in New York.

The National Museum of the American Indian has one of the finest and most extensive collections of material remains derived from the central Canadian

Haida pipe collected from the Tahltan, ca. 1820–1830. British Columbia, Canada. Wood, ivory, pitch, metal, paint; 32 x 10 x 4 cm. Collected by Lieutenant George Thornton Emmons. 9203

Arctic Inuit, including the Copper Inuit (Kitlinermiut), Netsilik Inuit (Netsilingmiut), and Caribou Inuit (Qairnirmiut, Harvaqtuurmiut, Paallirmiut, and Ahiarmiut). The Canadian Arctic Inuit collections were acquired in part by Christian Leden (1882–1957), an intrepid Norwegian ethnomusicologist and explorer who spent 1913 to 1916 traveling among the Inuit of the west coast of Hudson Bay, surviving shipwrecks, blizzards, and starvation.[10] Emerging from the wilderness, Leden learned of the outbreak of World War I and immediately returned to Europe, trusting his arduously gathered ethnology collections—more than 500 specimens—to the care of the Hudson's Bay Company, which eventually forwarded them to Montreal on the yearly supply barge that visited the remote trading posts. Mysteriously, Leden presumed his collection had been lost and never knew that George Heye had arranged for its acquisition in 1917.

Two other significant collections of central Canadian Arctic Inuit material culture were acquired by Heye. Donald Cadzow (1894–1960), the nephew of a Hudson's Bay Company fur trader, conducted archaeological and ethnographic work for Heye in the Northwest and Yukon territories, collecting hundreds of ethnographic specimens from Copper Inuit (as well as several thousand objects from Canadian Plains Indian tribes).[11] Rounding out the central Arctic collections are nearly a thousand mostly archaeological specimens collected by Therkel Mathiassen (1892–1967) during the Fifth Thule Expedition (1921–1923), which were received in an exchange with the National Museum of Denmark.

Heye cultivated a number of Alaskan entrepreneurs, an unusual and extremely productive source of artifacts. One such dealer-collector was Arnold Liebes (1889–1957), whose family had a profitable fur-trading, shipping, and mercantile business along the north coast of Alaska with posts at Wainwright, Barrow, and on St. Lawrence Island.[12] In 1923 Liebes arranged to send to Heye in New York a collection of 450 objects from the Yuit (Siberian Yup'ik) communities on St. Lawrence Island—a collection that is second to none in its breadth of traditional clothing, tools, and small commercial carvings. By far and away the most prolific purveyor of ethnographic objects and curios from a commercial source was J. E. Standley (1854–1940),

Kenneth Kaiona (Copper Inuit, ca. 1850–d.?), dance cap, ca. 1920. Coronation Gulf, Alaska. Caribou hide, ermine fur, yellow-billed loon skin, sinew, wool, cotton fabric; 20 x 23 x 32 cm. Gift of John D. Ferguson. 23/2297

who opened Ye Olde Curiosity Shop in Seattle in 1899.[13] More than 1,600 objects flowed from Stadley to Heye between 1904 and 1924.

While other institutions may house older individual items made by the Native peoples of the North American Arctic and Subarctic, few if any can rival the breadth and the time-depth of the museum's holdings. The National Museum of the American Indian's stewardship of the collection, its commitment to honor and conserve the material culture of Native lives and to make objects available to descent community members as well as students and scholars, is simultaneously the museum's principal goal and its greatest challenge. Dissemination of information about the scope and extent of these collections is complicated by their lack, in many cases, of detailed, supportive documentation.

Yuit (Siberian Yup'ik) utensils, ca. 1920. St. Lawrence Island, Alaska.
Ivory; 15 x 3 cm. Collected by Farrar Burn. 11/6743

cultural patrimony, have similarly to recognize the
responsibility we have to make these collections acces-
sible to the descendants of the people who made them
a long time ago. It is hoped that the presentation of the
extent of the collections, in this and other books and
increasingly online, will continue to promote the dialogue between museum caretakers and Native scholars
and elders that augments some of the lost knowledge
that once surrounded these items.

Still, the collections have an eloquent story to
tell if only we learn to listen to the language of
bark, stone, and skins, and read the messages in the
designs and craftsmanship that are integral to tools
and clothing. The objects are tangible links to the
lives of Native families during the preceding century,
to the dichotomy between life in the bush and life in
the village. They attest to an abiding dependence on
the resources provided by the land in the number and
variety of tools that gave hunters and their families a
high degree of mobility, in the sophistication of tools
used in resource procurement, and in the design and
craftsmanship of skin and fur clothing that was both
a product of the hunt and a medium for attending to
the deep spiritual relationships between hunters and
animals. Objects have always been powerful symbols,
so it is not surprising that the political representatives of the Innu Nation and Mamit Innuat incorporate a snowshoe into the logos of their organization,
and the Grand Council of the Cree has a stretched
beaver skin in theirs.

In a world of decreasing biological and cultural
diversity, the descent communities of Arctic and Subarctic hunters and foragers provide a desperately
needed perspective on nonhierarchical societies based
on principles of reciprocity and traditional ecological
knowledge. The collections from the northern regions
are a priceless heritage whose significance only deep-
ens with time. That they are treasured by museums is
a recognition of the value placed on northern Native
communities and their culture. These artifacts are
ambassadors of a way of life and a human perspective that connects the contemporary world to the very
roots of human existence in North America.

This is a legacy of George Heye's collecting zeal.
Although Heye bought the services of some of the best
professional anthropologists of the time, he had less
interest in their field notes and records, which could
have greatly enriched our knowledge of the collections.

In northern Native communities, it is easy to recognize the tremendous awe and respect with which
elders are held. In part this respect acknowledges the
profound weight of the responsibility the elders bear
to transmit and preserve pride, cultural integrity, and
knowledge. In the course of their long lives, they have
been intimately involved in the killing and handling
of animals. It is believed that through these experiences, the elders have obtained powers and perspectives that give them the responsibility to negotiate the
rituals and relations between the world of the animal
masters and the world of human beings. Museum
curators, privileged to work with powerful objects of

Iñupiaq ship carving

Iñupiaq ship carving, ca. 1880–1910. Point Barrow, Alaska. Ivory, sinew; 30 x 5 x 15 cm. Purchase. 21/4677

The Native peoples of Arctic North America and Siberia have carved walrus ivory for about 2,000 years. Early carvings were usually tools, some with artistic designs, and figurines that may have had religious significance. When European and American whalers sailed to the Alaskan Arctic in the mid-19th century, Iñupiat and Yupiit started selling their ivory carvings as souvenirs. Between 1848 and 1910, when commercial whaling came to an end in the western Arctic, there were approximately 2,100 annual whaling ship cruises, according to the research of John Bockstoce. Bockstoce states that the lure of profits by having early access to the bowhead led a few whaling ships to overwinter at various places in the Chukchi Sea beginning in 1858 and continuing off and on through the mid-1890s.[1] The carver of this ship would most likely have been quite familiar with the sight of whaling ships.

The artist carved the hull and railing for this model whaling ship from one large piece of tusk and then attached several pieces of ivory for the sails, masts, rudder, and other parts on the deck, showing great attention to detail. Such a carving, made from rather large pieces of ivory, would be unusual today. The decline of sea ice due to climate change makes hunting walrus harder for the Iñupiaq and Yup´ik hunters, and ivory is now in short supply. Climate change may also adversely affect walrus populations, which depend on moving sea ice floes to gain access to the clams they eat. Today's carvers tend to create smaller figurines to make the most of the tusks they do have.

—Deanna Paniataaq Kingston (King Island Iñupiaq)

Inuit *amauti* or *tuilli* (woman's parka), ca. 1890–1925. Iqluligaarjuk (Chesterfield Inlet), Nunavut, Canada. Parka: caribou skin, glass beads, stroud cloth, caribou teeth, and metal pendants; needlecase: ivory, seal hide; carrying strap with toggles: caribou hide, ivory; 143 x 65 cm. 13/7198.

Inuit *amauti* or *tuilli* (woman's parka)

This woman's parka is a striking example of the artistry of Inuit women's beadwork, which flourished during the whaling period on the west coast of Hudson Bay from 1860 to 1915. Although acquired after the demise of the whaling era in the central Canadian Arctic, the parka was collected near the former whaling station of Cape Fullerton (Qatiktalik). The beadwork, fashioned on a woolen stroud backing, has clearly been transferred from another parka. Regarded as a woman's treasured possession, beadwork was sometimes gifted from mother to daughter or daughter-in-law, suggesting that the beadwork on this parka may date from a generation before, at the height of the whaling era. The creation of an accomplished seamstress and graphic artist, this is one of a small number of Inuit beaded parkas preserved in museum collections.

Incorporating almost 160,000 beads, the seamstress has worked out an array of floral and anatomical designs, as well as geometric motifs, to decorate the parka's front, hood, shoulders (*tui*), and wrist cuffs. The parka is accompanied by a finely carved ivory needlecase, as well as a hide carrying strap anchored by a pair of ivory toggles, used to secure a baby carried in the back pouch (*amaut*). Together, the parka, needlecase, and carrying strap provide an image of the creative and maternal role of women within Inuit society.[1]

Frequented by the New England whaler Captain George Comer, the whaling station at Cape Fullerton was a lively outpost in the whaling economy and became an epicenter for the development of beaded parkas in the late 19th century. Working through the intermediary of an *isumataq* (Inuit leader), Captain Comer hired Inuit crews to man the whaleboats, guide hunting expeditions, and secure a constant supply of fresh meat and fish for the whalers; women were engaged to sew parkas, mitts, boots, and sleeping bags for the whaling crews.[2] At its height, the whaling station comprised a thriving community of about 100 persons, drawing Inuit from camps throughout a wide-ranging area.[3]

—Bernadette Driscoll Engelstad

I like the sound the beads make as I walk.
—ARVIAT (INUIT), SEAMSTRESS

We call these parkas *tuilli* because of their big shoulders. They were made this way so that nursing mothers could put their baby's feet in there, and there was plenty of room to nurse. This tuilli was made for a woman with a newborn baby, but she wouldn't wear something this beaded for everyday. It would be more for drum dancing or celebrations.

I have looked at different beadwork on tuillis and have concluded that each piece of work is about creative self-expression; it's about making something that is different and unique, a desire to be different, unique, and beautiful. The design and make are still the same—it's a most practical *amauti* for traveling. I have been told by various elders and elderly relatives that the late Captain Comer designed some of the patterns on my grandmother Shoofly's tuilli, which is in the collection of the American Museum of Natural History. Perhaps it was the stars on the chest piece. Another elder told me that the boots on her parka represent the boots that Captain Comer brought back to Shoofly. The actual boots were too small, so a replica of the boots went on the chest piece. Was it a symbol of their love for each other?

I would have to say my favorite part of Shoofly's beadwork is the caribou hunting scene on the back of the hood. Shoofly would be pleased to learn that her descendants still hunt caribou. And we still try to demonstrate the respect owed to the sacrifices made by such animals by using and making something practical, warm, and beautiful out of their skins.

—Bernadette Miqqusaaq Dean (Aivilingmiut Inuk)

Cree *misko takiy* (hide coat)

Cree *misko takiy* (coat), ca. 1780–1820. Alberta, Canada. Moose hide, paint, porcupine quill, hair; 125 x 160 cm. Purchase. 17/6343

This spectacular painted-hide coat is among a dozen coats of its type that survive in collections. Straight-cut coats with broad bands of geometric painting date to between 1770 and 1820. Made from a single large moose hide, the coat wraps around a man's body as it once wrapped around the animal. The wearer's spine, accented by painted elements, is aligned with the spine of the animal. The vertical column of alternating geometric shapes, echoing the vertebrae of the spinal column, crowned with a perpendicular band, identifies the coat as Northern Cree.

By 1743 fur traders on the shores of Hudson Bay had adopted the coat, which they called a "tockey" or "toggey," from the Cree *muska togy* or *misko takiy*. This was a winter garment, once trimmed with fur. The elaborate decoration at the shoulder is assembled from pieces of loom-woven quillwork and fine leather fringe wrapped with quill, accented by tufts of dyed red deer hair. Lines and circles were pressed or carved into the surface of the hide and the resulting forms filled with either indigenous paint or a clear substance that, over time, contrasted with the natural hide. While each artist drew from a common repertoire of motifs, no two coats are alike.

Cree women made these coats for both European and Cree men. The coats provide us with a window into a dynamic space where different systems of knowing the world came together. They also preserve a record of our earliest aesthetic practices.

—Sherry Farrell Racette
(Timiskaming First Nation)

Angokwazhuk (Happy Jack, Iñupiaq)

Walrus-ivory carving

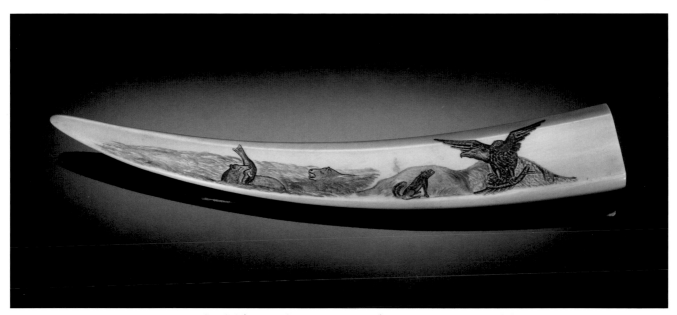

Angokwazhuk (Happy Jack, Iñupiaq, 1870?–1918), carving, ca. 1900. Nome, Alaska.
Walrus ivory tusk; 34 x 5 x 3 cm. Collected by J. E. Standley. 5/3086

When Happy Jack worked, he worked it perfectly, exactly. You can't even see the marks on his things. [Other carvers] tried hard like Happy Jack, but they don't do it like Happy Jack. I try, too; I can't do it even if I copy.

—BIG MIKE, HAPPY JACK'S
BROTHER-IN-LAW

Angokwazhuk, or Happy Jack, grew up on the Seward Peninsula of Alaska. In 1892, at the age of 19, he was living on Little Diomede Island when Captain Hartson Bodfish admired his carving and invited him onto his whaling ship. The sailors apparently named him Happy Jack and probably also showed him scrimshaw engraving. Although Happy Jack carved other objects, he is famous for detailed engravings in what Dorothy Jean Ray has called the "Western pictorial" style.[1]

While we may never know, I believe that the two hillside scenes on either side of this tusk depict the story of the Eagle–Wolf Dance. This dance recounts how a hunter, after killing a giant eagle, is taken to the giant eagle's mother's home so that she can teach him to sing, dance, and feast. She tells him that he must perform these activities when he returns home so that her son's spirit can return to her. This story was told, and the dance performed, among villages on the Seward Peninsula during the late 19th and early 20th centuries.

On one side of the tusk, Happy Jack has engraved an eagle larger than the wolf. On the other side, birds fly out of the den, startled by the snarling wolf at the entrance. In the story, the hunter sees a vision of a hillside den, from which birds fly away and a wolf emerges dancing. If the drawings do depict this story, this is a valuable and unique piece, as Happy Jack usually carved village and hunting scenes or scenes from photographs. In addition, contemporary carvers rarely engrave whole tusks because of the lack of ivory.

—Deanna Paniataaq Kingston (King Island Iñupiaq)

Bob Haozous (Warm Springs Chiricahua Apache, b. 1943), *Sleeping Man*, 1975.
Limestone, paint, wood; 70 x 50 x 56 cm. Gift of Hopewell Foundation. 265383

Future tense

LOOKING AT THE OBJECTS in this book, it is easy to find yourself trying to imagine the lives and thoughts of their makers who lived in the distant past. Yet our lives are quite different. The earliest makers hunted, gathered, and grew their food. They made or traded locally for the majority of their clothing and other goods. For the makers who lived in the not-so-distant past, whose names begin to emerge in the records, this sense of remoteness diminishes, but does not disappear. In contrast, the works in the modern and contemporary arts collection are made by people we know by name. Most of them were living when their work was acquired by the museum. Many are living today. These makers are not distant at all.

It is also entirely appropriate to depart at this point from the geographical organization of *Infinity of Nations*. There is no doubt that the artists represented in the modern and contemporary arts collection, like their historic peers, are influenced by culturally specific histories and traditions and by their connection to place. But these artists have chosen to embrace and incorporate modern media and materials and contemporary subjects in their work, and the majority regard themselves as members of a diverse international community creating and commenting on a global culture.

George Gustav Heye focused on collecting historical material culture and archaeological objects. By the 1960s, however, Heye's successors at the Museum of the American Indian had become interested in fine art drawings and paintings as well. Paintings collected at that time include important early work of Hopi artists Waldo Mootzka (1910–1940) and Fred Kabotie (1900–1986). The majority, however, were created during the 1930s in what was initially known as the Studio style. These include works by Andy Tsinahjinnie (Navajo, 1916–2000), Geronimo Cruz Montoya (San Juan, b. 1915), Awa Tsireh (San Ildefonso, 1898–1955), and other students of Dorothy Dunn—the founder of the Studio of the Santa Fe Indian School and a proponent and patron of "traditional" Indian painting—and regional evolutions of the genre from the 1940s, 1950s, and 1960s.[1]

Yet even in this early collection, vanguards in the field are represented. Oscar Howe (Yanktonai Sioux, 1915–1983) created work that defied conventional categorizations of American Indian art, and Joe Herrera (Cochiti, 1923–2001) and George Morrison (Ojibway, 1923–2000) are also recognized as important modernists. Native painting and art in other nontraditional media began to expand and diversify as regional movements beyond the Southwest took shape.

In the far north, the Inuit artist Kenojuak Ashevak (b. 1927) became known as early as the late 1950s for her lyrical printmaking, a medium introduced to the Inuit in the Cape Dorset region as part of an economic initiative. Kenojuak's work draws upon familiar imagery in her environment such as birds and other animals as well as Inuit women, but her spare and fantastical interpretations are powerful statements of beauty and design. Her masterful use of silhouette, patterning, and abstract designs may have been influenced by her experience sewing traditional clothing, which involves creating designs with piecework, and by other Inuit art practices such as scrimshaw. Her popularity increased through her regular contributions to the Cape Dorset print collections, and her work continues to be emblematic of Inuit print-making in design and subject.

Kenojuak Ashevak (Inuit, b. 1927), *Untitled*, ca. 1990–2000. Paper, graphite, ink; 50 x 66 cm. Gift of R. E. Mansfield. 26/5491

Jerome Tiger (Creek/Seminole, 1941–1967), *First Shot*, 1967. Tempera on paperboard; 50 x 35 cm. Unknown collector. 25/1081

Norval Morrisseau (Anishinaabe, 1932–2007), *Early Shaman*, 1973. Acrylic on canvas; 160 x 95 cm. Gift of R. E. Mansfield. 26/4094

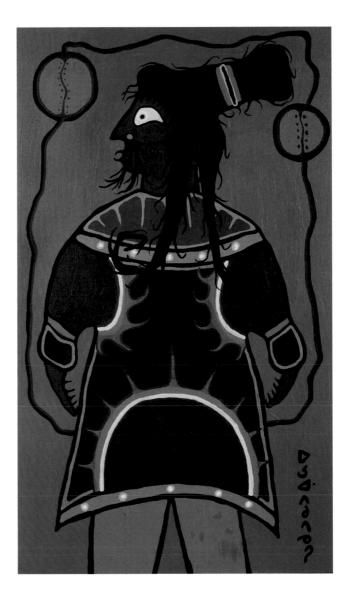

Many Native artists from this time did not attend college or university art programs. There are several significant collections of paintings by self-taught artists in the museum. Frank Day (1902–1976), a Maidu from California, began painting late in life during a long recovery after an accident. His narrative paintings find their subjects in traditional stories passed on through oral tradition. Bonita Wa Wa Calachaw Nuñez (Luiseño, 1888–1972) used her expressive paintings to explore her personal history. Largely unknown, she lived in upper Manhattan near the Museum of the American Indian and donated more than twenty-five paintings to the museum a few weeks before she passed away in 1972. Like Nuñez, Cathy Nelson-Rodriguez (Luiseño, b. 1953) is a self-taught painter from the La Jolla Reservation in Southern California, where she still lives. She uses her paintings to create autobiographical narratives and exorcise personal demons, as well as to make powerful self-portraits and portraits of people in her community.[2]

Another notable collection is a group of fourteen drawings and paintings on paper by Jerome Tiger (Creek/Seminole, 1941–1967). Tiger incorporated some of the techniques of traditional Indian painting in his work, such as sparse or empty backgrounds and the use of flat inpainting and outline, but with an emphasis on dimensionality, design, and action. *First Shot* (1967) exemplifies his work, its dynamic composition capturing the intensity of a hunt in brush. The diagonal composition draws attention away from the empty center of the painting, pulling us toward the corners where we see the hunter's muscles still taut from the release of the arrow and the bird in its last terrible moment of life, mid-air, before it hurtles to the ground. A prolific artist in his short lifetime, Tiger is still recognized for defining a distinctive painting style identified with the Southeast.[3]

The long and wide-ranging career of Norval Morrisseau (Ojibwe, 1932–2007) continues to influence new generations of artists. In the early 1970s, he and his colleagues in the Canadian artists' collective popularly known as the Indian Group of Seven became the cornerstone of the budding Woodland School. Morrisseau's work combines the modernist use of saturated blocks of vivid color with a bold linear style that references the pictorial traditions of rock art and Ojibwe birchbark drawings. Native traditional and ritual beliefs, especially stories of mythical beings and transformation, became his iconic subject. The painting *Early Shaman* (1973), an example from his early career, demonstrates his approach in color and composition, and shows a depiction of a shape-shifting shaman (a likely self-portrait indicated by the beard and mustache) whose hands have changed into claws.[4]

Allan Houser (Chiricahua Apache, 1914–1994) also enjoyed a long and iconic career. He influenced the entire field of Native art, in part through his tenure as a sculpture instructor at the Institute of American Indian Arts (IAIA) in Santa Fe, a center of innovation in the burgeoning Indian art scene of the 1970s. Like many of his peers, Houser was trained as a young man in traditional Indian painting techniques and subject matter under Dorothy Dunn and worked as a muralist with Gerald Nailor (Navajo, 1917–1952). In his monumental sculpture, however, rendered primarily in stone and bronze, he combined traditional subject matter with an emphasis on abstraction and a modernist approach to the figure. With few exceptions—such as his depictions of Geronimo—Houser's figures became anonymous, symbolic, and, some would say, romantic representations of Native people. Houser's heroic sculptural portraiture, such as *Seated Woman* (1992), was widely lauded and has been imitated throughout the American Southwest and beyond.[5]

Other artists in the region in the 1960s and 1970s shaped the direction of work in two-dimensional media. With his former IAIA student T. C. Cannon (Caddo/Kiowa, 1946–1978), Fritz Scholder (Luiseño, 1937–2005) created a colorful and dynamic approach to painting that combines commentary on the Indian as subject with pop art conventions. The museum's collection includes paintings and prints from throughout Scholder's career. R. C. Gorman (Navajo, 1931–2005), celebrated during the late 1970s and early 1980s for his bold nudes and masterful drawings of monumental Navajo madonnas, was one of the few living artists to be both collected and featured in a solo exhibition by the Museum of the American Indian before the collection was transferred to the Smithsonian in 1989. The collection contains early drawings by Gorman, as well as a number of print portfolios.[6]

Many artists, both Native and non-Native, have strived to succeed by creating idealistic depictions of

Larry Beck (Chnagmiut Yup'ik, 1938–1994), *Ooger Uk Inua (Walrus Spirit)*, 1982. Hubcaps, tires, chair legs, PVC plastic; 55.2 x 30.8 x 48.5 cm. Transferred from the Indian Arts and Crafts Board Collection, Department of the Interior. 25/5423

Native people. It is inevitable that other artists would react against these conventions, so palatable to a wide audience. The artist who is perhaps best known for avoiding safe subjects and embracing controversy is Bob Haozous (Chiricahua Apache/Navajo, b. 1943). Haozous rapidly became known for satirical and provocative sculpture that challenges romantic imagery and addresses contemporary issues. *Sleeping Man* (1975), representative of his early work in stone, slyly tweaks romantic, timeless representations of Native people. The figure's cowboy boots, blue jeans, concha belt, and garish shirt place him squarely in the northern New Mexico gallery scene of the 1970s. During this period Haozous created a number of sleeping people to show contemporary Indians who have lost their connection with Indian philosophy and metaphorically gone to sleep. Of *Sleeping Man* he states, "His spirit is Indian, but you can't tell—we don't even know who we are." By the mid-1980s, Haozous began working in cut and enameled steel and creating monumental sculpture that addresses death, sexuality, exploitation, racism, and environmental pillage, as well as the historical travails of the Apache.[7]

As the century drew to a close, many more artists began challenging conventions and the arbitrary divisions between traditional and nontraditional work, blending new materials with older forms. James Schoppert (Tlingit, 1947–1992) was at the forefront of this movement, disassembling and remixing Northwest formline carving traditions into innovative, dynamic sculptural works, breaking the rules of color and composition. Larry Beck (Yup'ik, 1938–1994), who had enjoyed a long career as a sculptor and installation artist in the Pacific Northwest, became interested in Yup'ik masking traditions in the late 1970s and began to experiment using found objects to craft contemporary masks. His mixed media sculpture *Ooger uk Inua (Walrus Spirit*, 1982) captures the whimsy of

Infinity of Nations

Bently Spang (Northern Cheyenne, b. 1960), *War Shirt #2, Modern Warrior Series*, 2003. Mixed media, photographs, imitation sinew, 16mm film, velvet, glass beads, metal, plastic; 148 x 63 cm. Purchase. 26/2745

contemporaneous American pop sculpture, yet evokes the elegance and gravitas of Northern masks. Though Schoppert and Beck died at the height of their careers, we can still see their influence in the work of younger artists from the region such as Nicholas Galanin (Tlingit/Aleut, b. 1970), Brian Jungen (Dunne-za, b. 1970), and Stephen Jackson (also known as Stron Softi, Tlingit, b. 1976).

The transmutation of new or alternative materials and traditional forms is found throughout recent Native art history. Joe Feddersen (Colville, b. 1953), known primarily as a printmaker who uses designs from both basketry and the urban landscape as sources for his abstract work, collaborated with master glass artist Preston Singletary (Tlingit, b. 1963) to create a series of glass baskets, including *Tire* (2003). Although the form is recognizably a Plateau basket, the designs are taken from such sources as HOV lane symbols, the painted lines in parking lots, and tire treads. Another nontraditional "basket" in the collection is the *Pieced Treaty: Spider's Web Treaty Basket* (2006–2007) by Shan Goshorn (Cherokee, b. 1957). In this instance, the artist critiques the renegotiation of the Tobacco Compact between the state of Oklahoma and the Cherokee Nation by printing copies of the agreements, cutting them into strips, and weaving the pieces into a Cherokee basket with the traditional spider's web design. Goshorn writes that the work "refers to the continual breaking of agreements. The basket has been deliberately left unfinished as these 'negotiations' appear to be ongoing."[8]

Repurposed photographic materials have provided a rich trove for many artists. Bently Spang (Northern Cheyenne, b. 1960) used photographic prints and 16mm film to create a powerful series of three war shirts in the late 1990s and early 2000s. The body of each shirt is composed of personal photos, including candid snapshots of family members and views of his family's

ranch on the Northern Cheyenne Reservation in southeast Montana. Spang, like his ancestors, used materials at hand to create these shirts, which honor and protect his family and culture as well as define his personal identity. *War Shirt #2* (2003) pays homage to the land with multiple photographs of the landscape strung together to form a panoramic vista.

The relationship between Native people and photography is laden with the weight of history. The camera was first the tool of the oppressor, used to define and control Native people. Even today, historic photographs of Indians serve as romantic templates of authenticity, a trope that contemporary Native artist Kent Monkman (Cree Métis, b. 1965) skewers in his work, including the series *The Emergence of a Legend* (2007). Shelley Niro (Mohawk, b. 1954) was first known for her playful hand-tinted photographic work *Mohawks in Beehives* (1991) and the self-referential series *This Land is Mime Land* (1992), in which she appears in various pop-cultural guises, such as Marilyn Monroe, to address issues of identity and cultural genocide. As her work has matured, her themes have become more abstract and meditative, and her process—now incorporating digital manipulation—has become more sophisticated. Her seven-panel work *La Pieta* (2007) is a multilayered commentary on war using images of water, land, and a young man's bare chest to memorialize loss. Each image is surrounded by a frame of wampum depicting poppies, a symbol for war deaths. By combining these images with the overarching theme of motherhood reflected in the title, Niro sought to create a work that is not didactic but visual poetry. The loss of land becomes an allegory for the loss of life. Emerging artist Will Wilson (Navajo, b. 1969) also uses digitally manipulated photography to create haunting images of the landscape that are both beautiful and foreboding of environmental peril in the series *Auto Immune Response* (2004).[9]

In addition to artists working in mixed media, photography, and new media (including video and digital arts), there are many contemporary Native painters in the "European" tradition. Judith Lowry (Mountain Maidu/Hamowi Pit River, b. 1948) creates monumental

Shelley Niro (Mohawk, b. 1954),
La Pieta (detail, using six of the
seven panels), 2007. Giclee print
on canvas. Purchase. 26/7463

narratives that retell family and tribal stories as well as make social statements in the idiom of illusionistic art traditions. In one of her more humorous and surreal paintings, *Fortune* (1994), European and pre-Columbian goddesses sit in a Chinese restaurant and react to the contents of their fortune cookies. Her work contrasts with the equally alluring, but highly abstract paintings of Mario Martinez (Yaqui, b. 1953), who synthesizes techniques and iconography from both Western and Yaqui traditions.[10]

Many people look at Native art, including art by living artists, expecting to find recognizable

iconography—feathers, horses, or tipis. In fact, abstraction has historically been the norm. Pueblo artists have an especially strong tradition of visual abstraction, expressed in their ceramics. Nora Naranjo-Morse (Santa Clara, b. 1953), one of the most celebrated artists from the region, began her career as a ceramicist creating figurative work, but has since ventured into more conceptual and abstract forms. The large-scale sculpture *Stories Upon Stories* (2005) is a meditation on centuries of Pueblo pottery traditions that continue to inspire artists today. "Pre-contact, contact, colonization, war, loss of language, resistance stories and more

stories . . . have flowed through these artists over the years expressing a universe of transitions. And yet, it is obvious these designs speak of an undeniable connection to the earth material that transcends and addresses something solid, forgiving, supportive, and ultimately life affirming. Each carved or painted design has the mark of balance while maintaining the fluidity of design concept. . . . I see these designs as marks of ceremony and the beginning breath of spiritual life." [11]

Naranjo-Morse's work, like all of the objects in this book, reflects the enduring values and dynamic nature of Native life and art. Although the materials at hand have changed over the centuries from natural substances, such as hide, wood, and feathers, to include synthetic products and digital processes, Native people are still incorporating and responding to their experiences through visual expression. The Modern and Contemporary Art collection—represented by the small sample of works shown here—demonstrates that Native artists today are members of an increasingly international cultural community engaged in a global exchange of ideas, trying to make sense of this complex world.

—Kathleen Ash-Milby (Navajo)

Nora Naranjo-Morse (Santa Clara, b. 1953) *Stories Upon Stories*, 2005. Aluminum, paint; 238 x 29 x 106 cm. Gift of Addison Arts, 26/5837

Judith Lowry (Mountain Maidu/ Hamowi Pit River, b. 1948), *Fortune*, 1993. Acrylic on canvas; 182 x 150 cm. Gift of R. E. Mansfield. 26/4322

Facing: Mario Martinez (Yaqui, b. 1953), *Yaqui Flashback II*, 1991. Acrylic, mixed media on canvas; 184 x 151 cm. Gift of Suzanne M. Rubel and Bill Rosenfeld. 26/5365

Joseph W. Keppler (1872–1956), portrait of George G. Heye, May 12th, 1927.
Watercolor. S02307

The collections of the National Museum of the American Indian

THE COLLECTIONS of the National Museum of the American Indian, numbering more than 825,000 objects today, have been augmented in recent decades through acquisitions and donations of powerful and compelling works of contemporary Native art. The growing and vibrant collection of contemporary works is continually enhanced in response to currents in the Native art world. Like James Luna's mixed media installation work, *Chapel for Pablo Tac*, created for the 2005 Venice Biennale's 51st International Art Exhibition in Venice, Italy, many works by living artists reflect a clear engagement with Western artistic currents and media, yet speak strongly to issues of Native identity. Still, the core of the NMAI's holdings is the collection of its forerunner institution, the Museum of the American Indian, Heye Foundation (MAI–HF).[1]

Essentially, this founding collection was assembled over the course of sixty years by one man: George Gustav Heye. It isn't news, of course, that by the time of his death in 1957, Heye had created the largest private collection in the world of American Indian arts and artifacts from North, Central, and South America and the West Indies.[2] Heye's stated aim was nothing less than "to gather and preserve for students everything useful in illustrating and elucidating the history and anthropology of aborigines of the Western [H]emisphere and to disseminate the knowledge gained by its researches."[3] Heye's collection not only spans the Americas, representing more than 1,200 indigenous cultures from the tip of Tierra del Fuego (Yámana and Selk´nam) to the Arctic tundra (Greenland Inuit), but ranges in time from 11,000 BC (Clovis projectile points) to the works of artists active in the late 1950s

(paintings by Southwest artists turning away from the Dorothy Dunn Studio). Comprising some 700,000 objects when Heye passed away, the collection includes simple and exquisitely wrought tools; basic and beautifully embellished weapons; unremarkable and intricately crafted containers; stringed, wind, and percussion musical instruments; plain and handsomely decorated clothing; objects of personal adornment; symbols of prestige and rank; dwellings; and objects of transportation—an exceptional reservoir of the heritage of Native American people.

George Gustav Heye was born into exclusive New York society on September 16, 1874, the son of Marie Antoinette Lawrence and Carl Friederich Gustav Heye. The Heye family home was located in the then-uptown neighborhood of Murray Hill, three blocks from the elegant brownstone built by financier John Pierpont Morgan in 1880. George Heye, who attended private schools and traveled to Europe as a youth, was heir to a tradition of respectability—and financial aggression. His father had entered the petroleum business just as the home lighting market was switching from whale oil to kerosene, and when the automobile was emerging on the American scene. In 1876 John D. Rockefeller bought the elder Heye's profitable Economic Refining Company. Usually, Rockefeller dismissed the owners of the small refineries he merged into his Standard Oil Company, but he was impressed by Heye and kept him on as president of the subsidiary. Heye rose within Standard Oil—the largest oil refinery in the world, controlling the transportation, production, refining, and marketing of petroleum products—eventually taking charge of the Foreign Shipping Department.

Given entrée by birth into the world of economic power, George Gustav Heye would eventually have access to the financial resources of industrial America.

With a degree in electrical engineering from the School of Mines of Columbia College—a school, it seems, his maternal great-grandfather helped establish[4]—in 1897 George Heye went to work for the White–Crosby engineering firm as an assistant superintendent on the construction of a seventeen-mile rail line to a mine near Kingman, Arizona. He returned to New York ten months later as chief engineer of the project and with a small collection of Indian objects. Back east, and following the social conventions of his class, in 1901 Heye co-founded the investment bank Battles, Heye, and Harrison, with offices in New York and Philadelphia. Heye would remain active in the affairs of the bank only until 1909. By then he had already emerged as a serious collector of Native American art, and his collection was attracting the attention of anthropologists keenly interested in its research potential.

As has often been repeated, Heye once reminisced about the first object he acquired, a Navajo shirt. He contended that from the moment he bought it, he was struck by the urge to collect Native-made objects.[5] In New York he began buying private collections. One of these—the large Henry E. Hales Collection of archaeological pottery from Socorro County, New Mexico, purchased in 1903—inspired Heye, under the influence of George H. Pepper of the American Museum of Natural History, to begin cataloguing his collection, regarding it not as simply a personal interest, but rather as a study collection.[6] According to Pepper, in 1904 Heye also began "actual field collecting,"[7] funding an archaeological expedition, led by Frank D. Utley, to Puerto Rico and Mexico to collect archaeological "specimens."

By 1906, Frederick Webb Hodge, of the Bureau of American Ethnology (BAE) in Washington, D.C., wrote in the *American Anthropologist*, "Noteworthy among private collections in American ethnology and archaeology made during recent years, if not, indeed, during any period, is that of Mr. George G. Heye of New York

City."[8] According to Hodge, Heye's collection encompassed more than 30,000 objects. It included historic Tlingit, Tahltan, Plains, and Iroquois objects, but mainly comprised archaeological material from the eastern United States, Midwest, and Southwest, and also from Mexico, Ecuador, Costa Rica, and the Caribbean.

Between that year and 1916, when the Museum of the American Indian, Heye Foundation was established, Heye and his mother would fund more than thirty archaeological and ethnographic expeditions,[9] and his collection would rapidly increase to include 400,000 objects. (Heye's mother supported his work until her death in 1915, at which time he inherited an estimated $10 million. His father had died in 1899.) Heye's most important archaeological expeditions during this period were conducted in Ecuador, Colombia, and the West Indies. Columbia University professor Marshall H. Saville, whom he met in 1906, is credited with planning Heye's first comprehensive research project, an archaeological survey of the coastal regions of Ecuador and Colombia.[10] Heye sent teams, some led by Pepper, to these areas every year from 1906 to 1910 and again in 1914. The Ecuador expeditions yielded important collections of stone sculptures, stelae, monoliths, and remarkable chairs with U-shaped seats resting on the backs of crouching human or animal figures (page 55). These seats are affiliated with the Manteño culture, which flourished from AD 500 to 1000. Heye had a special interest in exploring the region where Europeans first encountered the Native peoples of the Americas. In 1907 he funded the fieldwork of several individuals in the West Indies. These expeditions also created one of the finest Taíno collections extant, including a very strong collection of wooden objects—*duhos*, platters, drums, and sculptures—archaeological material that rarely survives.

The most intensive and extensive ethnographic fieldwork during this period was undertaken by Mark Raymond Harrington, whom Heye had met sometime between 1905 and 1908. Harrington, who had a master's in anthropology from Columbia University and operated Covert & Harrington, Commercial

Mark Raymond Harrington with a Seminole family, 1908. Florida. P37386

Ethnologists, had experience collecting among Native people. Between 1908 and 1916 Harrington collected some 7,453 objects for Heye from the Seminole, Choctaw, Creek, Cherokee, Chitimacha, Coushatta, Houma, Alibamu, and Catawba people in the southeastern United States; from the Delaware, Osage, and Shawnee in the Midwest; from the Meskwaki, Sac and Fox, Kiowa, Kiowa Apache, and Chiricahua Apache in Oklahoma; and from the Kickapoo in northern Mexico.

In April 1907, Heye entered into an agreement with George Byron Gordon and the University Museum in Philadelphia.[11] Heye provided Gordon with $2,000 to help fund a collecting expedition to Alaska and to purchase, on Heye's behalf, "duplicate specimens" amounting to one-third of the objects collected. Heye received northern Athapaskan, Tanana, and Kuskokwim Yup'ik material upon Gordon's return. Presumably wanting to cement relations with Heye, Gordon also gave him several Plains objects, including a shield collected by the painter George Catlin; Tsimshian, Makah, Kwakwaka'wakw, and Haida material collected by

Stewart Culin and Charles F. Newcombe; and archaeological material from Key Marco, Florida, collected by Frank Cushing of the BAE. Shortly thereafter, Gordon suggested that Heye house a portion of his collection in Philadelphia, with the assumption—on Gordon's part—that Heye would eventually donate his collection to the University Museum. Heye took Gordon up on the offer and was elected to the museum's board and named chairman of the Committee on the American Society. The museum publicly displayed part of Heye's collection, the first time that any of his pieces were exhibited. In a unique arrangement, Heye provided salary for assistants in the museum's American Section, but whatever was collected with Heye's funds was catalogued separately and stored with his collection. His holdings remained a distinct, private collection within the University Museum—and continued to grow.[12]

Heye was increasingly aware that he needed to find a suitable place to store, care for, and exhibit his entire collection. At some point he entered into conversations with millionaire and philanthropist Archer Milton

Huntington over a plot of land on which to build a museum. Huntington was creating a large cultural complex in upper Manhattan. The complex—Audubon Terrace—already housed, in stately Beaux-Arts buildings, the Hispanic Society, the American Geographical Society, and the American Numismatic Society. In the spring of 1916, Huntington offered Heye a plot on Broadway at 155th Street. Upon legally establishing and endowing the MAI–HF, Heye deeded to the trustees of the museum his entire collection of American Indian material.

Heye's inherited wealth allowed him to fund collecting expeditions in North, Central, and South America and to assemble what was already widely acknowledged as an exceptionally important collection of American Indian material culture. Yet his personal fortune would not be the only financial source drawn on to build and fill his museum. Heye counted among his friends industrial leaders in copper, rubber, and railways, as well as attorneys and bankers. His museum's founding trustees were United States Rubber Company vice president James B. Ford; United Fruit Company founder Minor C. Keith; director of Hendricks Brothers (dealers in metals, especially copper) Harmon W. Hendricks; Archer M. Huntington, son of railroad magnate Collis P. Huntington; corporate attorney F. Kingsbury Curtis; and a wealthy Philadelphia amateur archaeologist, Clarence B. Moore. At least half of these men were titans of industry.[13] Heye's trustees not only provided him with land for his museum, but contributed $350,000 for its design, construction, and infrastructure—including state-of-the-art mahogany display cabinetry. More than that, they bought individual objects of exceptional importance for the new museum, purchased large collections, and helped fund the museum's ambitious collecting expeditions. Heye's second wife, the former Thea Kowne Page, also purchased singular objects, such as an Olmec ceremonial axe dating to ca. 800 to 600 BC, bought from the art collector (and brother of Gertrude Stein) Leo Stein (page 86). Thea Heye also sponsored archaeological and ethnographic expeditions to Central America, Peru, and Chile.

With the financial support of his trustees and wife, Heye would fund more than one hundred collecting expeditions throughout the hemisphere over the next decade, often as many as twelve a year. To carry out this work, he employed a full-time staff whose chief responsibilities were to conduct archaeological excavations or collect objects directly from Native peoples, and to publish on the "knowledge gained and collections gathered" from their expeditions in the museum's series *Indian Notes, Indian Notes and Monographs, Contributions from the Museum of the American Indian, Heye Foundation,* and *Leaflets of the Museum of the American Indian, Heye Foundation.* Heye also employed "field collectors of ethnographic specimens" on a short-term basis, often avid collectors who collected directly from Indian peoples. Typically, upon learning about their pursuits, Heye purchased their personal collections and then hired them to collect for the MAI–HF. Heye covered the costs associated with their collecting trips and provided the funds with which they were to purchase objects and ship them back to New York City.

Heye understood one big anthropological idea—the culture area, conceived in the early 20th century as "a geographic area occupied by a number of peoples whose cultures show a significant degree of similarity with each other"[14] and dissimilarity from cultures of peoples of other areas. In 1916, Heye's staff went to work amassing ethnological and archaeological collections from every culture area into which the Americas had been classified. Heye's early advisor Marshall Saville—a member of the MAI–HF staff from 1918 to 1932, during which time he served one term (1927–1928) as president of the American Anthropological Association—excavated in Guatemala, Mexico, Ecuador, and Peru. Mark R. Harrington's expeditions involved both archaeological and ethnographic field collecting. Well documented for their day, the objects he collected form the nucleus of many of the MAI–HF's individual tribal collections. He would go on collecting for Heye until 1928, continuing his ethnographic work among eastern tribes, but also collecting in the Great Lakes region. In the Great Basin, he worked among the Paiute in Nevada and explored Lovelock

George G. Heye and Museum of the American Indian–Heye Foundation trustees, ca. 1920. New York. *From left to right:* Minor C. Keith, James B. Ford, Heye, F. K. Seward, F. Kingsbury Curtis, Samuel Riker Jr., Archer M. Huntington, and Harmon W. Hendricks. The first object catalogued by Heye, an archaeological Tularosa bowl, is displayed on the wall to the left. P11452

Cave where, in 1924, he and L. L. Loud of the University of California discovered a cache of 2,000-year-old decoy ducks—the oldest decoy ducks in the world (page 215). George Pepper's contributions to the collections were largely archaeological. Besides his earlier work with Saville at Manabi in Ecuador, Pepper excavated at Pueblo Bonito, in Chaco Canyon, New Mexico. Remarkable for the scale of its monumental public and ceremonial buildings, by AD 1050 Pueblo Bonito had the densest concentration of buildings in the Southwest. Among much else, Pepper uncovered a large number of tall, cylindrical vessels, sherds of which were recently discovered to have traces of cacao, indicating long-distance trade between Mesoamerica and ancestral

Pueblo peoples (page 113).[15] Among Heye's newer staff, Columbia University-educated Alanson B. Skinner collected for Heye mainly among the Menominee of Wisconsin, but also among the eastern Dakota tribes, that is, the Wahpeton and Sisseton, and in the east among the Seneca. He carried out archaeological work in Arkansas, Wisconsin, New York, and Costa Rica. Donald Cadzow collected extensively in Saskatchewan and Alberta, Canada, among the Loucheux, Slavey, Woodlands Cree, Prairie Cree, Bush Cree, Bungi or Plains Ojibwe, Assiniboine, and Pikuni. Cadzow also made large collections among the Baffin Island Inuit and Copper Inuit around Coronation Gulf in the north central Arctic. Joining the staff of the MAI–HF as

Donald Cadzow with Cree women, 1926. Files Hills Reserve, Saskatchewan. N23008

assistant director in 1919, Frederick Webb Hodge excavated Nacoochee Mound in Georgia with Heye and
Pepper. More important, from 1917 until 1923, he organized and directed the Hendricks–Hodge Expedition
to the historic A:shiwi (Zuni) villages of Hawikku and
Kechipan.[16] From one of the most extensive archaeological excavations conducted in the Southwest at the
time, thousands of wood, bone, textile, shell, and lithic
objects and architectural elements were recovered and
added to the museum's collection.

Lieutenant George T. Emmons, a U.S. Navy officer who spent most of his life acquiring objects from
the North Pacific and selling them to museums, was,
with Harrington, one of Heye's most important field
collectors.[17] Emmons collected primarily among the
Tlingit, Tahltan, and Tsimshian, but also among
the Kwakwaka´wakw, Bella Bella, Cowichan, Haida,
and Nootka. Heye bought the large personal collection of Indian art amassed by Edward H. Davis, a
transplanted New Yorker turned California rancher.
He then hired Davis to continue collecting for the
MAI–HF. Davis made significant collections among
the Cahuilla, Chemehuevi, Cocapah, Cora, Diegueño,
Huichol, Luiseño, Maricopa, Mayo, Opata, Panamint,

Edward H. Davis with Seri children, 1924. Tiburón Island, Mexico. N23816

Pima, San Carlos Apache, Quechan, Seri, Serrano,
Tohono O´odham, Walapia, White Mountain Apache,
and Yaqui between the years 1916 and 1933.[18] William
Wildschut, a Dutch businessman who is best known
for his recording of the life story of Two Leggings, an
Apsáalooke (Crow) warrior, as well as his MAI–HF publications on Apsáalooke medicine bundles and beadwork,[19] made important collections among northern
Plains tribes. From 1923 to 1928 Wildschut collected
extensively among the Apsáalooke, Arapaho, Bannock,
Blackfeet, Cheyenne, Flathead, and Shoshone. Melvin

R. Gilmore, an ethnobotanist and authority on the phylogeny of flowering plants, made important collections among the Arikara and Omaha, and among the Pawnee and Winnebago as well.

Intensive collecting among Native peoples in the early 20th century went hand in hand with conducting ethnographic fieldwork. Several ethnographers of note who did not serve on Heye's full-time staff also made collections for, or sold collections to, him. Frank G. Speck devoted the majority of his career to the study of eastern tribes ranging from the Labrador Eskimo and Innu in the north to the Yuchi in the south. One of Franz Boas's first graduate students and a firm disciple of the Boasian method, Speck saw collecting as an integral part of fieldwork, though he would sell objects to museums to fund future research. A. Irving Hallowell, a former student of Speck's who taught at the University of Pennsylvania, is best known for his studies of Ojibwe and their worldview. He made collections, acquired by Heye, among the Saulteaux band of Chippewa, Abinaki, Swampy Cree, Mashapee, and Nipissing Algonquin during his field studies. Christian Leden, the Norwegian explorer-anthropologist and early ethnomusicologist, worked among Inuit peoples in Greenland and along the west coast of the Hudson Bay. Frances T. Densmore, another pioneer ethnomusicologist—and pioneer woman anthropologist—had a fifty-year association with the BAE, for whom she made an important collection of wax cylinder sound recordings. She collected for Heye among the Lakota in 1917 on the Standing Rock Reservation in South Dakota. Archaeologist Samuel K. Lothrop had a long association with the Peabody Museum from 1915 through 1960, but he also undertook MAI–HF-sponsored expeditions, notably to Chile, El Salvador, and Peru. Lothrop also made important ethnographic collections among the Yámana and Selk´nam of Tierra del Fuego.

During the 1920s, while Heye was directing and participating in the collecting activities of the museum, he also served two terms as president of the Explorers Club. Heye's association with the club helps contextualize his personal and professional aims. Established in 1904, the club's membership doubles as a list of the most prominent explorers of the early 20th century, including Robert Peary, Adolphus Washington Greeley, and Sir Ernest Shackleton. The club welcomed archaeologists, ethnologists, biologists, naturalists, ornithologists, aviators, and those interested in their work. The bond uniting these men was that they traveled to remote regions, contacted indigenous tribes, "uncovered early civilizations," and otherwise investigated worlds not yet documented in the West. Members gathered at lectures and annual dinners to share stories of their research and plan future expeditions. Probably equally to Heye's liking, it was an association of New York's "cultured metropolitan elite" who felt a mission to seek out uncharted territory. Early rosters of the club's membership include a large number of individuals who collected for Heye. Perhaps some of these individuals—such as Cadzow, Gilmore, and Harrington—joined the Explorers Club at Heye's suggestion. But it was also through his connections at the club that Heye became acquainted with Arctic and Central and South American explorers. Notable among these men were Robert Bartlett, who collected for Heye in the Arctic; George Dyott, Francis Gow-Smith, and Gordon MacCreagh, who collected for him in the Amazon; paleoichthyologist William L. Bryant; western artists and illustrators Frederick S. Dellenbaugh and Edwin W. Deming; Tierra del Fuego explorer and ethnologist Charles Wellington Furlong; and naturalist George Bird Grinnell. Worth noting, too, MAI–HF trustee James B. Ford was an early member and president of the Explorers Club.

Heye also bought Indian material from a large number of professional dealers, many of whom are still well known in museum circles. Fred Harvey operated a chain of hugely profitable hotels and restaurants for passengers of the Santa Fe Railway in the Southwest. His Fred Harvey Company actively collected American Indian arts and artifacts from the early 1900s through the 1930s, many of which were sold to museums.[20] Heye acquired 321 Harvey objects from throughout the United States, including an ancestral Hopi bowl with stylized representations of birds (page 115). J. E.

Standley's Ye Olde Curiosity Shoppe in Seattle catered, in the early 1900s, to whalers, traders, gold seekers, and the like—anyone with Alaskan "curiosities" to sell for quick cash.[21] With these objects Standley organized a large exhibition for the Alaska–Yukon–Pacific Exposition, a world's fair held in Seattle in 1909. In 1916, Heye purchased 825 objects from Standley's exposition display. From Grace Nicholson, doyenne of the fine art curio trade, especially in Native basketry, Heye purchased 951 mainly Pomo, Karuk, Yurok, and Tolowa objects. After Heye's death, the MAI–HF acquired Nicholson's remarkable twenty-eight-year-long correspondence with William Benson, husband of Mary Benson—two of the finest Pomo basket-makers working at the turn of the 19th century. The correspondence presents a unique glimpse into their lives—and into their relationship with the dealer.[22]

Each of the museum's collections of cultural material—Tlingit, Pomo, Ancestral Pueblo, et cetera—was formed, in large part, through a combination of field collecting, purchases from professional dealers, trustee donations, and auction purchases. Even so, these varied sources represent only part of the chronicle of Heye's collecting, whose roots go deep into American history, and Indian–white relations. Before 1897, when Heye purchased his first Indian artifact, many individuals made small, but notable, collections of American Indian art. Many were people caught up in the making of America. Some of these men were involved in the very beginning of the transcontinental railroad project. Though his name is not well known today, painter and illustrator John Mix Stanley was a great rival of George Catlin. Like Catlin, he traveled extensively and painted, from life, portraits of Indians of different tribes.[23] In 1853 Stanley was a member of Governor Isaac Steven's survey to determine the best railroad route across the northern United States. The survey party cut through Blackfeet territory, and the collection Stanley made includes an early and powerful Blackfeet war shirt. Others participated in government-sponsored explorations of the American West. In 1871 Frederick S. Dellenbaugh, also an artist, took part in John Wesley Powell's second exploration down the Colorado River and into the Grand Canyon, believed to be the last great stretch of land and river still unknown in the United States. In 1899 Dellenbaugh joined the Harriman Expedition, a two-month survey of the Alaska coast sponsored by railroad tycoon Edward H. Harriman. Dellenbaugh's collection, numbering ninety-three objects, represents various tribes. Some collectors were present at the creation of merchant capitalism in America. William Henry Schieffelin was born into a prominent family that "held an important place in the social and business life of New York,"[24] directing for several generations the oldest pharmaceutical company in the country.[25] Shieffelin's sojourn out west in the early 1860s was apparently that of a privileged young man. At Fort Benton, on the Missouri River, he received, in an exchange of gifts, a rare and magnificent Apsáalooke war exploit robe, one of only two such robes in the United States today (pages 162–165). Finally, some individual collectors were successful doctors who contributed to important medical advances. Among the 347 catalog entries associated with Dr. George Jackson Fisher are a coat and pair of finger woven garters associated with the Seminole leader Osceola (page 193).

Even more salient, perhaps, than these privileged and often affluent 19th-century figures were the collectors who lived in prolonged contact with Indian peoples—usually during and just after the so-called Indian wars, the battles between the U.S. Army and Native tribes. Military officers whose collections were acquired by Heye include 2nd Lieutenant (later Brigadier General) Charles G. Sawtelle, Captain John G. Bourke, General Nelson A. Miles, and Colonel Eugene Beaumont, to name just a very few. There is much irony in the fact that men who fought to subjugate Indians also sought to form collections of their artisanship. Captain Bourke participated in the 1872 Tonto Basin Campaign in Arizona, which resulted in the deaths of hundreds of Western Apache men, women, and children. Yet he collected extensively among Western Apache peoples. In April 1881 he was assigned to "the duty of investigating the manners and customs of the Pueblo, Apache, and Navajo Indians." Strangely, considering his war record, Bourke was deeply interested in ethnological studies and had studied the "manners and customs" of Western Apache Indians since the early 1870s. Bourke's collecting was part of his "investigations." Stationed among the Northern Cheyenne and Lakota in the mid 1870s, he helped lead the U.S. Army's offensives against these tribes—and, at the same time, collected among them. In 1876 or 1877, he acquired a shirt from Little Big Man, which, he was told, had belonged to Crazy Horse (page 155).[26]

Heye also acquired the collections of a number of Office of Indian Affairs agents. U.S. Indian agents were responsible for administering, on behalf of the government, Native nations confined to reservations. Among other duties, the agents were to distribute the annuities to tribes stipulated in their treaties with the United States and encourage Indians to become farmers ("to force them to walk the white man's road"). Agents whose collections are represented in the MAI–HF include Thomas Twiss, Douglas Grier, and George H. Bingenheimer. Like Bourke a graduate of West Point, Twiss was named Indian agent for the upper Platte in 1855, a time of intense turmoil for Oglala Lakota peoples. Twiss was their agent until he was suspended for his dictatorial dealings with them.[27] He was reinstated only to be dismissed a second time. Formed in the 1850s, the Twiss collection numbers seventy-four objects, including many important pony beaded objects dating to this relatively early period.

Missionaries whose collections George Heye obtained include Thomas Crosby and Gilbert Wilson. The U.S. and Canadian governments passed prohibitions against the practice of Native traditional and religious ceremonies during the 19th century, but it was missionaries who daily and zealously enforced these laws. Often, missionaries targeted leaders and heads of large families for conversion, believing that their followers and families would follow. Crosby, an English Methodist, worked among First Nations people in British Columbia. Missionizing intensively throughout the province, especially among the Tsimshians at Fort Simpson, he insisted on the abandonment, or rather eradication, of Native traditions, all the while

collecting traditional arts among the Tsimshian, Kwakwa̲ka′wakw, Haida, Bella Coola, and Tlingit.[28]

The single thread connecting all of these collectors, of the 19th or early 20th century, whether private or professional, is that they collected with the belief that American Indians would and should succumb to what they regarded as the forces of progress. (Captain Bourke titled one of his many ethnographic works *Vesper Hours of the Stone Age*.)

George Gustav Heye, one of a number of extremely wealthy New Yorkers assembling large collections at the turn of the 20th century, inherited this pervasive way of thought. Yet he also stands apart from his peers. Other New York collectors—men like John Pierpont Morgan, Henry Clay Frick, and Benjamin Altman—were connoisseurs who collected fine art. Heye's was an entirely different kind of undertaking. Although he was not an intellectual, he conceived of the collection he formed as scientific. True, the intellectual framework for the MAI–HF's collecting was best articulated in letters and publications by academics George H. Pepper and Frederick Webb Hodge. But Heye had an archaeological and anthropological interest from the start, one that revolved around the questions, "Whence came the American Indian and when?"[29] To find the answers, Heye understood, would require not only an archaeological collection, but a hemispheric one as well. Hand in hand with the great questions of the New World's origins was the strong notion that contemporary American Indians were vestiges of a bygone time. The objects Heye collected—masterworks, but also, everyday tools and utensils—were for him all material evidence surviving from the past.

Finally, Heye formed his collection during the "great period of museum anthropology," when anthropological inquiry took place in museums (as opposed to universities) and objects were considered important to answering questions not just about extinct lifeways, but also about "others"—peoples whose differences from Westerners were considered profoundly problematic.[30] The perceived "otherness" of non-Western cultures was, of course, the product of the political and economic processes summarized as colonialism. But more immediately relevant, this perspective reflected the belief that Western societies were higher on the "scale of mankind"—a 19th-century notion of social evolution that placed Victorians at the apex. The assemblages of anthropology museums—decidedly 19th- and early-20th-century phenomena[31]—were, it is now accepted, based upon a cultural imperialism that diminished the communities from which objects were collected.[32]

While it is important to know how Heye acquired the objects in his collection—now the cornerstone of the collections of the National Museum of the American Indian—and the cultural context within which the collection was formed, what is of ultimate importance is to understand the Native history these objects embody and their significance to Native peoples today. It is a moving experience when Native communities come to view their tribal collections—sacred and ceremonial objects; men's, women's, and children's clothing; cradleboards; utensils; weapons; horse gear; musical instruments; and toys. Often a prayer ceremony is conducted before a group begins working with their collection. After an elder or other tribal member smudges all who are present, purifying everyone with smoke from burnt cedar or sage, the objects may be smudged as well. The day starts slowly as tribal members get accustomed, if they ever do, to the scale of the museum's holdings—the numbers of things that were made, worn, and used by their grandparents and great-grandparents—and to the strong emotions they feel when they see these objects laid out before them. To have it all seem so unreal and yet so familiar, and to feel it pull on their hearts. Eventually, some one thing, seemingly a very small thing, captures someone's attention. A pattern of shapes or colors on a beaded cradleboard or moccasin, and then the murmuring begins, sometimes in English, sometimes not. Someone, an elder, recalls aloud seeing her grandfather use a certain object. A thin, tapered stick about ten inches long and ornately carved. It was used by Kiowa men to part their hair. Or an Apache man picks up a pair of very small, unadorned moccasins, neither painted nor beaded, and points out sets

of barely visible, pin-sized holes in the hide. He tells those present that the moccasins belonged to a very sick child. The holes, he explains, were made to attach small turquoise beads during a healing ceremony. As is generally the case, sacred objects are looked at quietly, but are not touched except by those who have the religious authority to do so, and then only following certain prescriptions.

Two watershed acts of Congress went far in changing the ways in which museums and Indian peoples interact. The American Indian Religious Freedom Act (AIRFA) of 1978 acknowledged that American Indians have been denied the free exercise of their religions guaranteed in the First Amendment. It laid the groundwork for the Native American Graves Protection and Repatriation Act (NAGPRA) of 1990, which calls for museums that receive federal funds to produce inventories of their collections to tribal governments and provides for the repatriation to tribes of human remains, funerary objects, and objects of cultural patrimony.[33] The NMAI Act of 1989, which established the new museum and transferred in June 1990 the MAI–HF collection to the Smithsonian, also provides for the repatriation of human remains and certain categories of objects alienated from Native tribes.

While the NMAI continues to collaborate with tribal representatives to identify objects in its collection that fall under this legislation, the museum also continues to build its collection in ways responsive to Native aims. Emphasis has been placed upon the acquisition of modern and contemporary works. In 1999, the museum received the Indian Arts and Crafts Board (IACB) collection of 20th-century American Indian art. Part of Commissioner of Indian Affairs John Collier's economic initiative for Indian peoples under the New Deal, the IACB collection helped support the work of Native artists throughout the United States, from 1935 through the 1980s, by purchasing examples of their art. Encompassing great artistic diversity, this rich and important collection has filled a tremendous gap in the museum's collection.

The NMAI has also been fortunate to receive many examples of contemporary traditional works over the

Percy Medina (Quechua, b. 1976), carved gourd, 2008. Peru. Gourd; 25 x 26 cm. Gift of the artist. 26/6799

last twenty years through donations by contemporary artists and art collectors, as well as through purchases made in conjunction with exhibitions.[34] The Quechua carved and pyro-engraved gourd made in 2008 by Percy Medina, to give one example, carries on one of the oldest indigenous art forms in the Americas. In his virtuosic art, Medina introduces entirely new subject matter while maintaining the technical and compositional mastery of the most accomplished Quechua gourd carvers.

At the heart of the museum's mission is a commitment to demonstrate the vitality of traditional Native art forms. Also central to its work, however, is encouraging a deep understanding among the public of Native artistic expressions that transcend traditional media and techniques, and that engage a wide range of contemporary artistic issues. To this end the NMAI has acquired significant works by such singular artists as the Dunne-za sculptor Brian Jungen, whose monumental sculptures reference themes of globalization, pop culture, and the commodification of Indian culture.[35] Over the last twenty years, the NMAI has acquired nearly 3,000 works of art that reflect the breadth, diversity, and tenor of present-day Native America. The museum is committed to building one of the world's foremost collections of 20th- and 21st-century American Indian art, while remaining faithful to the stewardship of its historic collections.

—Cécile R. Ganteaume

Broadway revival

For more than seventy years, beginning in 1922, George Gustav Heye's Museum of the American Indian at Broadway and 155th Street in upper Manhattan was widely recognized as one of the best places in the world to see the material culture of the original peoples of the Americas. Now, *Infinity of Nations*, the companion exhibition to this book, again presents a survey of Heye's unparalleled collections on Broadway, through more than 700 particularly significant objects on view at the George Gustav Heye Center, at the southern end of that old Algonquin trail.

Both museum-goers who remember the exhibits at Audubon Terrace—and many New Yorkers do—and those who discovered the collections after Congress created the Smithsonian National Museum of the American Indian, will find familiar and challenging elements in the new exhibition. The Heye Center, which opened in 1994, and the museum on the National Mall in Washington, our larger, but younger (2004) sibling, are part of a new generation of museums that interpret cultural history from the inside out. Presenting objects and art made by American Indians in imaginative, intelligent, and beautiful ways remains important, and the Heye collections remain dazzling, but we now give greater emphasis to cultural context—the ideas objects embody and their relationship to living cultural values.

At the same time, the National Museum of the American Indian and other culturally based museums are seeking to be more significant to the communities we represent. By regarding our galleries, auditoriums, classrooms, screening rooms, collections and research facilities, and conservation labs as places where living cultures can express and renew their traditions, museums are becoming new kinds of civic spaces.

A recurring theme of *Infinity of Nations* is the interconnectedness of peoples and the important role contact and exchange have always played in the development of cultures and societies. By serving as contemporary centers for the exchange of ideas—bringing together intellectual and cultural values and contributions from many sources and disciplines, and people from throughout our communities and around the world—museums have the potential to play a unique part in cultural encounters on issues that have bearing on all our lives, indigenous and nonindigenous.

I hope this marvelous book spurs you to visit the museum. Reading Philip Deloria's introduction on the power of objects to move us, I realized that one emotion I so often feel in our galleries is gratitude. Arden Kucate touches on it in his discussion of a stone jar and the care Ancestral Pueblo people took to keep it safe. These objects have come through hundreds, sometimes thousands, of years of history.

Musing—Phil's perfect word—on a Mississippian shell gorget, my colleague Tom Evans observed, "We can only guess as to what the artist was recording. The people of that place and time knew the warrior being depicted. They understood what he was doing and why. It would have been inconceivable to them that we might one day look at these objects and wonder at the meaning of their universe." Yes, it would have been, but we are privileged to have that opportunity. Come and see these objects in person. Something you encounter will speak to you.

—John Haworth (Cherokee), director, George Gustav Heye Center, National Museum of the American Indian

Mexica Tlalchitonatiuh, setting sun god, ca. AD 1325–1521. Probably Tenochtitlan, Mexico. Basalt; 6 x 41 cm. Exchange with Morris De Camp Crawford. 11/8220

Acknowledgments

THE IMPRESSIVE SCOPE OF IDEAS presented on these pages is the result of years of collaboration and research, and I would like to thank the many contributors whose talents and wisdom are showcased in this book. The main essays were written by leading scholars in their fields, and I offer my gratitude to each of them. I would also like to thank the fifty-three Native scholars and community members who wrote texts about individual objects highlighted in this volume. These objects were selected because of their aesthetic, cultural, and historic importance, and each of the authors gives a personal interpretation of the object's significance, referencing his or her scholarly research and unique cultural insights. I am particularly indebted to scholars Steven J. Crum (Western Shoshone), Michael Witgen (Ojibwe), and Craig P. Howe (Lakota) for providing consultations on the Native contributors to this volume. Ten of the Native contributors co-wrote their texts with non-Native scholars, and I am very grateful to those collaborating authors.

Michael Witgen, a historian at the University of Michigan, also introduced me to the expression "infinity of nations," from his original research into 17th-century French colonial documents, and generously shared his scholarship on Anishinaabe and French relations, including the use of this expression in reference to Anishinaabe peoples. As early as 1626, French missionaries and colonial governors eager to establish commercial and diplomatic alliances throughout their colonial territories described the peoples of the New World as "an infinity of nations." The expression embodies multiple meanings, two of which seem most appropriate here. First, the phrase quite rightly captures France's impression of North America as a land populated with a multitude of indigenous peoples, rather than the uninhabited New World of European imagination. Second, the word "nations" acknowledges the sovereignty of the Native peoples—a sovereignty that was soon threatened by colonial and national powers—and a nation-to-nation status that Native peoples still fight to protect to this day. This volume pays tribute to those peoples, past and present, and to the deeply cultural, profoundly social objects they created.

I thank Philip J. Deloria (Standing Rock Sioux) for his reflective introduction and for offering a way to begin thinking about the objects made and used by Native peoples that, through the contingencies of history, have found their way into the collections of the National Museum of the American Indian.

There are many individuals to whom I turned for help in dating or identifying the cultural attributions of individual objects selected for the *Infinity of Nations* exhibition and illustrated in this book, or for further understanding of the cultural significance of objects. For generously sharing their expertise, I am very grateful to Joyce Bear (Muskogee [Creek]), Steve Bourget, Arni Brownstone, John Carlson, Bob Chenoweth, Janet Chernela, William Conklin, Nora Dauenhauer (Tlingit), Christopher Donnan, Celestino Gachupin (Zia), Robert Grumet, Stanley Guenter, Richard Hansen, Ira Jacknis, John Janusek, Adriano Jerozolimski, Jeff Kowalski, Peter Macnair, Joe Medicine Crow (Crow), Michael J. Moratto, Cath Oberholtzer, Steve Plog, Charles Redcorn (Osage), Ann Rowe, Abelardo Sandoval, Kristine Stenzel, Jay Stewart, André Toral, Anton Treuer (Ojibwe), Terence Turner, Alexei Vranich,

Herman Viola, and Juliet Wiersema. If I've inadvertently left anybody off this list, I sincerely apologize and offer my deepest thanks to them, too.

I offer my gratitude to NMAI Director Kevin Gover (Pawnee) and Associate Director for Museum Programs Tim Johnson (Mohawk), for their tutelage, unwavering support, and constant encouragement in bringing this book—and its related exhibition—to fruition. I am also deeply indebted to John Haworth (Cherokee), director of the George Gustav Heye Center in New York, and Peter Brill, deputy assistant director, for the invitation to serve as curator of *Infinity of Nations*, and for their vision and commitment to the project.

I would like to thank Tanya Thrasher (Cherokee), head of the museum's publications office, and her staff for their professionalism and dedication. Ann Kawasaki and Colleen Schreier provided invaluable administrative support. Alexandra Harris (Cherokee) assisted in the production of the map graphics, created by talented illustrator Gene Thorp. Alexandra, Sally Barrows, Megan Gray, Arwen Nuttall (Four Winds Band of Cherokee), and Charlotte Watter also provided editorial assistance. I am particularly grateful to editor Holly Stewart, and to senior designer Steve Bell, who created the book's beautiful design. It has been a pleasure to work with HarperCollins; editor Stephanie Meyers, production editor Diana Aronson, and production supervisor Karen Lumley, in particular, have gone out of their way to make this book successful.

I greatly appreciate the fine work of Cynthia Frankenburg and her staff in NMAI Photo Services, including Ernest Amoroso, Katherine Fogden (Mohawk), Will Greene, Walter Larrimore, and Roger A. Whiteside, for producing the book's exquisite photography. Thanks to NMAI head of conservation Marian Kaminitz; conservators Susan Heald, Emily Kaplan, and Kelly McHugh; Mellon Foundation conservation fellows; and NMAI interns for their expert preparation of the objects for photography and display. Thanks are due to Shelly Uhlir for ingeniously devising the object mounts. For their gracious help throughout the process, I would also like to thank NMAI photo archivists Lou Stancari and Emily Moazami. I am also most deeply grateful to Lynne Altstatt, librarian of the NMAI's Vine Deloria, Jr., Library.

I owe a special debt of gratitude to research assistant Maria Galban. She has been involved in every facet of this book's production, from object selection and organizing workshops, to researching current tribal names and writing informative object labels and captions. Her contributions are invaluable and very much evident on every page. I also offer my sincere thanks to the many colleagues who together created the *Infinity of Nations* exhibition, on view at the museum's George Gustav Heye Center in New York through 2020. Exhibition project managers Duane Blue Spruce (Laguna/Ohkay Owingeh) and Lindsay Stamm Shapiro provided outstanding assistance at every step of the way. Imrey Culbert LP designed the beautiful casework to house more than 700 particularly significant objects from the museum's extraordinary collections. Finally, I offer thanks to Associate Director for Museum Assets Jane Sledge and my curatorial colleagues Ann McMullen, Mary Jane Lenz, Emil Her Many Horses (Lakota), and Ramiro Matos (Quechua) for their encouragement.

—Cécile R. Ganteaume

Notes & references

A note on the maps

The tribal names and archaeological cultures identified on the regional maps in this book correspond to the cultural attributions of the objects illustrated in each chapter. Their locations correspond to the dates when those objects were made. These maps do not reflect a comprehensive identification and location of tribes and archaeological cultures present in any region at any point in time.

For more information on the collections

To see more about the objects in this book and the accompanying exhibition at the George Gustav Heye Center in New York, please visit the *Infinity of Nations* website at www.nmai.si.edu/exhibitions/infinityofnations.

INTRODUCTION

Philip J. Deloria

1. Benjamin, "On some motifs in Baudelaire," 188.

2. Benjamin, "On the mimetic faculty," 333–36.

3. Rabinbach, "Introduction to Walter Benjamin's 'doctrine of the similar,'" 60–64.

4. Prown, "Introduction."

5. Adorno, "Valéry Proust Museum," 176.

References

Adorno, Theodor. "Valéry Proust Museum." In *Prisms*, Samuel and Shierry Weber, trans. Cambridge MA: MIT, 1997.

Benjamin, Walter. "On some motifs in Baudelaire." In *Illuminations*, Hannah Arendt, ed., Harry Zohn, trans. New York: Schocken, 1969.

Benjamin, Walter. "On the mimetic faculty." In *Reflections*, Peter Demetz, ed., Edmund Jephcott, trans. New York: Schocken, 1978.

Prown, Jules. "Introduction." In *American Artifacts: Essays in Material Culture.* East Lansing: Michigan State University, 2000.

Rabinbach, Anson. "Introduction to Walter Benjamin's 'doctrine of the similar.'" *New German Critique* 17 (1979).

PATAGONIA, TIERRA DEL FUEGO, AND GRAN CHACO

Tom Dillehay

1. Bengoa, *Historia de los antiquos Mapuches*; Dillehay, *Monuments, Resistance and Empires*; Faron, *Hawks of the Sun*; Latcham, *Organización social y las creencias religiosas de los antiguos Araucanos*; Mandrini and Ortelli, "Los 'Araucanos' en las pampas"; Nacuzzi, *Identidades impuestas.*

2. Bengoa; Boccara, "Colonización, resistencia y etnogénesis"; Villalobos and Pinto, ed. *Araucanía.*

3. Aldunate, "Mapuche: Gente de la tierra."

4. Faron, *Hawks of the Sun.*

5. Foester, *Introducción a la religiosidad Mapuche*; Grebe et al, "Cosmovisión Mapuche"; Guevara, *Historia de Chile*; Latcham.

6. Alonqueo, *Instituciones religiosas del Pueble Mapuche*; Dillehay; Foester; Grebe; Titiev, *Araucanian Culture in Transition.*

7. Acuña et al., "Genetic variants of serum *Butyrylcholinesterase* in Chilean Mapuche Indians."

References

Acuña, M. P., L. Eaton, N. R. Ramírez, L. Cifuentes, and E. Llop. "Genetic variants of serum *Butyrylcholinesterase* in Chilean Mapuche Indians." *American Journal of Physical Anthropology* 121, no. 1 (2003): 81–85.

Aldunate, C. "Mapuche: Gente de la tierra." In *Etnografía: Sociedades Indígenas contemporáneas y su ideología*, 111–34. Santiago, Chile: Editorial Andrés Bello, 1996.

Alonqueo, M. *Instituciones religiosas del Pueble Mapuche.* Santiago, Chile: Ediciones Nueva Universidad, 1979.

Bengoa, J. *Historia de los antiquos Mapuches del Sur.* Santiago, Chile: Imprenta Catalonia, 2003.

Boccara, G. "Colonización, resistencia y etnogénesis en las fronteras Americanas." In *Colonización, resistencia y mestizaje en las Américas, siglos XVI–XX*, 47–82. Quito, Ecuador: Ediciones Abya–Yala, 2000.

Dillehay, T. D. *Monuments, Resistance and Empires: Araucanian Polity and Ritual Narratives.* Cambridge and New York: Cambridge University, 2007.

Faron, L. *Hawks of the Sun: Mapuche Morality and Its Ritual Attributes.* Pittsburgh: University of Pittsburgh, 1964.

Foester, R. *Introducción a la religiosidad Mapuche.* Santiago, Chile: Editorial Universitaria, 1993.

Grebe, M. E., S. Pacheco, and J. Segura. "Cosmovisión Mapuche." *Cuadernos de la realidad nacional* 14 (1972): 46–73.

Guevara, T. *Historia de Chile: Chile prehispánico*, vol. 1 and 2. Santiago, Chile: Imprenta Cervantes, 1929.

Latcham, R. E. *Organización social y las creencias religiosas de los antiguos Araucanos.* Santiago, Chile: Imprenta Cervantes, 1924.

Mandrini, R., and S. Ortelli. "Los 'Araucanos' en las pampas (ca. 1700–1850)." In *Colonización, resistencia y mestizaje en las Américas, siglos XVI–XX*, G. Bocarra, ed., 201–36. Quito, Ecuador: Ediciones Abya–Yala, 2002.

Nacuzzi, L. R. *Identidades impuestas: Tehuelches, aucas y pampas en el norte de la Patagonia.* Buenos Aires: Sociedad Argentina de Antropología, 1998.

Titiev, M. *Araucanian Culture in Transition.* Ann Arbor: University of Michigan, 1951.

Villalobos, S., and J. Pinto, ed. *Araucanía: Temas de historia fronteriza.* Temuco, Chile: Ediciones Universidad de la Frontera, 1984.

Paul Ossa

1. Borrero, "Early occupation in the Southern Cone"; Dillehay, "Profiles in pleistocene history."

2. Bolas are sets of stones (commonly three) wrapped in leather and connected by leather thongs. The hunter holds one stone, or the nexus of the thongs, and whirls the other stones about his head, before letting the bolas go in the direction of the prey. The thongs wrap about the legs or neck and body of the animal, bringing it down. Bolas are found early in the occupation of the area, with possibly the earliest being found at the archaeological site of Marazzi in Tierra del Fuego. Laming-Emperaire et al., "Le site de Marazzi en Terre de Feu."

3. The most famous Yámana was a young man called Jemmy Button (his Yámana name is recorded as Orundellico) by Fitz-Roy after he "purchased" him for a button. Jemmy Button was taken to England with three other Fuegian natives. There they were educated and discreetly exhibited for a year. On Fitz-Roy's second voyage on HMS *Beagle*—with Charles Darwin as his naturalist and gentleman companion—the three surviving Fuegians were returned to their homeland. They were left at Wulaia Cove on Navarino Island. In the report of his voyage, Fitz-Roy mentions the last encounter he had with the natives, whom he had named Fuegia Basket and

York Minster. "Fuegia looked clean and tidily dressed [Fitz-Roy certainly meant in contemporary English dress], and by her wigwam was a canoe, which York was building out of planks left for him by our party." Fuegia Basket and York Minster were not Yámana but Kawesqar, and had a long voyage to make to get to their homeland. Fitz-Roy added, "Jemmy's occupation was hollowing out the trunk of a large tree, in order to make such a canoe as he had seen at Rio de Janeiro." Fitz-Roy, *Narrative of the Surveying Voyages*, 224.

4. Kidd, "The morality of the Enxet people."

References

Borrero, Luis Alberto. "Early occupation in the Southern Cone." In *Handbook of South American Archaeology*, Helaine Silverman and William Isbell, ed., 59–72. New York: Springer, 2008.

Chapman, Anne. *The Selk´nam: Drama and Power in a Hunting Society*. Cambridge and New York: Cambridge University, 1982.

Dillehay, Tom D. "Profiles in pleistocene history." In *Handbook of South American Archaeology*, Helaine Silverman and William Isbell, ed., 29–43. New York: Springer, 2008.

Fitz-Roy, Robert. *Narrative of the Surveying Voyages of His Majesty's Ships "Adventure" and "Beagle," between the years 1826 and 1836, describing their examination of the southern shores of South America and the "Beagle" circumnavigation of the globe. Proceedings of the Second Expedition, 1931–1836, under the Command of Captain Robert Fitz-Roy*, vol. 2. London: Henry Colburn, 1839.

Gusinde, Martin. *Die Feuerland indianer; Ergebnisse meiner vier Forschungsreisen in den Jahren 1918 bis 1924. Unternommen im Auftrage des Ministerio de Instrucción pública de Chile. In drei Bänden herausgegeben von Martin Gusinde. Band 1: Die Selk´nam; vom Leben und Denken eines Jägervolkes auf der grossen Feuerlandinsel, 1931. Band 2: Die Yamana; vom Leben und Denken der Wassernomaden am Kap Hoorn, 1937. Band3/2: Antropologie der Feurland–Indianer, 1939. Band 3/1: Die Halakwulup; vom Leben und Denken der Wassernomaden im Westpatagonischen Inselreich*, 1974. Modling–Wien: Verlag St. Gabriel: Verlag der internationalen zeitschrift Anthropos, 1931–1974.

Kidd, Stephen W. "The morality of the Enxet people of the Paraguayan Chaco and their resistance to assimilation." In *Peoples of the Gran Chaco*, Elmer S. Miller, ed. Westport CT: Greenwood, 1999.

Laming-Emperaire, A., D. Lavallée, and R. Humbert. "Le site de Marazzi en Terre de Feu." *Rehué* 1 (1968): 133–43.

Musters, George Chaworth. *At Home with the Patagonians: A Year's Wanderings over Untrodden Ground from the Straits of Magellan to the Rio Negro*. London: John Murray, 1871.

Orquera, L. A., and E. L. Piana. *La vida material y social de los Yámana*. Buenos Aires: EUDEBA, Instituto Fueguino de Investigaciones Científicas, 1999.

THE ANDES
Tom Dillehay

1. Salomon and Schwartz, *South America*.

2. Silverman and Isbell, *Handbook of South American Archaeology*.

3. Labbe, *Colombia before Columbus*.

4. Burger, *Chavin and the Origins of Andean Civilization*; Moseley, *The Incas and Their Ancestors*.

5. Kosok, *Life, Land and Water in Ancient Peru*; Moseley.

6. Kaulicke, *Los origenes de la civilización Andina*; Moseley; Silverman and Isbell.

7. D'Altroy, *The Incas*; Moseley.

8. Salomon and Schwartz.

References

Burger, Richard L. *Chavin and the Origins of Andean Civilization*. London: Thames and Hudson, 1992.

D'Altroy, T. *The Incas*. London: Blackwell, 2003.

Kaulicke, Peter. *Los origenes de la civilización Andina: Arqueología del Perú. Historia general del Perú*, vol. 1. J. A. Del Busto, ed. Lima: Brasa, 1994.

Kosok, Paul. *Life, Land and Water in Ancient Peru*. New York: Long Island University, 1965.

Labbe, A. J. *Colombia before Columbus: The People, Culture, and Ceramic Art of Prehispanic Colombia*. New York: Rizzoli, 1986.

Lathrap, D. *Ancient Ecuador*. Chicago: Field Museum, 1975.

Moseley, Michael E. *The Incas and Their Ancestors: The Archaeology of Peru*. London: Thames and Hudson, 1972.

Salomon, Frank, and Stuart B. Schwartz, ed. *South America. The Cambridge History of the Native Peoples of the Americas*, vol. 3, part 1. Cambridge and New York: Cambridge University, 1999.

Silverman, H., and W. Isbell, ed. *Handbook of South American Archaeology*. New York: Springer, 2008.

THE AMAZON
Wlliam H. Fisher

I was fortunate to receive help and commentary from many people during the course of trying to understand the assemblage of pieces represented in this project. I therefore express great appreciation to the following people, who, of course, are not responsible for any of the interpretations I elaborate in this chapter: thanks are due to Martha Case, Janet Chernela, Maria Galban, Elisa Galli, Cécile Ganteaume, John Hemming, Alf Hornborg, Søren Hvalkof, Kohalue Karajá, Manuel Ferreira Lima Filho, Betty Meggers, George Mentore, Scott Mori, Steven Rubenstein, Glenn Shepard Jr., Hanne Veber, Gustaaf Verswijver, and Norman and Dorothea Whitten.

—William H. Fisher

A case in point for this project's theme of continental interactions is the pottery drinking horn described by Juan Carlos Jintiach and Richard Tsakimp on page 83 (22/8772). Amazonian peoples often manufacture things destined for other groups, so many objects in the collections can be traced in at least two ways—as products of a certain people and as incorporated into the practices and beliefs of another. Neighboring Canelos Quichua women make these kinds of cornets for the Shuar and Achuar, as well as for their own use. Achuar and Shuar shamans are primarily trained by Canelos shamans, and Achuar and Shuar not infrequently marry Canelos women (e.g. Taylor, "Sick of history," 138). The motif and color scheme of this horn are clearly Canelos (cf. Whitten and Whitten, *From Myth to Creation*, 4). The painted motif on the horn is *amaru*, the anaconda. Ceramic effigy vessels represent forms that emanate life force during festivals, and the blown cornet produces the sound of the trumpeter bird. Before being blown, the horn could be used to serve *asua*, a fermented manioc brew.

1. Slater, *Dance of the Dolphin*.

2. Lathrap, *The Upper Amazon*.

3. Schaan, "Into the layrinths of Marajoara pottery," 114.

4. Meggers, "The mystery of Marajoara."

5. Schaan, "The Camutins chiefdom," 143ff.

6. Myers, "Redes de intercambio tempranas," 70.

7. Vidal, "Secret religious cults and political leadership."

8. Chernela, *The Wanano Indians of the Brazilian Amazon*.

9. Sorenson, "Multilingualism in the Northwest Amazon," 682.

10. Chernela, "Social meanings and material transaction."

11. Hill, *Keepers of the Sacred Chants*; Hill and Granero, *Comparative Arawakan Histories*.

12. Reichel-Dolmatoff, *Amazonian Cosmos*, 110–23.

13. Guss, *To Weave and Sing*; Frechione, "The Yekuana of southern Venezuela."

14. Guss, 13.

15. Yde, *Material Culture of the Waiwái*, 246–47; Guss.

16. Yde, 62.

17. Rivière, *Individual and Society in Guiana*, 12–13.

18. Wilbert, *Survivors of Eldorado*, 157.

19. Guss, 79; Yde, 60. Despite the distance between their centers of settlement, the Waiwái and Ye´kuana have languages and cultures that approach one another quite closely. Guss, 236.

20. Lathrap, 34.

21. Le Moine and Raymond, "Leishmaniasis and Inca settlement."

22. See Veber, "External inducement and non-Westernization."

23. Weiss, "Campa cosmology," 171.

24. Glave, "The 'Republic of Indians' in revolt," 521–25.

25. Roe, *The Cosmic Zygote*, 42, citing DeBoer.

26. Morin, "Los Shipibo–Conibo," 289.

27. cf. Roe, "Marginal Men."

28. Morin, "Los Shipibo–Conibo," 334.

29. Lathrap, 184; Roe, "Art and residence among the Shipibo," 48.

30. Roe, "Art and residence"; cf. Gebhart-Sayer, *The Cosmos Encoiled*, Gebhart-Sayer, "The geometric designs of the Shipibo–Conibo."

31. Moseley, *The Incas and Their Ancestors*, 163ff; Bawden and Conrad, *The Andean Heritage*, 16–17.

32. Mannheim, *The Language of the Inka*.

33. Taylor, "Sick of history."

34. Descola, *The Spears of Twilight*, 159.

35. Taylor, 158.

36. Rubenstein, "Colonialism, the Shuar Federation, and the Ecuadorian state."

37. Descola, 93.

38. Chaim, *Os aldeamentos indígenas*.

39. Gallais, *Uma catechese entre os Indios do Araguaya Brazil*, 9 (author's translation).

40. Fisher, *Rain Forest Exchanges*, 19.

41. e.g., Baldus, *Tapirapé*, 359.

42. e.g., Lima and Ferreira, *Hetohoky*, 39.

43. Fisher, *Rain Forest Exchanges*, 69–70.

44. cf. Frikel, *Os Xikrin*.

45. Verswijver, "Only you may wear my ornament."

46. Fisher, "Name rituals and acts of feeling among the Kayapó."

47. Verswijver, "The intertribal relations between the Juruna and the Kayapo Indians."

48. Gregor, "Uneasy peace."

References

Baldus, Herbert. *Tapirapé: Tribo Tupí no Brasil Central*. São Paulo, Brazil: Companhia Editora Nacional, 1970.

Bawden, Garth, and Geoffrey W. Conrad. *The Andean Heritage*. Cambridge MA: Peabody Museum, 1982.

Chaim, Marivone M. *Os aldeamentos indígenas na Capitania de Goiás (1749–1811)*. Goiânia, Brazil: Oriente, 1974.

Chernela, Janet M. "Social meanings and material transaction: The Wanano–Tukano of Brazil and Colombia." *Journal of Anthropological Archaeology* 11 (1992): 111–24.

Chernela, Janet M. *The Wanano Indians of the Brazilian Amazon: A Sense of Space*. Austin: University of Texas, 1993.

Descola, Philippe. *The Spears of Twilight: Life and Death in the Amazon Jungle*, Janet Lloyd, trans. New York: New, 1996.

Faria, Luís de Castro. *A figura humana na arte dos Índios Karajá*. Rio de Janeiro: Universidade do Brasil–Museu National, 1959.

Fisher, William H. "Name rituals and acts of feeling among the Kayapó (Mebengokre)." *Journal of the Royal Anthropological Institute* 9, no. 1 (2003): 117–35

Fisher, William H. *Rain Forest Exchanges: Industry and Community on an Amazonian Frontier*. Washington: Smithsonian, 2000.

Frechione, John. "The Yekuana of southern Venezuela." *Cultural Survival Quarterly* 8, no. 4 (1984).

Frikel, Protasio. *Os Xikrin: Equipamento e técnica de subsistência*. Belém, Brazil: Museu Paraense Emílio Goeldi, 1968.

Gallais, Estevão. *Uma catechese entre os Indios do Araguaya Brazil*, Octaviano Esselin, trans. São Paulo, Brazil: Escola Typograhica Salesiana, 1903.

Gebhart-Sayer, Angelika. *The Cosmos Encoiled: India Art of the Peruvian Amazon*. New York: Center for Inter-American Arts, 1984.

Gebhart-Sayer, Angelika. "The geometric designs of the Shipibo–Conibo in ritual context." *Journal of Latin American Lore* 2, no. 2 (1985): 143–75.

Glave, Luis Miguel. "The 'Republic of Indians' in revolt (ca. 1680–1790)." In *The Cambridge History of the Native Peoples of the Americas*, vol. 3, part 2, Frank Salomon and Stuart B. Schwartz, ed., 502–57. Cambridge and New York: Cambridge University, 1999.

Granero, Fernando Santos. "Templos e ferrarias: Utopia e reinvenção no Oriente peruano." In *Amazônia: Etnologia e história indígena*, Eduardo Viveiros de Castro and Manuela Carneiro da Cunha, ed., 67–94. São Paulo, Brazil: FAPESP, 1993.

Gregor, Thomas. "Uneasy peace: Intertribal relations in Brazil's upper Xingu." In *The Anthropology of War*, Jonathan Haas, ed., 105–24. Cambridge and New York: Cambridge University, 1990.

Guss, David. M. *To Weave and Sing: Art, Symbol, and Narrative in the South American Rain Forest*. Berkeley: University of California, 1989.

Hill, Jonathan D. *Keepers of the Sacred Chants: The Poetics of Ritual Power in an Amazonian Society*. Tucson: University of Arizona, 1993.

Hill, Jonathan D., and Fernando Santos Granero. *Comparative Arawakan Histories: Rethinking Language Family and Culture Area in Amazonia*. Urbana: University of Illinois, 2002.

Lathrap, Donald W. *The Upper Amazon*. New York: Praeger, 1970.

Le Moine, Genevieve, and J. Scott Raymond. "Leishmaniasis and Inca settlement in the Peruvian jungle." *Journal of Historical Geography* 13, no. 2 (1987): 113–29.

Lima, Filho, and Manuel Ferreira. *Hetohoky: Um rito Karajá*. Goiânia, Brazil: Editora UCG, 1994.

Mannheim, Bruce. *The Language of the Inka since the European Invasion*. Austin: University of Texas, 1991.

Meggers, B. J. "The mystery of Marajoara: An ecological solution." *Amazoniana* 16, no. 3/4 (2001): 421–40.

Morin, Françoise. "Los Shipibo–Conibo." In *Guía Etnográfica de la Alta Amazonía*, vol. 3, Fernando Santos and Frederica Barclay, ed., 275–435. Panama/Quito: Smithsonian Tropical Research Institute/Ediciones Abya–Yala, 1998.

Moseley, Michael E. *The Incas and Their Ancestors: The Archaeology of Peru*. London: Thames & Hudson, 2001.

Myers, Thomas P. "Redes de intercambio tempranas en la hoya Amazonica," Luciana Proaño, trans. *Amazonia Peruana* 4, no. 8 (1983): 61–75.

Pétesch, Nathalie. *La pirogue de sable: Perennité cosmique e mutation social chez les Karajá du Brésil central*. Paris: Éditions Peeters, 2000.

Reichel-Dolmatoff, Gerardo. *Amazonian Cosmos: The Sexual and Religious Symbolism of the Tukano Indians*. Chicago: University of Chicago, 1971.

Rivière, Peter. *Individual and Society in Guiana*. Cambridge and New York: Cambridge University, 1984.

Roe, Peter. "Art and residence among the Shipibo Indians of Peru: A study in microacculturation." *American Anthropologist* (new series) 82, no. 1 (1980): 42–71.

Roe, Peter. "Marginal men: Male artists among the Shipibo Indians of Peru." *Anthropologica* 21, no. 2 (1979): 189–221.

Roe, Peter. *The Cosmic Zygote: Cosmology in the Amazon Basin*. New Brunswick NJ: Rutgers University, 1982.

Rubenstein, Steven. "Colonialism, the Shuar Federation, and the Ecuadorian state." *Environment and Planning D: Society and Space* 19 (2001): 263–93.

Schaan, Denise Pahl. "Into the layrinths of Marajoara pottery: Status and cultural identity in prehistoric Amazonia." In *Unknown Amazon: Culture in Nature in Ancient Brazil*, Colin McEwan, Cristiana Barreto, and Eduardo Neves, ed. London: British Museum, 2001.

Schaan, Denise Pahl. "The Camutins chiefdom: Rise and development of social complexity on Marajó Island, Brazilian Amazon." PhD thesis, University of Pittsburgh, 2004.

Slater, Candace. *Dance of the Dolphin: Transformation and Disenchantment in the Amazonian Imagination*. Chicago: University of Chicago, 1994.

Sorenson, Arthur P., Jr. "Multilingualism in the Northwest Amazon." *American Anthropologist* (new series) 69, no. 6 (1967): 670–84.

Taylor, Anne Christine. "Sick of history: Contrasting regimes of historicity in the upper Amazon." In *Time and Memory in Indigenous Amazonia: Anthropological Perspectives*, Michael Heckenberger and Carlos Fausto, ed., 133–68. Gainesville: University of Florida, 2007.

Veber, Hanne. "External inducement and non-Westernization in the uses of the Ashéninka cushma." *Journal of Material Culture* 1, no. 2 (1996): 155–82.

Veber, Hanne. "The salt of the montaña: Interpreting indigenous activism in the rain forest." *Cultural Anthropology* 13, no. 3 (1998): 382–413.

Verswijver, Gustaaf. "Only you may wear my ornament." In *Kaiapó, Amazonia: The Art of Body Decoration*, Gustaaf Verswijver, ed., 65–88. Tervuren, Belgium: Royal Museum of Central Africa, 1992.

Verswijver, Gustaaf. "The intertribal relations between the Juruna and the Kayapo Indians (1850–1920)." *Jahrbuch des Museums für Völkerkunde* 34 (1982): 305–15.

Vidal, Silvia M. "Secret religious cults and political leadership: Multiethnic confederacies from northwestern Amazonia." In *Comparative Arawakan Histories: Rethinking Language Family and Culture Area in Amazonia*, Jonathan D. Hill and Fernando Santos Granero, ed., 248–68. Urbana: University of Illinois, 2002.

Wagley, Charles. *Welcome of Tears: The Tapirapé Indians of Central Brazil.* New York: Oxford University, 1977.

Weiss, Gerald. "Campa cosmology." *Ethnology* 11, no. 2 (1972): 157–72.

Whitten, Dorothea Scott, and Norman E. Whitten Jr., ed. *From Myth to Creation: Art from Amazonian Ecuador.* Urbana: University of Illinois, 1988.

Whitten, Norman E., Jr., and Dorothea Scott Whitten. *Puyo Runa: Imagery and Power in Modern Amazonia.* Urbana: University of Illinois, 2008.

Wilbert, Johannes. *Survivors of Eldorado: Four Indian Cultures of South America.* New York: Praeger, 1972.

Yde, Jens. *Material Culture of the Waiwái.* Copenhagen: The National Museum of Copenhagen, 1965.

Peter Roe and Bahuan Mëtsa

1. DeBoer and Lathrap, "The making and breaking of Shipibo–Conibo ceramics"; Roe, *Arts of the Amazon.*

2. Roe, "Marginal men."

3. Heath, *An Ani šhëati in the Shipibo village of San Pablo*; Roe, *The Cosmic Zygote.*

4. Roe, "Art and residence."

5. Roe, "Marginal men."

6. There are at least two classes of shamans who use ayahuasca: *onaya* and the higher-level *muraya.*

7. Roe, "Panó Huëtsa Nëtë."

8. Heath, "Una ventana hacia el infinito."

9. Illius, "Arte traditional y comercial"; Lathrap, "Shipibo tourist art."

10. Hoffman, "Money, ecology, and acculturation."

11. Roe, *The Cosmic Zygote.*

References

Alvaréz, José, Peter Roe, Charles Swann, and Alfredo Tagle. "Materials in Native American Shipibo pottery." *Proceedings of the 4th International Conference on the Non-Destructive Testing of Works of Art*, vol. 2, 809–820. Berlin, Germany: Deutsche Gesellschaft für Zerstörungsfreie Prüfung e.V., 1994.

Bergman, Roland W. *Amazon Economics: The Simplicity of Shipibo Indian Wealth.* Department of Geography Dellplain Latin American Studies 6, Syracuse University. Ann Arbor MI: University Microfilms International, 1980.

Campos, Roberta. "Producción de pesca y caza de una aldea Shipibo en el Río Pisqui." *Amazonía Peruana* 1, no. 2 (1977): 53–74.

d'Ans, Andre-Marcel. "Reclasificatión de la lengua Pano y datos glotocronológicos para la etnohistoria de la Amazonía Peruana." *Revista del Museo Nacional*, no. 39 (1973).

DeBoer, Warren R. "Buffer zones in the cultural ecology of aboriginal Amazonia." *American Antiquity* 46, no. 2 (1981): 364–77.

DeBoer, Warren R. "Pillage and production in the Amazon: A view through the Conibo of the Ucayali Basin, eastern Perú." *World Archaeology* 18, no. 2 (1986): 231–46.

DeBoer, Warren R., and Donald W. Lathrap. "The making and breaking of Shipibo–Conibo ceramics." In *Ethnoarchaeology: Implications of Ethnography for Archaeology*, Carol Kramer, ed., 102–38. New York: Columbia University, 1979.

Gebhart-Sayer, Angelika. *The Cosmos Encoiled: Indian Art of the Peruvian Amazon.* Exhibition catalog. New York: Center for Inter-American Relations (The Americas Society), 1984.

Gebhart-Sayer, Angelika. "The geometric designs of the Shipibo–Conibo in ritual context." *Journal of Latin American Lore* 11 (1985): 143–75.

Heath, Carolyn. *An Ani šhëati in the Shipibo Village of San Pablo, Río Sinuya, Lower Ucayali River, Peru/ Un Ani šhëati en la ville Shipibo de San Pablo, Río Sinuya, Aguas Abajo del Río Ucayali, Perú.* Typescript. San Juan: Centro de Investigaciones Indígenas de Puerto Rico, 1991.

Heath, Carolyn. "El tiempo nos venció: Los Shipibo del Ucayali." In *Una ventana hacia el infinito: Arte Shipibo–Conibo*, Pedro Pablo Alayza and Fernando Torres, ed., 16–23. Lima: Instituto Cultural Peruano Norteamericano (ICPNA), 2002.

Heath, Carolyn. "Mitos y leyendas del grupo Shipibo–Conibo." In *Una ventana hacia el infinito: Arte Shipibo–Conibo*, Pedro Pablo Alayza and Fernando Torres, ed., 24–28. Lima: Instituto Cultural Peruano Norteamericano (ICPNA), 2002.

Heath, Carolyn. "Reproduciendo el cielo sobre la tierra: Textilería y alfarería del grupo Shipibo–Conibo." In *Una ventana hacia el infinito: Arte Shipibo–Conibo*, Pedro Pablo Alayza and Fernando Torres, ed., 34–42. Lima: Instituto Cultural Peruano Norteamericano (ICPNA), 2002.

Heath, Carolyn. "Una ventana hacia el infinito: El simbolismo de los diseños Shipibo–Conibo." In *Una ventana hacia el infinito: Arte Shipibo–Conibo*, Pedro Pablo Alayza and Fernando Torres, ed., 45–50. Lima: Instituto Cultural Peruano Norteamericano (ICPNA), 2002.

Hern, Warren M. "High fertility in a Peruvian Amazon Indian village." *Human Ecology* 5, no. 4 (1977): 355–68.

Hern, Warren M. "Family planning, Amazon style." *Natural History* 101, no. 12 (1992): 30–37.

Hoffman, Hans. "Money, ecology, and acculturation among the Shipibo of Peru." In *Explorations in Cultural Anthropology: Essays in Honor of George Peter Murdock*, Ward Goodenough, ed., 259–76. New York: McGraw-Hill, 1964.

Illius, Bruno. *Ani Shinan: Schamanismus bei den Shipibo–Conibo.* 2nd ed. Tübigen, Germany: Verlag S y F. Münster, 1991.

Illius, Bruno. "Die Grosse Boa. Kunst und Kosmologie der Shipibo–Conibo," In *Die Mythen Sehen*, vol. 2, Mark Münzel, ed., 705–28. Frankfurt, Germany: Stadt Frankfurt Dez. Kultur u. Freizeit, 1988.

Illius, Bruno. "La Gran boa: arte y cosmologia de los Shipibo–Conibo." *Schweizerishe Amerikanisten–Gesellshaft Bulletin* 55–56 (1991): 23–35.

Illius, Bruno. "The concept of Nihue among the Shipibo–Conibo of eastern Peru." In *Portals of Power: Shamanism in South America*, E. Jean Langdon and Gerhard Baer, ed., 63–77. Albuquerque: University of New Mexico, 1992.

Illius, Bruno. "Arte tradicional y comercial, los Shipibo–Conibo." In *Una ventana hacia el infinito: Arte Shipibo–Conibo*, Pedro Pablo Alayza and Fernando Torres, ed., 55–58. Lima: Instituto Cultural Peruano Norteamericano (ICPNA), 2002.

Lathrap, Donald W. *The Upper Amazon.* Ancient Peoples and Places Series, 70. New York: Praeger, 1970.

Lathrap, Donald W. "Shipibo tourist art." In *Ethnic and Tourist Arts: Cultural Expressions from the Fourth World*, Nelson H. H. Graburn, ed., 197–207. Berkeley: University of California, 1976.

Lathrap, Donald W. "Recent Shipibo–Conibo ceramics and their implications for archaeological interpretations." In *Structure and Cognition in Art*, Dorothy K. Washburn, ed., 25–39. New York: Cambridge University, 1983.

Meggers, Betty J., and Clifford Evans, Jr. "An experimental formulation of horizon styles in the tropical forest area of South America." In *Essays in Pre-Columbian Art and Archaeology*, Samuel K. Lothrop et al., ed., 372–88. Cambridge MA: Harvard University, 1961.

Morales Chocano, Daniel. "Los ancestros del grupo cultural Shipibo–Conibo del Ucayali central en la Amazonía Peruana." In *Una ventana hacia el infinito: Arte Shipibo–Conibo*, Pedro Pablo Alayza and Fernando Torres, ed., 29–33. Lima: Instituto Cultural Peruano Norteamericano (ICPNA), 2002.

Mujica Baquerizo, Ana. "Los tejidos Shipibo–Conibo." In *Una ventana hacia el infinito: Arte Shipibo–Conibo*, Pedro Pablo Alayza and Fernando Torres, ed., 43–44. Lima: Instituto Cultural Peruano Norteamericano (ICPNA), 2002.

Myers, Thomas P. "Defended territories and no-man's-lands." *American Anthropologist* 8 (1976): 354–55.

Myers, Thomas P. "Spanish contacts and social change on the Ucayali River, Peru." *Ethnohistory* 21, no. 2 (1974): 135–57.

Myers, Thomas P. "The expansion and collapse of the Omagua." *Journal of the Steward Anthropological Society* 20, no. 1–2 (1992): 129–52.

Myers, Thomas P. "Visión de la prehistoria de la Amazonía superior." *El Seminario de Investigaciones Sociales en la Amazonía Peruana*, 37–87. Iquitos: CAAAP/CETA/CIAAP-UNAP/CIPA/CONCYTEC/IINC/UNAP, 1988.

Raymond, J. Scott, Warren R. DeBoer, and Peter G. Roe. *Cumancaya: A Peruvian Ceramic Tradition*. Occasional Papers 2. Calgary, Canada: Department of Archaeology, University of Calgary, 1975.

Roe, Peter G. "Aboriginal tourists and artistic exchange between the Pisquibo and the Shipibo: 'Trade ware' in an ethnographic setting." In *Networks of the Past: Regional Interaction in Archaeology*, Peter D. Francis, F. J. Kense, and P. G. Duke, ed. Proceedings of the 12th Annual Conference, the Archaeological Association of the University of Calgary, 61–84. Calgary: University of Calgary, 1981.

Roe, Peter G. "Archaism, form and decoration: An ethnographic and archaeological case study from the Peruvian Montaña." *Ñawpa Pacha* 14 (1976): 73–94, plates 26–29.

Roe, Peter G. "Art and residence among the Shipibo Indians of Peru: A study in microacculturation." *American Anthropologist* 82 (1980): 42–71.

Roe, Peter G. *Arts of the Amazon*. Barbara Braun, ed. London and New York: Thames & Hudson, 1995.

Roe, Peter G. "At play in the fields of symmetry: Design structure and shamanic therapy in the upper Amazon." In *Symmetry Comes of Age*, Dorothy Washburn and Donald W. Crowe, ed., 215–303. Seattle: University of Washington, 2004.

Roe, Peter G. *The Cosmic Zygote: Cosmology in the Amazon Basin*. New Brunswick NJ: Rutgers University, 1982.

Roe, Peter G. "Estilo artístico e identidad étnica entre los Shipibo y los mestizos de la montaña peruana." In *Tramas de la Identidad*, vol. 4 of *De Palabra y Obra en el Nuevo Mundo* series, J. Jorge Klor de Alba, Gary H. Gossen, Miguel León Portilla, and Manuel Gutíerrez Estévez, ed., 343–408. Madrid and Mexico City: Siglo Veintiuno,1996.

Roe, Peter G. "The Joŝho Nahuanbo are all wet and undercooked: Shipibo views of the whiteman and the Incas in myth, legend and history." In *Rethinking History and Myth: Indigenous South American Perspectives on the Past*, Jonathan Hill, ed., 106–35. Urbana: University of Illinois, 1988.

Roe, Peter G. "The language of the plumes: 'Implicit mythology' in Shipibo, Cashinahua and Waiwai feather adornments." In *L.A.I.L. Speaks! Selected Papers from the Seventh International Symposium, Albuquerque, 1989*, Mary H. Preuss, ed., 105–36, plates A–F. Culver City CA: Labyrinthos, 1990.

Roe, Peter G. "Marginal men: Male artists among the Shipibo Indians of Peru." *Anthropologica* 21 (1979): 189–221.

Roe, Peter G. "Mythic substitution and the stars: Aspects of Shipibo and Quechua ethnoastronomy compared." In *Songs from the Sky: Indigenous Astronomical and Cosmological Traditions of the World*, Von del Chamberlain, John B. Carlson, and M. Jane Young, ed., 193–227. Selected proceedings of the First International Conference on Ethnoastronomy: Indigenous Astronomical and Cosmological Traditions of the World, Smithsonian, Washington, September 5–9, 1983. Bognor Regis UK: Ocarina, and College Park MD: Center for Archaeoastronomy, 2005. Also published as *Archaeoastronomy, the Journal of the Center for Archaeoastronomy* 12–13 (1996).

Roe, Peter G. "Of rainbow dragons and the origins of designs: The Waiwai Urufiri and the Shipibo Ronin ëhua." *Latin American Indian Literatures Journal* 5, no. 1 (1989): 1–67.

Roe, Peter G. "Panó Huëtsa Nëtë: The armadillo as scaly discoverer of the Lower World in Shipibo and comparative lowland South Amerindian perspective." *Latin American Indian Literatures Journal* 7, no. 1 (1991): 20–72.

Roe, Peter G. "The Pleiades in comparative perspective: The Waiwai Shirkoimo and the Shipibo Huishmabo." In *Astronomies and Cultures: Selected Papers from Oxford 3, International Conference on Archaeoastronomy*, Clive Ruggles and Nick Saunders, ed., 296–328. Boulder: University of Colorado, 1993.

Roe, Peter G. "Style, society, myth and structure." In *Style, Society, and Person*, Christopher Carr and Jill E. Neitzel, ed., 27–76. New York: Plenum, 1995.

Rowe, Ann P. *Warp Patterned Weaves of the Andes*. Washington: Textile Museum, 1977.

Weber, Ronald L. *Caimito: An Analysis of the Late Prehistoric Culture of the Central Ucayali, Eastern Peru*. PhD dissertation. Urbana–Champaign: The University of Illinois, 1975.

MESOAMERICA AND THE CARIBBEAN

George Stuart

1. This important Mesoamerican deity with goggle eyes and fangs also appears on a rectangular bowl from Copán, Honduras, and a clay portrait from an area in El Salvador settled by central Mexicans around AD 1000—both in the museum's collections.

References

Coe, Michael D. *The Maya Scribe and His World*. New York: The Grolier Club, 1973.

Coe, Michael D. *The Maya*. 7th ed. London: Thames & Hudson, 2005.

Martin, Simon, and Nikolai Grube. *Chronicle of the Maya Kings and Queens: Deciphering the Dynasties of the Ancient Maya*. London: Thames & Hudson, 2000.

Miller, Mary, and Simon Martin. *Courtly Art of the Ancient Maya*. London: Thames & Hudson, 2004.

Stuart, George, and David Stuart. *Palenque: Eternal City of the Maya*. London: Thames & Hudson, 2008.

Leonardo López Luján

1. Among earlier triple alliances in central Mexico, scholars include Tollan, Culhuacan, and Otompan before the fall of Tollan in the 12th century; Culhuacan, Tenayuca, and Xaltocan after the fall of Tollan; and Azcapotzalco, Coatlinchan, and Culhuacan. Through these and other coalitions in the Basin of Mexico, city-states joined together for mutual defense and to pursue other shared interests.

On the greenstone mask from Teotihuacán (2/6607, p. 91): This kind of mask was not used by the people of Teotihuacán to cover their faces in public ceremonies; stone masks are too heavy to wear, and they lack perforations for the eyes. It has been suggested that these masks were buried in graves, but they have never been found in that type of setting. Perhaps they were used to depict the divine images of perishable materials, like those represented in mural paintings.

Alejandro González Villarruel

References

Jiménez, Wigberto, and Paul Kirchoff. "Mesoamérica." In *Sociedad Mexicana de Antropología, Sobretiro Especial del Tomo VIII de la Enciclopedia de Mexico*. Mexico: Secretaria de Educacion Publica, 1975.

Malinowsky, Bronislaw, and Julio de la Fuente. "La economía de un sistema de mercados en Mèxico." *Acta Antropológica* epoca 2, vol. 1, no. 2 (1957).

Joanna Ostapkowicz

1. Taíno, from *nitaíno*, meaning "good" or "noble," has come to refer to the people inhabiting the islands of Hispaniola (Quisqueya), Puerto Rico (Boriquen), Jamaica (Xamayca), and Cuba at the time of European contact. The name, however, masks the cultural complexity and diversity that was present in the Greater Antilles at this time.

2. Wilson, *The Archaeology of the Caribbean*, 102–10.

3. Long-distance trade connections between the Greater Antilles and the South American mainland appear to have waxed and waned since the first ancestral migrations into the islands, and were filtered through the Lesser Antilles. These connections appear to have increased slightly during the 1200s to 1500s, with the development of complex chiefdoms in Hispaniola and Puerto Rico and their desire for valuables. Such exotics, acquired via long-distance trade networks, were interwoven into local value systems that were autonomous of mainland influences. More regular links—and, to a degree, greater influences—were maintained between the cultures of the Lesser Antilles and South America. Sued-Badillo, "The indigenous societies at the time of conquest," 259–60;

Hofman et al., "Island rhythms," 262; Allaire, "Agricultural societies in the Caribbean," 195–227.

4. Regarding cultural influence reaching into the Lesser Antilles, see Crock and Petersen, "Inter-island exchange," 14. Regarding Taíno outposts in the Leewards, see Hofman and Hoogland, "Social dynamics and change," 54; also Siegel, "What happened after AD 600 on Puerto Rico?"

5. *Cohoba*, a hallucinogenic drug (possibly involving *Anadananthera peregrina*) inhaled during the eponymous ceremony, was of central importance to the Taíno, facilitating communication with numinous powers who provided guidance on community decisions. The Taíno developed a unique repertoire of objects that were specifically linked to this ceremony, including snuff tubes, vomiting spatulas, and cohoba stands.

6. cf. Hofman et al., "Island rhythms," 258.

7. Martyr D'Anghera, *De Orbe Novo*, 259.

8. Carlson, *Strings of Command*.

9. Wilson, "Linking prehistory and history in the Caribbean," 270; Wilson, *The Archaeology of the Caribbean*, 149.

10. Oliver, *Caciques and Cemí Idols*, 168.

11. Ostapkowicz, "To be seated with 'great courtesy and veneration.'"

12. Symcox, *Italian Reports on America*, 32.

13. Las Casas, *Historia de las Indias*, 447.

14. Ober, *Camps in the Caribbees*, 222.

15. Colón, *The Life of the Admiral Christopher Columbus*, 83.

16. Chanca, "Letter of Dr. Chanca," 48.

17. Arrom, *An Account of the Antiquities of the Indians*, 19; Oliver, *Caciques and Cemí Idols*, 148–56.

References

Allaire, Louis. "Agricultural societies in the Caribbean: The Lesser Antilles." In *Autochthonous Societies. General History of the Caribbean*, vol. 1, Jalil Sued-Badillo, ed., 195–227. London: UNESCO–Macmillan, 2003.

Carlson, Lisbeth Anne. *Strings of Command: Manufacture and Utilization of Shell Beads among the Taíno Indians of the West Indies.* Master's

thesis, Gainesville: University of Florida, 1993.

Chanca, Diego Alvarez. "Letter of Dr. Chanca, written to the City of Seville." In *Second Voyage of Columbus*, C. Jane, trans., 20–73. London: Hakluyt Society, 1932.

Colón, Fernando. *The Life of the Admiral Christopher Columbus by His Son Ferdinand.* Benjamin Keen, trans. [1959]. New Brunswick NJ: Rutgers University, 1999.

Crock, John G., and James B. Petersen. "Inter-island exchange, settlement hierarchy and a Taíno-related chiefdom on the Anguilla Bank, Northern Lesser Antilles." In *Late Ceramic Age Societies in the Eastern Caribbean*, André Delpuech and Corinne L. Hofman, ed., 139–56. BAR International Series, 1273, Paris Monographs in American Archaeology. Oxford: Archaeopress, 2004.

Forte, Maximilian, ed. *Indigenous Resurgence in the Contemporary Caribbean: Amerindian Survival and Revival.* New York: Peter Lang, 2006.

Hofman, Corinne L., Alistair J. Bright, Arie Boomert, and Sebastiaan Knippenberg. "Island rhythms: The web of social relationships and interaction networks in the Lesser Antillean Archipelago between 400 BC and AD 1492." *Latin American Antiquity* 18, no. 3 (2007): 243–68.

Hofman, Corinne L., and Menno L. P. Hoogland. "Social dynamics and change in the Northern Lesser Antilles." In *Late Ceramic Age Societies in the Eastern Caribbean*, André Delpuech and Corinne L. Hofman, ed., 47–58. BAR International Series, 1273, Paris Monographs in American Archaeology. Oxford: Archaeopress, 2004.

Las Casas, Bartolomé de. *Historia de las Indias.* 3 vols. Serie de Cronistas de Mexico 15–17, Augustín Millares Carlo and Lewis Hanke, ed. Mexico City: Fondo de Cultura Economica, 1951. (Originally published ca. 1525).

Martyr D'Anghera, Peter. *De Orbe Novo: The Eight Decades of Peter Martyr D'Anghera.* Francis Augustus MacNutt, trans. New York: Burt Franklin, 1970.

Ober, Frederick A. *Camps in the Caribbees: The Adventures of a Naturalist in the Lesser Antilles.* Boston: Lee and Shepard, 1880.

Oliver, Jose. *Caciques and Cemí Idols: The Web Spun by Taíno Rulers between Hispaniola and Boriquen.*

Birmingham: University of Alabama, 2009.

Ostapkowicz, Joanna. "To be seated with 'great courtesy and veneration': Contextual aspects of the Taíno duho." In *Taíno: Pre-Columbian Art and Culture from the Caribbean*. Oxford: Monacelli, 1997.

Pané, Ramon. *An Account of the Antiquities of the Indians: Chronicles of the New World Encounter.* José Juan Arrom, ed. Susan Griswold, trans. Durham NC and London: Duke University, 1999.

Siegel, Peter E. "What happened after AD 600 on Puerto Rico? Corporate groups, population restructuring, and post-Saladoid social changes." In *Late Ceramic Age Societies in the Eastern Caribbean*, André Delpuech and Corinne L. Hofman, ed. BAR International Series, 1273, Paris Monographs in American Archaeology. Oxford: Archaeopress, 2004.

Sued-Badillo, Jalil. "The indigenous societies at the time of conquest." In *Autochthonous Societies*, vol. 1 of *General History of the Caribbean*, Jalil Sued-Badillo, ed. London: UNESCO–Macmillan, 2003.

Symcox, Geoffrey, ed., *Italian Reports on America, 1493–1522: Accounts of Contemporary Observers.* Repertorium Columbianum, vol. 12. Turnhout, Belgium: Brepols, 2002.

Wilson, Samuel. *The Archaeology of the Caribbean.* Cambridge and New York: Cambridge University, 2007.

Wilson, Samuel. "Linking prehistory and history in the Caribbean." In *Late Ceramic Age Societies in the Eastern Caribbean*, André Delpuech and Corinne L. Hofman, ed., 269–72. BAR International Series, 1273, Paris Monographs in American Archaeology. Oxford: Archaeopress, 2004

José Barreiro

1. Reciting his tobacco prayer—a ceremony of appreciation to the Seven Powers of Nature—Panchito Ramirez, Taíno cacique from Caridad de los Indios, Cuba, implores first the four cardinal directions and then the Mother Earth. In his autobiographical testimony, don Panchito tells of a visitation by the Mother Earth spirit in the dream–vision that has guided his leadership of the Native community. Barreiro,

José. *Panchito: Mountain Cacique—Guajiro—Taíno Testimony.* Santiago de Cuba: Ediciones Catedral, 2001.

THE SOUTHWEST
Linda Cordell

1. Cordell, *Archaeology of the Southwest*; Kantner, *Ancient Puebloan Southwest*; Minnis, "Earliest plant cultivation"; Plog, *Ancient Peoples of the American Southwest*.

2. Cordell.

3. Fields and Zamudio-Taylor, "Aztlan."

4. Lipe, "The basketmaker II period."

5. Huckell, "The first 10,000 years in the Southwest"; Lipe; Smiley, "Early farmers in the Southwest."

6. Crown and Hurst, "Evidence of cacao use"; Crown and Judge, *Chaco and Hohokam*; Judge, "Chaco culture National Historical Park"; Mathien, "Ornaments of the Chaco Anasazi."

7. Crown and Judge; Lekson, "Chaco matters"; Neitzel, *Pueblo Bonito*.

8. Brody, *Mimbres Painted Pottery*; Nelson, *Mimbres during the Twelfth Century*.

9. Nelson.

10. Wilshusen, "The genesis of Pueblos."

11. Varien and Wilshusen, *Seeking the Center Place*.

12. Lipe.

13. Cordell et al., "Mesa Verde settlement history and relocation"; Lipe; Naranjo, "We came from the south. We came from the north."

14. Doyel, "Irrigation, production, and power"; Fish and Fish, *The Hohokam Millennium*.

15. Fish and Fish.

16. Bayman, "Artisans and their crafts in Hohokam society."

17. Fish and Fish.

18. Lopez, "Huhugam."

19. Woosley, "Shadows on a silent landscape."

20. Di Peso, *Casas Grandes*, 758.

References

Bayman, James M. "Artisans and their crafts in Hohokam society." In *The Hohokam Millennium*, Suzanne K. Fish and Paul R. Fish, ed., 75–83. Santa Fe: School of American Research, 2008.

Brody, J. J. *Mimbres Painted Pottery*. Revised edition. Santa Fe: School of American Research, 2004.

Cordell, Linda. *Archaeology of the Southwest*. 2nd ed. San Diego CA: Academic, 1997.

Cordell, Linda S., Carla Van West, Jeffrey S. Dean, and Deborah A. Muenchrath. "Mesa Verde settlement history and relocation: Climate change, social networks, and Ancestral Pueblo migration." *Kiva* 72 (2007): 379–406.

Crown, Patricia L., and W. Jeffrey Hurst. "Evidence of cacao use in the Prehispanic American Southwest." *PNAS* 106, no. 7 (2009): 2110–13.

Crown, Patricia L., and W. James Judge, ed. *Chaco and Hohokam, Prehistoric Regional Systems in the American Southwest*. Santa Fe: School of American Research, 1991.

Di Peso, Charles C. *Casas Grandes, a Fallen Trading Center of the Gran Chichimeca*, vol. 3. Flagstaff AZ: Amerind Foundation, Dragoon and Northland, 1974.

Doyel, David E. "Irrigation, production, and power in Phoenix Basin Hohokam society." In *The Hohokam Millennium*, Suzanne K. Fish and Paul R. Fish, ed., 83–90. Santa Fe: School of American Research, 2008.

Fields, Virginia M., and Victor Zamudio-Taylor. "Aztlan: Destination and point of departure." In *The Road to Aztlan, Art from a Mythic Homeland*, Virginia M. Fields and Victor Zamudio-Taylor, ed., 38–85. Los Angeles County Museum of Art, 2001.

Fish, Suzanne L., and Paul R. Fish. "The Hohokam millennium." In *The Hohokam Millennium*, Suzanne K. Fish and Paul R. Fish, ed., 1–12. Santa Fe: School of American Research, 2008.

Fish, Suzanne L., and Paul R. Fish, ed. *The Hohokam Millennium*. Santa Fe: School of American Research, 2008.

Huckell, Bruce B. "The First 10,000 years in the Southwest." In *Southwest Archaeology in the Twentieth Century*, Linda S. Cordell and Don D. Fowler, ed., 142–156. Salt Lake City: University of Utah, 2005.

Judge, W. James. "Chaco Culture National Historical Park, NM: The Place and Its People." In *American Indian Places, a Historical Guidebook*, Frances H. Kennedy, ed., 192. Boston: Houghton Mifflin, 2008.

Kantner, John. *Ancient Puebloan Southwest*. Cambridge and New York: Cambridge University, 2004.

Lekson, Stephen H. "Chaco matters." In *The Archaeology of Chaco Canyon, an 11th-century Pueblo Regional Center*, Stephen H. Lekson, ed., 3–44. Santa Fe: School of American Research, 2006.

Lipe, William D. "The basketmaker II period in the Four Corners area." In *Basketmaker Anasazi, Papers from the 1990 Wetherill-Grand Gulch Symposium*, Victoria M. Atkins, ed., 1–12. Cultural Resource Series No. 24. Salt Lake City UT: Bureau of Land Management, 1993.

Lipe, William D. "Mesa Verde National Park, CO." In *American Indian Places, a Historical Guidebook*, Frances H. Kennedy, ed., 199–200. Boston: Houghton Mifflin, 2008.

Lopez, Daniel. "Huhugam." In *The Hohokam Millennium*, Suzanne K. Fish and Paul R. Fish, ed., 117–22. Santa Fe: School of American Research, 2008.

Mathien, Frances Joan. "Ornaments of the Chaco Anasazi." In *Ceramics, Lithics, and Ornaments of Chaco Canyon*, vol. 3, Frances Joan Mathien, ed., 1119–1207. Publications in Archeology 18G, Chaco Canyon Studies. Santa Fe: National Park Service, 1997.

Minnis, Paul E. "Earliest plant cultivation in the desert borderlands of North America." In *The Origins of Agriculture, an International Perspective*, C. Wesley Cowan and Patty Jo Watson, ed., 121–42. Tuscaloosa: University of Alabama, 2006.

Naranjo, Tessie. "'We came from the south. We came from the north': Some Tewa origin stories." In *The Mesa Verde World, Explorations in Ancestral Pueblo Archaeology*, David Grant Noble, ed., 49–58. Santa Fe: School of American Research, 2006.

Neitzel, Jill E., ed. *Pueblo Bonito, Center of the Chacoan World*. Washington: Smithsonian, 2003.

Nelson, Margaret C. *Mimbres during the Twelfth Century: Abandonment, Continuity, and Reorganization*. Tucson: University of Arizona, 1999.

Plog, Stephen. *Ancient Peoples of the American Southwest*, 2nd ed. London: Thames and Hudson, 2008.

Smiley, Francis E. "Early farmers in the Southwest: A view from Marsh Pass." In *Basketmaker Anasazi, Papers from the 1990 Wetherill-Grand Gulch Symposium*, Victoria M. Atkins, ed., 243–56. Cultural Resource Series No. 24. Salt Lake City UT: Bureau of Land Management, 1993.

Varien, Mark D., and Richard Wilshusen, ed. *Seeeking the Center Place: Archaeology and Ancient Communities in the Mesa Verde Region*. Salt Lake City: University of Utah, 2000.

Wilshusen, Richard. "The genesis of Pueblos." In *The Mesa Verde World, Explorations in Ancestral Pueblo Archaeology*, David Grant Noble, ed., 19–28. Santa Fe: School of American Research, 2006.

Woosley, Anne I. "Shadows on a silent landscape: Art and symbol at prehistoric Casas Grandes." In *The Road to Aztlan, Art from a Mythic Homeland*, Virginia M. Fields and Victor Zamudio-Taylor, ed., 164–83. Los Angeles CA: Los Angeles County Museum, 2001.

Shelby Tisdale

1. Riley, *Becoming Aztlan*, 69.

2. Sando, *Pueblo Nations*, 248.

3. Spicer, *Cycles of Conquest*, 159.

4. Dillingham, *Acoma & Laguna Pottery*, 132.

5. Tisdale, *Cocopah Identity and Cultural Survival*; Williams, "Cocopah."

6. Tisdale, "Maria Poveka Martinez," 54.

7. Spivey, *The Legacy of Maria Poveka Martinez*, 185.

8. Batkin, *Pottery of the Pueblos of New Mexico*, 78.

9. Spier, *Yuman Tribes of the Gila River*, 316–17.

10. Kaufman and Selser, *The Navajo Weaving Tradition*, 53.

11. Ganteaume, "Western Apache tailored deer hide shirts," 52.

12. Ganteaume.

13. Opler, "Chiricahua Apache," 407–09.

References

Batkin, Jonathan. *Pottery of the Pueblos of New Mexico, 1700–1940*. Colorado Springs: The Taylor Museum of the Colorado Springs Fine Arts Center, 1987.

Bee, Robert L. "Quechan." In *Handbook of North American Indians: Southwest*, vol. 10, Alfonso Ortiz, ed., 86–98. Washington: Smithsonian, 1983.

Cirillo, Dexter. *Southwestern Indian Jewelry*. New York: Abbeville, 1992.

Dillingham, Rick. *Acoma & Laguna Pottery*. Santa Fe: School of American Research, 1992.

Ezell, Paul H. "History of the Pima." In *Handbook of North American Indians, Southwest*, vol. 10, Alfonso Ortiz, ed., 149–60. Washington: Smithsonian, 1983.

Ganteaume, Cécile R. "Naiche's deer hide paintings: A consideration." *American Indian Art Magazine* 28, no. 1 (2002): 44–55, 86.

Ganteaume, Cécile R. "Western Apache tailored deer hide shirts: Their resemblance to full-dress coats worn by officers in U.S. Army and possible meaning." *American Indian Art Magazine* 23, no. 2 (1998): 44–55, 104.

Harlow, Francis H., and Dwight P. Lanmon. *The Pottery of Zia Pueblo*. Santa Fe: School of American Research, 2003.

Jernigan, E. W. *White Metal Universe: Navajo Silver from the Fred Harvey Collections*. Phoenix AZ: Heard Museum, 1981.

Kaufman, Alice, and Christopher Selser. *The Navajo Weaving Tradition: 1650 to the Present*. Tulsa OK and San Francisco: Council Oak, 1999.

Opler, Morris E. "Chiricahua Apache." In *Handbook of North American Indians: Southwest*, vol. 10, Alfonso Ortiz, ed., 401–18. Washington: Smithsonian, 1983.

Powell, Melissa S. "Secrets of Casas Grandes." In *Secrets of Casas Grandes: Precolumbian Art & Archaeology of Northern Mexico*, Melissa S. Powell, ed., 13–37. Santa Fe: Museum of New Mexico, 2006.

Riley, Carroll L. *Becoming Aztlan: Mesoamerican Influence in the Greater Southwest, AD 1200–1500*. Salt Lake: University of Utah, 2005.

Sando, Joe S. *Pueblo Nations: Eight Centuries of Pueblo Indian History*. Santa Fe: Clear Light, 1992.

Spicer, Edward H. *Cycles of Conquest: The Impact of Spain, Mexico, and the United States on the Indians of the Southwest, 1533–1960*. Tucson: University of Arizona, 1989.

Spier, Leslie. *Yuman Tribes of the Gila River*. New York: Dover, 1978. (Originally published by the University of Chicago in 1933.)

Spivey, Richard L. *The Legacy of Maria Poveka Martinez*. Santa Fe: Museum of New Mexico, 2003.

Stewart, Kenneth M. "Mohave." In *Handbook of North American Indians: Southwest*, vol. 10, Alfonso Ortiz, ed., 55–70. Washington: Smithsonian, 1983.

Struever, Martha H. *Painted Perfection: The Pottery of Dextra Quotskuyva*. Santa Fe: Wheelwright Museum of the American Indian, 2001.

Tisdale, Shelby. *Cocopah Identity and Cultural Survival: Indian Gaming and the Political Ecology of the Lower Colorado River Delta, 1850–1996*. PhD dissertation, University of Arizona, Tucson, 1997.

Tisdale, Shelby. *Fine Indian Jewelry of the Southwest*. Santa Fe: Museum of New Mexico, 2006.

Tisdale, Shelby. "Marjorie Ferguson Lambert: Including American Indian and Hispanic peoples in Southwestern anthropology." In *Their Own Frontier: Women Intellectuals Re-Visioning the American West*, Shirley A. Leckie and Nancy J. Parezo, ed., 181–207. Lincoln and London: University of Nebraska, 2008.

Tisdale, Shelby. "Maria Poveka Martinez: Her life, her pottery, her legacy at the Millicent Rogers Museum." *American Indian Art Magazine* 31, no. 1 (2005): 54–63.

Trimble, Stephen. *The People: Indians of the American Southwest*. Santa Fe: School of American Research, 1993.

Williams, Anita Alvarez de. "Cocopah." In *Handbook of North American Indians: Southwest*, vol. 10, Alfonso Ortiz, ed., 113–24. Washington: Smithsonian, 1983.

Wheat, Joe Ben. "Navajo blankets." In *Woven by the Grandmothers*, Eulalie Bonar, ed., 69–85. Washington: Smithsonian, 1996.

THE PLAINS AND PLATEAU
Janet Catherine Berlo

The author wishes to thank Emil Her Many Horses for his contributions in editing this essay.

1. For a discussion of these tropes, see Liebersohn, *Aristocratic Encounters*.

2. In subsequent generations, as anthropologists fanned out over these regions, a more diverse sampling of cultural artifacts was collected, including many objects made and used by women. Her Many Horses and Cutschall, *Identity by Design*.

3. Catlin, *Letters and Notes*, 145. His full account of Mato-Tope occurs on pp. 144–154.

4. Horse Capture and Horse Capture, *Beauty, Honor, and Tradition*. When George Catlin spent some weeks with Mato-Tope in 1832, the Mandan chief presented him with a painted replica of the hide robe he wore, along with an explanation of its meaning. See Maurer, *Visions of the People*, figure 148. This is not the exact hide painting that Mato-Tope gave to Catlin; the Mandan artist repainted the history of his exploits several times as gifts to distinguished visitors from other cultures. This was one acquired by a Swiss explorer who followed in Catlin and Bodmer's footsteps later in the 1830s.

5. Wied, *People of the first man*.

6. For a succinct biography, see Victor Douville, "History of Sinte Gleska (Spotted Tail) 1823–1881," at http://www.sintegleska.edu/about/spottedTail.html. Despite its occasional dated and condescending language, no one has surpassed the detail and scope of Hyde, *Spotted Tail's Folk*.

7. The early ethnographic sources are not in agreement about the number of councilors, chiefs, *wakikonza*, or shirt wearers that existed under the head chief. Sometimes these terms are used interchangeably. Red Feathers told James Walker that there were four or six head chiefs, called wakikonza, while Walker's own summaries describe one wakikonza and a council made up of an indefinite number. Black Elk says there were six councilors who made up the laws and a group of men (*wicasa yatapika* usually glossed as "shirt wearers") who elected the chiefs. It is likely that these offices and the number of men who held them were flexible and perhaps differed among the bands or varied at different times. The size of these leadership offices might have depended upon the size of the band or whether there were multiple bands. See Walker, *Lakota Society*, 38, 58. For Black Elk, see DeMallie, *The Sixth Grandfather*, 320. See also Berlo, *Spirit Beings and Sun Dancers*, figure 9 and plates 22 and 23, for drawings of such individuals made by late-19th-century Lakota artists.

8. Hyde, *Spotted Tail's Folk*, 64.

9. Charles G. Sawtelle (1834–1913), who served with the Sixth Infantry, was later a general in the U.S. Army.

10. Hyde, 65.

11. This trip is well described in Poole, *Among the Sioux of Dakota*, chapters 23–31, for Poole was the Indian Agent who accompanied them.

12. Hyde, 286–293.

13. See http://www.sintegleska.edu.

14. Larry McMurtry's fine short biography, *Crazy Horse, a Life*, takes up the issues of his fame and provides an annotated bibliography. A fuller account is provided by Bray, *Crazy Horse: A Lakota Life*.

15. For his own account of this service, see Bourke, *On the Border with Crook*.

16. As quoted from his diary by Porter, *Paper Medicine Man*, 67.

17. For an account of the fascinating transformation of Bourke from military officer to ethnologist, see Porter, *Paper Medicine Man*. Portions of his voluminous diaries, collected at West Point, have been published. See Robinson, *The Diaries of John Gregory Bourke*. Some of the drawings Bourke collected are published in Berlo, *Plains Indian Drawings*, 41, 92–95, and 129.

18. For the Battle of Rosebud, see Porter, 42–48; for the Sun Dance, see 91, 94.

19. Her Many Horses and Cutschall.

20. Barbara Hail, *Gifts*, 132 and fig. 10.1.

21. Clark and Webb, "Susette and Susan La Flesche."

22. Wilson, *Bright Eyes*. Tibbles's account of the massacre can be found in Tibbles, *Buckskin and Blanket Days*, chapters 31–34.

23. Personal communication from clothing historian Dr. Melissa Jurgena, August 21, 2008.

24. Clark and Webb.

25. Powell, "High Bull's victory roster," 14–21.

26. Bourke, 392–93; Wheeler, *Buffalo Days*, 142–47.

27. Grinnell, "Double trophy roster."

28. Price, *The Oglala People*, 71.

29. Price, 109.

30. Careful examination of the 52 drawings in the book reveals several artists' hands at work. Horses are drawn in at least three different styles, as are their riders. Some of the men may have drawn their own images, while others deferred to their peers who were more skilled at drawing.

31. Hardorff, *Lakota Recollections*, 29–34.

32. Dr. Valentine McGillycuddy (1849–1939) had been a surgeon with the army stationed at Fort Robinson before his appointment as Indian Agent. See McGillycuddy, *Blood on the Moon*; Red Dog is mentioned only once, on page 169.

33. A comparison of this book with another drawn by men in Red Dog's band perhaps a decade later shows that by the 1890s, Lakota artists selling drawing books to whites had fewer reservations about depicting scenes of battles waged against the U.S. Army. See Red Hawk's drawing book in Berlo, *Plains Indian Drawings*, 210–15, and Ritzenthaler, "Sioux Indian drawings." For a more comprehensive Sioux pictorial history, see the hundreds of drawings by Bad Heart Bull in Blish, *A Pictographic History of the Oglala Sioux*.

34. Sherman, whose ruthless ideas about military behavior were forged in the Civil War, was well known for his unyielding position: "During an assault," he insisted, "the soldiers can not pause to distinguish between male and female, or even discriminate as to age. As long as resistance is made, death must be meted out." As quoted in Marszalek, *Sherman: A Soldier's Passion for Order*, 379. Red Dog's drawing book was given to the museum by Eleanor Sherman Fitch, the general's granddaughter. Many military men commissioned such books, sometimes from Indian scouts they knew personally. For example, see Greene, both "Artists in Blue" and *Silver Horn*.

35. Curtis, *The North American Indian*, vol. 4, p. 47.

36. Arapoosh's exploits were recorded in several early sources. In addition to Curtis, who makes brief mention of him, see also Bradley, "The Bradley manuscript," 299–307; Denig, *Five Indian Tribes*, 161–84. Writing

in 1856, with more than two decades' experience as a fur trader, Denig provides the most thorough account by someone who knew Arapoosh. See also Hoxie, *Parading through History*, 56, 75–76, who relies on the same sources.

37. Lowie, "The religion of the Crow Indians," 407–08.

38. Denig, *Five Indian Tribes*, 162.

39. For a description of a vision of Thunder Beings by another Crow man that is remarkably consistent with those reported by Lakota, see Lowie, "The religion of the Crow Indians," 337–38.

40. Corey, "Coveted stripes," 131–46.

41. Wildschut, *Crow Indian Medicine Bundles*, 71.

42. The most extensive collection of Crow shields was made by George Dorsey and Stephen Simms in 1902 for the Field Museum in Chicago. Many of these were published in color in Hoxie, *The Crow*, 73–80. A shield illustrated on the cover of Hoxie's *The Crow*, remarkably similar to Arapoosh's (but with the standing figure painted in red on a black background, rather than the reverse), belonged to Wraps Up His Tail, also known as Sword Bearer (ca. 1863–1887).

43. Stirling, *Three Pictographic Autobiographies of Sitting Bull*, 1–56. See drawings of Thunder Beings made by the Lakota holy man Black Hawk in the 1880s in Berlo, *Spirit Beings and Sun Dancers*, plates 1 and 2. For Black Elk, see DeMallie, *The Sixth Grandfather*, 132. For Bush Otter, see Dorsey, *A Study of Siouan Cults*, 442. Another round Lakota drum with horns attached is in the collection of the Montana Historical Society (#1982.44.57). Painted in its front is a spirit figure, also with horns, and zigzag lines of power emanating from its mouth. There are no records as to its history (Bill Mercer, Montana Historical Society Museum Services Manager, personal communication, August 2008).

References

Berlo, J. C. *Plains Indian Drawings 1865–1935: Pages from a Visual History*. New York: Abrams, 1996.

Berlo, Janet Catherine. *Spirit Beings and Sun Dancers: Black Hawk's Vision of the Lakota World*. New York: George Braziller, 2000.

Blish, Helen. *A Pictographic History of the Oglala Sioux*. Lincoln: University of Nebraska, 1967.

Bourke, John Gregory. *On the Border with Crook*. Chicago: Rio Grande, 1962. (Originally published in 1891.)

Bradley, James H. "The Bradley manuscript." In *Contributions to the Historical Society of Montana*, vol. 9. Helena: Historical Society of Montana, 1923.

Bray, Kingsley. *Crazy Horse: A Lakota Life*. Norman: University of Oklahoma, 2006.

Brownstone, Arni. "Seven war-exploit paintings: A search for their origins." In *Studies in American Indian Art: A Memorial Tribute to Norman Feder*, Christian Feest, ed., 69–85. Seattle: University of Washington, 2001.

Campbell, Walter Stanley (writing as Stanley Vestal). *Sitting Bull: Champion of the Sioux*. Boston: Houghton Mifflin, 1932.

Catlin, George. *Letters and Notes on the Manners, Customs, and Conditions of the North American Indian* (1844). New York: Dover, 1973.

Clark, Jerry E., and Martha Ellen Webb. "Susette and Susan La Flesche: Reformer and missionary." In *Being and Becoming Indian: Biographical Studies of North American Frontiers*, James A. Clifton, ed. Chicago: Dorsey, 1989.

Corey, Carolyn. "Coveted stripes: The origin of 'Stroud' and 'Saved List' cloth for the North American trade." In *The People of the Buffalo*, vol. 2, Colin Taylor and Hugh Dempsey, ed. Wyk auf Foehr, Germany: Tatanka, 2005.

Curtis, Edward. *The North American Indian*. Seattle: E. S. Curtis, 1907–1930. The complete 20-volume work is available online via the Northwestern University Library at http://curtis.library.northwestern.edu/.

DeMallie, Raymond J. *The Sixth Grandfather: Black Elk's Teachings Given to John G. Neihardt*. Lincoln: University of Nebraska, 1984.

Denig, Edwin Thompson. *Five Indian Tribes of the Upper Missouri*, John C. Ewers, ed. Norman: University of Oklahoma, 1961.

Dorsey, James. *A Study of Siouan Cults*. Washington: Smithsonian Bureau of Ethnology, 1894.

Greene, Candace. "Artists in blue: The Indian scouts of Fort Reno and Fort Supply." *American Indian Art Magazine* 18, no. 1 (1992): 50–57.

Greene, Candace. *Silver Horn: Master Illustrator of the Kiowa People*. Norman: University of Oklahoma, 2001.

Grinnell, George Bird. "Double trophy roster." Undated, unpublished manuscript, object file 10/8725, National Museum of the American Indian.

Hardorff, Richard, ed. *Lakota Recollections of the Custer Fight: New Sources of Indian–Military History*. Spokane WA: Arthur Clark Co., 1991.

Her Many Horses, Emil, and Colleen Cutschall. *Identity by Design*. Washington and New York: NMAI, 2007.

Horse Capture, Joseph D., and George P. Horse Capture. *Beauty, Honor, and Tradition: The Legacy of Plains Indian Shirts*. Washington and New York: NMAI, 2001.

Hoxie, Frederick E. *Parading through History: The Making of the Crow Nation in America, 1805–1935*. New York: Cambridge University, 1995.

Hoxie, Frederick. *The Crow*. New York: Chelsea House, 1989.

Hyde, George. *Spotted Tail's Folk: A History of the Brulé Sioux*. Norman: University of Oklahoma, 1961.

Liebersohn, Harry. *Aristocratic Encounters: European Travelers and North American Indians*. Cambridge: Cambridge University, 1998.

Lowie, Robert H. "The religion of the Crow Indians." *Anthropological Papers of the American Museum of Natural History*, vol. 25, pt. 2. New York: American Museum of Natural History, 1922.

Marszalek, John F. *Sherman: A Soldier's Passion for Order*. New York: Free, 1993.

Maurer, Evan. *Visions of the People: A Pictorial History of Plains Indian Life*. Minneapolis: Minneapolis Institute of Arts, 1992.

McGillycuddy, Julia. *Blood on the Moon: Valentine McGillycuddy and the Sioux*. Lincoln: University of Nebraska, 1990. (Originally published in 1941.)

McMurtry, Larry. *Crazy Horse, a Life*. New York: Penguin Group, 1999.

Poole, D. C. *Among the Sioux of Dakota: Eighteen Months' Experience as an Indian Agent, 1869–70*. St. Paul: Minnesota Historical Society, 1988.

Porter, Joseph. *Paper Medicine Man: John Gregory Bourke and His American West*. Norman: University of Oklahoma, 1986.

Powell, Peter. "High Bull's victory roster." *Montana: The Magazine of Western History* 25, no. 1 (1975): 14–21.

Price, Catherine. *The Oglala People 1841–1879, A Political History*. Lincoln: University of Nebraska, 1996.

Ritzenthaler, Robert. "Sioux Indian drawings." Primitive Art Series 1, portfolio and unpaginated brochure. Milwaukee: Milwaukee Public Museum, 1961.

Robinson, Charles M., III, *The Diaries of John Gregory Bourke*. Denton: University of North Texas, 2009.

Stirling, Matthew. *Three Pictographic Autobiographies of Sitting Bull*. Smithsonian Miscellaneous Collections 97 (5). Washington: Smithsonian, 1938.

Tibbles, Thomas. *Buckskin and Blanket Days: Memoirs of a Friend of the Indians*. New York: Doubleday, 1957.

Utley, Robert M. *The Lance and the Shield: The Life and Times of Sitting Bull*. New York: Henry Holt, 1993.

Walker, J. R. *Lakota Society*. Raymond J. DeMallie, ed. Lincoln: University of Nebraska, 1984,

Wheeler, Homer W. *Buffalo Days: The Personal Narrative of a Cattleman, Indian Fighter, and Army Officer*. Lincoln: University of Nebraska, 1990.

Wildschut, William. *Crow Indian Medicine Bundles*, John C. Ewers, ed. 2nd ed. New York: Museum of the American Indian, Heye Foundation, 1975.

Wied, Maximilian. *People of the first man: Life among the Plains Indians in their final days of glory: the firsthand account of Prince Maximilian's expedition up the Missouri River, 1833–34*. New York: Promontory, 1982.

Wilson, Dorothy Clark. *Bright Eyes: The Story of Suzette La Flesche, an Omaha Indian*. New York: McGraw-Hill, 1974.

Donovin Sprague

References

Greene, Candace S., and Russell Thornton, ed. *The Year the Stars Fell*. Washington: Smithsonian, 2007.

Hyde, George. *Red Cloud's Folk.* Norman: University of Oklahoma, 1937.

Jensen, Richard, ed. *The Indian Interviews of Eli S. Ricker, 1903–1919, Voices of the American West,* vol. 1. Lincoln NE and London: University of Nebraska, 2005.

McMaster, Gerald, and Clifford E. Trafzer, ed. *Native Universe, Voices of Indian America.* Washington and New York: NMAI and National Geographic, 2004.

Patrick J. Hill and Timothy P. McCleary

1. The term "Blackfoot" is used to describe the larger confederacy of three politically, culturally, and linguistically related groups, the Blackfoot, Bloods, and Piegans. Since the collector did not distinguish the affiliation of the seller, the term Blackfoot in its general sense is used in this document.

2. Ewers, "Artists' choice," 45.

3. Van West, *A Traveler's Companion to Montana History,* 28.

4. Hoxie and Rzeczkowski, *Grapevine Creek Battle,* 18–19.

5. Brownstone, *"Seven war-exploit paintings,"* 69–72; Lowie, *Crow Indian Art,* 320.

6. Lowie, "Notes on the social organization and customs of the Mandan," 82–85.

7. Lowie, "Social life of the Crow Indians," 230–31; Old Horn and McCleary, *Apsáalooke Social and Family Structure,* 20.

8. McCoy, "Every picture tells a story," 173.

References

Brownstone, Arni. "Seven war-exploit paintings: A search for their origins." In *Studies in American Indian Art: A Memorial Tribute to Norman Feder.* Seattle: University of Washington, 2001.

Ewers, John C. "Artists' choice." *American Indian Art Magazine* 7, no. 2 (1982): 40–49.

Hoxie, Frederick E., and Frank Rzeczkowski. *Grapevine Creek Battle.* Denver CO: Lee Ballentine Production, 1998.

Lowie, Robert H. "Social life of the Crow Indians." *Anthropological Papers of the American Museum of Natural History,* vol. 9, no. 2 (1912): 179–253.

Lowie, Robert H. "Notes of the social organization and customs of the Mandan, Hidatsa, and Crow Indians." *Anthropological Papers of the American Museum of Natural History,* vol. 21, no. 1 (1917): 1–99.

Lowie, Robert H. "Crow Indian art." *Anthropological Papers of the American Museum of Natural History,* vol. 21, no. 4 (1917): 271–322.

McCoy, Ron. "Every picture tells a story: Plains Indian warrior art: The state of the art." *Reviews in Anthropology* 29 (2000): 171–184.

Old Horn, Dale D., and Timothy P. McCleary. *Apsáalooke Social and Family Structure.* Crow Agency MT: Little Big Horn College, 1995.

Van West, Carroll. *A Traveler's Companion to Montana History.* Helena: Montana Historical Society, 1986.

THE WOODLANDS

David W. Penney

1. Fenton, "This island," 292–94; Hale, "Huron folklore," 180–82; Hewitt, "Iroquois cosmology," 195–332.

2. Leland, *Algonquin Legends of New England,* 1.

3. Barnouw, *Wisconsin Chippewa Myths and Tales*; Blackbird, *History of the Ottawa and Chippewa Indians,* 73; Corbiere, "Nenaboozhoo giinmetoon"; Great Lakes Indian Fish and Wildlife Commission (GLIFWC), *Ojibwa Treaty Rights.*

4. An atlas created recently of ceded territories in what are now parts of Upper Michigan, Minnesota, and Wisconsin recovered nearly 700 Anishinaabemowin place names describing geographic features, resource areas, landmarks, and locations tied to events and stories. GLIFWC, *Gidakiiminaan (Our Earth).*

5. Quarries of the Munsungun Lakes region of Maine; Normanskill chert located near the southern New York–Massachusetts border; the Onondaga formations of northwest New York state; the Upper Mercer and Flint Ridge quarries of northwest Ohio; the Wyandot–Harrison County quarries of southern Indiana; and the Burlington, Dover, and Mill Creek outcrops of southern Illinois and Missouri—all exerted their gravitational pull on orbiting bands of paleoindian hunter-gatherers.

6. Seeman, "Intercluster lithic patterning"; Ellis and Lothrop, *Eastern Paleolindian Resource Use.*

7. Sigstad, *The Age and Distribution of Catlinite and Red Pipestone.* The stone catlinite is named for George Catlin, the frontier painter who visited the quarry site in 1834, one of several to write about stone-quarrying observed there. Catlin offered a rather confused and unattributed account of the mythic origins of red pipestone: "The Great Spirit at an ancient period here called the Indian nations together . . . and made a huge pipe . . . and smoked it over them." Unfortunately, Catlin was not a very skilled listener. From a Lakota perspective, historians Jace and Sam Decory write, "We believe that the red pipestone is the blood and flesh of the Lakota nation." Catlin, *North American Indians,* 429; Decory and Decory, "The gift of the sacred pipe," 18.

8. Bray and Bray, *Joseph N. Nicollet on the Plains and Prairies,* 42–108; White, "A trip to the pipestone quarry."

9. Byers, "Intentionality, symbolic pragmatics, and material culture," 277.

10. Copper plates and ornaments cut or engraved with religious imagery are among the most visually and metaphorically rich, and presumably sacred, categories of objects of the Middle Woodland Hopewell (200 BC–AD 400) and Mississippian (AD 900–1700) ideological complexes. Trader, traveler, and memoirist James Adair (1709–1783) reported that five copper plates kept at the Creek town of Tuckabatchee, Alabama, were regarded as their most sacred community possessions. They were transported in solemn procession, each wrapped in a buckskin bag and strapped to the back of a venerable and senior male, when the community was forced to remove to Arkansas in 1836. Swanton, "Social organization and social usages," 503–05. Similarly, the Jesuit missionary Allouez wrote in 1666 of the Anishinaabe that objects of copper were kept "as so many divinities, or as presents which the gods dwelling beneath the water have given them . . . they preserve these pieces of copper, wrapped up, among their most precious possessions." Thwaites, *The Jesuit Relations and Allied Documents,* 265–66. In 1842 the Anishinaabe historian William Warren saw one such copper plate, "inscribed with rude hieroglyphs," when it was shown to him by its keeper, Chief Tug-waug-aun-ay of the Crane clan, at La Pointe, Wisconsin. Warren, *History of the Ojibway People,* 89.

11. See Schroeder and Ruhl, "Metallurgical characteristics."

12. Sayles, "Banded glacial slates."

13. Buikstra and Charles, "Centering the ancestors."

14. Hamell, "Strawberries, floating islands, and rabbit captains," 77.

15. Axtell, *The Invasion Within,* 7–8.

16. Turner, "Socio-political organization." Smith demurred and Pocahontas eventually married another British official, John Rolfe.

17. Hamell, "Strawberries, floating islands, and rabbit captains"; Hamell, "The Iroquois and the world's rim."

18. Bailey, *The Conflict of European and Eastern Algonkian Cultures,* 49.

19. Swanton, *Indian Tribes of the Lower Mississippi Valley,* 56.

20. Kinietz, *The Indians of the Western Great Lakes,* 9–14, 233–34.

References

Axtell, James. *The Invasion Within: The Contest of Cultures in Colonial North America.* Oxford: Oxford University, 1985.

Bailey, Alfred G. *The Conflict of European and Eastern Algonkian Cultures 1504–1700: A Study in Canadian Civilization.* Toronto: University of Toronto, 1969.

Barnouw, Victor. *Wisconsin Chippewa Myths and Tales.* Madison: University of Wisconsin, 1977.

Blackbird, Andrew J. *History of the Ottawa and Chippewa Indians of Michigan.* Harbor Springs MI: Little Traverse Bay Historical Society, 1887.

Bray, Edmund C., and Martha Coleman Bray. *Joseph N. Nicollet on the Plains and Prairies: Expeditions of 1838–39 with Journals, Letters, and Notes on the Dakota Indians.* St. Paul: Minnesota Historical Society, 1976.

Byers, A. Martin. "Intentionality, symbolic pragmatics, and material culture: Revisiting Binford's view of the Old Copper Complex." *American Antiquity,* vol. 64, no. 2 (1999): 265–287.

Buikstra, Jane, and Douglas K. Charles. "Centering the

ancestors: Cemeteries, mounds, and sacred landscapes of the ancient North American midcontinent." In *Archaeologies of Landscape: Contemporary Perspectives*, W. Ashmore and A. B. Knapp, ed., 201–28. Oxford: Blackwell, 1999.

Catlin, George. *North American Indians*, P. Matthiessen, ed. London: Penguin, 1989. (Originally published in 1841.)

Corbiere, Alan. "Nenaboozhoo gii-nmetoon: Nanabush left his mark." *Kinoomaadiwag Cultural Research* 3, no. 1 (2004): 7–9.

Decory, Sam, and Jace Decory. "The gift of the sacred pipe." *Coteau Heritage: Journal of the Pipestone County Historical Society* 2, no. 1 (1989): 18–19.

Ellis, Christopher J., and Jonathan C. Lothrop, ed. *Eastern Paleoindian Resource Use*. Boulder CO: Westview, 1989.

Fenton, William N. "This island, the world on the turtle's back." *Journal of American Folklore* 75, no. 298 (1962): 283–300.

Great Lakes Indian Fish and Wildlife Commission (GLIFWC). *Gidakiiminaan (Our Earth): An Anishinaabe Atlas of the 1836 (Upper Michigan), 1837, and 1842 Treaty Ceded Territories*. Odanah WI: GLIFWC, 2007.

Great Lakes Indian Fish and Wildlife Commission (GLIFWC). *Ojibwa Treaty Rights: Understanding Impact*. Odanah WI: GLIFWC, 2006.

Hale, Horatio. "Huron folklore. I. Cosmogonic myths, the good and evil twins." *Journal of American Folklore* 1, no. 3 (1888): 177–83.

Hamell, George R. "Strawberries, floating islands, and rabbit captains: Mythical realities and European contact in the Northeast during the sixteenth and seventeenth centuries." *Journal of Canadian Studies* 21, no. 4 (1986/87): 72–94.

Hamell, George R. "The Iroquois and the world's rim: Speculations on color, culture, and contact." *American Indian Quarterly* 16, no. 4 (1992): 451–69.

Hewitt, J. N. B. "Iroquois cosmology." *Annual Report of the Bureau of American Ethnology* 21 (1903): 127–339.

Kinietz, W. Vernon. *The Indians of the Western Great Lakes 1615–1760*. Ann Arbor: University of Michigan, 1940.

Leland, Charles G. *Algonquin Legends of New England*. Boston: Houghton Mifflin, 1884.

Sayles, Robert W. "Banded glacial slates of a permo-carboniferous age, showing possible seasonal variations in deposition." *Proceedings of the National Academy of Sciences* 2 (1916): 167–70.

Schroeder, David L., and Katherine C. Ruhl. "Metallurgical characteristics of North American prehistoric copper work." *American Antiquity* 33, no. 2 (1968): 162–69.

Seeman, Mark F. "Intercluster lithic patterning at Nobles Pond: A case for 'disembedded' procurement among early Paleoindian societies." *American Antiquity* 59, no. 2 (1994): 273–88.

Sigstad, John S. *The Age and Distribution of Catlinite and Red Pipestone*. PhD dissertation, University of Missouri, 1973.

Swanton, John R. *Indian Tribes of the Lower Mississippi Valley and the Adjacent Coast of the Gulf of Mexico*. Bulletin 43. Washington: Bureau of American Ethnology, 1911.

Swanton, John R. "Social organization and social usages of the Indians of the Creek Confederacy." *Bureau of American Ethnology, Annual Report* 42 (1928): 23–472.

Thwaites, Ruben G., ed. *The Jesuit Relations and Allied Documents: Lower Canada, Iroquois, and Ottawa 1664–1666*, vol. 50. Cleveland OH: Burrows Brothers, 1899.

Turner, E. Randolph. "Sociopolitical organization within the Powhatan chiefdom and the effects of European contact, AD 1607–1634." In *Cultures in Contact: The European Impact on Native Cultural Institutions in Eastern North America, AD 1000–1800*, W. W. Fitzhugh, ed., 193–224. Washington: Smithsonian, 1985.

Warren, William W. *History of the Ojibway People*. St. Paul: Minnesota Historical Society, 1984. (Originally published in 1885.)

White, C. A. "A trip to the pipestone quarry." *Coteau Heritage: Journal of the Pipestone County Historical Society* 2, no. 1 (1989): 20–22.

James A. Brown

1. Reilly and Garber, *Ancient Objects and Sacred Realms*; Lankford et al., *Visualizing the Sacred*.

2. Milner, *The Moundbuilders*.

3. Silverberg, *Mound Builders of Ancient America*; Squier and Davis, *Ancient Monuments of the Mississippi Valley*.

4. This connection has achieved popular visibility in the writing of Malcolm Gladwell, who cites studies showing the importance of logging 10,000 hours of practice to achieving distinction in all manner of skills. The 10,000-hour rule applies to ancient societies in the same way that it does for our own. Gladwell, *Outliers*.

5. Penney, "The archaeology of aesthetics."

References

Gladwell, Malcolm. *Outliers: The Story of Success*. New York: Little-Brown, 2008.

Lankford, George E., F. Kent Reilly, III, and James Garber, ed. *Visualizing the Sacred: Cosmic Visions, Regionalism, and the Art of the Mississippian World*. Austin: University of Texas, 2010.

Milner, George R. *The Moundbuilders: Ancient Peoples of Eastern North America*. London: Thames & Hudson, 2004.

Penney, David W. "The archaeology of aesthetics." In *Hero, Hawk, and Open Hand: American Indian Art of the Ancient Midwest and South*, R. F. Townsend and R. V. Sharp, ed., 42–55. Chicago: Art Institute of Chicago, 2004.

Reilly, F. K., III, and J. F. Garber, ed. *Ancient Objects and Sacred Realms: Interpretations of Mississippian Iconography*. Austin: University of Texas, 2007.

Silverberg, Robert. *Mound Builders of Ancient America: The Archaeology of a Myth*. Greenwich CT: New York Graphic Society, 1968.

Squier, Ephraim G., and Edwin H. Davis. *Ancient Monuments of the Mississippi Valley*. Smithsonian Contributions to Knowledge, no. 1, 1848.

Ruth B. Phillips and Michael Witgen

1. Nearly all these officers and officials passed through Halifax, Quebec, and Montreal and eagerly sought out finely crafted wares made for the curio market, such as Mi'kmaq quilled boxes, convent-made moosehair-embroidered bark wares, canoe models, and elegantly decorated moccasins. It is striking that although Foster spent time in these cities, his collection includes no examples of these things. Phillips and Idiens, "A casket of curiosities"; Phillips, *Patterns of Power*.

2. From an inscription on the portrait Caldwell commissioned of himself arrayed in his Indian outfit we know that the garments were presented to him on the occasion of his adoption by Anishinaabeg in the Ohio Territory in 1780, a ceremony that reaffirmed the Anishinaabe alliance with the British. The majority of the Caldwell Collection is now in the Canadian Museum of Civilization. The portrait survives in two copies: one in the Kings Regiment Collection, Liverpool Museums, and the other (with the inscription) at Castle Caldwell, in Ireland. See Jones, "Caldwell and DePeyster."

3. The fragmentary information about Foster's activities in official correspondence reports him as venturing out of Michilimackinac with an Indian Department interpreter named Guillaume La Mothe, taking charge of surveying for a new fort at Ile St. Joseph, distributing Indian corn and maple sugar to "distressed Chippewa," and trying to prevent the murder of Wawaness, a Chippewa from Lake Superior. Boston, unpublished research notes.

4. Letter from Charles Foster to George Terasaki, October 9, 1966.

5. "They are extremely handsome, and have a superior air to any I have seen," Elizabeth Simcoe wrote. ". . . Some wore black silk handkerchiefs, covered with silk brooches, tied right round the head, others silver bands, silver arm bands, and their shirts ornamented with brooches; scarlet leggings or pantaloons, and black, blue or scarlet blankets." Simcoe, *The Diary of Mrs. John Graves Simcoe*, 308.

6. When Great Lakes leaders wore such outfits at councils and ceremonial events, they signaled their prestige and efficacy in looking after their people. Shannon, "Dressing for success along the Mohawk frontier."

7. It is linguist Richard Rhodes' observation that "there are only two general terms in Ojibwa for categories of people with respect to membership in Ojibwa society: *inawemaagen*, 'relative,' and *meyaagizid*, 'foreigner.' . . . Notably absent are separate categories of unrelated cultural insiders

which would correspond to English 'friend' and 'stranger.'" Rhodes, "Ojibwa politeness and social structure," 172–73.

8. For a discussion of these failed expeditions and the subsequent campaign of General Anthony Wayne, see Dowd, *A Spirited Resistance*, 105–09. This would have been the political and diplomatic climate in which Foster acquired his outfit. Native peoples on the Ohio frontier struggled to maintain a united Indian opposition to America's influence and expansion. An important part of this opposition involved reaching out to the "back nations" of the upper Great Lakes, such as the Anishinaabeg, with the hope of also drawing the British—who still maintained posts in the region—into the alliance. For a Native perspective on the politics behind this coalition, see *A Narrative of an Embassy to the Western Indians*, especially 103–05.

References

A Narrative of an Embassy to the Western Indians from Original Manuscript of Hendrick Auppamut. Memoirs of Historical Society of Pennsylvania, 2 (1827).

Boston, John. Unpublished research notes, Archives, National Museum of the American Indian, VX–4.

Dowd, Gregory Evans. *A Spirited Resistance: The North American Indian Struggle for Unity, 1745–1815*. Baltimore MD: Johns Hopkins University, 1992.

Foster, Charles. Letter to George Terasaki, October 9, 1966, Archives, National Museum of the American Indian, VX–4.

Jones, Simon. "Caldwell and DePeyster: Two collectors from the King's Regiment on the Great Lakes in the 1770s and 1780s." In *Three Centuries of Woodlands Indian Art*, J. C. H. King and Christian F. Feest, ed., 41. Altenstadt, Germany: ZKF, 2007.

Phillips, Ruth B. *Patterns of Power: The Jasper Grant Collection and Great Lakes Indian Art of the Early Nineteenth Century*. Kleinburg ON: McMichael Canadian Collection, 1984.

Phillips, Ruth B., and Dale Idiens. "A casket of curiosities: Eighteenth-century objects from northeastern North America in the Farquharson Collection." *Journal of the History of Collecting* 6, no. 1 (1994): 21–33.

Rhodes, Richard A. "Ojibwa politeness and social structure." In *Papers of the Nineteenth Algonquian Conference*, William Cowen, ed. Ottawa: Carleton University, 1988.

Shannon, Timothy J. "Dressing for success on the Mohawk frontier: Hendrick, William Johnson, and the Indian fashion." *The William and Mary Quarterly* (January 1996): 13–42.

Simcoe, Elizabeth Posthuma. *The Diary of Mrs. John Graves Simcoe: Wife of the First Lieutenant-Governor of the Province of Upper Canada, 1792–6*. Toronto: Briggs, 1911.

CALIFORNIA AND THE GREAT BASIN

Steven M. Karr

1. Today, while beading still abounds, brain-tanning in some regions is on the wane. Traditional use of deer brain has fallen off for years as deer hunters choose to keep trophy heads. Tanners first turned to cow brain an alternative, but with the onset of mad cow disease, that practice is now illegal. Increasingly tanners have begun to use pig brain—many believe the higher fat content lends a more supple hide—enabling artists to continue traditional practices with necessary accommodations.

2. This is true even in Southern California, where Mission peoples incorporated the horse into their cultural orientation earlier than most groups within the state.

3. Similar braided horsehair belts can be found in the Southwest Museum of the American Indian, Autry National Center Collection in Los Angeles—one there, like this one, is attributed to the Shasta, the other to their immediate western neighbors, the Karuk people.

4. The Cupeño are not to be mistaken for the Agua Caliente Band of Cahuilla Indians, who have long lived in the Palm Springs area.

For further reading

Anderson, M. Kat. *Tending the Wild: Native American Knowledge and the Management of California's Natural Resources*. Berkeley: University of California, 2006.

Cook, Sherburne F. *The Conflict between the California Indians and White Civilization*. Berkeley: University of California, 1976.

Cuero, Delfina. *Delfina Cuero: Her Autobiography*. Slyvia Brakke Vane, ed., Rosalie Pinto Robertson, trans. Banning CA: Malki-Ballena Press, 1991.

Gutiérrez, Ramon A., and Richard J. Orsi, ed. *Contested Eden: California before the Gold Rush*. Berkeley: University of California, 1998.

Heizer, Robert F. *The Destruction of California Indians: A Collection of Documents from the Period 1847 to 1865*. Santa Barbara: Peregrine Smith, 1974.

Heizer, Robert F., ed. *Handbook of North American Indians: California*, vol. 8. Washington: Smithsonian, 1978.

Heizer, R. F., and M. A. Whipple, ed. *The California Indians: A Source Book*. Berkeley: University of California, 1971.

Hurtado, Albert L. *Indian Survival on the California Frontier*. New Haven: Yale University. 1988.

Karr, Steven M. "Pablo Tac: Native peoples in precontact California." In *The Human Tradition in California*, 1–15, Clark Davis and David Igler, ed. Lanham MD and Oxford: SR Books, 2002.

Karr, Steven M. "The Warner's ranch Indian removal: Cultural adaptation, accommodation, and continuity." *California History* 86, no. 4 (2009).

Karr, Steven M. "'Water We Believed Could Never Belong to Anyone': The San Luis Rey River and the Pala Indians of Southern California." *American Indian Quarterly* 24, no. 3 (2000): 381–99.

Lightfoot, Kent, and Otis Parrish. *California Indians and Their Environment: An Introduction*. Berkeley: University of California, 2009.

Powers, Stephen. *Tribes of California*. Introduction and notes by Robert F. Heizer. Berkeley: University of California, 1976. (Originally published in 1877.)

Rawls, James J. *Indians of California: The Changing Image*. Norman: University of Oklahoma, 1984.

Sandos, James A. *Converting California: Indians and Franciscans in the Missions*. New Haven: Yale University, 2004.

Margolin, Malcolm, ed. *The Way We Lived: California Indian Stories, Songs and Reminiscences*. Berkeley: Heyday, 1993. (Originally published in 1933 by the California Historical Society.)

Catherine S. Fowler

Suggested reading

Bates, Craig D. "An artistic style uniquely their own: Basketry, parfleches and clothing of the Ute people." In *Ute Indian Arts and Culture from Prehistory to the New Millennium*, William Wroth, ed., 143–78. Colorado Springs: Taylor Museum of the Colorado Springs Fine Art Center, 2000.

d'Azevedo, Warren L., ed. *Handbook of North American Indians: Great Basin*, vol. 2, William C. Sturtevant, ed. Washington: Smithsonian, 1986.

Fowler, Catherine S. *Tule Technology: Northern Paiute Uses of Marsh Resources in Western Nevada*. Smithsonian Folklife Studies no. 6. Washington: Smithsonian, 1990.

Her Many Horses, Emil, ed. *Identity by Design: Tradition, Change, and Celebration in Native Women's Dresses*. New York: NMAI and HarperCollins, 2007.

THE NORTHWEST COAST

Mary Jane Lenz

1. Levi-Strauss, "The art of the Northwest Coast."

2. William Reid quoted from an unpublished manuscript in Reid, "Silent speakers."

3. Drucker, *Indians of the Northwest Coast*. Some scholars extend the Northwest Coast into northern California. For a discussion, see Suttles, *The Northwest Coast*, 1–15 (Introduction).

4. Indeed, speculation regarding connections with Asia appears in a body of scholarly literature that references not only armor and the presence of Chinese coins, but design elements such as splayed figures and double-headed serpents, as well as carved pillars and house posts that evoke totem poles. See Covarrubias, *The Eagle*, 189–90, for a list of Asiatic and Pacific traits in Northwest Coast art. Also see Coe, "Asiatic sources of Northwest Coast art."

5. Chowning, "Raven myths."

6. When Vancouver visited Puget Sound in 1792, he reported that the people kept small dogs whose white, fluffy hair was sheared to make yarn for weaving blankets. The artist Paul Kane sketched such a dog in 1847. The existence of "dog hair blankets" has puzzled scholars ever since. At

present, consensus appears to be that these early blankets were probably a mixture of dog hair and mountain goat wool. The yarn was used to make the white ceremonial blankets with thin red striping, which are worn by Salish people even today. This Salish blanket is a distinctly different type, incorporating the bright colors and complex patterns of what is known as "nobility blankets." Speculation holds that the design may have been inspired by patchwork quilts made by Euro-American farmers' wives. Only a few of these blankets are still in existence. They were apparently commissioned by Joseph W. McKay, manager of the Yale Hudson's Bay Company trading post. Records indicate that McKay purchased it from "the chief of the Tsakum [Spuzzum River?] band of Cowichan Salish at Yale."

7. Shotridge, "Ghost of Courageous Adventurer."

8. In an 1805 letter sent from Sitka to the directors of the Russian American Company, the imperial envoy Rezanov wrote, "The brutal massacre committed by the Americans [referring to the Tlingit] has taught us to take precautions. Our cannons are always loaded. . . ." Russian gunboats used their cannons to fire on the Native population on several occasions. The early Yakutat Tlingit pipe shown on page 227 depicts a Russian ship's cannon. The barrel doubtless produced a realistic effect as smoke poured out of its mouth.

9. Argillite flutes with holes were copies of European recorders. (Often, as in the flute on page 228, the mouthpiece was cast of lead.) Like the panel pipes, early flutes were often decorated with floral patterns, rosettes, and sculptured figures of humans and animals. And, like the pipes, they could be used, but the spacing of the holes would not produce a true sound scale. This flute was acquired by Lady Jane Franklin, widow of the Arctic explorer Sir John Franklin, whose Northwest Passage expedition perished in the Arctic 1845–1848. Lady Franklin supported several expeditions to search for the lost expedition, and she traveled to Canada and Alaska where, presumably, she acquired this flute.

References

Chowning, Ann. "Raven myths in northwestern North America and northeast Asia." *Arctic Anthropology* 1 (1962): 1–5.

Coe, Ralph T. "Asiatic sources of Northwest Coast art." In *American Indian Art: Form and Tradition*, 85–91. Minneapolis: Walker Art Center, Minneapolis Institute of Arts, 1972.

Covarrubias, Miguel. *The Eagle, the Jaguar, and the Serpent*, vol. 1. New York: Alfred A. Knopf, 1954.

Drucker, Philip. *Indians of the Northwest Coast*. Garden City NY: Natural History, 1955.

la Pérouse, Jean-François de Galaup. *The Journal of Jean-François de Galaup de la Pérouse 1785–1788*. John Dunmore, ed. and trans. London: Hakluyt Society, 1994.

Levi-Strauss, Claude. "The art of the Northwest Coast at the American Museum of Natural History." *Gazette des Beaux Arts* 6, no. 24 (1943): 175–82.

Reid, Martine J. "Silent speakers: The arts of the Northwest Coast." In *The Spirit Sings: Artistic Traditions of Canada's First People*. Toronto: McClelland & Stewart, Glenbow Museum, 1988.

Shotridge, Louis. "Ghost of Courageous Adventurer." *Museum Journal* 11 (1920): 11–26.

Suttles, Wayne, ed. *Handbook of North American Indians: The Northwest Coast*, vol. 7. Washington: Smithsonian, 1983.

Robert Joseph | Aaron Glass

1. Holm, *Smoky-Top*, 35.

2. For thorough background on the potlatch prohibition, see Cole and Chaikin, *An Iron Hand upon the People*. For Kwakwaka'wakw perspectives, see Sewid-Smith, *Prosecution or Persecution*; Webster, "From colonization to repatriation"; and the film *Potlatch! A Strict Law Bids Us Dance*.

References

Cole, Douglas, and Ira Chaikin. *An Iron Hand upon the People: The Law Against the Potlatch on the Northwest Coast*. Vancouver: Douglas and McIntyre, 1990.

Holm, Bill. *Smoky-Top: The Art and Times of Willie Seaweed*. Seattle: University of Washington, 1983.

Potlatch! A Strict Law Bids Us Dance. Movie directed by Dennis Wheeler and produced by the U'mista Cultural Society, Alert Bay BC, 1975.

Sewid-Smith, Daisy. *Prosecution or Persecution*. Cape Mudge BC: Nuyum-balees Society, 1979.

Webster, Gloria Cranmer. "From colonization to repatriation." In *Indigena: Contemporary Native Perspectives*, Gerald McMaster and Lee-Ann Martin, ed. Vancouver: Douglas and McIntyre, 1992.

THE ARCTIC AND SUBARCTIC
Stephen Loring

Nalungiaq's wonderful description of the relationship between human beings and animals is from Field, *Songs and Stories of the Netsilik Eskimos*, 7–8. Field has taken Inuit testimony and formatted it as poetry (which, of course, it is).

1. The literature of the North and the peoples of the Arctic and Subarctic regions is as vast and diverse as the landscape and cultures it seeks to contain. Significant source volumes with extensive bibliographies to guide research include the Smithsonian's *Handbook of North American Indians* (vol. 5: *Arctic*, vol. 6: *Subarctic*, and vol. 15: *Northeast*); for Greenland, Malaurie, *Ultima Thule*; for Canada, Glenbow Museum, *The Spirit Sings*; for Alaska, Fitzhugh and Crowell, *Crossroads of Continents*, and Fitzhugh and Kaplan, *Inua*; and for the Aleutian Islands, Black, *Aleut Art*.

2. For an appreciation of the extraordinary challenges faced by Arctic-adapted pioneering populations of "paleoindians"—the original discoverers and colonizers of the Western Hemisphere—see Bonnichsen and Turnmire, *Ice Age People of North America*; Haynes, *The Early Settlement of North America*; Meltzer, *First Peoples in a New World*; Storck, *Journey to the Ice Age*. For later Arctic migrations, see Fitzhugh, *Arctic and Circumpolar Regions*.

3. Some indication of the ingenuity, craftsmanship, and creativity that are hallmarks of northern peoples' tools and clothing is apparent in Duncan, *Northern Athapaskan Art*; Hail and Duncan, *Out of the North*; Issenman, *Sinews of Survival*; King et al., *Arctic Clothing of North America*; Oakes and Riewe, *Our Boots*; and Thompson, *Pride of the Indian Wardrobe*.

4. Andrews and Zoe, "The Įdaà Trail"; Andrews, Zoe, and Herter, "On Yamòzah's Trail"; Tanner, *Bringing Home Animals*.

5. Clark and Clark, *Batza Tena*; Denton, "From the source to the margins and back"; Loring, "And they took away the stones from Ramah."

6. Fitzhugh, "Maritime archaic cultures" and "Settlement, social and ceremonial change"; Tuck, *Ancient Peoples of Port au Choix, Newfoundland*.

7. Bennett and Rowley, *Uqalurait*; Brody, *Maps and Dreams*; Fienup-Riordan, *Boundaries and Passages: Rule and Ritual in Yup'ik Eskimo Oral Tradition*, *The Living Tradition of Yup'ik Masks*; Lowenstein, *Ancient Land*; Rasmussen, "Intellectual culture of the Iglulik Eskimos," "Observations on the intellectual culture of the Caribou Eskimos," "The Netsilik Eskimos," and "Intellectual culture of the Copper Eskimos."

8. The extraordinary eloquence of material culture to convey meaning and insight about northern Native cultures, especially when coupled with the knowledge of community elders and traditional culture bearers, is perhaps most elegantly revealed by the work of Ann Fienup-Riordan and her Yup'ik colleagues and associates (Fienup-Riordan, *The Living Tradition of Yup'ik Masks*, *Where the Echo Began*, *Ciuliamta Akluit*, and *Yuungnaqpiallerput*). The decorations and designs on traditional Innu tools and clothing epitomize the spiritual underpinnings characteristic of northern Athapaskan and Algonkian material culture; see Burnham, *To Please the Caribou*; Speck and Heye, "Hunting charms of the Montagnais and the Mistassini"; and VanStone, *Davis Inlet and Barren Ground Naskapi*.

9. James G. Smith prepared a wonderful exhibit and accompanying catalog on Arctic, primarily Alaskan Eskimo (Iñupiaq, Yup'ik, Inuit) ivory carvings from the Heye collections for the former Museum of the American Indian Heye Foundation in New York. See Smith, *Arctic Art*.

10. Leden, *Across the Keewatin Icefields*.

11. Cadzow, "Native copper objects."

12. Jablonski et al., "A history of anthropology at the California Academy of Sciences."

13. Duncan, 1001 *Curious Things*.

References

Andrews, Thomas D., and John B. Zoe. "The Įdaà Trail: Archaeology and the Dogrib cultural landscape, Northwest Territories, Canada." In *At a Crossroads: Archaeology and First Peoples in Canada*, George P. Nicholas and Thomas D. Andrews, ed., 160–77. Burnaby BC: Archaeology, Simon Fraser University, 1997.

Andrews, Thomas D., John B. Zoe, and Aaron Herter. "On Yamòzah's Trail: Sacred sites and the anthropology of travel." In *Sacred Lands: Claims, Conflicts and Resolutions*, Jill Oaks, Rick Riewe, Kathi Kinew, and Elaine Maloney, ed., 305–20. Occasional Publication no. 43. Edmonton: Canadian Circumpolar Institute, 1998.

Bennett, John, and Susan Rowley, ed. *Uqalurait: An Oral History of Nunavut*. Montreal: McGill-Queen's University, 2004.

Black, Lydia. *Aleut Art, Unangam Aguqaadangin*. Fairbanks: University of Alaska, 2003.

Bonnichsen, Robson, and Karen Turnmire, ed. *Ice Age People of North America*. Corvallis: Oregon State University, 1999.

Brody, Hugh. *Maps and Dreams: Indians and the British Columbia Frontier*. Vancouver: Douglas and McIntyre, 1981.

Burnham, Dorothy. *To Please the Caribou: Painted Caribou-Skin Coats Worn by the Naskapi, Montagnais, and Cree Hunters of the Quebec–Labrador Peninsula*. Toronto: Royal Ontario Museum, 1992.

Cadzow, Donald. *Native Copper Objects of the Copper Eskimo*. Indian Notes and Monographs. New York: Museum of the American Indian, Heye Foundation, 1920.

Clark, Donald, and A. McFayden Clark. *Batza Tena: Trail to Obsidian: Archaeology at an Alaskan Obsidian Source*. Archaeological Survey of Canada Mercury Series 147. Hull QC: Canadian Museum of Civilization, 1994.

Denton, David. "From the source to the margins and back—Notes on Mistassini quartzite and archaeology in the area of the Colline Blanche." In *L'eveilleur et l'ambassadeur: essais archéologiques et ethnohistoriques en hommage à Charles Martijn*, Roland Tremblay, ed., 17–32. Recherches amérindiennes au Québec. Collection Paléo-Québec no.27, 1998.

Duncan, Kate C. *Northern Athapaskan Art: A Beadwork Tradition*. Seattle: University of Washington, 1989.

Duncan, Kate C. *1001 Curious Things: Ye Olde Curiosity Shop and Native American Art*. Seattle: University of Washington, 2000.

Field, Edward, ed. *Songs and Stories of the Netsilik Eskimos: Based on Texts Collected by Knud Rasmussen on the Fift Thule Expedition, 1921–1924*. Cambridge MA: Education Development Center, 1970.

Fienup-Riordan, Ann, ed. *Ciuliamta Akluit: Things of Our Ancestors*. Seattle: University of Washington, 2005.

Fienup-Riordan, Ann. *The Living Tradition of Yup'ik Masks: Agayuliyararput (Our Way of Making Prayer)*. Seattle: University of Washington, 1996.

Fienup-Riordan, Ann, ed. *Where the Echo Began*. Fairbanks: University of Alaska, 2000.

Fienup-Riordan, Ann. *Yuungnaqpiallerput: The Way We Genuinely Live: Masterworks of Yup'ik Science and Survival*. Seattle: University of Washington, 2007.

Fitzhugh, William. "Arctic and Circumpolar Regions." In *Encyclopedia of Archaeology*, Deborah M. Pearsall, ed., 247–71. New York: Academic/Elsevier, 2008.

Fitzhugh, William. "Maritime archaic cultures of the central and northern Labrador coast." *Arctic Anthropology* 15, no. 2 (1978): 61–95.

Fitzhugh, William. "Settlement, social and ceremonial change in the Labrador maritime archaic." In *The Archaic of the Far Northeast*, David Sanger and M. A. P. Renouf, ed., 47–81. Orono: The University of Maine, 2006.

Fitzhugh, William, and Aaron Crowell. *Crossroads of Continents: Cultures of Siberia and Alaska*. Washington: Smithsonian, 1988.

Fitzhugh, William, and Susan Kaplan. *Inua: Spirit World of the Bering Sea Eskimo*. Washington: Smithsonian, 1982.

Glenbow Museum, *The Spirit Sings: Artistic Traditions of Canada's First Peoples*. Toronto: McClelland & Stewart, 1987.

Hail, Barbara A., and Kate C. Duncan. *Out of the North: The Subarctic collection of the Haffenreffer Museum of Anthropology*. Bristol RI: Haffenreffer Museum, Brown University, 1989.

Haynes, Gary. *The Early Settlement of North America, the Clovis Era*. Cambridge: Cambridge University, 2002.

Issenman, Betty Kobayashi. *Sinews of Survival, the Living Legacy of Inuit Clothing*. Vancouver: University of British Columbia, 1997.

Jablonski, Nina G., Dinah Houghtaling, Russell Hartman, and June Anderson. "A history of anthropology at the California Academy of Sciences." *Proceedings of the California Academy of Sciences*, 4th series 58, no. 9 (2007): 135–54.

King, J. C. H., Birgit Pauksztat, and Robert Storrie, ed. *Arctic Clothing of North America—Alaska, Canada, Greenland*. Montreal: McGill-Queen's University, 2005.

Leden, Christian. *Across the Keewatin Icefields: Three Years among the Canadian Eskimos, 1913–1916*, Leslie Neatby, trans. Winnipeg: Watson & Dwyer, 1990.

Loring, Stephen. "'And they took away the stones from Ramah': Lithic raw material sourcing and eastern Arctic archaeology." In *Honoring Our Elders: A History of Eastern Arctic Archaeology*, William Fitzhugh, Stephen Loring, and Daniel Odess, ed., 163–85. Contributions to Circumpolar Anthropology, vol. 2. Washington: Arctic Studies Center, Smithsonian, 2002.

Lowenstein, Tom. *Ancient Land: Sacred Whale*. New York: Farrar, Strauss, and Giroux, 1994.

Malaurie, Jean. *Ultima Thule: Explorers and Natives in the Polar North*. New York: W. W.Norton & Co., 2003.

Meltzer, David J. *First Peoples in a New World, Colonizing Ice Age America*. Berkeley: University of California, 2009.

Oakes, Jill, and Rick Riewe. *Our Boots: An Inuit Woman's Art*. Vancouver: Douglas and McIntyre, 1995.

Rasmussen, Knud. "Intellectual culture of the Copper Eskimos." *Report of the Fifth Thule Expedition 1921–24*, vol. 9. Copenhagen: Gyldendal, 1932.

Rasmussen, Knud. "Intellectual culture of the Iglulik Eskimos." *Report of the Fifth Thule Expedition*, vol. 7, no. 1. Copenhagen: Gyldendal, 1929.

Rasmussen, Knud. "Observations on the intellectual culture of the Caribou Eskimos." *Report of the Fifth Thule Expedition 1921–24*, vol. 7, no. 3. Copenhagen: Gyldendal, 1930.

Rasmussen, Knud. "The Netsilik Eskimos, social life and spiritual culture." *Report of the Fifth Thule Expedition 1921–24*, vol. 8, no. 1–2. Copenhagen: Gyldendal, 1931.

Smith, J. G. E. *Arctic Art: Eskimo Ivory*. New York: Museum of the American Indian, Heye Foundation, 1980.

Speck, Frank G., and G. G. Heye. "Hunting charms of the Montagnais and the Mistassini." *Museum of the American Indian, Heye Foundation, Indian Notes and Monographs*, misc. series 13, 1–19, 1921.

Storck, Peter L. *Journey to the Ice Age, Discovering an Ancient World*. Vancouver: University of British Columbia, 2004.

Tanner, Adrian. *Bringing Home Animals*. Institute of Social and Economic Research, Social and Economic Studies No.23. St. John's: Memorial University of Newfoundland, 1979.

Thompson, Judy. *Pride of the Indian Wardrobe, Northern Athapaskan Footwear*. Toronto: University of Toronto, 1989.

Tuck, James A. *Ancient Peoples of Port au Choix, Newfoundland*. Institute of Social and Economic Research, Social and Economic Studies no. 17. St. John's: Memorial University of Newfoundland, 1976.

VanStone, James W. *Material Culture of the Davis Inlet and Barren Ground Naskapi: The William Duncan Strong Collection*. Fieldiana Anthropology 7. Chicago: Field Museum of Natural History, 1985.

Deanna Paniataaq Kingston

(Iñupiaq ship carving)

1. Dorothy Jean Ray, *Artists of the Tundra and the Sea*.

Reference

Dorothy Jean Ray, *Artists of the Tundra and the Sea*. Seattle: University of Washington, 1961.

Bernadette Driscoll Engelstad

1. Driscoll, "Sapangat"; "Pretending to be caribou."

2. Joe Curley in Eber, "Inuit memories of the whaling days," 108–111.

3. Eugenie Tatoonie Kablutok in Eber, 121.

References

Driscoll, Bernadette. "Pretending to be caribou: The Inuit parka as an artistic tradtion." In *The Spirit Sings: Artistic Traditions of Canada's First Peoples*. Glenbow Museum. Toronto: McClelland and Stewart, 1987.

Driscoll, Bernadette. "Sapangat—Inuit beadwork in the Canadian Arctic." *Expedition* 26, no. 2 (1984): 40–47.

Eber, Dorothy, et al. "Inuit memories of the whaling days: Interviews on South Baffin Island." May 1982 (ms. IV-C-138M). Archives of the Canadian Museum of Civilization, Ottawa.

Deanna Paniataaq Kingston

(Inuit *amauti* or *tuilli*)

1. Bockstoce, *Whales, Ice & Men*.

Reference

Bockstoce, John. *Whales, Ice & Men: The History of Whaling in the Western Arctic*. Seattle: University of Washington, 1986.

CONTEMPORARY ART

Kathleen Ash-Milby

1. For a comprehensive overview of the early collection of paintings in the Museum of the American Indian collection, see Callandar and Fawcett, *Native American Painting*.

2. For more about Frank Day and Bonita Wa Wa Chaw Nuñez, see Dobkins, *Memory and Imagination*, and Ash-Milby, "Bonita Wa Wa Calachaw Nuñez."

3. Tiger and Babcock, *The Life and Art of Jerome Tiger*.

4. Hill, *Norval Morrisseau*. Founded by painter Daphne Odjig (Ojibwe, b. 1919), the Indian Group of Seven included Alex Janvier (Dene Suline/Salteaux, b. 1935), Jackson Beardy (Ayisini [Cree], 1944–1984), Eddy Cobiness (Ojibwa, 1933–1996), Carl Ray (Sandy Lake Cree, 1943–1978), and Joseph Sanchez (White Mountain Apache, b. 1948).

5. For more about Allan Houser and reproductions of his art in the NMAI collections, see Lowe, *Native Modernism*.

6. Sims, *Fritz Scholder: Indian/Not Indian*.

7. Conversation with the author, May 2009. For a survey of Bob Haozous's work, see Sanchez, *Bob Haozous: Indigenous Dialogue*.

8. *Potlatch Woven Hat* by Preston Singletary, *Tire* by Joe Feddersen, and other art from this collection can be seen in NMAI, *Indigenous Motivations*. For more about Joe Feddersen, see *Joe Feddersen: Vital Signs*. Shan Goshorn quotation: unpublished artist statement, 2009.

9. See the essay NMAI, "Landscape: Through an Interior View," and the exhibition catalogue NMAI, *Off the Map*, for discussion of contemporary Native art that engages the landscape, including other work in the NMAI collection. Selections from Kent Monkman's photographic series, *Emergence of a Legend* (2007), are reproduced in Baker and McMaster, *Remix: New Modernities*.

10. See McMaster, *New Tribe New York*, for more about Mario Martinez.

11. See NMAI, *The Land Has Memory*, for more about Nora Naranjo-Morse and the site-specific public art commission *Always Becoming* (2007) outside of the National Museum of the American Indian on the Washington Mall. Artist quote: personal communication, June 2009.

References

Ash-Milby, Kathleen. "Bonita Wa Wa Calachaw Nuñez: An Indian princess painter." In *Painters, Patrons and Identity: Essays in Honor of J. J. Brody and the University of New Mexico*, Joyce M. Szabo, ed. Albuquerque: University of New Mexico, 2001.

Baker, Joe, and Gerald McMaster, ed. *Remix: New Modernities in a Post–Indian World*. Washington and New York: NMAI, 2007.

Callandar, Lee A., and David M. Fawcett. *Native American Painting*. New York: Museum of the American Indian, Heye Foundation, 1982.

Dobkins, Rebecca J., with Carey T. Caldwell and Frank R. La Pena. *Memory and Imagination: The Legacy of Maidu Indian Artist Frank Day*. Oakland: Oakland Museum of California, 1997.

Hill, Greg A. *Norval Morrisseau: Shaman Artist*. Ottawa: National Gallery of Canada, 2006.

Joe Feddersen: Vital Signs. Salem OR: Hallie Ford Museum of Art, Willamette University, in association with the University of Washington, 2008.

Lowe, Truman T., ed. *Native Modernism: The Art of George Morrison and Allan Houser*. Washington and New York: NMAI, 2004.

McMaster, Gerald, ed. *New Tribe New York: The Urban Vision Quest*. Washington and New York: NMAI, 2005.

National Museum of the American Indian. *Indigenous Motivations: Recent Acquisitions from the National Museum of the American Indian*. Washington and New York: NMAI, 2006.

National Museum of the American Indian. "Landscape: Through an Interior View." In *The Land Has Memory*. Washington and New York: NMAI, 2008.

National Museum of the American Indian. *Off the Map: Landscape in the Native Imagination*. Washington and New York: NMAI, 2007.

National Museum of the American Indian. *The Land Has Memory*. Washington and New York: NMAI, 2008.

Sanchez, Joseph M. *Bob Haozous: Indigenous Dialogue*. Santa Fe: Institute of American Indian Arts Museum, 2005.

Sims, Lowery Stokes, ed. *Fritz Scholder: Indian/Not Indian*. Washington and New York: NMAI, 2008.

Tiger, Peggy, and Molly Babcock. *The Life and Art of Jerome Tiger: From War to Peace, Death to Life*. Norman: University of Oklahoma, 1980.

THE COLLECTIONS OF THE NMAI

Cécile R. Ganteaume

1. In 1989 U.S. Public Law 101–185 created the National Museum of the American Indian (NMAI) under the authority of the Smithsonian. At the same time, it called for the transfer of the collection of a much older museum, the Museum of the American Indian–Heye Foundation, to the NMAI.

2. See, for example, Hodge, "Recent progress in American anthropology" and "Aims and objects of the Museum"; Kidwell, "Every last dishcloth"; Lenz, "George Gustav Heye"; Mason, "George G. Heye, 1874–1957"; McMullen, "Reinventing George Heye"; Pepper, "The Museum of the American Indian, Heye Foundation"; Wallace, "Slim-Shin's Monument"; Wilcox, "The Museum of the American Indian, Heye Foundation."

3. Museum of the American Indian, Heye Foundation, "Museum of the American Indian," 1.

4. Mason, "George G. Heye, 1874–1957," 7.

5. See Mason, 11.

6. Hodge, "Aims and objects of the Museum," 3–4; Pepper, "The Museum of the American Indian, Heye Foundation," 403. The largest part of this collection is from what is now Catron County, New Mexico.

7. Pepper, "The Museum of the American Indian, Heye Foundation," 406.

8. Hodge, "Recent progress in American anthropology," 537.

9. *New York Times*, "Museum of Indians," 7; *The Sun*, "Great Indian Museum," 1.

10. Hodge, 4; Pepper, 406.

11. The University Museum (officially known today as the University of Pennsylvania Museum of Archaeology and Anthropology) was known as the Free Museum of Science and Art at the time Heye was affiliated with it.

12. King and Little, "George Byron Gordon," 33.

13. To take but one example, Minor C. Keith, founder of the United Fruit Company, a "multinational colossus more powerful than many nation-states," was responsible for monopolizing and globalizing the production of bananas in the early 20th century. Taking bananas out of the jungle and turning them into a commodity, his company built several hundred miles of railways in Costa Rica, Guatemala, and Honduras and owned the world's largest private navy of refrigerated ships to transport its fruit. Keith did for the banana business what John D. Rockefeller did for oil. He pushed small growers out of business by undercutting their prices and buying up their land until he had no real competition. His profits and power were enormous. See Chapman, *Bananas*.

14. Spencer et al., *The Native Americans*, xviii. Classification by culture areas allowed museums to build and catalogue collections systematically.

15. Pepper, a founder of the American Anthropological Association, also had a special

interest in Navajo weaving, and the large collection of southwestern material he acquired for the museum includes a number of early Navajo texiles—*biil*, mantas, chief blankets, and sarapes.

16. Samuel K. Lothrop and George H. Pepper worked with Hodge—in addition to at least 39 Zuni men.

17. Lenz, "George Gustave Heye," 179.

18. Besides being in the NMAI archives, many of Edward H. Davis's field notes are housed in the Division of Rare Manuscript Collections, Cornell University Library. His photographic collection and some field books are housed in the San Diego Historical Society.

19. Nabokov, *Two Leggings*.

20. See *Fred Harvey: Fine Arts Collection, An Exhibition Organized by the Heard Museum*, published by the Heard Museum of Anthropology and Primitive Art in 1976.

21. Duncan, *1001 Curious Things*.

22. See Gasser, *"My Dear Miss Nicholson,"* and also McClendon, "Pomo Basket Makers." Additionally, in the 1960s the MAI–HF acquired from Thyra Maxwell more than 100 objects collected by Grace Nicholson.

23. Although a good number of his paintings still survive, approximately 200 were lost in a fire at the Smithsonian in 1865; fires in New York and Detroit also destroyed many of his paintings.

24. Reynolds, *Genealogical and Family History*, 1297.

25. Pelletreau, *Historical Homes*; Reynolds, *Genealogical and Family History*.

26. Bourke wrote of the shirt, "It was presented to me by Little Big Man, who led me to believe that it had once belonged to the great chief of the Sioux, Crazy Horse, or had at least been worn by him." Bourke, "Medicine men of the Apache," 476.

27. Thrapp, *Encyclopedia of Frontier Biography*, 1453.

28. Cole, *Captured Heritage*.

29. Pepper, "The Museum of the American Indian, Heye Foundation," 401; *The Sun*, "Great Indian Museum." Grounded in British antiquarianism, the beginnings of archaeology in the Americas were concerned with learning, "Who were the first inhabitants of the New World; where did they come from and when." Hurst, *Predicting the Past*, 2.

30. Stocking, *Objects and Others*, 4.

31. Stocking cites the establishment of the Peabody Museum of Archaeology and Ethnology in 1866 as an early milestone. Stocking, 7.

32. Price, *Primitive Art*, 5.

33. Even before the enactment of the NAGPRA legislation, tribes were seeking the return of certain objects from museums. The Zuni Pueblo of New Mexico sought, for many years, the return of its Ahayu:da, or War Gods, from museums throughout the United States. Zuni War Gods are placed in shrines outside the Zuni's village to protect the Zuni people from harm. Their removal contrary to Zuni religious practices was unethical, if not illegal. In May 1990 the MAI–HF returned the two War Gods in its collection to the Zuni, as it turned out, just days before the MAI–HF collection was transferred to the NMAI.

34. NMAI, *Indigenous Motivations*.

35. NMAI presented *Brian Jungen: Strange Comfort*, a major exhibition of the artist's works, October 16, 2009, through August 8, 2010.

References

Bourke, John G. "Medicine men of the Apache." In *Ninth Annual Report of the Bureau of American Ethnology* (1887–1888). Washington: Bureau of American Ethnology, 1892.

Chapman, Peter. *Bananas: How the United Fruit Company Shaped the World*. Edinburg: Canongate, 2007.

Cole, Douglas. *Captured Heritage: Scramble for Northwest Coast Artifacts*. Seattle: University of Washington, 1985.

Duncan, Kate C. *1001 Curious Things: Ye Olde Curiosity Shoppe and Native American Art*. Seattle: University of Washington, 2000.

Gasser, María del Carmen, ed. *"My Dear Miss Nicholson": Letters and Myths by William Benson, A Pomo Indian*. Carmel NY: M. d. C. Gasser, 1995.

Hodge, F. W. "Aims and objects of the Museum, Heye Foundation." In *Indian Notes and Monographs*, No. 36. 3rd ed. New York: Museum of the American Indian, Heye Foundation, 1923.

Hodge, F. W. "Recent progress in American anthropology: A review of the activities of institutions and individuals from 1902 to 1906." *American Anthropologist*, n.s., 8, no. 1 (1906): 537–38.

Hurst, Thomas. *Predicting the Past: An Introduction to Anthropological Archaeology*. New York: Holt, Rinehart and Winston, 1974.

Kidwell, Clara Sue. "Every last dishcloth: The prodigious collecting of George Gustav Heye." In *Collecting Native America 1870–1960*. Washington: Smithsonian, 1999.

King, Eleanor M., and Bryce P. Little. "George Byron Gordon and the early development of the university museum." In *Raven's Journey: The World of Alaska's Native People*, Susan A. Kaplan and Kristin J. Barsness, ed. Philadelphia: University of Pennsylvania, 1986.

Lenz, Mary Jane. "George Gustav Heye." In *Spirit of a Native Place: Building the National Museum of the American Indian*. Washington and New York: NMAI, in association with National Geographic, 2004.

Lenz, Mary Jane. "Learning to See from Within." In *Listening to Our Ancestors: The Art of Native Life along the North Pacific Coast*. Washington and New York: NMAI and National Geographic, 2005.

Lothrop, Samuel K. "George Gustav Heye." *American Antiquity* 23 (1957–1958): 66–67.

Mason, J. Alden. "George G. Heye, 1874–1957." In *Leaflets of the Museum of the American Indian, Heye Foundation*, no. 6. New York: Museum of the American Indian, Heye Foundation, 1957.

McLendon, Sally. "Pomo Basket Makers: The Legacy of William and Mary Benson." *Native Peoples*, vol. 4, no. 1 (1990): 26–33.

McMullen, Ann. "Reinventing George Heye: Nationalizing the Museum of the American Indian and its collections." In *Contesting Knowledge: Museums and Indigenous Perspectives*, Susan Sleeper-Smith, ed. Lincoln and London: University of Nebraska, 2009.

Museum of the American Indian, Heye Foundation. *Museum of the American Indian, Heye Foundation: Its Aims and Objects*. New York: Museum of the American Indian, Heye Foundation, 1921.

Museum of the American Indian, Heye Foundation, 1923.

Nabokov, Peter. *Two Leggings, the Making of a Crow Warrior*. Lincoln: University of Nebraska, 1967.

National Museum of the American Indian. *Indigenous Motivations: Recent Acquisitions from the National Museum of the American Indian*. Washington and New York: NMAI, 2006.

New York Times. "Museum of Indians will cost $250,000," May 6, 1919.

Pelletreau, William S. *Historical Homes and Institutions and Genealogical and Family History of New York*, vol. 1. New York: Lewis, 1907.

Pepper, George H. "The Museum of the American Indian, Heye Foundation." *Geographical Review* 2, no. 6 (1916).

Price, Sally. *Primitive Art in Civilized Places*. Chicago: University of Chicago, 1989.

Reynolds, Cuyler. *Genealogical and Family History of Southern New York and the Hudson River Valley*. New York: Lewis, 1914.

Spencer, Robert F., and Jessse D. Jennings, et al. *The Native Americans: Ethnology and Backgrounds of the North American Indians*. New York: Harper & Row, 1977.

Stocking, George, Jr. *Objects and Others: Essays on Museums and Material Culture*. History of Anthropology, vol. 3. Madison: The University of Wisconsin, 1985.

The Sun. "Great Indian Museum to seek solution of mystery of red man," May 28, 1916.

Thrapp, Dan L. *Encyclopedia of Frontier Biography*. Spokane WA: Arthur H. Clark, 1988.

Wallace, Kevin. "Slim-Shin's monument." *The New Yorker*, November 19, 1960.

Wilcox, Vincent U. "The Museum of the American Indian, Heye Foundation." *American Indian Art Magazine* 3, no. 2 (1978).

Wildschut, William, and John C. Ewers. *Crow Indian Beadwork: A Descriptive and Historical Study*. Contributions from the Museum of the American Indian, Heye Foundation, vol. 16. New York: Museum of the American Indian, Heye Foundation, 1959.

Wildschut, William, and John C. Ewers. *Crow Indian Medicine Bundles*. Contributions from the Museum of the American Indian, Heye Foundation, vol. 17. New York: Museum of the American Indian, Heye Foundation, 1960.

Infinity of Nations

Authors

Uremirĩ Aprigio Azevedo (Tukano) is a knowledge keeper and traditional bench-maker in the Pirarara community of Amazonas, Brazil. He is also concerned with documenting biodiversity and climate change along the Rio Tiquié.

Kathleen Ash-Milby (Navajo) is an associate curator at the NMAI George Gustav Heye Center in New York, focusing on contemporary art and new media. Her recent exhibitions and publications include *HIDE: Skin as Material and Metaphor; Off the Map: Landscape in the Native Imagination*; and, with Truman Lowe, *Edgar Heap of Birds: Most Serene Republics*, a public art installation and collateral project for the 52nd International Art Exhibition/Venice Biennale (2007).

Vilmar Azevedo, with his grandfather Uremirĩ Aprigio Azevedo, is a knowledge keeper and traditional bench-maker in the Pirarara community of Amazonas, Brazil.

José Barreiro (Taíno) is director of the Office for Latin America within the Museum Scholarship Group at NMAI. His research interests focus on Caribbean studies, indigenous social movements, oral narratives, and indigenous community development.

Tomás Barrientos Q. is director of the Archaeology Department at the Universidad del Valle de Guatemala. He has worked extensively at various archaeological sites in Guatemala, including Kaminaljuyú and La Corona. With Marcello Canuto, he co-directs Proyecto Regional Arqueológico La Corona in northeastern Petén.

Janet Catherine Berlo is professor of art history and visual and cultural studies and co-director of the Graduate Program in Visual and Cultural Studies at the University of Rochester. Her many publications include *A Kiowa's Odyssey: A Sketchbook from Fort Marion* and *Quilting Lessons: Notes from the Scrap Bag of a Writer and Quilter*.

Alden Big Man (Apsáalooke, Crow Nation), is a PhD candidate in history at the University of New Mexico. His background includes studying and teaching Indian history, mainly that of the Northern Plains and the American West.

Ned Blackhawk (Western Shoshone) is professor of history at Yale University. He has received numerous awards for his writing, including the 2007 Frederick Jackson Turner Award from the Organization of American Historians.

Lisa Brooks (Abenaki) is assistant professor of history, literature, folklore, and mythology at Harvard University. She is the author of *The Common Pot: The Recovery of Native Space in the Northeast* and co-author of *Reasoning Together: The Native Critics Collective*.

James A. Brown is professor of archaeology at Northwestern University. His research examines the evolutionary process of social and cultural complexities in the Eastern Woodlands of North America.

Marcello Canuto is director of the Middle American Research Institute and associate professor in the Anthropology Department at Tulane University. He is co-director, with Tomás Barrientos, of Proyecto Regional Arqueológico La Corona, a research project in Guatemala studying southern lowland Maya civilization.

María Catrileo (Mapuche) is a linguist at the Universidad Austral de Chile and author of many articles and books about the phonology, grammar, and lexicon of the Mapuche language, Mapudungun.

Elizabeth Chanco (Quechua) is a textile artist and oral historian.

Brenda J. Child (Red Lake Ojibwe) is a professor in the Department of American Indian Studies at the University of Minnesota, where she received the President's Multicultural Research Award in 2002. She is the author of *Boarding School Seasons: American Indian Families, 1900–1940*.

Tomah Joseph (Passamaquoddy, 1837–1914), Birchbark box, ca. 1900. Maine. Birchbark, spruce root; 10.5 x 6.5 x 8 cm. The Helen Pep Grodka Collection. Presented by Mr. and Mrs. Harry W. Blumenthal. 25/1662

Linda Cordell is a senior scholar at the School of American Research and professor emerita of anthropology at the University of Colorado. She received the Alfred Vincent Kidder Medal of Eminence in American Archaeology from the American Anthropological Association in 2002, and in 2005, she was elected to the National Academy of Sciences.

Robert Davidson (Haida) is a master carver of totem poles and masks as well as a printmaker, painter, and jeweler. Davidson's work is found in a number of private and public collections, including the National Gallery of Canada, the Canadian Museum of Civilization, and the Southwest Museum.

Bernadette Miqqusaaq Dean (Aivilingmiut Inuk), from Rankin Inlet, Nunavut, Canada, is development coordinator for Somebody's Daughter, a program to help Inuit women learn traditional sewing and survival skills.

Philip J. Deloria (Standing Rock Sioux) is Carroll Smith-Rosenberg Collegiate Professor in the Department of History, the American Culture Program, and the Native American Studies Program at the University of Michigan. The author of several publications, including *Playing Indian* and *Indians in Unexpected Places*, he is currently a trustee of the National Museum of the American Indian.

Ernestine Ygnacio-De Soto (Barbareño Chumash), a Chumash elder and daughter of the last speaker of the Barbareño Chumash language, has worked extensively with researchers to preserve ethnographic and archaeological information about her tribe.

Tom Dillehay is a distinguished professor and chair of the Department of Anthropology at Vanderbilt University. He has published fifteen books and more than two hundred journal articles and has received numerous international and national awards for his research, books, and teaching.

Bernadette Driscoll-Engelstad is an independent curator, researcher, and writer with a specialty in Inuit art and material culture. She has conducted fieldwork among Inuit artists and seamstresses in communities across the Canadian Arctic.

R. David Edmunds (Cherokee) is the Anne and Chester Watson Chair in History at the University of Texas Dallas School of Arts and Humanities. He is the author and editor of numerous books, including *Enduring Nations: Native Americans in the Midwest* and *The Fox Wars: The Mesquakie Challenge to New France*.

Oliver Enjady (Mescalero Apache) is an artist whose work has been exhibited in museums and galleries in Santa Fe, Albuquerque, Ruidoso, and Carlsbad, New Mexico. In 1996 he received the prestigious First Place in Painting award at the Santa Fe Indian Market.

Jim Enote (A:shiwi) is director of the A:shiwi A:wan Museum and Heritage Center in Zuni, New Mexico, established by A:shiwi tribal members in 1992. He practices the traditional Zuni method of high-altitude farming and received his BS in agriculture from New Mexico State University.

Tom Evans (Skidi Pawnee) is a collections specialist at NMAI. His research interests include Pawnee and Mississippian cultural history. He is a contributing author of *Born of Clay: Ceramics from the National Museum of the American Indian*.

Sherry Farrell Racette (Timiskaming First Nation), associate professor of art history at Concordia University, is the 2009–2010 Ann Ray Resident Scholar at the School of American Research. Her research interests focus on Cree painted hide coats as encoded objects and memory.

William H. Fisher is associate professor of anthropology at the College of William and Mary. He has published research on gender relations, ritual and social movements, and the book *Rain Forest Exchanges: Industry and Community on an Amazonian Frontier*.

Donald L. Fixico (Shawnee/Sac and Fox/Muscogee Creek/Seminole) is Distinguished Foundation Professor of History at Arizona State University. He is the author of numerous publications, including *American Indians in a Modern World*, *Daily Life of Native Americans in the Twentieth Century*, and *The American Indian Mind in a Linear World: American Indian Studies and Traditional Knowledge*.

Jorge A. Flores Ochoa (Quechua) is an anthropologist and professor at the Universidad Nacional San Antonio, Abad del Cusco. He is the author of several publications, including *El Centro del Universo Andino* and "Q'eros: Arte Inka en vasos ceremoniales" in *Colección Arte y Tesores del Perú*.

Fernando Flores Zuñiga is a member of the Instituto Riva Aguero de la Pontificia Universidad Catolica del Peru and a scholar specializing in agrarian reform and archival research. He has also worked as an editor and publisher, and served as an academic advisor to the Congress of the Republic of Peru.

Catherine S. Fowler, former professor of anthropology at the University of Nevada, has authored and co-authored numerous articles and publications on various topics in anthropology, research, and museum studies. Currently, she serves as the chair of the Research Committee on the NMAI Board of Trustees.

Lois George-Kane (Fallon Paiute–Shoshone Tribe of Stillwater) is the granddaughter of Wuzzie George, a traditional educator of Northern Paiute ways who was known for sharing her knowledge freely with those who wanted to learn about the culture and traditions of her people. Lois is a descendant of the Cattail-Eater Band and Trout-Eater Band of Northern Paiute.

Doug George-Kanentiio (Akwesasne Mohawk) is a journalist and former NMAI trustee. He is a co-founder of the Native American Journalists Association.

Aaron Glass holds a dual fellowship at the American Museum of Natural History and Bard Graduate Center in New York, where he teaches anthropology of museums and material culture and coordinates a research program into the museum's Northwest Coast collection. He has published articles on various aspects of First Nations art and performance and is co-author, with Aldona Jonaitis, of the forthcoming book *The Totem Pole: An Intercultural Biography*.

Alejandro González Villarruel is deputy director of ethnography at the Museo Nacional de Antropología in Mexico City.

Patrick J. Hill (Apsáalooke), an artist and tribal historian, worked for several years as an interpretive ranger for the National Park Service at the Little Bighorn Battlefield National Monument. He has also served as historical consultant for Little Bighorn College, the University of Indiana, and Sarah Lawrence College.

Harold Jacobs (Hít Tlein [Big House] of the T'aakhu *khwaan*) is a cultural resource specialist for the Tlingit–Haida Central Council in Juneau, Alaska.

Juan Carlos Jintiach (Shuar), coordinator of international economic cooperation and strategic development for the Coordinating Body of the Indigenous Organizations of the Amazon Basin, is president of the Shuar Nation Corporation (Shuar Territory, Ecuador), executive co-director of the Amazon Alliance, and a fellow at the University of Florida.

John Johnson is curator of anthropology at the Santa Barbara Museum of Natural History. He has written extensively on the culture and history of Chumash Indians, as well as Native peoples elsewhere in central and southern California. Recently Johnson collaborated with Ernestine De Soto to write and produce the hour-long documentary *6 Generations*, which tells the story of De Soto's Barbareño Chumash family.

Robert Joseph (Kwakwaka'wakw) is a hereditary chief of the Gwawaenuk First Nation, the former president of the Indian Residential School Survivors Society, and CEO of the Residential Schools Commission for British Columbia. His essays appear in many publications, including *Listening to Our Ancestors: The Art of Native Life along the North Pacific Coast*.

Vicki Kane (Reno–Sparks Indian Colony) is a traditional knowledge keeper. Her family is descended from the Stillwater Paiute.

Steven M. Karr is acting director and Ahmanson Curator at the Southwest Museum of the American Indian, Autry National Center. Previously, he worked at the Natural History Museum of Los Angeles County and the Phoebe A. Hearst Museum of Anthropology at the University of California, Berkeley, where he also taught Native American studies. He continues to teach at the University of California, Los Angeles.

Piydjô Kayapó (Kayapó) is a traditional knowledge keeper. Born in the Kayapó village of Kubenkrankei, Piydjô Kayapó now lives in Kikretum, a Kayapó village founded in 1978.

Deanna Paniataaq Kingston (King Island Iñupiaq) is associate professor of anthropology at Oregon State University. She has contributed chapters to many collections, including *To Harvest, to Hunt: Stories of Resource Use in the American West* and *Words of the Real People*.

Arden Kucate (A:shiwi) has served as a tribal councilman for the Pueblo of Zuni for more than eight years. He has certification in the Native American Graves Protection and Repatriation, National Historic Preservation, and National Environmental Policy acts, and has worked with the Center for Research on Education, Diversity and Excellence at the University of California, Santa Cruz.

Mary Jane Lenz is a museum specialist in NMAI's Collections Documentation and Research unit. She has worked with the Heye collections for more than thirty years, curating several exhibitions of Northwest Coast art and contributing to publications on the Northwest Coast, Native American Dance, and the history of NMAI. She is the author of *Small Spirits: Native American Dolls from the National Museum of the American Indian*.

Barnaby Lewis (Akimel O'odham) is a traditional singer, knowledge keeper, and cultural preservation officer for the Gila River Indian Community. He received a 2009 Arizona Humanities Council Award for his oral history project studying the internment of Japanese Americans at Gila River during World War II.

Leonardo López Luján is senior researcher and professor of archaeology at Museo del Templo Mayor, Instituto Nacional de Antropología e Historia in Mexico City. Since 1991, López Luján has served as the director of the excavation project of the Templo Mayor (Grand Temple) in Mexico City.

Stephen Loring is Arctic archaeologist and museum anthropologist with the Arctic Studies Center at the Smithsonian National Museum of Natural History. He has conducted research in New England, Quebec, Labrador, Arkansas, Peru, Argentina, and the Brooks Range, and on the outermost Aleutian Islands.

John N. Low (Pokagon Band Potawatomi) is a PhD candidate in American culture at the University of Michigan. He served as executive director of the Mitchell Museum of the American Indian in Evanston, Illinois, and as a 2009–2010 Scholar in Residence at the Newberry Library in Chicago.

Bradley Marshall (Hoopa) is tribal liaison for the Phoebe A. Hearst Museum of Anthropology at the University of California, Berkeley. He received his BA in Native American studies with an emphasis in federal Indian law from Humboldt State University in Arcata, California.

Ramiro Matos (Quechua), an archaeologist and curator at NMAI, is the author of numerous articles on Andean archaeology, including "Inca ceramics" in *The Incas: Arts and Symbols* and—with Jeffrey Parson and Charles Hastings—*Prehispanic Settlement Patterns in the Upper Mantaro and Tarma Drainages, Junín, Peru*.

Timothy P. McCleary is a professor at Little Big Horn College, the Crow tribal college, having received his PhD from the University of Illinois, Urbana-Champaign. He works with the Crow Nation to record and share their history, traditions, and culture and has published widely on Crow culture, including the book *The Stars We Know: Crow Indian Astronomy and Lifeways*.

Michelle McGeough (Métis) is currently a faculty member of the Institute of American Indian Arts Museum Studies Department in Santa Fe, New Mexico. Previously, she was assistant curator at the Wheelwright Museum of the American Indian.

Percy Medina (Quechua) is a member of a long and distinguished family of gourd artists with roots in the Andean village of Cochas Chico, Huancayo, Peru. He is recognized as one of the most talented gourd carvers of his generation, with work in the collections of the Smithsonian and many other museums.

Bahuan Mëtsa (Manuel Rengifo Barbaran, Shipibo) is an elder of the Shipibo village of San Francisco de Yarinacocha, Peru.

Robert J. Miller (Eastern Shawnee Tribe of Oklahoma) is professor of law at Lewis and Clark Law School in Portland, Oregon, and chief justice of the Court of Appeals of the Grand Ronde Tribe. He authored the book *Native America, Discovered and Conquered: Thomas Jefferson, Lewis and Clark, and Manifest Destiny*.

Les Namingha (Zuni/Tewa–Hopi), a highly respected ceramist, credits his aunt, renowned Hopi potter Dextra Quotskuyva, for teaching him the art. He is best known for his modernist treatment of traditional motifs and for invigorating the long-standing tradition of Hopi pottery.

Jo Ann Nevers (Washoe) is a tribal historian and author of *WA SHE SHU: "The Washoe People" Past and Present*.

Paul Ossa is an archaeologist with Arqueologia Austral/ Southern Archaeology in Berkeley, California. Previously, he was a lecturer at LaTrobe University, spending a year as a visiting professor at the Universidad de Chile.

Joanna Ostapkowicz is curator of the Americas collections at the World Museum in Liverpool, England. She also serves as principal investigator in the Pre-Hispanic Caribbean sculptural arts in wood project, supported by the Getty Foundation and the British Academy.

David W. Penney, vice president of exhibitions and collections strategies and curator of Native American art at the Detroit Institute of Arts, is the author of *Great Lakes Indian Art*, *Art of the American Indian Frontier: A Portfolio*, and, with George Horse Capture (A'aninin), *North American Indian Art*.

Ruth Phillips is Canada Research Chair in Modern Culture and professor of art history at Carleton University in Ottawa. Her research and publications focus on museum representation and on Anishinaabe and Haudenosaunee artistic traditions from the Great Lakes.

Allen Pinkham, Sr. (Ni Mii Puu), is a tribal elder and founding member of the NMAI board, where he also served as secretary. He has served on the Nez Perce Tribe Executive Committee, with some years as chairman. He is now retired and raises buffalo on the Nez Perce Indian Reservation in Idaho.

Gloria Quidel (Mapuche), a scholar of Mapuche language and culture, received her MA in intercultural bilingual education and is currently teaching Mapuche language and methodology at the Universidad Católica de Temuco in Chile.

Erin Rentz (Karuk) is a botanist with the U.S. Forest Service in Klamath National Forest. Her research interests include the traditional management and natural history of plant species used in Native Californian basketry. She has been a basket-weaver for ten years.

Peter Roe is professor of anthropology at the University of Delaware. His research interests include the material culture of Native South America, ceramic technology, ethno- and archaeo-astronomy, and Caribbean ceramic analysis. He has also served as a consultant for several museum exhibitions in the U.S. and Puerto Rico.

Teri Rofkar (Ch´ais-koowu-tla´a T´ak dein taan, Ta´aх´ hit, Tlingit Raven Clan, Snail House) has been weaving baskets and ceremonial robes since 1986, using the traditional Tlingit styles and techniques passed down to her by her elders.

Nicolasa I. Sandoval (Santa Ynez Band of Chumash) is a lecturer in the Education Department at the University of California, Santa Barbara, where she also earned a PhD. She serves on the board of directors of the Santa Barbara Museum of Natural History and the California Indian Museum and Cultural Center.

Sherrie Smith-Ferri (Dry Creek Pomo/Bodega Bay Miwok) is director of the Grace Hudson Museum and Sun House in Ukiah, California. She has extensively researched collections of Pomo material culture and ethnographic manuscripts in museums and archives nationwide.

Donovin Sprague (Minnicoujou Lakota) is a historian and instructor at Black Hills State University in Spearfish, South Dakota. The author of several books, he serves as director of education at Crazy Horse Memorial, Crazy Horse, South Dakota.

George Stuart founded the Center for Maya Research, a non-profit organization to promote research on the archaeology, iconography, and epigraphy of the Maya. He has also worked at the National Geographic Society for more than forty years.

Edgar Suyuc (Kaqchikel Maya) is an archaeologist and co-director of the Proyecto Arqueológico Cuenca Mirador, which is currently exploring the origins and processual dynamics of pre-Classic Maya civilization in Guatemala.

Jan Timbrook, curator of ethnography at the Santa Barbara Museum of Natural History, has collaborated on many books and has authored more than a dozen scientific papers on topics ranging from herbal medicine to environmental management by the Chumash. Her 2007 book *Chumash Ethnobotany* is based on nearly thirty years of research on Chumash plant knowledge.

George E. "Tink" Tinker (wazhazhe, Osage Nation) is Clifford Baldridge Professor of American Indian Cultures and Religious Traditions at Iliff School of Theology in Denver, Colorado. He is the author of several books including *American Indian Liberation: A Theology of Sovereignty*.

Shelby Tisdale, director of the Museum of Indian Arts and Culture/Laboratory of Anthropology in Santa Fe, New Mexico, has more than twenty-five years of museum and archaeological experience working for such institutions as the Millicent Rogers Museum, Philbrook Museum of Art, and Indian Arts Research Center at the School of American Research.

Richard Tsakimp (Shuar) is head shaman for the Shuar, a traditional healer, and president of the Shaman Association of the Andes. He is a repository of deep knowledge of the history, culture, spirituality, and traditional medicine of the Shuar.

William Hiłamas Edward Wasden Jr. ('Na̱mg̱is Kwakwa̱ka̱'wakw), works as a cultural advisor and researcher at the U'mista Cultural Society in Alert Bay, British Columbia. He was taught traditional artwork by the late chief and master carver Pa̱l'nakwa̱laga̱lis Wakas Douglas Cranmer and also by Haida artist Don Yeomans.

Paula Whitlow (Mohawk) has been the curator at the Chiefswood National Historic Site, Ohsweken, Ontario, since 1995.

Michael Witgen (Ojibwe) is assistant professor of American culture and history at the University of Michigan. His interests include the national histories of Native American peoples and nation states, American–Canadian borderlands, and pre-confederation Canada.

Gordon L. Yellowman (Southern Cheyenne) is adjunct professor teaching Native American art at the Cheyenne and Arapaho Tribal College and Southwestern Oklahoma State University. He received the 2002 Native American Cultural Heritage Award from the Denver Museum of Nature and Science.

INFINITY OF NATIONS

Art and History in the Collections of the National Museum of the American Indian

Director: Kevin Gover (Pawnee)

Associate director for museum programs: Tim Johnson (Mohawk)

Director, George Gustav Heye Center: John Haworth (Cherokee)

General editor: Cécile R. Ganteaume

Publications manager: Tanya Thrasher (Cherokee)

Project editor: Holly Stewart

Designer: Steve Bell

Managing editor: Ann Kawasaki

Research: Maria Galban

Map illustrations: Gene Thorp

Editorial assistance: Alexandra Harris (Cherokee), Megan Gray, Charlotte Watter

Administrative assistance: Colleen Schreier

Design assistance: Julie Allred

Object photography and photo services: Cynthia Frankenburg, Ernest Amoroso, R.A.Whiteside, Katherine Fogden (Mohawk), Walter Larrimore, William Greene

Photo archives: Lou Stancari, Emily Moazami

Separations: Robert J. Hennessey

Exhibition curator: Cécile R. Ganteaume

Curatorial research assistant: Maria Galban

Librarian: Lynne Altstatt

Contemporary art curator: Kathleen Ash-Milby (Navajo)

Project manager: Duane Blue Spruce (Laguna/ Ohkay Owingeh)

Exhibition manager: Lindsay Stamm Shapiro

Exhibition design liaison: Peter Brill

Exhibition advisor: Kerry Boyd

Exhibition script editor: Holly Stewart

Exhibition writers: José Barreiro (Taíno), Mark Hirsch

Project assistant: Robert Mastrangelo

Exhibition design: Gerry Breen

Exhibition graphic design: Susanna Stieff, Eileen Moore, Patricia Beirne, Kate Johnson

Exhibit fabrication: Stacey Jones, Rick Pelasara, John Richardson

Collections conservation: Jessie Johnson, Susan Heald, exhibit liaisons; Anne Kingery, Anne Gunnison, Luba Dougan-Nurse, asst. liaisons; Marian Kaminitz, Emily Kaplan, Kelly McHugh, NMAI Andrew W. Mellon Fellows, and interns

Exhibition and photo mountmaking: Shelly Uhlir

Registration: Ann Drumheller (Onondaga), Ellen Simmons, Sharla Blanche, Margaret Cintron, Heather Farley, Rajshree Solanki

Collections management: Linda Greatorex, Maria McWilliams, Tori Cranner, Tom Evans (Pawnee), Janet Pasiuk, Tony Williams

Exhibition media: Kathy Suter, Kevin Cartwright, Augusta Lehman

Exhibition audioguides: Daniel Davis

Website: Cheryl Wilson, Jason Wigfield

Information technology: Abby Campbell, Dwight Schmidt, Erin Weinman, James S. Smith

NMAI collections web search: Ann McMullen, DucPhong Nguyen

Development: Lucia DeRespinis, Farhana Rahman

Executive Planning Office: Justin Estoque, Doug Gillis

Education: Johanna Gorelick, Edwin Schupman (Muskogee)

Public programs: Shawn Termin (Lakota), Jorge Estevez (Taíno)

Administration: Scott Merritt, Tamara Levine

Public relations: Ann Marie Sekeres, Quinn Bradley (Navajo/Assiniboine)

Special events: Trey Moynihan

Visitor services: Samir Bitar

Special thanks to Eric Monsonis and Janice Slivko, Smithsonian Institution Office of Facilities Engineering and Operations; Jia-Sun Tsang, Allison Martin, Sara Babo, Smithsonian Museum Conservation Institute; Nora Lockshin, Smithsonian Archives; Cathleen Zaret, conservation volunteer; Tina Jones, Carol Monahan, and Willard Powell, Smithsonian Institution Office of Contracting; William Chimborazo, Angela Friedlander, and Cody Harjo, GGHC Cultural Interpreters; the GGHC administration and facilities staff; and all other NMAI and Smithsonian staff for making this project possible.

NMAI object photography

Ernest Amoroso: 1, 2, 4, 6 bottom right, 12, 18, 23, 25, 27, 28, 30, 31, 32, 34, 35, 36, 40 upper, 42, 45, 46 lower, 47 upper, 48, 49, 50, 52, 53, 54, 55, 56, 57 upper, 58, 60, 63 upper, 67, 70, 75, 84, 88, 91, 95, 96, 98 upper, 99, 100, 108–09, 116 upper, 119, 120, 126, 127, 128, 130, 132, 134, 135, 137, 138, 139, 141, 145, 146, 147, 149, 151, 153, 154, 158, 159, 161, 162–65, 166, 171, 172 upper & lower right, 174, 175, 176 lower, 182, 183, 186, 189, 190, 193, 194, 196, 199, 201, 202, 205, 206, 207 lower, 210, 211, 215, 216, 218, 219, 220, 223, 224, 227, 228, 231, 232, 233, 236, 240, 242, 243, 244, 245, 246, 250, 253, 255, 256, 262, 264 upper, 268, 270–71, 272, 273, 286, upper back cover

Katherine Fogden: 267

Cynthia Frankenburg: 209

David Heald: 103 right, 111, 143, 155, 205

Justin Kerr: 57 lower (rollout detail)

Walter Larrimore: cover, 7 center left, low right, 26, 39, 40 lower, 43, 44, 47 lower, 63 lower, 64, 68, 71, 72, 76, 77, 78, 81, 82, 83, 86, 90, 92–93, 98 lower, 104, 105, 106, 112, 115, 116 lower, 117, 131, 136, 144, 152, 156, 157, 160, 169, 170, 172 upper & lower left, 176 upper, 177, 178, 180, 181, 185, 188, 195, 197, 200, 207 upper, 208, 212, 217, 225, 235, 237, 249, 251, 252, 254, 257, 258, 260, 261, 264 lower, 265, 273, 306, lower back cover

R.A.Whiteside: 3, 5, 19, 46 upper, 94, 103 left, 192, 234, 238

NMAI Move Team: 110

Index

I

Ica, 47, 48
  figural vessel, **47**
Iconographic Workshop, Texas State University, 184
Indian Arts and Crafts Board (IACB) Collection, 284–285
Indigenous and Tribal Peoples Convention of 1989, 99
Inka, 37, 51–52
  accounting system, 52
  architecture, 52
  aryballus vessel, **52**
  creation stories, 49, 51
  drinking vessels, 57
  goldsmiths and jewelers, 41
  government, 51–52
  influence, 53
  khipu, **53**
  Mapuche contact with, 21, 23, 25
  pottery, 52, 56
  qero, **57**
  stonemasonry, 52
  terraced vessel, **56**
  weaving, 52
Innu, 246, 248, 256
  ceremonial robe, **253**
  family on the Crooked River, **246**
Inshata-Theumba (Susette La Flesche), 16, 147–148, 157
Institute of American Indian Arts (IAIA), 266
Inuit, 241, 248, 251–253, 263
  amauti or tuilli (parka), **258**
Iñupiaq (pl. Iñupiat), 241, 257, 261
  bow drill, **246**
  cribbage board, **251**
  man's parka, **240**
  model *qasgiq*, **250**
Iowa Nation, 168
  drop, **152**
Iromagaja (Rain-in-the-Face, Hunkpapa Lakota), **149**
Ishi, 218
Itiba Cahubaba, 110

J

Jackson, Sheldon, 228
Jackson, Stephen, 269
James Bay Cree hood, **244**
Jamestown colony, 170
Javaé, 77
Jennings, Vanessa Paukeigope, 147

Jesuits, *see also* missionaries, 73
jewelery
  in Andes, 41, 49
  Hohokam, 119, 121
Jivaroan peoples, 74
Johnson, Emily Pauline, *see* Tekahionwake
Johnson, Terrol, 125
Jónibo or Jónicobo, 73
Joseph, Chief Robert, 239
Joseph Brant (Gilbert Stuart), 173
Juan Santos Atahualpa, 72
Jungen, Brian, 269, 285
Juruna Indians, 80

K

Kabotie, Fred, 263
Kachemak lamp, **243**
Kaiona, Kenneth, 255
Kaminaljuyú, 87, 105
Karajá, 77, 79
  ijasò mask and rattles, 76, **77**
  war club, **75**
Kariña, 66
Karuk rod-armor vest, **197**
Kattenanit, Job, 189
Kawesqar (Alakaluf), 26
Kayapó, *see* Mebêngôkre
Keith, Minor C., 278
Keokuk, Chief, *see* Kiyo'kaga
Keppler, Joseph W., 274
Keyser, Louisa, *see* Dat so la lee
Kickapoo hair ornament, **172**
Kina initiation ceremony, 29–30
King Philip's War, 189
Kiyo'kaga, 194
Kogi, 41
Kootenai baby carrier, **147**
Kotlean, 226, 227
Krajás, 75, 77, 79
Kupangaxwichem (Cupeño) saddle blanket, 200, **201**
Kwakwaka'wakw, 221, 223–225, 228, 230, 232, 239
  gikiwe', **239**
  Ḵumugwe' (Chief of the undersea), 230, **231**
Kwii.aang (Isabella Edenshaw), 227, 237

L

La Flesche, Susette, *see* Inshata-Theumba
Laguna Pueblo, 123
  pottery, 124
Lakota, 142–143, 145, 153, 155, 158
  square hand drum, **153**
Lambayeque
  effigy vessel, 37, **51**
  gold discs, **40**, 41
  goldsmiths and jewelers, 41, 47
  road system by, 52
  urban centers, 48, 49
languages
  in Amazon, 66, 69, 74
  in Ancestral cultures, 121
  in Andes, 53, 72
  in Great Basin, 210
  Mapuche, 25
  Mohawk, 195
  Muskogean, 182
  in Northwest Coast, 221
  Otomian, 94
  Uru, 53
La Pieta (Shelley Nero), 269
lapis, 141
Lawrence, Nellie, 30
Leden, Christian, 253–254, 281
Leeward Islands, 101, 102
Lesser Antilles, 101, 102
Liebes, Arnold, 254
Ligeex, Chief, 225
Lima culture, urban centers, 48
Little Big Man, 145, 155
The Long Walk, 129
Looking Glass, Chief, 156
Lothrop, Samuel K., 281
Loud, L. L., 279
Lowie, Robert, 150
Lowry, Judith, 269–270, 272
Lucayan, 101
  duho (seat), **103**

M

MacCreagh, Gordon, 281
Machalilla, 42
Machu Picchu, 51
Mackenzie, Joe, 251
Magellan, Ferdinand, 29
Magus, John, 189
Mah-to-tóh-pa, Four Bears (Catlin), **141**

Makah, 221
Makuxi, 68
Mamit Innuat, 256
Mandan, 150
Manek'enk (Haush), 26
manioc, 61,62, 73, 75, 79
Manteño culture, 55
  seat, **55**
Mapuche
  ancestors, 24
  breast ornament, **25**
  in Chilean society, 23–24
  contact with Andeans, 25
  death, view of, 24
  deity Ngünechen, 24, 31, 33
  historical background, 21, 23
  kultrung, **20**, **32**
  late pre-Hispanic culture, 25
  machi, 20, 24, 33, 35
  poncho, 24, **25**
  rewe, **20**, **35**
  rituals and celebrations, 20, 24, 31, 33
  stirrups with tapaderos, **31**
  textiles and pottery, 24–25
Maquinna, 226
Marajoara culture, 62, 63
  bowls, **63**, **64**
  jar, **63**
Maritime Archaic people, 247
Marta, María, 213
Martinez, Julian, 137
Martinez, Maria, 125, 137
Martinez, Mario, 270, 273
masks
  bô, 76, **77**
  contemporary, 266
  Karajá, 77, 79
  Kwakwaka'wakw, 230, 231
  Mississippian long-nosed gods, 178
  Taíno, 103
  Teotihuacán, 91
  Yámana, 30
  Yup'ik, 242
Mathiassen, Therkel, 254
Matlatzinca, 94
Mato-Tope, 140–141
Mawayéna people, 68
Maximilian, Prince, 141, 150
Maya
  bas-relief depicting a ball player, **106**, 107
  Classic period, 107

Southwest Museum of the American Indian, 200

Spang, Bently, 269

Spanish
in Amazon, 61, 66, 72, 73
impact of contact with, 53, 64
Mapuche contact with, 21, 23, 25
in Northwest Coast, 226
in Southwest, 123, 134
treaty with Araucanian nation, 23

Speck, Frank G., 252, 281

Speen, James, 189

Spivey, Richard, 125

St. Louis Universal Exposition of 1904, 229

St. Michael's Cathedral (Sitka), 227

Standing Bear, 157

Standing Rock Reservation, 153

Standley, J. E., 254, 282

Stanley, John Mix, 282

Stein, Leo, 278

Steven, Isaac, 282

Stikine people, 235

Stiles, William, 252

Stockbridge Nation, 175

stone clubs, **225**

Stone Forehead, 154

Stories Upon Stories (Nora Naranjo-Morse), 270, **272**

Stuart, Gilbert, 173

Studio of the Santa Fe Indian School, 263

Subarctic region, *see* Arctic/ Subarctic region

Sulupcucagele, Juan Mariano, 214

Sunka Luta (Red Dog), 149–150, **158**

Suyuc, Edgar, 104, 105

T

Ta:ʹaltul (Boat Dance), 217

Tafoya, Margaret, 125, 130

Tahltan, 225, 227, 235
bag, **249**

Taíno
description, 101–103
dieties, 110, 111
guaíza mask, **103**
zemí of Deminán Caracaracol, 111

zemí of Itiba Cahubaba, **110**

Tairona, 41
bowl, **42**

Taku Tlingit, 225

Tambos, *see also* Inkas, 51

tanning, 199

Tapirapé, 77, 79

Tashunca-uitco (Crazy Horse), 144–145, 150, 155, 283

Tatoosh, 226

Tecumseh, Chief (Shawnee), 16, 19, 192

Tehuelche, *see* Aónikenk

Teixeira, Germano, **65**

Tekahionwake (Emily Pauline Johnson), 16, 195

Tenochtitlan, 91

Teotihuacán, 87
mask, **91**

Tepanec, 91
Ehecatl (wind god), **96**
Quetzalcoatl (feathered serpent), **108, 109**

Tetzcoco, 91

textiles, *see also* clothing, weaving
in Amazon, 69, 72
in contemporary Mexico, 101
in Andes, 38, 44
Inka, 52
Mapuche, 24, 25, **25**
in Southwest, 125

Thayendanegea (Joseph Brant), 16, 173, 174

This Land is Mime Land (Shelley Nero), 269

Thom, Princess, 228

Thunder Beings, 152

Tibbles, Thomas, 147, 157

Tierra del Fuego
archaeological sites, 26
rainfall and climate, 28
settlers, 29

Tiger, Jerome, 264

Tikal, 87

Tire (Preston Singletary), 269

Tiwanaku
art style and religious symbolism in, 48
historical background, 37, 38
mirror, **39**

Tlacopan, 91

Tlahuica, 94

Tlaloc, 91

Tlaltecuhtli, 108

Tlaxcala, 94

Tłįcho, 10, 246

Tliliuhquitepec, 94

Tlingit, 221, 223–227
basketry hat, 15–16, 221, **234**
knife and sheath, **235**
pipe, **233**

tobacco, 66, 69, 85, 110, 111, 123, 140, 153, 170, 173, 174, 225, 227, 233, 269

tombs
Moche ornaments, 47
Paracas promontory, 44

Tonatiuh, 97

Tonto Basin Campaign, 282

toqui cura (Mapache), **23**, 24

Toribio, Rosalia Medina, 125, 131

Totonac Danza de los Ormegas belt, **98**

trade
in Amazon, 64, 68, 73, 74, 77, 80
in Andes, 41, 48
fur, 226–227, 260
in Mesoamerica, 87, 95
in Northwest Coast, 222–227
in Plains and Plateau, 141–142
in Southwest, 123, 126, 134

Triple Alliance, *see excan tlatoloyan*

Truckee River agreement, 204, 207

Tsakimp, Richard, 83

Tsimshian, 221, 223, 224

Tsinahjinnie, Andy, 263

Tsireh, Awa, 263

Tukano, 66, 82

Tukanoan bench, **82**
headring, **67**

Tumbaga, 41

Tupi-Guarani language, 25

Turks and Caicos, 101, 103

turquoise, 41

Twiss, Thomas, 283

Twitchell, Adams Hollis, 253

U

Uaupés River, 64, 65, 67, 82

Ucayali River, 73

Uliggaq (Ella Pavil), 247

University Museum (Philadel-

phia), 277

Upper Yanktonai, 153

urban developments, *see also* architecture
of Ancestral Puebloans, 113, 118
in Andes, 41, 44, 47–49, 51

Uru language, 53

U.S. Army scouts, 159

Ute, 126
shirt, **209**

Utley, Frank D., 276

Uto-Aztecan linguistic family, 210

Uxmal, 91

V

Valdivia, 41–42, 54
female figurines, **54**

Valenzuela, Candelaria, 214

Ventureño Chumash, 214

Vicús, 49

Virgen de la Caridad del Cobre, 110

W

Waiwái, 68
pakara, **68**

wakikonza, 142, 145

Walker River Northern Paiute fish trap, **206**

Walla Walla
dress, **146**
pouch, **145**

Warm Springs Apache, 129

War Shirt #2: Modern Warrior Series (Bently Spang), **268**, 269

war shirts, 142–145, 155

war with the Indians of New England, 189

Washoe, 210
basket, **208, 216**

Washoe or Northern Paiute basket, **208**

water drum, 161

water rights, in Great Basin, 204, 207

weaving, *see also* basketry; textiles
in Amazon, 69, 72
in Andes, 38, 44
in Great Basin, 208–209, 213
Inka, 52

PHOTO CREDITS

Images from the NMAI Photo Archives are identified where they appear by photo number. All images © the source unless otherwise noted.

p. 10, T. Andrews/GNWT.

p. 20, Dr. Rene San Martin, NMAI.

p. 25, Barnert, NMAI.

p. 27, Charles Wellington Furlong. Rauner Special Collections, Courtesy of Dartmouth College Library.

p. 30, Martin Gusinde. Courtesy of Anthropos Institut.

p. 38, Wayne Smith, NMAI.

p. 42 Bobby Haas/National Geographic Stock.

p. 51, William Albert Allard/ National Geographic Stock.

p. 53, José Luis Stephens, NMAI.

p. 65, Janet Chernela.

p. 69, John Bodley.

p. 73, Philippe Descola.

p. 77, William Fisher.

p. 80, William Fisher.

p. 89, Otis Imboden. Courtesy of Boundary East Archaeological Research Center.

p. 100, Rachel Cobb.

p. 114, upper, Martin Gray/ National Geographic Stock; lower, Adriel Heisey.

p, 124, Charles M. Wood, NMAI.

p. 125, upper, E. H. Davis, NMAI; lower, William Henry Jackson, NMAI.

p. 142, Smithsonian American Art Museum. Gift of Mrs. Joseph Harrison, Jr.

p. 148, Glenbow Archives, NA-1897-5.

p. 173, The Northumberland Estates, Alnwick Castle, Collection of the Duke of Northumberland.

p. 177, photographer unknown. Photo courtesy of Richard Pohrt.

p. 201, P1046, George Wharton James Collection, Braun Research Library, Autry National Center.

p. 208, Courtesy of Sue Coleman.

p. 226, P39-0788, Alaska State Library, Case and Draper Photograph Collection.

p. 229, Charles Carpenter. © The Field Museum, CSA13583.

p. 246, William Brooks Cabot Collection. Smithsonian Institution, National Anthropological Archives.

p. 247, Leuman M. Waugh. NMAI

p. 251, T. Andrews/GNWT.

Captions for images pages 1–6:

p. 1: Sunka Luta (Red Dog, Oglala Lakota, ca. 1848–d.?), ledger book drawing (detail), ca. 1884. Pine Ridge Reservation, South Dakota. Paper, leather, graphite, ink, colored pencil; 20 x 14 cm. Presented by Eleanor Sherman Fitch. 20/6230. (See page 158.)

p. 2: Iñupiaq bow drill (detail), ca. 1880–1920. Kotzebue Sound, Alaska. Ivory, paint; 43 x 1.5 cm. Purchase. 19/1629. (See page 246.)

p. 3: Hiłamas (Willie Seaweed or Smoky Top, 'Nak'waxda'xw Kwakwaka'wakw, 1873–1967), *gikiwe'* (chief's headdress, detail), ca. 1949. Vancouver Island, British Columbia. Cedar wood, paint, velveteen; 50 x 22 cm. Purchased from Wilhelm Helmer. 23/8252. (See pages 238–39.)

p. 4: Recuay vessel depicting an Andean leader and a llama, AD 900–1300. Recuay, Ancash, Peru. Clay, paint; 18 x 10 x 19 cm. Purchased from Leon J. Buki. 24/7646

p. 5: Winnebago moccasins, ca. 1890. Nebraska. Hide, beads: 24 x 14 x 12 cm. 14/1035

pp. 6–7: all of the objects on the title page appear elsewhere in the book, with the exception of the woven bag (p. 6, bottom right): Ska-ba-quay (Mrs. Joseph Tesson, Meskwaki, ca. 1846–1929) bag, ca. 1900. Iowa. Wool, cotton; 60 x 45 cm. Collected by Mark R. Harrington. 2/7911